Fasting: Unlocking Spiritual Power and Breakthrough

Volume 1

Sheldon Juell

Fasting: Unlocking Spiritual Power and Breakthrough, Volume 1

Copyright © 2015 by Sheldon Juell

All Rights Reserved.

ISBN: 978-1-59755-386-5

Published by: Advantage Books ™
                         Longwood Florida, USA
                         www.advbookstore.com

Library of Congress Catalog Number: 2015942743

Cover Designed by: Calvin Wray
                                  Juice Creative
                                  www.juiceonline.ca

First Printing: February 2016
15 16 17 18 19 20 21   10 9 8 7 6 5 4 3 2 1
Printed in the United States of America

Acknowledgements

I, first of all, want to thank my Lord and Saviour Jesus Christ for His gracious gift of salvation that has been freely given to me, and the Holy Spirit who guided, directed and empowered me to complete this project. I never dreamed that I could start and complete a project of this magnitude, but I did by the grace of God. Second, to God's gift of love, my wife, Ivone who inspires, supports, and encourages me to go after my dreams, and to become the person that God intends for me to be. I love you very much.

I am grateful and sincerely appreciate the following men of God who took time out of their busy schedules to read *Fasting: Unlocking Spiritual Power and Breakthrough* and write an endorsement.

To my friend, Pastor and author, Dr. Barry Buzza, Northside Church, Coquitlam BC. Thank you for writing such an inspiring Foreword. You are truly a living example of Jesus Christ as you reveal the profound truths of the Word of God through your life and ministry.

To President Steve Falkiner, The Canadian Foursquare Church, may the Lord bless you and give you wisdom as you continue to give leadership, guidance, and direction to pastors and church leaders across Canada and throughout the world.

To Dr. Ken Deeks, Vice President for Academic Affairs. May the Lord bless you and give you wisdom as you continue to give academic leadership and direction to the faculty and in educating, equipping, and empowering the students to academic excellence at Pacific Life Bible College.

Foreword by Dr. Barry Buzza

It's Fall in British Columbia as I write this foreword to my friend, Sheldon Juell's, classic book on *Fasting: Unlocking Spiritual Power and Breakthrough*. I'm sitting in my living room, looking out at the front yards of my neighbor's and our homes. Our front lawn is carpet green and free of weeds, while our neighbor's lawn is littered with an unattractive mixture of crabgrass, clover, buttercups and dandelions. I'm happy with our lush grass and my neighbor is discouraged with his carpet of weeds.

Two weeks ago, as we were chatting outside, he asked me what my secret of success was. I didn't want to insult or discourage my friend. I really like him, but I had to tell the truth. I said that our healthy lawn was due to a combination of good fertilizer and regularly attacking weeds. Just by keeping my lawn well nourished, the good strong grass pushes out weeds that don't belong, but I still need to keep careful watch out for weeds and deal ruthlessly with them as soon as they appear.

In the formula I shared with my neighbor that day, is a life lesson that will help us keep our souls as healthy as my front lawn. The twofold secret of daily nourishment of our souls, plus regularly dealing with invasive predators, will keep our hearts pure and soft.

In each of our lives, there are enemies who want to see our souls get tangled up in destructive weeds. As Jesus illustrated in the third soil of his parable of the farmer who scattered seeds, those weeds, if not dealt with severely, will ultimate kill any fruitfulness we are meant to produce.

In Sheldon Juell's newest book, *Fasting: Unlocking Spiritual Power and Breakthrough*, I believe he has clearly introduced us to one of Jesus' most powerful weed killers and fertilizers. Maybe we could think of the Spiritual Fast as "Weed and Feed" for our souls.

As far back as the Bible story goes, we can see the battle that all of us face with this enemy called "the flesh". Adam and Eve were instructed by Jesus himself to not eat the fruit in middle of the garden. We can easily picture the conversation between the Angel of Light and Eve.

"Why don't you try it? It's the best tasting fruit in the entire Garden!"

"Well yes, it certainly does look delicious!"

It didn't seem like it took too much convincing for him to get Eve to pick the fruit and taste it.
And it was sumptuous! "Adam, you have to try it. You'll really like it!"

Even more quickly than Eve had succumbed, Adam dove in and joined her. The weeds of their flesh had easily taken root; they'd "*leaned to their own understanding*" and away from the way of God's Word. Before they knew what was happening, Adam's and Eve's souls were polluted with weeds of self-centeredness.

Story after story throughout the Bible record, we see in the lives of our Bible heroes, this same battle between the flesh and the spirit. Cain followed in his parents' footsteps, then Noah, Abraham, Jacob, Achan, Samson, Saul and David. Each of their lawns, from time to time, became infected with weeds.

Turn the page to the New Testament. Maybe daily walking with Jesus would help his followers keep healthy.

One of the stories that shocks us the most was set in a spiritually dynamic scene near the end of the earthly ministry of Jesus. It was Passover, April 30AD. On the very night that Jesus was to die for the sins of the world, he got up after dinner, disrobed and tied a towel around his waist. Then Jesus Christ, God himself, knelt down before each of his disciples and began to wash their feet. He was teaching by his example that the way to be great in the Kingdom of God is to be a servant.

I'm not sure how long it was after that, maybe minutes, that Jesus interrupted his disciples in the middle of an argument. Believe it or not, they were verbally jesting over the question, "Who is the greatest?"

Jesus was righteously disturbed. "Guys, don't you get it? *Among you it is supposed to be different. Those who are the greatest among you should take the lowest rank, and the leader should be like a servant.*"

What had happened? The same thing as happened to Adam and Eve. It's the same battle we have each faced over and over. The weeds of our flesh blow over our souls, and too often take root.

What are we to do? What kind of "Weed and Feed" do we need?

Jesus taught that unless a grain of wheat falls into the ground and dies it abides alone. Paul said that he had to die daily to himself. The weeds of self-centeredness have to die and our souls must be nourished.

There are many nourishing fertilizers with which we can feed our souls. Worship, Bible reading and study, meditation, Christian fellowship, communion ... The list goes on. But I believe one of the most powerful antidotes to infection of the flesh, and health promoting nutrients we can apply to our souls is the discipline of fasting.

Sheldon Juell's treatise on how to unlock spiritual power and breakthrough through fasting is the best I have ever read. This valuable book has been thoroughly researched through meticulous Bible study and historical examples. Everything we need to know about this priceless key to spiritual vitality is in these pages. When I first read *Fasting: Unlocking Spiritual Power and Breakthrough*, I was encouraged and stimulated in the discipline of fasting like never before.

If my neighbor would simply listen to my teaching and follow my example, when it comes to lawn care, he would have a lush green carpet of lawn by next summer. How much more important is it that we hear this expert teaching on fasting, and follow the example of spiritual leaders who have gone before! We would live in Spiritual Power and Breakthrough like Jesus has promised. "*This kind will only come out through fasting and prayer!*" I heartily recommend this book to you. Apply its lessons liberally to the lawn of your souls. You'll be glad you did.

Dr. Barry Buzza
Lead Pastor, Northside Church
Author of "Teach Us To Pray"
Coquitlam, BC Canada

Table of Contents

Introduction

I had just been laid off from work and was applying for work daily within the educational and academic disciplines; with no success. I was praying and seeking the Lord for work, but with all my educational and academic qualifications, I was rarely receiving a phone call for an interview. I constantly prayed and asked the Lord: What was happening? Is there something wrong with me? Should I change my resume? Was I doing something in the interviews that I needed to change? Should I look to other jobs that are in management outside of education? I changed my resume many times thinking that this would help, but it did not seem to help. Nothing changed. Rare job interviews. No job. We needed a breakthrough in our finances.

Then I thought Jesus, priests, kings, prophets, and others in Scripture spoke about fasting and how it could bring healing and break cycles of defeat in a person's life. I started to talk to people about fasting to hear their perspective and response to fasting. However, the majority of their thoughts, views, and responses were negative. I would make comments like fasting seems to be lacking in many of our churches today and their response was one of indifference and/or irrelevance to the Christian and their walk with the Lord.

More than ever, in the day in which we live, we need to practice the spiritual discipline of fasting combined with prayer to bring healing, deliverance, fresh vision and focus to our lives as Christians and to churches. The local church today needs to practice both individual and corporate fasting. Some believed in both, but were reluctant to practice, some did not believe in corporate fasting, even though I gave them examples of corporate fasting in Scripture (e.g., Est. 4:1-3, 12-17, 9:29-32). Some viewed fasting as only having personal benefits, which is true, but there are also corporate benefits such as confession of sin and repentance, unity of purpose, prophetic revelation, the favour of God, empowerment to reach the lost, sharpening our spiritual senses, and exposing those areas in our lives where we lack self-control, to name a few. These are instruments that the Holy Spirit uses to bring about necessary individual and corporate transformation to our lives.[1] Some of the reactions included: laughing, joking, and changing the subject. Very few people that I spoke with took seriously the spiritual discipline of fasting, which disturbed me, since they are Christians and some of them were pastors. The Lord began to show me that those who do not see the relevance of fasting today are those who need to fast the most. Why? Their flesh and/or carnal nature is too alive and fasting is necessary since it cuts at the heart of our sinful nature and brings it under submission to Jesus Christ.

There seems to be many people today in our churches who struggle with various issues—whether, physical, emotional, mental, spiritual, and financial. Many of us experience the breakthrough and freedom we need as we seek the Lord. However, many of us experience some level of breakthrough, but may not sense a complete breaking of the chains of bondage that was holding us captive. Many pray for what seems to be endless hours of prayer and experienced some level of breakthrough, but not a complete breakthrough. This led me to ask the Lord, what else is there? How can I experience a complete breaking of these chains or bondage?

---

[1] For a further discussion on the corporate benefits of fasting, please refer to "The Benefits of Fasting".

When I first contemplated writing on the subject of fasting, I wanted to make sure that it was not only a theoretical study—it also needed to include practical aspects and personal reflections. A lot of prayer and fasting was not only a vital part before beginning to write, but also the highest priority during the research and writing on this book. I began to pray, fast, and contemplate this research early spring of 2012. I then began to seek the Lord in fasting, but then as a diabetic I needed to be cautious so that I would not place my health in danger. The Lord brought to mind how His grace is sufficient,

But he said to me, "My grace is sufficient for you, for my power is made perfect in weakness". Therefore I will boast all the more gladly about my weaknesses, so that Christ's power may rest on me. That is why, for Christ's sake, I delight in weaknesses, in insults, in hardships, in persecutions, in difficulties. For when I am weak, then I am strong (2 Cor. 12:9-10).

One of my greatest struggles was to experience and prove that through fasting we can experience spiritual power and breakthrough. I began to fast lunch from 11:00am to 5:00pm and after a few weeks I thought that I would begin to see some results, but did not. I became discouraged and wanted to stop fasting since it seemed like it was not working, which was based upon my own preconceived conception of fasting. I felt the Lord tell me to continue until He had released me from fasting. It is so easy to become discouraged when we do not see the results we desire. We need to remember to allow the Lord to have His way in our lives, and not our way. I would fast, waiting for the breakthrough that I desired, with no results. I sensed the Lord telling me to stop, but there were no results. Then I sensed the Lord telling me to fast again, but why, since the last time there were no results. This occurred a number of times, and once again I became discouraged.

Then finally, the breakthroughs started to occur slowly, but not in the way that I expected. The Lord started to increase my wife's income. I thought wonderful, but I need to experience this spiritual power and breakthrough in my own life. The Lord started to open the door, not for a job at first though, but through the entire time that I was unemployed the Lord was miraculously supplying our needs, even though times were tough—the Lord is always faithful. During this time, the Lord pressed upon my heart to make some financial decisions which lead to financial breakthroughs that I had been fasting and praying. These breakthroughs came in the form of being approved for two (b) Mastercards, even though I was not working. We had also fallen behind in paying rent, which I kept track of how much we had paid and how much we still owed, based upon what the manager had told me. However, on a number of occasions when I went to pay rent, the amount remaining was approximately $250.00 less than what was owed.

Early 2013, I contacted Logos Bible Software to have my master's thesis entitled "Community Life in the Early Church" added and available for purchase and download. It was subsequently launched in April 2013. Four months later, I received my first royalty check for the sale of 200 books. I had expected maybe fifteen to twenty books and was completely blown away and humbled by this number of books that were sold in such a short period of time. Moreover, in February 2014, we opened a professional counselling clinic called the Door of Hope Counselling Clinic in Port Coquitlam, BC and are seeing many lives being transformed. We also believe that the Lord has many more breakthroughs waiting for us and that this is only the beginning. We sense the favour of the Lord upon our lives as we commit ourselves and our plans to the Lord and allow Him to direct our steps.

> Let love and faithfulness never leave you; bind them around your neck, write them on the tablet of your heart. Then you will win favor and a good name in the sight of God and man. Trust in the LORD with all your heart and lean not on your own understanding; in all your ways acknowledge him, and he will make your paths straight. Do not be wise in your own eyes; fear the LORD and shun evil. This will bring health to your body and nourishment to your bones. Honor the LORD with your wealth, with the firstfruits of all your crops; then your barns will be filled to overflowing, and your vats will brim over with new wine (Pr. 3:3-10).

> In their hearts humans plan their course, but the LORD establishes their steps. (Pr. 16:9)

> A man's steps are directed by the LORD. How then can anyone understand his own way? (Pr. 20:24)

Fasting: Unlocking Spiritual Power and Breakthrough argues that there is both biblical and historical evidence to support the fact that fasting is a worthy subject for Christians to not only study and understand, but more importantly to put into practice. In decades past, conversations concerning fasting and prayer occurred on a constant basis and likewise were practiced. However, in Western society, it seems as though a small percentage of Christians and churches regularly practice, and the topic is often ridiculed and its importance has eroded away to the place to almost becoming extinct.

Arthur Wallis in his book "God's Chosen Fast" states,

> For nearly a century and a half, fasting has been out of vogue, at least in the churches in the West. The very idea of someone actually fasting today seems strange to most twentieth-century Christians. They associate it with medieval Christianity, or perhaps with High Church practice. They may recall that political leaders, like Mahatma Ghandi, have used it as a weapon of passive resistance. As a spiritual exercise, it is confined, they would think, to believers who appear to be a little extreme or fanatical.
>
> There are others whose misgivings concern the practical aspect. To them fasting and starving are synonymous terms, and they fear it will have harmful results. Because "no man ever hates his own flesh, but nourishes and cherishes it" (Eph. 5:29), they oppose fasting almost instinctively.
>
> Why such attitudes to a practice that is so obviously scriptural? One answer is that fasting was one of the dominant features of an asceticism which began to appear in the post-apostolic age and became extreme in form as well as widespread in influence in medieval times. The pendulum began to swing the other way as people revolted against anything that savored of asceticism. The church today is still suffering from that reaction. We have not yet recovered the spiritual balance of New Testament Christianity.[2]

Arthur Wallis, in relation to how traditional views can affect us, further states

---

[2] Arthur Wallis, *God's Chosen Fast: A Spiritual and Practical Guide to Fasting* (Fort Washington, PA: CLC Publications, 1968), 9.

When our minds are conditioned by prejudice or paralyzed by traditional views, we may face a truth in Scripture again and again without ever touching us. Our spiritual inhibition concerning that truth permits us to see, but not to perceive. The truth lies dormant within, mentally apprehended but not spiritually applied. This is particularly true in relation to fasting.

When, however, such a truth is first ignited by the Holy Spirit, there is immediate conflict in the minds of most people. The truth of the Bible has suddenly become "alive and powerful," and there is an assault upon our traditional attitudes and prejudices.

The outcome of the struggle reveals whether or not we are open to receive and obey fresh light about God, and so grow in the knowledge of the truth.[3]

Arthur Wallis raises the question as to whether or not we will allow our current perception of fasting or lack of one to be challenged by the truth of God's Word and then live out these truths in our daily walk with Him (1 Cor. 4:6). Moreover, he continues this thought concerning fasting in the New Testament,

In New Testament times fasting was a channel of power. As spirituality waned and worldliness flourished in the churches, the power of the gifts of the Spirit was withdrawn. With the loss of that inward power, men could only cling to what they had left, its outward accompaniment. More and more emphasis was placed upon the outward act of fasting, though bereft of the inward spirit that alone could give it value. Asceticism became the mark of piety and spirituality. Paul's prediction about "the form of religion but denying the power" (1 Tim. 3:5) was being fulfilled.[4]

Jesus in the Sermon on the Mount addressed the outward form of Pharisaic practice. He first addressed their practice of almsgiving (Mt. 6:1-4); second, their practice of prayer (Mt. 6:5-15); third, their practice of fasting and their attempt to demonstrate how righteous they were (Mt. 6:16-18). They loved to put on an external show of spirituality (Mt. 6:16-18), yet inwardly they were full of greed, self-indulgence, and wickedness (Mt. 23:25-26; Lk. 11:39). In the day in which we live and the soon return of our Saviour Jesus Christ, we must follow the advice of the apostle Paul who exhorts believers to focus and live our lives according to the Spirit,

Those who live according to the flesh have their minds set on what the flesh desires; but those who live in accordance with the Spirit have their minds set on what the Spirit desires. The mind governed by the flesh is death, but the mind governed by the Spirit is life and peace. The mind governed by the flesh is hostile to God; it does not submit to God's law, nor can it do so. Those who are in the realm of the flesh cannot please God. You, however, are not in the realm of the flesh but are in the realm of the Spirit, if indeed the Spirit of God lives in you. And if anyone does not have the Spirit of Christ, they do not belong to Christ. But if Christ is in you, then even though your body is subject to death because of sin, the Spirit gives life because of righteousness. And if the Spirit of him who raised Jesus from the dead is living in you, he who raised Christ from the dead will also give life to your mortal bodies because of his Spirit who lives in you. Therefore, brothers and sisters, we have an obligation—but it is not to the flesh, to live according to it. For if you live according to the flesh, you will die; but if by the Spirit you put to death the misdeeds of the body, you will live (Rom. 8:5-13).

---

[3] Wallis, *God's Chosen Fasting*, 10.
[4] Wallis, *God's Chosen Fasting*, 14.

It is time for the church today to rediscover the lost treasure—the Holy Spirit—who was prevalent in the Early Church and walk daily in the spiritual power and breakthrough that is released through the biblical and spiritual discipline of fasting. Wallis certainly brings the point home concerning the truth that is found in the Word of God.

> When people do not like the plain, literal meaning of something in the Bible, they are tempted to spiritualize it and so rob it of its potency. Once the truth becomes nebulous, it ceases to have any practical application. They have blunted its edge; it can no longer cut.[5]

This is what has happened to fasting that is taught throughout the Word of God. We have spiritualized fasting to the point where we have deprived ourselves of receiving the fullest extent of the power of the Holy Spirit and the Word of God in our lives. We have explained away His truth as being irrelevant due to our own ignorance and/or our own biases. The power of the gospel, the work of the Holy Spirit in our lives, and the Word of God have been given to us to unlock spiritual power and breakthrough so that we can walk in the freedom that Jesus Christ gave us through His life, crucifixion, death, and resurrection. We only need to activate the truth of God's Word by obeying His precepts and living out His Word in our lives daily.[6]

When we look at the biblical and spiritual discipline of fasting in other parts of the world, fasting along with prayer are regularly practiced and people are being healed, delivered from demonic strongholds, and living the victorious Christian life. J. I. Packer has a wonderful summation,

> When Christians meet, they talk to each other about their Christian work and Christian interests, their Christian acquaintances, the state of the churches, and the problems of theology—but rarely of their daily experience of God.
> Modern Christian books and magazines contain much about Christian doctrine, Christian standards, problems of Christian conduct, techniques of Christian service—but little about the inner realities of fellowship with God.
> Our sermons contain much sound doctrine—but little relating to the converse between the soul and the Saviour.
> We do not spend much time, alone or together, in dwelling on the wonder of the fact that God and sinners have communion at all; no, we just take that for granted, and give our minds to other matters.
> Thus we make it plain that communion with God is a small thing to us.[7]

John Piper continues this thought and adds,

---

[5] Wallis, *God's Chosen Fasting*, 13.

[6] John F. Walvoord and Roy B. Zuck, eds., *The Bible Knowledge Commentary: An Exposition of the Scriptures*, Vol. 2 (Wheaton, IL: Victor Books, 1985), 790.

[7] J. I. Packer, *A Quest for Godliness: The Puritan Vision of the Christian Life* (Wheaton, IL: Crossway Books, 2010), 215, in John Piper, *A Hunger for God: Desiring God Through Fasting and Prayer* (Wheaton, IL: Crossway, 1997), 9f.

We seem to find it easier to talk much of plans and principles for proclaiming the gospel and planting churches, and to talk little of the power of God that is necessary for this gospel to be proclaimed and the church to be planted.

If we really want to be a part of seeing disciples made and churches multiplied throughout North America and to the ends of the earth, we would be wise to begin on our knees. . . . apart from dependence on and desperation for God, we will not only miss the ultimate point of our mission, but we will also neglect the ultimate need of our souls.[8]

We were made to feast on God. In the words of the psalmist, we were created to cry:

O God, you are my God, earnestly I seek you; my soul thirsts for you, my body longs for you, in a dry and weary land where there is no water. I have seen you in the sanctuary and beheld your power and your glory. Because your love is better than life, my lips will glorify you. I will praise you as long as I live, and in your name I will lift up my hands. My soul will be satisfied as with the richest of foods; with singing lips my mouth will praise you (Ps. 63:1-5).

Sometimes we earnestly seek after things *from* God rather than God Himself. It is hard for us to imagine anyone leaving the presence of the living God—the maker and sustainer of heaven and earth—and looking for something better! But, isn't this exactly what we struggle with and often fall back into our old ways like the Israelites did throughout their history, and today, we are no different.

---

[8] Piper, *A Hunger for God*, 9f.

Chapter 1: Fasting and the Christian Life

The purpose of this chapter is to describe some of the reasons why fasting seems to be neglected in the lives of Christians. It also describes our physical and spiritual appetites and how these appetites affect our lives, being transformed by the power of the Holy Spirit, and developing a deeper level of hunger and thirst in our relationship with God. We conclude this chapter by addressing the questions: why and when should Christians fast.

The Word of God gives us many reasons why fasting is a necessary part of the Christian life: (a) we fast because we're hungry for God's Word and the Holy Spirit in our lives; (b) we fast because we long for God's glory to resound in the church and God's praise to resound among the nations; (c) we fast because we yearn for the Son of God to return and Kingdom of God to come; and (d) we fast simply because we want God more than we want anything this world has to offer us.[9]

Fasting: Why Is It Neglected Today?

We live in a day where fasting, to some extent, has faded away and people either fear or have misunderstood the spiritual discipline of fasting. We live in a society where self-indulgences have become the norm. Cornelius Plantinga, Jr., sums up self-indulgence and gluttony as sin, which spoils our appetite for God,

> Self-indulgence is the enemy of gratitude, and self-discipline usually its friend and generator. That is why gluttony is a deadly sin. The early desert fathers believed that a person's appetites are linked: full stomachs and jaded palates take the edge from our hunger and thirst for righteousness. They spoil the appetite for God.[10]

When the subject of fasting is raised, many do not know how to respond, and through our own ignorance we explain it away as irrelevant. When we look at why fasting is feared by some, the possibility arises that we could become something that we do not want or something could happen or issues exposed that we do not want to be exposed. We fear that we will suffer for no reason, resulting in a negative experience. Likewise, people may see us as being a fanatic or literally going off the deep end—shaving our heads, demonstrating a behaviour that makes us look like someone in need of being admitted to a psychiatric ward. As with any subject, it is too easy to take a subject to an extreme, which is wrong since it is out of balance. Some people have exalted religious fasting beyond all Scripture and reason, while others believe that fasting in not necessary, not to be desired, and therefore disregarded; yet others believe that fasting is to be conjoined as a matter of faith (i.e., baptism).[11]

Moreover, fasting has become a spiritual discipline that has been misunderstood due to a lack of awareness—taught, preached, and practiced. Among Christians, and in many of our churches, there is a

---

[9] Piper, *A Hunger for God*, 10f.

[10] Cornelius Plantinga, Jr., quoted in The Reformed Journal (November, 1988). Donald S. Whitney, *Spiritual Disciplines for the Christian Life* (Colorado Springs, CO: NavPress, 1991), 159.

[11] Mark A. Copeland, *Fasting: A Special Study*, 1992-2007, In Rick Meyers, e-Sword, Version 10.2.1, 2000-2012, <http://www.e-sword.net>.

famine of information concerning the physical and spiritual benefits, the defining of and preparation for fasting, the why and when, and the occasions for fasting. However, the Word of God mentions fasting about the same number of times as repentance, confession, and baptism.

> Christians in a gluttonous, denial-less, self-indulgent society may struggle to accept and to begin the practice of fasting. Few Disciplines go so radically against the flesh and the mainstream of culture as this one. But we cannot overlook its biblical significance. Of course, some people, for medical reasons, cannot fast. But most of us dare not overlook fasting's benefits in the disciplined pursuit of a Christlike life.[12]

Part of the reason why many struggle to accept and practice of fasting can be due to its scope of denying fleshly desires. Those who negate the value of fasting in the Christian life, are probably in the most need of practicing fasting since their sin nature is too alive and active. The fear of fasting and being misunderstood has kept many from benefiting from its spiritual richness and deepening of one's relationship with God.[13] Richard Foster defines fasting as "the voluntary denial of a normal function for the sake of intense spiritual activity".[14]

When we think about the practice of fasting in the church, a few issues come to mind. First of all, there is church tradition. People are not accustomed to fasting since it is not part of their Christian tradition. Fasting seems to be rarely preached, discussed, and/or practiced. However, for those in our church that have come from non-Western cultures, it is often a spiritual discipline that is regularly practiced by church leadership and church members. Second, in society today, there is an increase of self-indulgence and lack of discipline—not going without, or having to wait for what we want. It is as if we are living in a society of convenience in which our wants and desires must be immediately satisfied. In other words, we are impatient to wait. In this type of society, no wonder fasting has lost its relevance and self-control and discipline have fallen by the wayside.[15] Many Christians lack this profound intimacy with God which results from fasting.

Through fasting we are reminded of Jesus' words during His forty day fast, "It is written: 'Man does not live on bread alone, but on every word that comes from the mouth of God'" (Mt. 4:4; cf. Deut. 8:3). Likewise, Jesus responded "Do not test the LORD your God as you did at Massah. Be sure to keep the commands of the LORD your God and the stipulations and decrees he has given you" (Deut. 6:16-17) and

> Fear the LORD your God, serve him only and take your oaths in his name. Do not follow other gods, the gods of the peoples around you; for the Lord your God, who is among you, is a jealous God and his anger will burn against you, and he will destroy you from the face of the land" (Deut. 6:13-15).

---

[12] Whitney, *Spiritual Disciplines for the Christian Life*, 160.

[13] Whitney, *Spiritual Disciplines for the Christian Life*, 160.

[14] LaVonne Neff, et al., ed., *Practical Christianity* (Wheaton, IL: Tyndale House, 1987), 300.

[15] <http://www.rcnzonline.com/fnf/a191.html>, Accessed on September 3, 2013.

It is interesting that each time Jesus responded to the three temptations, He quoted from Deuteronomy, which was all spoken by Moses to the Israelites concerning their time of testing in the wilderness. Moses speaks of Yahweh raising up "a prophet like me".

> The nations you will dispossess listen to those who practice sorcery or divination. But as for you, the LORD your God has not permitted you to do so. The LORD your God will raise up for you a prophet like me from among your own brothers. You must listen to him. For this is what you asked of the LORD your God at Horeb on the day of the assembly when you said, "Let us not hear the voice of the LORD our God nor see this great fire anymore, or we will die". The LORD said to me: "What they say is good. I will raise up for them a prophet like you from among their brothers; I will put my words in his mouth, and he will tell them everything I command him. If anyone does not listen to my words that the prophet speaks in my name, I myself will call him to account (Deut. 18:14-19).

The context here speaks of the Israelites were to heed the words of the prophets of the Lord and that Yahweh would raise up a succession of Israelite prophets beginning with Moses. The Israelites for too long had followed the dark magic of the Canaanite diviners, witches, and spiritists. The Lord was calling them to obey what Yahweh had spoken to Moses on Mount Sinai that He would be their mediator (Deut. 5:23-27). This succession would lead to the ultimate prophet, Jesus Christ. These prophets were to live after the example of Moses until the Mediator of the New Covenant had arrived.[16]

This specifically refers to the Old Testament shadow being replaced by New Testament reality. It is through a new Joshua (יְהוֹשֻׁעַ *yehôshua*ʾ), Jesus (Ἰησοῦς *Iēsous*)[17], that He will gather a people from both Jews and Gentiles and as their representative He was led by the Holy Spirit into the wilderness as the Israelites were led into the wilderness. As the Israelites wandered in the wilderness for forty years so Jesus wandered in the wilderness for forty days. Jesus was tested as Israel was tested; hungered as Israel hungered; and triumphed as Israel triumphed and were led into the Promised Land of forgiveness and eternal life.[18]

Moreover, the forty days of fasting not only prepared Jesus for testing; it was part of His testing as hunger was a test of faith for the Israelites in the wilderness.

> Be careful to follow every command I am giving you today, so that you may live and increase and may enter and possess the land the LORD promised on oath to your ancestors. Remember how the LORD your God led you all the way in the desert these forty years, to humble you and to test you in order to know what was in your heart, whether or not you would keep his commands. He humbled you, causing you to hunger and then feeding you with manna, which neither you nor your fathers had known, to teach you that man does not live on bread alone but on every word that comes from the mouth of the LORD. Your clothes did not wear out and your feet did not

---

[16] Walvoord and Zuck, eds., *The Bible Knowledge Commentary*, Vol. 1, 296-97.

[17] יְהוֹשֻׁעַ *yehôshua*ʾ "3193", In Thoralf Gilbrant, ed., *The Complete Biblical Library Hebrew-English Dictionary, Heth-Yodh* (Springfield, IL: World Library Press, Inc., WORDsearch CROSS e-book, 1998). Ἰησοῦς *Iēsous* "2400", In Thoralf Gilbrant, ed., *The Complete Biblical Library Greek-English Dictionary, Zeta-Kappa* (Springfield, MO: Complete Biblical Library, WORDsearch CROSS e-book, 1991).

[18] Piper, *A Hunger for God*, 56.

swell during these forty years. Know then in your heart that as a man disciplines his son, so the LORD your God disciplines you (Deut. 8:1-5).

The Holy Spirit led Jesus into the wilderness to let Him be hungry to test and see what was in His heart—did He love God more or bread more. Through fasting we become aware of where our heart is. As with the Israelites and with Jesus, "fasting is God's testing ground—and healing ground. . . . Fasting is a way of revealing to ourselves and confessing to our God what is in our hearts. Where do we find our deepest satisfaction—in God or in his gifts?"[19] Jesus stated,

Do not store up for yourselves treasures on earth, where moth and rust destroy, and where thieves break in and steal. But store up for yourselves treasures in heaven, where moth and rust do not destroy, and where thieves do not break in and steal. For where your treasure is, there your heart will be also (Mt. 6:19-21).

The life of Job is a great example "I have not departed from the commands of his lips; I have treasured the words of his mouth more than my daily bread" (Job 23:12). We must come to the place that God is our source of life—He alone is our provider. Food does not sustain us, God sustains us. Therefore, when we are fasting, it is more than abstaining from consuming food; we are feasting on the Word of God. One of the obstacles to fasting and one of the reasons that keeps us from fasting is that more than any other type of discipline, fasting exposes the areas where we lack discipline and especially those areas which control us. In this way, fasting makes us vulnerable, exposes sin in our lives, and takes us to a place where we just do not want to go. In relation to this, Richard Foster states, "more than any other discipline, fasting reveals the things that control us. This is a wonderful benefit to the true disciple who longs to be transformed into the image of Jesus Christ. We cover up what is inside of us with food and other things".[20] Fasting forces us to choose to allow either our issues to control us or allow the Holy Spirit to transform us,

Now the Lord is the Spirit, and where the Spirit of the Lord is, there is freedom. And we, who with unveiled faces all reflect the Lord's glory, are being transformed into his likeness with ever-increasing glory, which comes from the Lord, who is the Spirit (2 Cor. 3:17-18).

Foster states that fasting will expose our pain, pride, anger, bitterness, jealousy, strife, fear,

If pride controls us, it will be revealed almost immediately. David said, "I humbled my soul with fasting (Ps. 35:13). Anger, bitterness, jealousy, strife, fear—if they are within us, they will surface during fasting. At first, we will rationalize that our anger is due to our hunger. And then, we know that we are angry because the spirit of anger is within us. We can rejoice in this knowledge because we know that healing is available through the power of Christ.[21]

The Bible is very careful to warn us about certain types of people

---

[19] Piper, *A Hunger for God*, 57.

[20] Richard Foster, *The Celebration of Discipline* (New York: Harper & Row, 1978), 48.

[21] Foster, *The Celebration of Discipline*, 48.

The Spirit clearly says that in later times some will abandon the faith and follow deceiving spirits and things taught by demons. Such teachings come through hypocritical liars, whose consciences have been seared as with a hot iron. They forbid people to marry and order them to abstain from certain foods, which God created to be received with thanksgiving by those who believe and who know the truth (1 Tim. 4:1-3).

Paul was disappointed with those whom he had discipled and who had submitted themselves to the principles of this world,

Since you died with Christ to the basic principles of this world, why, as though you still belonged to it, do you submit to its rules: "Do not handle! Do not taste! Do not touch!"? These are all destined to perish with use, because they are based on human commands and teachings. Such regulations indeed have an appearance of wisdom, with their self-imposed worship, their false humility and their harsh treatment of the body, but they lack any value in restraining sensual indulgence (Col. 2:20-23).

But not everyone knows this. Some people are still so accustomed to idols that when they eat such food they think of it as having been sacrificed to an idol, and since their conscience is weak, it is defiled. But food does not bring us near to God; we are no worse if we do not eat, and no better if we do (1 Cor. 8:7-8).

Paul presents a strong warning against any simplistic form of fasting that will inevitably lead to a person's spiritual good. "Harsh treatment of the body" may only feed a person's flesh with more self-reliance. C. S. Lewis gives a stern warning against this type of behaviour:

Fasting asserts the will against the appetite—the reward being self-mastery and the danger pride: involuntary hunger subjects appetites and will together to the Divine will, furnishing an occasion for submission and exposing us to the danger of rebellion. But the redemptive effect of suffering lies chiefly in its tendency to reduce the rebel will. Ascetic practices which, in themselves, strengthen the will, are only useful insofar as they enable the will to put its own house (the passions) in order, as a preparation for offering the whole man to God. They are necessary as a means; and as an end, they would be abominable, for in substituting will for appetite and there stopping, they would merely exchange the animal self for the diabolical self. It was therefore truly said that "only God can mortify".[22]

The true mortification of our sinful nature is more than just simple denial and discipline. It is an internal, spiritual matter of finding more contentment in Christ than in satisfying our own appetite. Jesus, in His Sermon on the Mount, did not prohibit people from owning material possessions (cf. Mt. 27:57; Lk. 19:2, 8-9).

Do not store up for yourselves treasures on earth, where moth and rust destroy, and where thieves break in and steal. But store up for yourselves treasures in heaven, where moth and rust do not destroy, and where thieves do not break in and steal. For where your treasure is, there your heart will be also (Mt. 6:19-21).

---

[22] C. S. Lewis, *The Problem of Pain* (New York: Macmillan, 1962), 112.

Rather, He addressed the issue of making these possessions the object of the heart of their affections, which included valuable goods, money, clothing, and household furnishings. These "treasures" had become the focus of their attention since they required more and more of their time and energy to maintain. Their hunger and thirst for God had been replaced by a hunger and thirst for material possessions, which is the issue that Jesus confronted.[23] We must remember that the issue is not only food. The issue is anything and everything past, present or future that is a substitute for God, as Martyn Lloyd-Jones writes,

> Fasting if we conceive of it truly, must not . . . be confined to the question of food and drink; fasting should really be made to include abstinence from anything which is legitimate in and of itself for the sake of some special spiritual purpose. There are many bodily functions which are right and normal and perfectly legitimate, but which for special peculiar reasons in certain circumstances should be controlled. That is fasting.[24]

As Jesus later states,

> No one can serve two masters. Either he will hate the one and love the other, or he will be devoted to the one and despise the other. You cannot serve both God and Money (Mt. 6:24).

Jesus confronts the Pharisees whose spiritual eyes had become contaminated by wealth and money, which had resulted in becoming a slave to the god of greed (Mt. 6:22). The Apostle Paul warns us that what controls us or becomes our master will become our god as Paul addresses this issue "to all the saints in Christ Jesus at Philippi" (Phil. 1:1) since "their god is their stomach",

> All of us, then, who are mature should take such a view of things. And if on some point you think differently, that too God will make clear to you. Only let us live up to what we have already attained. Join with others in following my example, brothers, and take note of those who live according to the pattern we gave you. For, as I have often told you before and now say again even with tears, many live as enemies of the cross of Christ. Their destiny is destruction, their god is their stomach, and their glory is in their shame. Their mind is on earthly things (Phil. 3:17-19).

The Apostle Paul in addressing the Philippians begins in chapter 3 with an exhortation to the Philippian believers, which seems as though he was boasting of his life. However, when we take a close look at his message, he makes it very clear that believers should "put no confidence in the flesh" and he warns them against such a lifestyle (Phil. 3:3). Paul begins by describing his past with boldness and pride, his wonderful achievements, and then recounts his conversion experience on the road to Damascus (Acts 9). He stresses the fact that the unity of the Philippian church was being threatened by Judaizers, who were masquerading as believers (2 Cor. 11:13) and requiring the Philippian believers to adhere to the Law

---

[23] Gilbrant, ed., *The Complete Biblical Library Commentary, Matthew* (Springfield, IL: World Library Press, Inc., WORDsearch CROSS e-book, 1988), 115. Walvoord and Zuck, eds., *The Bible Knowledge Commentary*, Vol. 2, 33.

[24] Martyn Lloyd-Jones, *Studies in the Sermon on the Mount*, Vol. 2 (Grand Rapids, MI: William B. Eerdmans Publishing Company, 1972), 38, in Piper, *A Hunger for God*, 19.

of Moses and become Jews. Paul warns them, "Watch out for those dogs, those men who do evil, those mutilators of the flesh" (Phil. 3:2). Paul's credentials far outweighed Jewish credentials,

> If anyone else thinks he has reasons to put confidence in the flesh, I have more: circumcised on the eighth day, of the people of Israel, of the tribe of Benjamin, a Hebrew of Hebrews; in regard to the law, a Pharisee; as for zeal, persecuting the church; as for legalistic righteousness, faultless (Phil. 3:4-6).

However, Paul states that in coming to Jesus, "I consider them rubbish, that I may gain Christ"—to know Him, His life, and His resurrection power (Phil. 3:8, 9-11). He lists seven benefits that he used to have, but counted as loss. He now states one of the most familiar verses in the New Testament and maybe in the entire canon of Scripture, "Forgetting what is behind and straining toward what is ahead, I press on toward the goal to win the prize for which God has called me heavenward in Christ Jesus" (Phil. 3:13-14). He states the purpose for the exhortations and urges the believers to develop a mature attitude, follow his example, and "live up to what we have already attained" (Phil. 3:16; cf. 3:15-17).

Paul next presents the reasons for the preceding exhortations, which he had spoken before and now with tears: "many live as enemies of the cross of Christ" (Phil. 3:18). According to Paul, believers should be able to discern the truth from error (cf. 1 Jn. 4:6) and it was their spiritual welfare that deeply concerned him.

> For, as I have often told you before and now say again even with tears, many live as enemies of the cross of Christ. Their destiny is destruction, their god is their stomach, and their glory is in their shame. Their mind is on earthly things (Phil. 3:18-19).

He solemnly warns them that those who "live as enemies of the cross of Christ" were destined for destruction, since how could they look at Jesus' sacrifice on the cross and still continue to live for themself and indulge in habitual sin. Paul uses the noun ἀπώλεια *apōleia*, which refers to eternal consequences contrasted with *sōtēria*, "salvation". It also meant more than "just annihilation but rather ruination by separation from the presence of God in eternal judgment".[25] Paul warned them against the emerging Gnosticism and those who trusted in their own achievements and not in the sufficiency of Christ alone. Their purpose and ultimate fulfillment in life came through indulging in the lusts of the flesh. Instead of controlling their appetites they allowed their appetites to control them. Moreover, they found their ultimate happiness in the sensuality of eating and drinking and not in the life, death, and resurrection of Jesus Christ.[26]

---

[25] ἀπώλεια *apōleia* "677", In Thoralf Gilbrant, ed., *The Complete Biblical Library Greek-English Dictionary, Alpha-Gamma* (Springfield, MO: Complete Biblical Library, WORDsearch CROSS e-book, 1991). Walvoord and Zuck, eds., *The Bible Knowledge Commentary*, Vol. 2, 662.

[26] Roger Ellsworth, *Opening Up Philippians*, Opening Up Commentary (Leominster: Day One Publications, 2004), 76.

Paul then describes three characteristics of how to identify these false teachers: first, "their god is their stomach", which was indicative of those with physical desires and unrestrained gluttony or literally meant "they honour sensual appetite like a god".

> For such people are not serving our Lord Christ, but their own appetites. By smooth talk and flattery they deceive the minds of naive people (Rom. 16:18).

This list of sins (Phil. 3:18-19) fits the Greek false teachers or Gnostics more than the Jews, but the identity of these heretics is unknown. It is quite possible that some believers had returned to their pagan way of life. This reminds us of the Israelites when the Lord drove in quail from the sea for two days and a night and continued until every person had gathered at least 10 homers (*ca.* 60 bushels) of quail (Num. 11:30-35). With this abundance of food, the people began their orgy of unrestrained gluttony and the Lord unleashed His wrath by sending a severe plague that killed many of the Israelites. This location was known as Kibroth Hattaavah קִבְרוֹתהַתַּאֲוָה *qivrôth hatta'ăwāh* or "the graves of craving" since at this location these Israelites were buried for craving other food. Their sin was a rejection of the Lord's abundant provision and had chosen a restrained appetite. The Israelites became terrified by everyone who had died and therefore relocated to Hazeroth חֲצֵרוֹת *chătsfirôth*.[27] It is possible that Paul is describing Gentiles with Epicurean tendencies,

> The Epicureans constituted a Greek school of philosophy with the basic views that satisfaction of the physical appetites was the highest purpose of mankind. In addition to describing these people as enemies of the Cross, Paul designated their end as destruction, a reference to eternal separation from God. A person's god is that to which he gives himself. These people had made their own unbridled lusts their gods. Although they gloried in their "freedom" to live as they pleased, their perverted actions only brought them shame. Paul's closing description of these false teachers is a very straightforward one—"who mind earthly things".[28]

Paul uses the noun κοιλία *koilia* which in the earliest Greek references (5th century BC) referred to "hollow of the body"; i.e., the abdominal area, which denotes a hollow place or cavity (Rom. 16:18). Jesus refers to that which disrupts the relationship between man and God is not located in what is external and/or physical, which He addressed the Jewish superficial view of purification. He states that evil is rooted in a person's innermost part of their being.[29]

---

[27] Walvoord and Zuck, eds., *The Bible Knowledge Commentary*, Vol. 1, 228. Robert James Utley, *New Testament Survey: Matthew-Revelation* (Marshall, TX: Bible Lessons International, 2000), 84.

[28] Gilbrant, ed., *The Complete Biblical Library Commentary, Galatians-Philemon* (Springfield, IL: World Library Press, Inc., WORDsearch CROSS e-book, 1995), 221.

[29] κοιλία *koilia* "2809", In Gilbrant, ed., *The Complete Biblical Library Greek-English Dictionary, Zeta-Kappa*. Gerhard Kittel, Geoffrey W. Bromiley and Gerhard Friedrich, eds. *Theological Dictionary of the New* Testament electronic ed. Vol. 4 (Grand Rapids, MI: William B. Eerdmans Publishing Company, 1964), 788.

Again Jesus called the crowd to him and said, "Listen to me, everyone, and understand this. Nothing outside a man can make him 'unclean' by going into him. Rather, it is what comes out of a man that makes him 'unclean'" (Mk. 7:14-15)

In the New Testament, the belly is a necessary part of the body to maintain earthly life, but is corruptible. The Pauline perspective of the κοιλία was not founded upon the Greek world, which viewed the "belly" as the seat of unrestrained sensuality, gluttony or sexual licentiousness and doomed for destruction. The issue here in relation to fasting was gluttony or the lack of self-control or abuse of a normal appetite for food.[30]

Second, "their glory is in their shame". The term "glory" is often used in the Old Testament for God (Ps. 106:20) and "shame" is the Old Testament term contemptuously given to an idol (Jdg. 6:32). Instead of giving glory to God these teachers heaped praise upon themselves. Ironically, their morality and spiritual values were so backwards and chaotic that they boasted in the things that brought them shame.[31] Paul was a man who could boast in his own life and achievements. However, he chose not to, and would only boast in his weaknesses and in Christ,

> I will boast about a man like that, but I will not boast about myself, except about my weaknesses. Even if I should choose to boast, I would not be a fool, because I would be speaking the truth. But I refrain, so no one will think more of me than is warranted by what I do or say. . . . But he said to me, "My grace is sufficient for you, for my power is made perfect in weakness". Therefore I will boast all the more gladly about my weaknesses, so that Christ's power may rest on me. That is why, for Christ's sake, I delight in weaknesses, in insults, in hardships, in persecutions, in difficulties. For when I am weak, then I am strong (2 Cor. 12:5-6, 9-10; cf. 1 Cor. 1:31; 2 Cor. 10:17; 11:30).

Paul addressed individuals within the church and society that had become completely self-indulgent and unable to feel shame. When individuals progress to the point of boasting of shameful behaviours, they are on the edge of becoming beyond hope. They had arrived at what can be described as inverted spiritual values, proud of their gluttonous appetites for food, sexual gratification, and unrestrained lifestyle. They placed the shame on those who lived according to the standards of Jesus Christ, while they lived a perverted life of indulgences. They called the followers of Jesus Christ religious fanatics, very cruel, and someone without emotions.[32]

Third, "their mind is on earthly things". The issue that Paul addresses here is not that God's people should neglect earthly matters, but he warns them that they should not look to earthly things to achieve merit with God. The apostle frequently alerted the people of God against such a lifestyle (cf. Gal. 4:3, 9-

---

[30] Kittel, Bromiley and Friedrich, eds., *Theological Dictionary of the New Testament*, Vol. 4, 788. "Philippians 3:19", In Daniel D. Wheddon, *Whedon's Commentary on the Old and New Testaments* (Hunt & Eaton, 1875), Rick Meyers, e-Sword, Version 10.2.1, 2000-2012, <http://www.e-sword.net>. "Philippians 3:1-21", In J. R. Dummelow, ed., *A Commentary on the Holy Bible*, Rick Meyers, e-Sword, Version 10.2.1, 2000-2012, <http:// www.e-sword. net>.

[31] "Philippians 3:1-21", In Robert Jamieson, A. R. Fausset, and David Brown, *Commentary Critical and Explanatory on the Whole Bible* (Oak Harbor, WA: Logos Research Systems, Inc., 1997).

[32] Ellsworth, *Opening Up Philippians*, 76-77.

11; Col. 2:21-22). They were living as though God is dead, as though heaven and hell are myths, and as though this life is all there is.[33]

In the end of chapter 3, Paul boasts

> But our citizenship is in heaven. And we eagerly await a Savior from there, the Lord Jesus Christ, who, by the power that enables him to bring everything under his control, will transform our lowly bodies so that they will be like his glorious body (Phil. 3:20-21).

Paul, first of all, contrasts those whose citizenship is in heaven with those of verse 19 whose "mind is on earthly things". The true believer anticipates the return of their Saviour. The Greek phrase for "eagerly await" ἀπεκδεχόμεθα *apekdechometha*, is used eschatologically in the sense "to wait for, to expect", but even more "to wait for expectantly, intense expectation, to wait anxiously" (Rom. 8:19, 23, 25; 1 Cor. 1:7; Gal. 5:5; Heb. 9:28). Paul emphasizes that to those who believe and follow Jesus Christ, this world is not their home, but heaven.[34]

Second, Paul speaks of Christ's return and He "will transform" μετασχηματίζω *metaschēmatizō* our bodies, which means "transforming, altering" or "changing" the outward appearance of a person or thing. The LXX uses this verb to describe the transformation of the martyrs into incorruptibility (4 Macc. 9:22) and 1 Samuel 28:8 (1 Kings 28:8, LXX) uses the verb in reference to the disguising of Saul. There is a distinct difference between the two verbs μετασχηματίζω *metaschēmatizō* and μεταμορφόω *metamorphoō*. While both verbs share the first part of the word *meta* they also are distinctly different root meanings *schēma* and *morphē*. The root word *schēma* refers to something that is changeable, such as a person's speech, gestures, or clothing to name a few. The Greeks believed that the outward appearance was a reflection of a person's internal state, and the outward appearance could be deceptive. Therefore, *schema* could likewise denote the apparent contrasted with the actual. The only New Testament occurrence of the root word *morphoō* is Galatians 4:19.[35]

> Becoming a Christian is here depicted in terms of birth, and the goal is the forming of Christ in man. According to the apostle's view Christ lives in Christians (Gal. 2:20; Rom. 8:10; 2 Cor. 13:3, 5; Col. 1:27; 3:11). He dwells in their hearts (Eph. 3:17). They have σπλάγχνα Χριστοῦ Ἰησοῦ (Phil. 1:8) etc. In order that this Christ-life may come into being in believers, Christ must take form in them. He must in some sense be incarnate afresh in each individual. The nerve of

---

[33] Walvoord and Zuck, eds., *The Bible Knowledge Commentary*, Vol. 2, 662.

[34] ἀπεκδέχομαι *apekdechomai* "549", In Gilbrant, ed., *The Complete Biblical Library Greek-English Dictionary, Alpha-Gamma.*

[35] μετασχηματίζω *metaschēmatizō* "3215", In Thoralf Gilbrant, ed., *The Complete Biblical Library Greek-English Dictionary, Lambda-Omicron* (Springfield, MO: Complete Biblical Library, WORDsearch CROSS e-book, 1991). μεταμορφόω *metamorphoō* "3209", In Gilbrant, ed., *The Complete Biblical Library Greek-English Dictionary, Lambda-Omicron.* σχῆμα *schēma* "4828", In Thoralf Gilbrant, ed., *The Complete Biblical Library Greek-English Dictionary, Sigma-Omega* (Springfield, MO: Complete Biblical Library, WORDsearch CROSS e-book, 1991). μορφόω *morphoō* "3308", In Gilbrant, ed., *The Complete Biblical Library Greek-English Dictionary, Lambda-Omicron.*

this metaphor, which is based on the development of the child in the mother's womb, is that Christ should come to full growth, to maturity, in the Christian.[36]

The Greek phrase σπλάγχνοις Χριστοῦ Ἰησοῦ (*splanchnois Iēsou Christou*) literally means that we are to have the "inner affections of Christ Jesus". The word *morphoō* refers to the unique character and essence of a person or entity. In the Transfiguration of Jesus, the Greek verb that Matthew uses is not *metaschēmatizō*, but μετεμορφώθη *metemorphōthē* from *metamorphoō*, expressing an inner transformation—a change deeper than Christ's clothing (Mt. 17:2). The Apostle Paul in referring to false prophets transforming themselves into apostles or "Satan himself masquerades as an angel of light" (2 Cor. 11:14), uses the verb *metaschēmatizō*, conveying an outward change only, but not touching their essence.[37]

> For such men are false apostles, deceitful workmen, masquerading as apostles of Christ. And no wonder, for Satan himself masquerades as an angel of light. It is not surprising, then, if his servants masquerade as servants of righteousness. Their end will be what their actions deserve (2 Cor. 11:13-15).

When Jesus returns for His Church, He will transform *metaschēmatisei* "change the outward form of" our earthly bodies so that they will be like συμμορφούμενος *summorphoumenos* from συμμορφόω *summorphoō*, meaning "identical in essential character" (Phil. 3:10) His glorious body. Then "when he appears, we shall be like him, for we shall see him as he is" (1 Jn. 3:2)—all believers will receive glorified bodies, like His body. We will no longer have earthly limitations, including disease and sin and our sanctification will be completed.[38] Likewise, Paul states that he was not "mastered by anything" and that our "body is a temple of the Holy Spirit", therefore, we must honour the Lord with our body,

> "Everything is permissible for me"—but not everything is beneficial. "Everything is permissible for me"—but I will not be mastered by anything. "Food for the stomach and the stomach for food"—but God will destroy them both. The body is not meant for sexual immorality, but for the Lord, and the Lord for the body. . . . Do you not know that your body is a temple of the Holy Spirit, who is in you, whom you have received from God? You are not your own; you were bought at a price. Therefore honor God with your body (1 Cor. 6:12-13, 19-20).

Fasting and Our Physical and Spiritual Appetites

Jesus, in the Parable of the Sower, addresses "the desires for other things", which speaks of lusting after anything that would stand between themselves and their relationship with God. John Piper states,

---

[36] Kittel, Bromiley and Friedrich, eds., *Theological Dictionary of the New Testament*, Vol. 4, 753-54.

[37] μετασχηματίζω *metaschēmatizō* "3215", In Gilbrant, ed., *The Complete Biblical Library Greek-English Dictionary, Lambda-Omicron*. μεταμορφόω *metamorphoō* "3209", In Gilbrant, ed., *The Complete Biblical Library Greek-English Dictionary, Lambda-Omicron*.

[38] Walvoord and Zuck, eds., *The Bible Knowledge Commentary*, Vol. 2, 663. συμμορφούμενος *summorphoumenos* "4684", In Gilbrant, ed., *The Complete Biblical Library Greek-English Dictionary, Sigma-Omega*. Ellsworth, *Opening Up Philippians*, 77-78.

And the only weapon that will triumph is a deeper hunger for God. The weakness of our hunger for God is not because he is unsavory, but because we keep ourselves stuffed with "other things". Perhaps, then, the denial of our stomach's appetite for food might express, or even increase, our soul's appetite for God. . . . When the sense of God diminishes, fasting disappears.[39]

There are many things that in and of themselves are not evil, but anything may become evil if it becomes an obstacle to growing in the Word of God and becoming fruitful.[40]

Still others, like seed sown among thorns, hear the word; but the worries of this life, the deceitfulness of wealth and the desires for other things come in and choke the word, making it unfruitful (Mk. 4:18-19).

Likewise, Luke says that even though there is an appearance of fruit this fruit does "not mature",

The seed that fell among thorns stands for those who hear, but as they go on their way they are choked by life's worries, riches and pleasures, and they do not mature (Lk. 8:14).

This is a wakeup call for us to allow the Holy Spirit to speak to us regarding both our physical and spiritual appetites as Saint Basil the Great states,

In the physical fast, the body abstains from food and drink. In the spiritual fast, the faster abstains from evil intentions, words and deeds. One who truly fasts abstains from anger, rage, malice, and vengeance. One who truly fasts abstains from idle and foul talk, empty rhetoric, slander, condemnation, flattery, lying and all manner of spiteful talk. In a word, a real faster is one who withdraws from all evil. As much as you subtract from the body, so much will you add to the strength of the soul. By fasting, it is possible both to be delivered from future evils, and to enjoy the good things to come. We fell into disease through sin; let us receive healing through repentance, which is not fruitful without fasting. True fasting lies is rejecting evil, holding one's tongue, suppressing one's hatred, and banishing one's lust, evil words, lying, and betrayal of vows.[41]

Moreover, St. Ignatiy Brianchaninov states, "The reason that fasting has an effect on the spirits of evil rests in its powerful effect on our own spirit. A body subdued by fasting brings the human spirit freedom, strength, sobriety, purity, and keen discernment".[42]

In regards to our physical appetite, Elmer L. Towns states, "When you take control of your physical appetite, you develop strength to take control of your emotional appetite".[43] We can see that fasting brings "a superior satisfaction in God"—it takes us to a deeper level of intimacy with Him. Christian fasting is

---

[39] Piper, *A Hunger for God*, 13, 16.

[40] Gilbrant, ed., *The Complete Biblical Library Commentary, Mark* (Springfield, IL: World Library Press, Inc., WORDsearch CROSS e-book, 1988), 103.

[41] Saint Basil the Great, 329-379 AD; Doctor of the Catholic Church, <http://www.sfaturiortodoxe.ro/orthodox/orthodox_advices_fasting.htm>, Accessed on September 3, 2013.

[42] St. Ignatiy Brianchaninov, 1807-1867 AD, was a bishop and theologian of the Russian Orthodox Church, <http://www.sfaturiortodoxe.ro/orthodox/orthodox_advices_fasting.htm>, Accessed on September 3, 2013.

[43] Elmer L. Towns, *Fasting for Spiritual Breakthrough* (Ventura, CA: Regal Books, 1996), 31.

also God's chosen weapon to break the control of anything that could rob us of "a superior satisfaction in God". This is why fasting must be of the utmost importance along with prayer in our lives. John Piper states that at the root of Christian fasting

> is the hunger of a homesickness for God. . . . Half of Christian fasting is that our physical appetite is lost because our homesickness for God is so intense. The other half is that our homesickness for God is threatened because our physical appetites are so intense. In the first half, appetite is lost. In the second half, appetite is resisted. In the first, we yield to the higher hunger that is. In the second, we fight for the higher hunger that isn't. Christian fasting is not only the spontaneous effect of a superior satisfaction in God; it is also a chosen weapon against every force in the world that would take that satisfaction away.[44]

Likewise, in regards to the root of Christian fasting, the following points can be seen: first, there are more than seventy biblical references that discuss the topic of fasting in Scripture and that appropriate biblical fasting is a valid form of spiritual devotion. Both the prophets and Jesus denounced pretentious and unrighteous fasting. However, proper fasting that comes from a right heart, backed up with a righteous life and a right attitude, is affirmed and accepted by God.

Second, Scripture presents the great cloud of witnesses in the Old Testament in relation to fasting. There is Moses (Ex. 34:28), Samuel (1 Sam. 7:6), David (Ps. 69:10-21), Jonathan (1 Sam. 20:34), Jehoshaphat (2 Chr. 20:3), Ezra (Ezra 10:6), Nehemiah (Neh. 1:4-10), Daniel (Dan. 9:3), Esther (Est. 4:10-17), Elijah (2 Kgs. 19:8), Joel (Joel 1:14), and Zechariah (Zech. 8:18). Moreover, there is only one specific Scripture that God commands a fast, the Day of Atonement (Lev. 16:29). The Mosaic Law stated that fasting was to be adhered to on the Day of Atonement (Lev. 16:29-31; 23:27) and that any other fasting was voluntary. The only exception to this was a fast declared in times of national emergency (Jdg. 20:26; 2 Chr. 20:3; Joel 2:15). The destruction of Jerusalem and the subsequent Exile encouraged annual fasts in observance of this national trauma

> The people of Bethel had sent Sharezer and Regem-Melek, together with their men, to entreat the LORD by asking the priests of the house of the LORD Almighty and the prophets, "Should I mourn and fast in the fifth month, as I have done for so many years?" Then the word of the LORD Almighty came to me: "Ask all the people of the land and the priests, 'When you fasted and mourned in the fifth and seventh months for the past seventy years, was it really for me that you fasted? (Zech. 7:2-5; cf. 8:19).

Third, there are many New Testament examples of fasting, Anna the prophetess (Lk. 2:37), John the Baptist and his disciples (Lk. 5:33), Jesus (Mt. 4:2), Paul and Barnabas (Acts 14:23), and the elders at Antioch (Acts 13:3). Fourth, Jesus echoed the sentiments of the Old Testament prophets in opposing ostentatious fasting as commonly practiced by the Pharisees (Mt. 6:16-18; cf. Isa. 58:3-7; Jer. 14:12; Zech. 7:5). He considered voluntary fasting a legitimate means of attaining humility and for reflecting on God's word (Mt. 9:14-15). In the early Church, fasting was observed as a preparation for important

---

[44] Piper, *A Hunger for God*, 17f.

decisions (e.g., Acts 13:2-3; 14:23). Weekly fasts became a regular practice on Wednesday and Friday (*Didache* 8:1).[45] Jesus assumes that His followers will fast on certain occasions, i.e., His statements in reference to fasting indicate that it is a normal and acceptable part of the Christian life,

> When you fast, do not look somber as the hypocrites do, for they disfigure their faces to show men they are fasting. I tell you the truth, they have received their reward in full. But when you fast, put oil on your head and wash your face, so that it will not be obvious to men that you are fasting, but only to your Father, who is unseen; and your Father, who sees what is done in secret, will reward you (Mt. 6:16-18).

Last, there are numerous giants of the faith throughout church history who fasted, these include: the early church fathers, Augustine, Martin Luther, John Calvin, John Knox, Jonathan Edwards, David Brainard, the Wesleys, and many others. All of these men regularly prayed and fasted. As Gordon P. Broadbent III states, "while there is always a danger of falling prey to false teaching in regard to fasting, extremes in practice, and distortions of the biblical perspective on fasting, the weight of evidence indicates it is a subject for believers to study and apply".[46] Keyan Soltani states that fasting is "not just for mystics and the monastics, but for every Christian. Fasting is not about us, nor is it about our devotion to God, as so many prescribe. We are a culture of abundance that indulges and abuses, but fasting is a means of God's grace to embrace someone greater than our appetites".[47]

John Piper also writes concerning fasting and our hunger for a deeper level of relationship with God, "When God is the supreme hunger of our hearts, He will be supreme in everything". A final thought concerns our contentment in our relationship with the Lord, "The absence of fasting is indicative of our comfort with the way things are. No one fasts to express how content they are. People only fast out of dissatisfaction. . . . The absence of fasting is the measure of our contentment with the absence of Christ".[48] We need to take a close look at whom or what is supreme in our hearts, in everything that affects us, and also our contentment with our relationship with Jesus Christ.

Jentezen Franklin states that through fasting we break free from the world's routine,

> fasting is a constant means of renewing yourself spiritually. The discipline of fasting breaks you out of the world's routine. It is a form of worship—offering your body to God as a living sacrifice is holy and pleasing to God (Rom. 12:1). The discipline of fasting will humble you, remind you of your dependency on God, and bring you back to your first love. It causes the roots of your relationship with Jesus to go deeper. . . . Fasting makes you more sensitive to the timing and voice of the Holy Spirit. . . . Fasting does such a work in your life that the lost are often drawn to you and to what God is doing. It's not that we manipulate God through our works, forcing His hand. Fasting simply breaks you and brings your faith to a new level.[49]

---

[45] Allen C. Myers, *The Eerdmans Bible Dictionary* (Grand Rapids, MI: William B. Eerdmans Publishing Company, 1987), 377.

[46] Gordon P. Broadbent III, *A Call to Biblical Fasting: A Written Sermon*, Doctoral unpublished manuscript (Sun Valley, CA: The Master's Seminary, October 30, 2006), 3-4.

[47] Piper, *A Hunger for God*, i.

[48] Piper, *A Hunger for God*, 14, 87.

[49] Jentezen Franklin, *Fasting* (Lake Mary, FL: Charisma House, 2008), 71, 104, 105.

He also states that fasting stirs up within our spirits a spiritual hunger that reaches a deeper level of hunger than can never be experienced through our physical hunger. There were cities where Jesus could not perform miracles due to their lack of hunger for God. Jesus, in His hometown of Nazareth, "did not do many miracles there because of their lack of faith" (Mt. 13:58). This kind of hunger was stirred up within the centurion who with "his family were devout and God-fearing; he gave generously to those in need and prayed to God regularly" (Acts 10:2).

> Hungry people are desperate people, and they are hungry for more of God than they have ever been. They are breaking out of religious rules, regulations, and traditional thinking and breaking through to more of His presence, more of His power to turn situations around, more of His healing power, and more of His miracle-working power! Only Jesus satisfies that hunger.[50]

Why Should Christians Fast?

Christians should practice the spiritual discipline of fasting since Jesus taught His disciples to fast. Jesus taught "**when you fast**" not "**if**" (Mt. 6:16) and taught that God looks favourably upon those who fast with proper motives,

> When you fast, do not look somber as the hypocrites do, for they disfigure their faces to show men they are fasting. I tell you the truth, they have received their reward in full. But when you fast, put oil on your head and wash your face, so that it will not be obvious to men that you are fasting, but only to your Father, who is unseen; and your Father, who sees what is done in secret, will reward you (Mt. 6:16-18).

Jesus also taught that the bridegroom would soon be taken from them and then they would fast. Likewise, fasting should be done only when circumstances necessitate its practice,

> Then John's disciples came and asked him, "How is it that we and the Pharisees fast, but your disciples do not fast?" Jesus answered, "How can the guests of the bridegroom mourn while he is with them? The time will come when the bridegroom will be taken from them; then they will fast (Mt. 9:14-15).

Furthermore, occasions would arise when prayer needed to be added to fasting, "But this kind does not go out except by prayer and fasting" (Mt. 17:21). Saint Athanasius the Great stated,

> Seest thou what fasting does: it heals illnesses, drives out demons, removes wicked thoughts, makes the heart pure. If someone has even been seized by an impure spirit, let him know that this kind, according to the word of the Lord, "goeth not out but by prayer and fasting" (Matthew 17:21).[51]

Today, many Christians struggle with the question "why should Christians fast?" Elmer L. Towns suggests nine reasons why Christians today need to practice the spiritual discipline of fasting:

---

[50] Franklin, *Fasting*, 81.

[51] Saint Athanasius the Great, ca. 296-373 AD, 20th Bishop of Alexandria, Christian Theologian and Church Father, <http://www.sfaturiortodoxe.ro/orthodox/orthodox_advices_fasting.htm>, Accessed on September 3, 2013.

1. More than ever before, believers are in bondage to demonic powers and need strength to stand against sin;
2. Believers throughout the world need solutions to many complex problems and threatening situations they are facing;
3. The Church is in desperate need of revival, and every tribe and tongue and nation is in desperate need of evangelization;
4. The world in general and the Church in particular are crying out for people of character and integrity—people who have found in Christ the emotional healing and strength to overcome sinful and destructive habits;
5. The abundance of food has insulated North American believers from the realities of starvation and malnutrition in the two-thirds world;
6. The media has so captured the national attention that even believers are operating according to principles completely alien to God's will for their lives;
7. Even with the abundance of food and medical technology in North America, people are not necessarily healthier;
8. A great many believers have become so entangled in economic and social pursuits that they need to be set free to establish their testimonies and to influence others for Christ;
9. The growing influence of demonic forces and the waning influence of biblical Christianity in North America and the fact that believers need protection from the evil one.[52]

When Should Christians Fast?

Now we need to answer the question, when should we as Christians fast. The discipline of fasting should be practiced anytime that we need divine help, which includes,

1. personal issues;
2. difficult temptations;
3. serious illness of a family member or friend;
4. appointing elders;
5. sending out missionaries.

When we are faced with circumstances where we need to persist in prayer, fasting can empower our prayers if we persistent (cf. Lk. 18:1-8) and if we follow God's method of true fasting

> When you fast, do not look somber as the hypocrites do, for they disfigure their faces to show others they are fasting. Truly I tell you, they have received their reward in full. But when you fast, put oil on your head and wash your face, so that it will not be obvious to others that you are fasting, but only to your Father, who is unseen; and your Father, who sees what is done in secret, will reward you (Mt. 6:16-18; cf. Isa. 58).

First of all, there are many examples in the early church when people fasted.[53]

---

[52] Elmer L. Towns, *Fasting for Spiritual Breakthrough Study Guide*, <http://digitalcommons.liberty.edu/towns_books/17>, Accessed on September 3, 2013.

[53] Copeland, *Fasting: A Special Study*, <http://www.e-sword.net>. Accessed on June 12, 2014.

1. The church in Antioch (Acts 13:1-3):

    a. fasted in their service to the Lord;
    b. fasted and prayed before sending out Paul and Barnabas on their missionary journey.

2. The churches of Galatia (Acts 14:21-23):

    a. fasted in each church;
    b. fasted before appointing elders in each church and committing them to the Lord.

Second, Paul as a minister of Christ listed fasting as a discipline that proved him as a minister of the Lord, "I have known hunger and thirst and have often gone without food" (2 Cor. 11:23-28). He also states that we should "follow my example, as I follow the example of Christ" (1 Cor. 11:1). Therefore, Christians should fast for various reasons:

1. voluntarily for health reasons;
2. voluntarily in an effort to gain self-control;
3. involuntarily in times of grief and sorrow.

As Christians, we should fast when we need the help of the Lord.

1. Fasting was practiced by many in the Old Testament:

    a. in times of war or threats of war—Israel;
    b. when a family member was sick—David;
    c. when seeking God for forgiveness—Ahab and Daniel;
    d. when seeking God's protection—Ezra.

2. Fasting was practiced by many in the New Testament:

    a. when confronted with temptation—Jesus (Mt. 4:1-11; Mk. 1:9-13; Lk. 4:1-13);
    b. when serving the Lord—Antioch;
    c. when starting a new mission—Antioch;
    d. when selecting and appointing elders—Galatia.

3. Fasting should be done in conjunction with prayer. God listens to the prayers of a humble person (Ezra 8:21-23).[54]

    a. to humble the soul (Ps. 35:13);
    b. to chasten the soul (Ps. 69:10).

We are often faced with overwhelming circumstances and in need of divine intervention. It is through fasting that we can attain God's favour. Some examples include:

---

[54] Copeland, *Fasting: A Special Study*, <http://www.e-sword.net>. Accessed on June 12, 2014.

1. A method of seeking God with sincerity: "you will seek me and find me when you seek me with all your heart" (Jer. 29:13);
2. Protection, Repentance and Blessing: "even now", declares the Lord, "return to me with all your heart, with fasting and weeping and mourning" (Joel 2:12; 2:13-32; Ezra 8:21-23, 31);
3. Direction and Guidance (Acts 13:1-3);
4. Illness/Severe Illness/Grief: (2 Sam. 12:15-19);
5. Humility (Ps. 35:13; 1 Kgs. 21:25-27);
6. Communication with God and the Holy Spirit (Ex. 34:28, Acts 13:1-3);
7. Fighting evil / casting out demons: in the account of the healing of a boy with an evil spirit, Jesus responds to His disciples question privately; "why couldn't we drive it out?" He replied, "This kind can come out only by prayer [and fasting]" (Mk. 9:28-29).

Chapter 2: Fasting and the Spiritual Disciplines

The purpose of this chapter is to describe the spiritual disciplines of almsgiving, prayer, and fasting and how this "cord of three strands" is not easily broken. It also discusses the heart of fasting and the necessity of disciplining our physical and spiritual appetites, its root which can be traced back to Sodom and Gomorrah, and conquering these appetites will lead to an increasing level of intimacy with the Lord. We finally discuss fasting and prayer, which is referenced throughout this study and Christian fasting in relation to the major religions of the world.

Three Spiritual Disciplines

> As the deer pants for streams of water, so my soul pants for you, O God. My soul thirsts for God, for the living God. When can I go and meet with God? My tears have been my food day and night, while men say to me all day long, "Where is your God?" (Ps. 42:1-3)

Fasting is a vital part of the Christian life and those who practice this spiritual discipline enter into a deeper, more intimate relationship with the Lord. As David says in Psalms 42, "deep calls to deep" (v. 7) and as Franklin says, "When you eliminate food from your diet for a number of days, your spirit becomes uncluttered by the things of this world and amazingly sensitive to the things of God".[55] As David was fasting here, his desire for a more intimate relationship—hunger and thirst for God—became a higher priority than his desire for food. David from the depths of his spirit cried out to the depths of God during his struggles.

Jesus, in His Sermon on the Mount, emphasizes the Christian disciplines of almsgiving, praying, and fasting (Mt. 6:1-18). Franklin links these Christian disciplines together to show that fasting should be practiced equally as almsgiving and praying. Murphy writes that

> prayer, fasting, and charity . . . are the three pillars of Old Testament piety that were taken over and confirmed in the New Testament. . . . The first charge given in the gospels by Jesus to his disciples is, "Repent and believe the gospel!" (Mk. 1:15). This is why the obligations to pray, fast, and do works of charity are so central. They are the most important means to accomplish our repentance, our turning away (literally, "conversion") from sinfulness. As the *Catechism of the Catholic Church* teaches through fasting, our conversion is directed to ourselves; through prayer, our conversion focuses us upon God; and through almsgiving, our conversion expresses itself in compassionate concern for our neighbor. . . . Just as there is no substitute for working out in the gym in order to train the body, so there is no substitute for fasting—for example, by doing works of charity—in order to achieve the purity of heart that we seek. The ancients, we realize, were correct in their conviction that prayer and fasting are needed if true charity, unhindered by our selfishness, is to take place at all.[56]

These Christian disciplines create, as Solomon writes, "a cord of three strands is not quickly broken" (Eccl. 4:12) and was the strongest cord made in the ancient world. Some scholars explain "a cord of three

---

[55] Franklin, *Fasting*, 10.

[56] Charles M. Murphy, *The Spirituality of Fasting, Rediscovering A Christian Practice* (Notre Dame, IN: Ave Maria Press, 2010), 4-5.

strands" as referring to the Father, Son, and Holy Spirit, or the three monastic vows of poverty, chastity, and obedience, or the theological virtues of faith, hope, and love. Moreover, the number three is used as the symbol of union, completeness, perfection, finality, of definitiveness. The context here speaks of friendship and a single cord was easy to break; two cords would require more strength, but "a cord of three strands" woven together was difficult to break. This style of writing was typical of Hebrew literature (cf. Pr. 6:16; Am. 1:3, 6, 9). According to Solomon, this was more than about numbers; he was thinking of the unity of three cords woven together as a unit.[57]

Likewise, Isaiah 5:18 says "Woe to those who draw sin along with cords of deceit, and wickedness as with cart ropes". This Chaldeen paraphrase helps clarify the Lord's woe, "To those who begin to sin by little and little, drawing sin by cords of vanity: these sins grow and increase till they are strong and are like a cart rope". The term "cart rope" as used by Isaiah was used to fasten loads on a cart and for yoking or harnessing animals to the cart, i.e., the Ark of the Covenant. In the context of Isaiah, it was used as "a symbol of the power of sinful pleasures or habits over him who indulges them".[58] This describes how sin that is practiced increases and gains a stronger foothold in our lives. Isaiah refers to these individuals as wicked

> The wicked at first draw sin with a slender cord; but by-and-by their sins increase, and they are drawn after them by a cart rope. . . . "The meaning is that the persons described were not satisfied with ordinary modes of provoking the Deity, and the consequent ordinary approach of his vengeance, but, as it were, yoked themselves in the harness of iniquity, and, putting forth all their strength, drew down upon themselves, with accelerated speed, the load of punishment which their sins deserved".[59]

It is interesting that the strength of the cord is dependent upon the quality and support of each individual strand. Its strength lies in the strength of its weakest strand and if one strand has a flaw, it weakens the whole cord. However, if "a cord of three strands" are weaved or united together they are able to conquer any enemy, "*vis unita fortior est*". Jesus referred to a kingdom divided against itself will not stand, "Jesus knew their thoughts and said to them, 'Every kingdom divided against itself will be ruined, and every city or household divided against itself will not stand'" (Mt. 12:25), but if united, it has the strength to stand against anything. However, if these cords become untwisted and unloosed, they can then

---

[57] "Ecclesiastes 4:12", In George Leo Haydock, *Haydock Catholic Bible Commentary*, Rick Meyers, e-Sword, Version 10.2.1, 2000-2012, <http://www.e-sword.net>. "Ecclesiastes 4:1-16", In H. D. M. Spence, *Pulpit Commentary*, Rick Meyers, e-Sword, Version 10.2.1, 2000-2012, <http://www.e-sword.net>. שָׁלֹשׁ *šālōš* "2403", In Harris, R. Laird, Gleason L. Archer, Jr. and Bruce K. Waltke, eds. *Theological Wordbook of the Old Testament*, electronic ed., (Chicago, IL: Moody Press, 1999), 933. Warren W. Wiersbe, *Be Satisfied*, "Be" Commentary Series (Wheaton, IL: Victor Books, 1996), 19.

[58] "Cart", In M. G. Easton, *Easton's Bible Dictionary* (New York: Harper & Brothers, 1893).

[59] "Cord", In Easton, *Easton's Bible Dictionary*.

be easily broken.[60] It is "a cord of three strands" of sin that requires fasting to break its power in our lives, since it has taken up root in our lives and must be uprooted so that we can mature in the Lord.

The Heart of Fasting

> I have been crucified with Christ and I no longer live, but Christ lives in me. The life I live in the body, I live by faith in the Son of God, who loved me and gave himself for me (Gal. 2:20).

The heart of fasting is about crucifying anything that hinders us from developing a more intimate relationship with the Lord. This means that we need to discipline the part of our body that becomes an obstacle to the deeper things of God—our appetite or stomach. The more we conquer our appetite the deeper we will grow in the Lord. Scripture has many examples, but only a few will be emphasized. The first example refers to Sodom and Gomorrah and the sin that was rampant throughout the Cities of the Plain: Sodom, Gomorrah, Admah, Zeboiim, and Zoar. After the destruction of these cities, they became "a potent biblical metaphor symbolizing the wrath of God.[61] Even though it seems that the sin that led to the fall of these Cities of the Plain as selfishness and homosexuality, it was much more than this as the prophet Ezekiel describes,

> Look, this was the iniquity of your sister Sodom: She and her daughter had pride, fullness of food, and abundance of idleness; neither did she strengthen the hand of the poor and needy. And they were haughty and committed abomination before Me; therefore I took them away as I saw *fit* (Eze. 16:49-50, NKJV).

The primary sin of Sodom and Gomorrah was pride, self-exaltation, defiance of God, false security, apathy, a luxurious life of ease, contempt, and neglect of the poor and needy. In Ezekiel, this is known as the parable of the three sisters (16:48-52). Israel and Judah (Jer. 3:7), and Jerusalem and Samaria (Eze. 16:46) are called sisters, referring to their common bloodlines. Sodom and Gomorrah was plagued by sexual perversion and its destruction is well documented in the book of Genesis (Gen. 19). It was Sodom and Gomorrah's "fullness of food" and "abundance of idleness" that resulted in her becoming full of pride, arrogance, and a haughty spirit. It was this elitism that resulted in neglecting to "strengthen the hand of the poor and needy". Their "fullness of food" and "abundance of idleness" had produced the crimes that have been previously stated, but they lacked the self-control and discipline that would produce good fruit. It was the mercy of the Lord that had blessed them with "fullness of food" and it was their sin

---

[60] Frank E. Gaebelein, ed., *The Expositor's Bible Commentary, Volume 5: Psalms, Proverbs, Ecclesiastes, Song of Songs* (Grand Rapids, MI: Zondervan Publishing House. Database © 2010 WORDsearch CROSS e-book, 1991), 1166. "Ecclesiastes 4:12", In John Gill, *John Gill's Exposition of the Entire Bible*, Rick Meyers, e-Sword, Version 10.2.1, 2000-2012, <http://www.e-sword.net>.

[61] "Sodom and the Cities of the Plain", In John D. Barry and Lazarus Wentz, eds., *The Lexham Bible Dictionary* (Bellingham, WA: Logos Bible Software, 2012).

that they abused this bountiful blessing. This heartless arrogance led Sodom to commit abominations before the Lord and subsequent judgment and destruction.[62]

Ezekiel discusses a number of areas of concern: first of all, there was an absence of praying, which resulted in an attitude of arrogance, pride, and idleness. Ezekiel uses the noun גָּאוֹן *gā'ôn* for pride, known as rebellion, defiance, or simply sin. In Israel, both individual and national pride had led them to destruction. On the individual level, the righteous found it better to identify with the "poor and needy" than to identify with the proud. They reaped what they had sown, "This is what they will get in return for their pride, for insulting and mocking the people of the LORD Almighty" (Zeph. 2:10).[63]

It is also interesting that Ezekiel does not mention the sexual perversion of homosexuality for which Sodom and Gomorrah were infamous,

> In a similar way, Sodom and Gomorrah and the surrounding towns gave themselves up to sexual immorality and perversion. They serve as an example of those who suffer the punishment of eternal fire (Jude 7).

However, the prophet Ezekiel's focus was upon the pride or arrogant or haughty spirit of the people. It is the root of pride that had produced various types of wickedness and fruit in the lives and cultures in which the spirit of pride had dominated. Ezekiel uses the adjective for pride גָּאוֹן *gā'ôn* (v. 49) and the verb for haughty גָּבַהּ *gāvahh* (v. 50). Even though there is a positive side of pride, here it presents the negative concept of arrogance.[64] This refers to their self-importance and self-centeredness in the eyes of others while neglecting those who they were called to serve as leaders. The root word used for pride is גָּאָה *gā'â*, which was an attitude referring back to Sodom and Gomorrah "In his arrogance the wicked man hunts down the weak, who are caught in the schemes he devises" (cf. Ps. 10:2). These leaders were guilty of arrogance, cynical insensitivity to the poor and needy, and presumption. It is both a behavioural tendency and a form of deportment, which are inseparably connected. Pride can be seen in Scripture as ultimately leading to destruction (Pr. 15:25; 16:18; Jer. 13:9; Isa. 13:11, et al).[65]

---

[62] "Chapter 28: Parable of the Three Sisters (Eze. 16:44-63)", In James E. Smith, *The Major Prophets*, Old Testament Survey Series (Joplin, MO: College Press, 1992). אָחוֹת *'āchôth* "269", In Thoralf Gilbrant, ed., *The Complete Biblical Library Hebrew-English Dictionary, Aleph-Beth* (Springfield, IL: World Library Press, Inc., WORDsearch CROSS e-book, 1998). Samuel J. Schultz and Gary V. Smith, *Exploring the Old Testament* (Wheaton, IL: Crossway Books, 2001), 191. "Ezekiel 16:48-50", In Joseph S. Exell, ed., *The Biblical Illustrator*, 1849, Rick Meyers, e-Sword, Version 10.2.1, 2000-2012, <http://www.e-sword.net>. "Ezekiel 16:49", In Gill, *John Gill's Exposition of the Entire Bible*.

[63] גָּאוֹן *gā'ôn* "1377", In Thoralf Gilbrant, ed., *The Complete Biblical Library Hebrew-English Dictionary, Gimel-Zayin* (Springfield, IL: World Library Press, Inc., WORDsearch CROSS e-book, 1998).

[64] "Ezekiel 16:49-50", In Thoralf Gilbrant, ed., *The Complete Biblical Library Commentary, Ezekiel* (Springfield, IL: World Library Press, Inc., WORDsearch CROSS e-book, 1996). גָּאוֹן *gā'ôn* "1377", In Gilbrant, ed., *The Complete Biblical Library Hebrew-English Dictionary, Gimel-Zayin.* גָּבַהּ *gāvahh* "1391", In Gilbrant, ed., *The Complete Biblical Library Hebrew-English Dictionary, Gimel-Zayin.*

[65] גָּאָה "299", In Harris, Archer, Jr., and Waltke, eds., *Theological Wordbook of the Old Testament*, 143. "Ezekiel 16:49-50", In Gilbrant, ed., *The Complete Biblical Library Commentary, Ezekiel.*

Second, there was an absence of fasting. Ezekiel uses the noun שִׂבְעַת־לֶחֶם *śib'at-leḥem* meaning satiety of food. This is the only reference in Scripture, used as an allegory, in which Ezekiel portrays Judah to Samaria as prostitutes. The root of this lied in their extravagant material ("fullness of food") or in today's culture, gluttony. The imagery that Ezekiel uses here focuses upon the leaders and their lack of faith in Yahweh, yet portrays their confidence in political alliances. These leaders acknowledged and worshipped the pagan gods and made alliances with them, but neglected worshipping the One true God. The sins of Judah's leaders was their oppression of the poor and needy contrary to their "fullness of food".[66]

Ezekiel also uses the phrase הַשְׁקֵטוּשַׁלְוַת *wĕšalwat hašqēṭ* ("abundance of idleness") meaning "careless ease" or "carefree peace". This lifestyle fostered sexual perversion (Gen. 13:13; 18:20; 19:4-5) and Ezekiel in this passage both exhorts and warns against wickedness and continuing to live in a lifestyle contrary to living a life of holiness. Even though wickedness was rampant in Sodom, it was insignificant as compared to that of the prophets of Jerusalem, which Jeremiah speaks of,

> And among the prophets of Jerusalem I have seen something horrible: They commit adultery and live a lie. They strengthen the hands of evildoers, so that no one turns from his wickedness. They are all like Sodom to me; the people of Jerusalem are like Gomorrah. Therefore, this is what the LORD Almighty says concerning the prophets: "I will make them eat bitter food and drink poisoned water, because from the prophets of Jerusalem ungodliness has spread throughout the land" (Jer. 23:14-15).

Jeremiah writes concerning the influence of the prophets upon the people, which was equated with the wickedness of Sodom and Gomorrah. God's only response to such wickedness was to discipline the prophets, since they poisoned the nation's spiritual springs. This discipline was described as bitter food "wormwood" which was a bitter herb used figuratively to denote "bitterness", "calamity" or "a curse". Likewise, they would "drink poisoned water" מֵי־רֹאשׁוְהִשְׁקִתִים *wĕhišqitîm mê-rō'š*, which the false prophets of Jerusalem had poured out into the land. In retribution, God would make them drink this polluted and poisonous water.[67]

Third, there was an absence of giving and/or serving which manifested itself in not helping "the poor and needy" in spite of their wealth which came from God. Ezekiel uses the phrase לֹא וְאֶבְיוֹןוְיַד־עָנִי הֶחֱזִיקָה *wĕyad-'ānî wĕ'ebyôn lō' heḥĕzîqâ* "neither did she strengthen the hand of the poor and needy".

---

[66] שִׂבְעָה *siv'āh* "7886", In Thoralf Gilbrant, ed., *The Complete Biblical Library Hebrew-English Dictionary, Sin-Taw* (Springfield, IL: World Library Press, Inc., WORDsearch CROSS e-book, 1998).

[67] "Jeremiah 23:13-15", In Thoralf Gilbrant, ed., *The Complete Biblical Library Commentary, Jeremiah-Lamentations* (Springfield, IL: World Library Press, Inc., WORDsearch CROSS e-book, 1996). Gaebelein, ed., *The Expositor's Bible Commentary, Volume 6: Isaiah, Jeremiah, Lamentations, Ezekiel* (Grand Rapids, MI: Zondervan Publishing House. Database © 2010 WORDsearch CROSS e-book, 1986), 521. לַעֲנָה *la'ănāh* "4081", In Gilbrant, ed., *The Complete Biblical Library Hebrew-English Dictionary, Kaph-Mem* (Springfield, IL: World Library Press, Inc., WORDsearch CROSS e-book, 1998). Gaebelein, ed., *The Expositor's Bible Commentary*, Vol. 6, 817. שִׂבְעָה *siv'āh* "7886", In Gilbrant, ed., *The Complete Biblical Library Hebrew-English Dictionary, Sin-Taw.*

The prophet declares that the mistreatment of the "poor and needy" is a dangerous sin since those who treat others in this way will face the wrath of God who cares for those who are looked down upon by society. Elihu recognized this truth (Job 36:6, 15), which caught the Lord's attention (Job 34:28). God commended King Josiah who "defended the cause of the poor and needy" (Jer. 22:16), and Isaiah declared that God's chosen fast was "to share your food with the hungry and to provide the poor wanderer with shelter" (Isa. 58:7). John Gill writes concerning "neither did she strengthen the hands of the poor and needy",

> though she had such abundance of food to supply them with, and so much leisure to attend to their distress; but her pride would not suffer her to do it; and she was too idle and slothful to regard such service; perhaps more is intended than is expressed; that she weakened the hands of the poor and needy, and cruelly oppressed them; which is often done by proud men, in great affluence and at leisure, which they abuse to bad purposes.[68]

There are numerous examples in the Old Testament which speak of the wicked oppressing and afflicting the poor and needy. The Psalms describe the cry of the poor and needy and how our ears need to hear their distress and help deliver them from their oppressors (Ps. 9:12; 10:12; 69:29; 70:5; 74:19; 86:1; 109:22). He responds with compassion (Isa. 49:13), saves the afflicted (Ps. 34:6; 35:10), provides for the poor (Ps. 68:10) and sustains the cause of the oppressed (Ps. 140:12). The adjective עָנִי *ʿānî* emphasizes the character quality of humility that comes from a proper response to affliction. The humble are contrasted with the haughty (2 Sam. 22:28; Ps. 18:27), the proud (Pr. 16:19) and the scoffer (Pr. 3:34). This humility is a Messianic trait as Jesus rides into Jerusalem as King on a donkey.[69]

> Rejoice greatly, Daughter Zion! Shout, Daughter Jerusalem! See, your king comes to you, righteous and victorious, lowly and riding on a donkey, on a colt, the foal of a donkey (Zech. 9:9).

There is also the example of Esau (עֵשָׂו *ʿēśāw*, "the red man") who was overcome by his physical appetite for red stew (v. 30) and was deceived by Jacob (יַעֲקֹב *yaʿăqōv*, "the heel-grabber") into selling his birthright in exchange for the "red stew".

> Once when Jacob was cooking some stew, Esau came in from the open country, famished. He said to Jacob, "Quick, let me have some of that red stew! I'm famished!" (That is why he was also called Edom.) Jacob replied, "First sell me your birthright". "Look, I am about to die", Esau said. "What good is the birthright to me?" But Jacob said, "Swear to me first". So he swore an oath to him, selling his birthright to Jacob. Then Jacob gave Esau some bread and some lentil stew. He ate and drank, and then got up and left. So Esau despised his birthright" (Gen. 25:29-34).

---

[68] "Ezekiel 16:49", In Gill, *John Gill's Exposition of the Entire Bible*, <http://www.e-sword.net>.

[69] עָנִי *ʿānî* "6270", In Gilbrant, ed., *The Complete Biblical Library Hebrew-English Dictionary*, Nun-Ayin (Springfield, IL: World Library Press, Inc., WORDsearch CROSS e-book, 1998).

The focus here is upon birthright or primogeniture. Moses uses the noun בְּכֹרָה *bekhōrāh* (πρωτότοκος, *prōtotokos*) which occurs ten times in the Old Testament and refers to the rights of the first-born in a family. Of all the occurrences, the most well-known is when Esau sells his birthright to Jacob to satisfy his appetite. Therefore, the inheritance that should have belonged to Esau, the first-born, was given to Jacob. Even though the first-born received a "double share of all he has", this did not always happen.

> He must acknowledge the son of his unloved wife as the firstborn by giving him a double share of all he has. That son is the first sign of his father's strength. The right of the firstborn belongs to him (Deut. 21:17).

In the case of Jacob, his first-born son Reuben forfeited his rights to the sons of Joseph when he slept with Jacob's concubine Bilhah (Gen. 35:22). Likewise, Simeon and Levi, who were next in line, forfeited their rights concurrently by their deceitful acts against Shechem and Judah thinking that he had slept with a temple prostitute later found out that she was his daughter-in-law. Judah then repented of his behaviour while there is no record of his brothers repenting. Due to Judah's repentance the first-born rights and the messianic line remained with Judah.[70] The birthrights of the eldest son is a known fact in the ancient Near East,

> This preferential treatment of the eldest son is known throughout the ancient Near East (Mari, Nuzi, Alalakh, Ugarit, Assyria), although the law codes of Lipit-Ishtar (20th century BC.) and Hammurabi (18th century BC.) both legislate an equal sharing of the inheritance by all the male heirs. In the Old Testament, the law of Deuteronomy 21:15-17 protects the birthright of the eldest son, although the sale of the birthright to a younger son is known from Nuzi as well as from the Old Testament (Gen. 25:27-34). The disregarding of primogeniture by the choice of a younger rather than the eldest son is witnessed both in the Old Testament (Gen. 48:12-20; cf. Rom. 9:12) and in texts from Nuzi, Alalakh, and Ugarit.[71]

Moreover, this birthright privileges established with the first-born son (Num. 3:12-13; 8:18; 2 Chr. 21:3), could be doubled (Deut. 21:15-17), forfeited (Gen. 49:4; 1 Chr. 5:1), or transferred (Gen. 25:33). The birthright privileges, in the New Testament, were designated to Jesus the Messiah (Rom. 8:29; Col. 1:18; Heb. 1:4-6).[72] "Esau became a skillful hunter, a man of the open country while Jacob was a quiet man, staying among the tents" (v. 27). God had a plan and purpose for Esau, however, his appetite and craving for food and indulgence for the immediate pleasures in life outweighed his birthright. The context of Esau and Jacob presents two types of people: the first is seen in Esau, whose birthright was of great

---

[70] בְּכֹרָה *bekhōrāh* "1112", In Gilbrant, ed., *The Complete Biblical Library Hebrew-English Dictionary, Aleph-Beth*.

[71] "Birthright", In Paul J. Achtemeier, ed., *Harper's Bible Dictionary*, 1st ed (San Francisco, CA: Harper & Row, 1985), 134-35.

[72] "Birthright", In Barry and Wentz, eds., *The Lexham Bible Dictionary*. "Birthright", In Chad Brand, Charles Draper, Archie England et al., eds., *Holman Illustrated Bible Dictionary* (Nashville, TN: Holman Bible Publishers, 2003), 220.

spiritual value, which he did not understand what he had until it was given away. The second is seen in Jacob, who initially served himself through deception,

> Sadly, things of great spiritual value are often handled in profane or crafty ways (Esau). Some people treat spiritual and eternal things with contempt, for they see them as of no value. And others, though regarding such things highly, make the higher cause serve themselves through craft and manipulation. . . . Jacob recognized the spiritual value of the birthright.[73]

Through this example, we can see how the life of Esau can be a warning for Israel who too often sacrificed their God-given provisions for selfish reasons. Esau in the end "despised his birthright" (Gen. 25:34) and realized his error in sacrificing his birthright to satisfy his appetite for just one meal (cf. Gen. 3:6). The Book of Hebrews speaks of Esau despising his birthright,

> See to it that no one misses the grace of God and that no bitter root grows up to cause trouble and defile many. See that no one is sexually immoral, or is godless like Esau, who for a single meal sold his inheritance rights as the oldest son. Afterward, as you know, when he wanted to inherit this blessing, he was rejected. He could bring about no change of mind, though he sought the blessing with tears (Heb. 12:15-17).

This account in Genesis 25, depicts Esau has being "famished" (v. 29). The Hebrew adjective עָיֵף 'āyfiph used here means "weary, exhausted, and faint". This same adjective is used of the Israelites who were exhausted from their wandering in the wilderness (Deut. 25:18) and were susceptible to attack from the Amalekites. In the case of Gideon, when his 300 soldiers had become exhausted, they continued to pursue the Midianites (Jdg. 8:4f.). Likewise, this can also be seen as King David and all the people fled from Absalom stopped to refresh themselves from exhaustion

> The king and all the people with him arrived at their destination exhausted. And there he refreshed himself (2 Sam. 16:14).

> They also brought wheat and barley, flour and roasted grain, beans and lentils, honey and curds, sheep, and cheese from cows' milk for David and his people to eat. For they said, "The people have become hungry and tired and thirsty in the desert" (2 Sam. 17:28-29).

In the Book of Job, Eliphaz accused Job of refusing to help the weary and the hungry, "You gave no water to the weary and you withheld food from the hungry" (Job 22:7). The Book of Proverbs states "Like cold water to a weary soul is good news from a distant land" (Pr. 25:25). The lesson here is that Esau in allowing his appetite to control him inevitably led him to despising spiritual things. Likewise, Jacob had an appetite and craved, but this was something of value. However, there is a caution presented here in regards to spiritual ambition: we should strive for those things which contain spiritual value and at

---

[73] Walvoord and Zuck, eds., *The Bible Knowledge Commentary*, Vol. 1, 70.

the same time avoid the devices of the flesh. Jacob later repented of his expedience, and became a capable servant since he had placed his priorities in their proper place.[74]

> See to it that no one misses the grace of God and that no bitter root grows up to cause trouble and defile many. See that no one is sexually immoral, or is godless like Esau, who for a single meal sold his inheritance rights as the oldest son. Afterward, as you know, when he wanted to inherit this blessing, he was rejected. He could bring about no change of mind, though he sought the blessing with tears (Heb. 12:15-17).

The third example refers to Moses delivering the "mixed multitude" (NKJV) of Israelites from Egyptian bondage after 400 years of slavery, sustaining them through the Red Sea, the forty years of wandering through the wilderness on their journey to the Promised Land. God provided for their every need, "During the forty years that I led you through the desert, your clothes did not wear out, nor did the sandals on your feet" (Deut. 29:5). However, they "began to crave other food" תַּאֲוָה *ta'ăwāh* "longing, eager desire, delight" and "lust" in a negative sense.[75]

> The rabble with them began to crave other food, and again the Israelites started wailing and said, "If only we had meat to eat! We remember the fish we ate in Egypt at no cost—also the cucumbers, melons, leeks, onions and garlic. But now we have lost our appetite; we never see anything but this manna!" (Num. 11:4-6).

Moses uses a rare noun "rabble" אֲסַפְסֻף *'ăsaphsuph* meaning "a disorderly collection" which describes the "mixed multitude" that followed the Israelites in the Exodus from Egyptian bondage.[76] During the forty years of wandering through the wilderness, the Israelites complained and rejected the provision of the Lord "we have lost our appetite; we never see anything but this manna!" (Num. 11:6). However, rejecting the provision of the Lord resulted in divine discipline,

> Tell the people: "Consecrate yourselves in preparation for tomorrow, when you will eat meat. The LORD heard you when you wailed, "If only we had meat to eat! We were better off in Egypt!" Now the LORD will give you meat, and you will eat it. You will not eat it for just one day, or two days, or five, ten or twenty days, but for a whole month—until it comes out of your nostrils and you loathe it—because you have rejected the, who is among you, and have wailed before him, saying, "Why did we ever leave Egypt?" (Num. 11:18-20).

> But while the meat was still between their teeth and before it could be consumed, the anger of the LORD burned against the people, and he struck them with a severe plague. Therefore the place was named Kibroth Hattaavah, because there they buried the people who had craved other food (Num. 11:33-34).

---

[74] Walvoord and Zuck, eds., *The Bible Knowledge Commentary*, Vol. 1, 70. עָיֵף *'āyfiph* "6106", In Gilbrant, ed., *The Complete Biblical Library Hebrew-English Dictionary, Nun-Ayin.*

[75] תַּאֲוָה *ta'ăwāh* "8707", In Gilbrant, ed., *The Complete Biblical Library Hebrew-English Dictionary, Sin-Taw.*

[76] אֲסַפְסֻף *'ăsaphsuph* "642", In Gilbrant, ed., *The Complete Biblical Library Hebrew-English Dictionary, Aleph-Beth.*

It is interesting that the place named Kibroth Hattaavah קִבְרוֹתהַתַּאֲוָה *qivrôth hatta'ăwāh* was one of the places where the Israelites journeyed in the wilderness, which is between the Desert of Sinai and Hazeroth (Num. 33:16f.). It is at Kibroth Hattaavah that the Israelites craved or lusted after meat resulting in the Lord sending them quail. Moreover, their rejection of the Lord's provision resulted in the deaths of many Israelites and is referred to as "the graves of craving".[77]

> Therefore the place was named Kibroth Hattaavah, because there they buried the people who had craved other food. From Kibroth Hattaavah the people traveled to Hazeroth and stayed there (Num. 11:34-35; cf. Deut. 9:22).

Matthew Henry writes concerning this,

> David longed for the water of the well of Bethlehem, but would not drink it when he had it, because it was obtained by venturing; much more reason these Israelites had to refuse this flesh, which was obtained by murmuring, and which, they might easily perceive, by what Moses said, was given them in anger; but those that are under the power of a carnal mind will have their lusts fulfilled, though it be to the certain damage and ruin of their precious souls.[78]

The Lord addresses the key issue "you have rejected the Lord" and the sin of disbelief in God as their provider. In today's language, it would be as if saying to Jesus, "leave me alone, you died in vain for me" which places this context in its proper perspective.[79]

> He is near in grace, but they have turned their back on him. He is in their midst, and they wish he were not. He has come down, and they wish he would go away. The issue was not just failure to demonstrate proper gratitude to the Lord who was in their midst and who was their constant source of good; it was turning from him entirely and grudgingly rejecting his many acts of mercy on their behalf.[80]

> Anyone who rejected the law of Moses died without mercy on the testimony of two or three witnesses. How much more severely do you think a man deserves to be punished who has trampled the Son of God under foot, who has treated as an unholy thing the blood of the covenant that sanctified him, and who has insulted the Spirit of grace?" (Heb. 10:28-29).

This context leaves us with the question, "what is the promised land in my life?" When we are so focused on allowing our own promised land to rule, reign, and control our lives, there is no place for God and allowing Him to take us into His Promised Land. Through fasting our promised land—our desires, lusts, craving—are removed so that the Lord can fill us with His provision and take us into His Promised Land.

---

[77] קִבְרוֹתהַתַּאֲוָה *qivrôth hatta'ăwāh* "7198", In Thoralf Gilbrant, ed., *The Complete Biblical Library Hebrew-English Dictionary, Pe-Resh* (Springfield, IL: World Library Press, Inc., WORDsearch CROSS e-book, 1998). תַּאֲוָה *ta'ăwāh* "8707", In Gilbrant, ed., *The Complete Biblical Library Hebrew-English Dictionary, Sin-Taw.*

[78] "Numbers 11:31-35", In Matthew Henry, *Matthew Henry's Commentary on the Whole Bible: Complete and Unabridged in One Volume* (Peabody, MA: Hendrickson Publishers, 1994).

[79] Frank E. Gaebelein, ed., *The Expositor's Bible Commentary, Volume 2: Genesis, Exodus, Leviticus, Numbers* (Grand Rapids, MI: Zondervan Publishing House. Database © 2010 WORDsearch CROSS e-book, 1990), 793.

[80] Gaebelein, ed., *The Expositor's Bible Commentary, Volume 2*, 793.

The Lord has supernatural blessings for us, but we are too often controlled by our physical appetites that His blessings for us will never be realized unless we seek the Lord through fasting and prayer.

Fasting and Prayer

When we consider the spiritual disciplines of fasting and prayer, we must remember that an acceptable fast will be connected with prayer and/or worship. When we merge prayer with fasting and dedicate them for the glory of God, they will reach their maximum effectiveness in our lives. This is not about manipulating God to fulfilling our desires, it's about forcing ourselves to focus and depend upon God for strength, provision, spiritual power, wisdom, and the breakthrough that only He can provide. The Word of God is full of examples of those who fasted and prayed. However, only a few will be included:

Samuel and the people of Israel (1 Sam. 7:5-6)	Nehemiah (Neh. 1:4)
Elijah (1 Kgs. 19:8)	Anna (Lk 2:37)
Jehoshaphat and Judah (2 Chr. 20:3-13)	John the Baptist (Mt. 11:18; Lk. 7:33)
Hannah (1 Sam. 1:7-8)	church at Antioch (Acts 13:2-3)
Esther and the Jews (Est. 4:16)	Paul and Barnabas (Acts 14:23)

Moreover, it is possible to pray without fasting, but a person cannot practice biblical fasting without prayer. As Broadbent III states, it is "A calling out to God in sorrow, seeking His presence in worship, wanting to submit to His Lordship in your life"[81]. John MacArthur, Jr., clarifies this when he says,

> Fasting is an affirmation of intense prayer, a corollary of deep spiritual struggle before God. It is never an isolated act or a ceremony or ritual that has some inherent efficacy or merit. It has no value at all–in fact becomes a spiritual hindrance and a sin–when done for any reason apart from knowing and following the Lord's will.[82]

The spiritual disciplines of fasting and prayer has been referenced throughout this study, therefore, there will not be separate section that addresses this highly important topic.

Christian Fasting and Other Religions

Fasting is an almost universal phenomenon within both Eastern and Western cultures. Over the centuries, abstaining from food has been undertaken by many for a variety of purposes, one of the most significant being religious reasons. For anyone who is spiritual, fasting redirects the mind away from physical urges—after the first few days at least, when food is the only thing you can think about.

For Christians, a forty day fast recalls Christ's forty days without food in the wilderness as He prayed to be shown His mission. Jews participate in the *Yom Kippur* fast on the theory that deliberately causing

---

[81] Broadbent III, *A Call to Biblical Fasting*, 16.

[82] John MacArthur, Jr., *The MacArthur New Testament Commentary*, Vol. 1 (Chicago, IL: Moody, 1985-90), 404.

yourself mild discomfort shows respect for the great suffering of the faithful of the past. Muslims fast to develop self-control, show adherence to their faith, and so that as each Ramadan day ends and food is served, they will have a keener appreciation of the bounty God has offered Earth. Both Christian fasting and Hindu fasting seek results. Hindu fasting focuses on the self and tries to get something for a perceived sacrifice. However, Christian fasting focuses on our relationship with God. The results are spiritual that glorify God—both in the person who fasts and for whom we fast and pray.[83]

People can also fast for medical or health reasons, and this too has been an accepted practice for centuries. Fasting can also be used as a political act, as observed by Mohandas Karamchand Gandhi, known by many as Mahatma, in his struggle against the British colonialism in the Indian sub-continent during 1940s. More commonly known as hunger strike, political fasting has been used by personalities all over the world including Martin Luther King, Jr., and Lanza del Vasto.

A modern day cross over between religious and political fast can be seen in a forty hour famine, an event run annually by the World Vision Australia. Likewise, there is the International Solidarity Fast for Darfur and Fast for Peace. The following chart highlights fasting or an equivalent among some of the primary belief systems within the world in which we live:[84]

Religion	When they fast	How they fast	Why they fast
Baha'i	The Baha'i fast takes place during Ala, the 19th month of the Baha'í year, from March 2-20.	Abstain from food and drink from sunrise to sunset.	To focus on love of God and spiritual matters.
Buddhist	All the main branches of Buddhism practice some periods of fasting, usually on full-moon days and other holidays.	Depending on the Buddhist tradition, fasting usually means abstaining from solid food, with some liquids permitted.	A method of purification. Tendai and Theravadin Buddhist monks fast as a means of freeing the mind. Some Tibetan Buddhist monks fast to aid yogic feats, like generating inner heat.
Catholic	Catholics fast and abstain from meat on Ash Wednesday and Good Friday, and abstain from meat on all Fridays in Lent. For many centuries, Catholics were forbidden to eat meat on all Fridays, but since the mid-1960s, abstaining from meat on Fridays outside of Lent has been a matter of local discretion.	On Ash Wednesday and Good Friday, two small meals and one regular meal are allowed; meat is forbidden. On Fridays in Lent, no meat is allowed. For the optional Friday fast, some people substitute a different penance or special prayer instead of fasting.	Teaches control of fleshly desires, penance for sins, and solidarity with the poor. The Lenten fast prepares the soul for a great feast by practicing austerity. The Good Friday fast commemorates the day Christ suffered.
Eastern Orthodox	There are several fast periods, including Lent, Apostles' Fast,	In general, meat, dairy products, and eggs are	Strengthens resistance to gluttony; helps open a person

---

[83] Towns, *Fasting for Spiritual Breakthrough*, 18.

[84] "Diversity at Work Series: Fasting in World Religions", RRAE Unit, OPC September 05, <http://www.beliefnet.com/Faiths/2001/02/Fasting-Chart.aspx>, Accessed on September 3, 2013.

	Dormition Fast, and the Nativity Fast, and several one-day fasts. Every Wednesday and Friday is considered a fast day, except those that fall during designated "fast-free weeks".	prohibited. Fish is prohibited on some fast days and allowed on others.	to God's grace.
Hindu	Fasting is commonly practiced on New Moon days and during festivals such as Shivaratri, Saraswati Puja, and Durga Puja (also known as Navaratri). Women in North India also fast on the day of Karva Chauth.	Depends on the individual. Fasting may involve 24 hours of complete abstinence from any food or drink, but is more often an elimination of solid foods, with an occasional drink of milk or water.	A way to enhance concentration during meditation or worship; purification for the system; sometimes considered a sacrifice.
Jewish	*Yom Kippur*, the Day of Atonement, is the best-known fast day. The Jewish calendar has six other fast days as well, including Tisha B'Av, the day on which the destruction of the Jewish Temple took place.	On *Yom Kippur* and Tisha B'Av, eating and drinking are forbidden for a 25-hour period, from sundown to sundown. On the other fast days, eating and drinking are forbidden only from sunrise to sundown.	Atonement for sins and/or special requests to God.
Mormon	The first Sunday of each month is a fast day. Individuals, families, or wards may hold other fasts at will.	Abstaining from food and drink for two consecutive meals and donating food or money to the needy. After the fast, church members participate in a "fast and testimony meeting".	Closeness to God; concentration on God and religion. Individual or family fasts might be held to petition for a specific cause, such as healing for one who is sick or help with making a difficult decision.
Muslim	Ramadan, the ninth month of the Muslim calendar, is a mandatory fasting period that commemorates the period when the Qur'an was first revealed to Prophet Muhammad. Various Muslim customs recommend days and periods of fasting in addition to Ramadan.	Abstain from food, drink, smoking, profane language, and sexual intercourse from before the break of dawn until sunset for the entire month.	Some Muslims fast every Monday (some say Thursday) because Prophet Muhammad was said to do this, and some fast during the month of Sha'baan, which precedes Ramadan, and especially during the three days leading up to Ramadan.
Pagan	No organized fast days, but some pagans choose to fast in preparation for Ostara (Spring Equinox).	At the discretion of the individual--some totally abstain from food, others reduce how much they eat.	Intended to purify a person energetically; often used to raise vibrational levels as preparation for magical work. Ostara fasting is used to cleanse oneself from heavier winter foods.
Protestant (Evangelical)	At the discretion of individuals, churches, organizations, or communities.	Though some people abstain from food or drink entirely, others drink only water or juice, eat only certain foods,	Evangelical fasts have become increasingly popular in recent years, with people fasting for spiritual

		skip certain meals, or abstain from temptations, edible or not.	nourishment, solidarity with impoverished people, a counterbalance to modern consumer culture, or to petition God for special needs.
Protestant (Mainline)	Not a major part of the tradition, but fasts can be held at the discretion of communities, churches, other groups, and individuals.	Discretion of those fasting.	For spiritual improvement or to advance a political or social-justice agenda. One example: the ELCA's "Campaign of Prayer, Fasting, and Vigils".

Chapter 3: The Practical Aspects of Fasting

The purpose of this chapter is to describe the key spiritual characteristics in preparing to fast and how unconfessed sin will hinder the purpose and breakthrough that we desire through fasting and prayer. It also highlights the benefits that affect every area of our lives and that seeking the Lord for direction and being led by the Holy Spirit in fasting is essential to growing in the Lord. It also describes the various lengths of fasts that can be seen throughout Scripture.

Spiritual Preparation to Fasting

The key to attaining the benefits of fasting is spiritual preparation. Moreover, the key component to fasting and prayer is repentance, which can be seen throughout this study. Any unconfessed sin will hinder our purpose for fasting and our prayers. The following are several ways that we can be spiritually prepared to fast:

1. Ask God to search your heart (Ps. 139:23);
2. Confess every sin the Holy Spirit brings to your attention and accept God's forgiveness (1 Jn. 1:9);
3. Seek forgiveness from all you have knowingly offended and forgive all who have hurt you.
4. Make restitution as the Holy Spirit leads you;
5. Ask God to fill you with His Holy Spirit;
6. Yield your mind, body, and spirit to the Lordship and leadership of Christ (Rom. 12:1-2);
7. Meditate on the attributes of God: His love, sovereignty, power, wisdom, faithfulness, grace, and holiness;
8. Begin your time of fasting and prayer with an expectant heart (Heb. 11:6).
9. Do not underestimate spiritual opposition (Gal. 5:16-17).

The Benefits of Fasting

The benefits of fasting have widespread implications, influences and/or effects. These benefits are transformational / life-changing in a person's life, whether personal, physiological, psychological, emotional, and spiritual. Some of these benefits include:

1. Scripture suggests that God recognizes fasting as a sign of deep sincerity;
2. Physicians assert that regular moderate fasting is a physical benefit to one's health. Fasting allows our bodies to occasionally cleanse themselves;
3. The mind is able to reach greater depths of concentration during fasting;
4. Fasting as a spiritual discipline helps us with self-discipline;
5. Fasting strengthens our appreciation for the abundance of good things;
6. Through fasting we become more spiritually sensitive to the things of God;
7. Fasting produces spiritual introspection, spiritual examination, spiritual confession, and spiritual intercession.[85]

---

[85] Towns, *Fasting for Spiritual Breakthrough*, 43-60, 176-80.

The following table highlights the various benefits of fasting:

Fasting Enables You to Hear and Heed God's Divine Will	Then the Israelites, all the people, went up to Bethel, and there they sat weeping before the LORD. They fasted that day until evening and presented burnt offerings and fellowship offerings to the LORD. And the Israelites inquired of the LORD. (In those days the ark of the covenant of God was there, with Phinehas son of Eleazar, the son of Aaron, ministering before it.). They asked, "Shall we go up again to battle with Benjamin our brother, or not?" The LORD responded, "Go, for tomorrow I will give them into your hands" (Jdg. 20:26-28).
Fasting Delivers Us From Strongholds and Bondages	Then Samuel said, "Assemble all Israel at Mizpah and I will intercede with the LORD for you". When they had assembled at Mizpah, they drew water and poured it out before the LORD. On that day they fasted and there they confessed, "We have sinned against the LORD". And Samuel was leader of Israel at Mizpah (1 Sam. 7:5-6).
Fasting Can Avert God's Judgment Through A Contrite Heart	So Ahab went home, sullen and angry because Naboth the Jezreelite had said, "I will not give you the inheritance of my fathers". He lay on his bed sulking and refused to eat (1 Kgs. 21:4).
	So she wrote letters in Ahab's name, placed his seal on them, and sent them to the elders and nobles who lived in Naboth's city with him. In those letters she wrote: "Proclaim a day of fasting and seat Naboth in a prominent place among the people. But seat two scoundrels opposite him and have them testify that he has cursed both God and the king. Then take him out and stone him to death". So the elders and nobles who lived in Naboth's city did as Jezebel directed in the letters she had written to them. They proclaimed a fast and seated Naboth in a prominent place among the people. Then two scoundrels came and sat opposite him and brought charges against Naboth before the people, saying, "Naboth has cursed both God and the king". So they took him outside the city and stoned him to death. Then they sent word to Jezebel: "Naboth has been stoned and is dead" (1 Kgs. 21:8-14).
	(There was never a man like Ahab, who sold himself to do evil in the eyes of the LORD, urged on by Jezebel his wife. He behaved in the vilest manner by going after idols, like the Amorites the LORD drove out before Israel.). When Ahab heard these words, he tore his clothes, put on sackcloth and fasted. He lay in sackcloth and went around meekly. Then the word of the LORD came to Elijah the Tishbite: "Have you noticed how Ahab has humbled himself before me? Because he has humbled himself, I will not bring this disaster in his day, but I will bring it on his house in the days of his son" (1 Kgs. 21:25-29).
	"Even now", declares the LORD, "return to me with all your heart, with fasting and weeping and mourning". Rend your heart and not your garments. Return to the LORD your God, for he is gracious and compassionate, slow to anger and abounding in love, and he relents from sending calamity (Joel 2:12-13).
	The Ninevites believed God. They declared a fast, and all of them, from the greatest to the least, put on sackcloth. When the news reached the king of Nineveh, he rose from his throne, took off his royal robes, covered himself with sackcloth and sat down in the dust. Then he issued a proclamation in Nineveh: "By the decree of the king and his nobles: Do not let any man or beast, herd or flock, taste anything; do not let them eat or drink. But let man and beast be covered with sackcloth. Let everyone call urgently on God. Let them give up their evil ways and their violence. Who knows? God may yet relent and with compassion turn from his fierce anger so that we will not perish". When God saw what they did and how they turned from their evil ways, he had compassion and did not bring upon them the destruction he had threatened (Jon. 3:5-4:1).

	It was a long time, twenty years in all, that the ark remained at Kiriath Jearim, and all the people of Israel mourned and sought after the LORD. And Samuel said to the whole house of Israel, "If you are returning to the LORD with all your hearts, then rid yourselves of the foreign gods and the Ashtoreths and commit yourselves to the LORD and serve him only, and he will deliver you out of the hand of the Philistines". So the Israelites put away their Baals and Ashtoreths, and served the LORD only. Then Samuel said, "Assemble all Israel at Mizpah and I will intercede with the LORD for you". When they had assembled at Mizpah, they drew water and poured it out before the LORD. On that day they fasted and there they confessed, "We have sinned against the LORD". And Samuel was leader of Israel at Mizpah (1 Sam. 7:2-6).
Fasting Gets God's Attention When In Need of Help	After this, the Moabites and Ammonites with some of the Meunites came to wage war against Jehoshaphat. Some people came and told Jehoshaphat, "A vast army is coming against you from Edom, from the other side of the Dead Sea. It is already in Hazezon Tamar" (that is, En Gedi). Alarmed, Jehoshaphat resolved to inquire of the LORD, and he proclaimed a fast for all Judah. The people of Judah came together to seek help from the LORD; indeed, they came from every town in Judah to seek him (2 Chr. 20:1-4).
Fasting Releases God's Favour and Anointing and Empowers Us To Bring in the Lost	For if you remain silent at this time, relief and deliverance for the Jews will arise from another place, but you and your father's family will perish. And who knows but that you have come to royal position for such a time as this?" Then Esther sent this reply to Mordecai: "Go, gather together all the Jews who are in Susa, and fast for me. Do not eat or drink for three days, night or day. I and my maids will fast as you do. When this is done, I will go to the king, even though it is against the law. And if I perish, I perish". So Mordecai went away and carried out all of Esther's instructions (Est. 4:14-17; Neh. 1:4; 2:6; cf. Dan. 10).
Fasting Releases Prophetic Revelation	At that time I, Daniel, mourned for three weeks. I ate no choice food; no meat or wine touched my lips; and I used no lotions at all until the three weeks were over. On the twenty-fourth day of the first month, as I was standing on the bank of the great river, the Tigris, I looked up and there before me was a man dressed in linen, with a belt of the finest gold around his waist. His body was like chrysolite, his face like lightning, his eyes like flaming torches, his arms and legs like the gleam of burnished bronze, and his voice like the sound of a multitude (Dan. 10:2-6).
Fasting Delivers Us From the Snares of the Enemy	There, by the Ahava Canal, I proclaimed a fast, so that we might humble ourselves before our God and ask him for a safe journey for us and our children, with all our possessions. I was ashamed to ask the king for soldiers and horsemen to protect us from enemies on the road, because we had told the king, "The gracious hand of our God is on everyone who looks to him, but his great anger is against all who forsake him". So we fasted and petitioned our God about this, and he answered our prayer. . . . On the twelfth day of the first month we set out from the Ahava Canal to go to Jerusalem. The hand of our God was on us, and he protected us from enemies and bandits along the way (Ezra 8:21-23, 31).
Fasting Helps Us To Live A Long and Healthy Life	"Is not this the kind of fasting I have chosen: to loose the chains of injustice and untie the cords of the yoke, to set the oppressed free and break every yoke? Is it not to share your food with the hungry and to provide the poor wanderer with shelter—when you see the naked, to clothe him, and not to turn away from your own flesh and blood? Then your light will break forth like the dawn, and your healing will quickly appear; then your righteousness will go before you, and the glory of the LORD will be your rear guard (Isa. 58:6-8).
	There was also a prophetess, Anna, the daughter of Phanuel, of the tribe of Asher. She was very old; she had lived with her husband seven years after her marriage, and then

	was a widow until she was eighty-four. She never left the temple but worshiped night and day, fasting and praying (Lk. 2:36-37).
Fasting Helps Us To Persevere and Conquer Temptations	Then Jesus was led by the Spirit into the desert to be tempted by the devil. After fasting forty days and forty nights, he was hungry. The tempter came to him and said, "If you are the Son of God, tell these stones to become bread". Jesus answered, "It is written: 'Man does not live on bread alone, but on every word that comes from the mouth of God'" (Mt. 4:1-4).
Fasting Gives Us Spiritual Power To Cast Out Demons	He replied, "Because you have so little faith. I tell you the truth, if you have faith as small as a mustard seed, you can say to this mountain, 'Move from here to there' and it will move. Nothing will be impossible for you". But this kind does not go out except by prayer and fasting (Mt. 17:20-21).
Fasting Connects You On A Deeper Level With God	Jesus, full of the Holy Spirit, returned from the Jordan and was led by the Spirit in the desert, where for forty days he was tempted by the devil. He ate nothing during those days, and at the end of them he was hungry. The devil said to him, "If you are the Son of God, tell this stone to become bread". Jesus answered, "It is written: 'Man does not live on bread alone'". The devil led him up to a high place and showed him in an instant all the kingdoms of the world. And he said to him, "I will give you all their authority and splendor, for it has been given to me, and I can give it to anyone I want to. So if you worship me, it will all be yours". Jesus answered, "It is written: 'Worship the LORD your God and serve him only'". The devil led him to Jerusalem and had him stand on the highest point of the temple. "If you are the Son of God", he said, "throw yourself down from here. For it is written: "'He will command his angels concerning you to guard you carefully; they will lift you up in their hands, so that you will not strike your foot against a stone'". Jesus answered, "It says: 'Do not put the LORD your God to the test'". When the devil had finished all this tempting, he left him until an opportune time (Lk. 4:1-13).
Fasting Helps Us Discern A Person's Character	Paul and Barnabas appointed elders for them in each church and, with prayer and fasting, committed them to the LORD, in whom they had put their trust (Acts 14:23).
Fasting Breaks Self-Pursuit	The husband should fulfill his marital duty to his wife, and likewise the wife to her husband. The wife's body does not belong to her alone but also to her husband. In the same way, the husband's body does not belong to him alone but also to his wife. Do not deprive each other except by mutual consent and for a time, so that you may devote yourselves to prayer. Then come together again so that Satan will not tempt you because of your lack of self-control. I say this as a concession, not as a command (1 Cor. 7:3-6).
Fasting: The Practical Way of Self-Denial	Do you not know that in a race all the runners run, but only one gets the prize? Run in such a way as to get the prize. Everyone who competes in the games goes into strict training. They do it to get a crown that will not last; but we do it to get a crown that will last forever. Therefore I do not run like a man running aimlessly; I do not fight like a man beating the air. No, I beat my body and make it my slave so that after I have preached to others, I myself will not be disqualified for the prize (1 Cor. 9:24-27).
Fasting Sharpens Your Spiritual Senses	We all have the natural senses of feeling, sight, hearing, smell and taste, but we also have spiritual equivalents, "taste and see that the LORD is good" (Ps. 34:8); "He that has ears to hear, let him hear what the Spirit says" (Rev. 2-3); "blessed are the pure in heart for they will see God" (Mt. 5:8); "the eyes of your heart may be enlightened" (Eph. 1:18). Fasting sharpens our spiritual senses and enables us to perceive, eagerly sieze the things of the Lord, and give us clear guidance and direction.

Fasting Helps You Physically	Fasting gives your body a vacation. A lot of food that we consume contains toxins and poisons like preservatives, artificial colours, and other forms of chemicals. Fasting for 14 or 21 days cleanses our digestive system by removing toxins and poisons. If cleansing these toxins and poison is true in the natural realm, it's also true in the spiritual realm. Fasting cleanses our soul from these toxins and poisons: deep hurts, bitterness, resentment, judgmental spirit, childhood bondage's, and things of the past will be revealed when you commit yourself to fasting and prayer. Fasting gives the Holy Spirit freedom to reveal areas of bondage that have become toxic or poisonous in our lives and relationships and then receive healing.[86]

According to Charles Stanley, Scripture describes seven benefits to prayer and fasting:

1. *Our attitudes, feelings, and thoughts get sifted, pruned and purified so that God might entrust us with a greater ministry.* By fasting and praying, we become more disciplined toward the things of the Father. We give Him opportunity to cut away from us those things that will slow us down, do us in, or keep us from His plans and purposes.
2. *We are able to discern more clearly the will of God for our lives.* Fasting clears our spiritual eyes and ears so we can accurately discern what God desires to reveal to us.
3. *We are confronted with our sins and shortcomings so we might confess them to God, receive forgiveness for them, and walk in greater righteousness.* Many times we break stubborn, sinful habits when we fast and pray. Fasting and prayer cleanse us and purify us from the errors that have kept us entangled in sin and folly.
4. *We experience a release of supernatural power.* Genuine fasting and prayer result in spiritual growth, including a renewed outpouring of supernatural power. Certain problems and situations cannot be resolved apart from fasting and prayer.
5. *We can influence national issues and concerns through our prayers.* As we fast and pray for our nation, God will move. He will pour out His Spirit, in His ways and in His timing. We can count on it.
6. *We can help build up God's people.* Prayer is the generator of the church. It gives power to its ministers. It propels outreach to the lost. It creates a climate in which evangelistic efforts succeed.
7. *Our minds are sharpened.* When we fast and pray, we begin to understand the Scriptures as never before. We become sensitive to God's timing and direction, with an increased awareness and ability to discern. We become keenly aware of what God desires to do and accomplish not only in our lives, but also in the lives of those around us.[87]

Types of Biblical Fasting

The types of biblical fasting have one thing in common which is to deny one's sensual appetites for a period of time to focus on spiritual growth. Biblically, fasting is a humbling experience and a time of self-denial when an individual draws near to God through prayer.

While the purpose of fasting in the Bible has nothing to do with losing weight, a number of popular diets have come about through the reading of Scripture. It changed their attitude about food and helped them to reach healthy weights as a result. The same has happened when people have studied what the

---

[86] Silva Moodley, *A Practical Guide to Fasting*, <http://www.lpm.org.za/sermon2.html>. Accessed on September 3, 2013. Towns, *Fasting for Spiritual Breakthrough*, 224-31.
[87] Charles Stanley, *The Benefits of Prayer and Fasting*, <http://www.northsidecitychurch.com/pdf/bopf.pdf>, Accessed on June 1, 2013.

Bible teaches about fasting. For example, in the Daniel Fast, there are different versions based on different interpretations of the Scripture.[88]

The Daniel Fast is one type of fasting modeled after biblical accounts. Biblical fasting is the restriction of food for spiritual reasons, and we find people fasting throughout the Old and New Testaments. In Ezra 10, we find the prophet so distraught over the actions of the people that he went into great mourning and praying before the Lord. At this time he neither ate nor drank for at least one night or perhaps longer. There are a few examples of forty day absolute fasts where the men must have been sustained supernaturally. Moses, on two separate occasions when he was before God, neither ate nor drank. Elijah traveled across the desert for forty days while eating no food nor drinking any water and was ministered to by an angel who gave him water and cakes.

There are many more, and not necessarily a standard. Daniel fasted for twenty-one days, Jesus for forty days, Ezra for one night, Cornelius for four days, and Paul for three days. It seems that all these people were seeking God through their fasting and perhaps the Lord led them in the "design" of their fast. The important point to remember in fasting is not to have a specific pattern or legalistic form but that we are led by the Holy Spirit. Before a person decides on the form of fasting, it is paramount to seek the Lord, asking for direction, trusting that He will reveal the method of fasting as you enter into this spiritual discipline and draw closer to Him.[89]

The Lengths of Fasts

The length of a fast varies throughout Scripture and depends upon the purpose for the fast. The first length of fast is that of one day, from sunrise to sunset, and after sunset food would be eaten. This first example refers to the battle between the Israelites and the Benjaminites (Jdg. 20), where Israel had neglected sacrificial worship and the Lord permits defeat so that they would repent and return to Him weeping and fasting until evening

> Then all the Israelites, the whole army, went up to Bethel, and there they sat weeping before the LORD. They fasted that day until evening and presented burnt offerings and fellowship offerings to the LORD (Jdg. 20:26).

The Lord responds positively "Go, for tomorrow I will give them into your hands" (Jdg. 20:28). The second example is seen where Samuel assembles all of Israel at Mizpah and he intercedes on their behalf (1 Sam. 7:5-6). The Israelites "drew water and poured it out before the Lord", fasted and confessed their sins before the Lord.

The third example, Saul had placed the Israelites under an oath "Cursed be anyone who eats food before evening comes, before I have avenged myself on my enemies!" (1 Sam. 14:24). This verse along with 1 Kings 8:31 and 2 Chronicles 6:22 refer to the "swearing" between neighbors. If and when the

---

[88] <http://diet.lovetoknow.com/wiki/9_Types_of_Biblical_Fasting>, Accessed on September 3, 2013. Copeland, *Fasting: A Special Study*, <http://www.e-sword.net>. Accessed on June 12, 2014.
[89] <http://danielfast.wordpress.com/2007/12/13/types-of-fasting>, Accessed on September 3, 2013.

disagreement is brought to the temple altar, judgment is pronounced upon the guilty party and the innocent party is vindicated. The guilty party then faced the consequences of the oath, which was common in the Old Testament.[90]

Saul commanded all his men to fast until they had completely annihilated the Philistines. Even though the Israelites were starving, they feared breaking Saul's oath even when they went into the woods and "saw the honey oozing out" (1 Sam. 14:26). Jonathan was not aware of this oath "reached out the end of the staff that was in his hand and dipped it into the honeycomb . . . and his eyes brightened" (1 Sam. 14:27). After they defeated the Philistines, the army was so hungry that they slaughtered Philistine animals and ate them without draining the blood (1 Sam. 14:32-33; cf. Lev. 17:10-14). Saul was so distressed that he quickly built an altar to offer a propitiatory sacrifice to the Lord (1 Sam. 14:35).[91]

The fourth example is seen as David and his men mourned, wept and fasted until evening upon receiving the news that King Saul and Jonathan had been killed in battle. "Then David and all the men with him took hold of their clothes and tore them. They mourned and wept and fasted till evening for Saul and his son Jonathan, and for the army of the Lord and for the nation of Israel, because they had fallen by the sword" (2 Sam. 1:11-12). David had been a respected man under King Saul's leadership; he without question recognizes the crown and armlet in the hands of the Amalekite.

But the messenger could scarcely have been prepared for the response of David and his men, who tear their clothes (v. 11) for the same reason that the Amalekite had earlier torn his clothes. David felt genuine and heartfelt expressions of grief over the loss of Saul and Jonathan (cf. 2 Sam. 1:17-27) and the other fallen Israelite warriors, that he and all his men mourn (v. 12; cf. 2 Sam. 11:26; 1 Sam. 25:1; 28:3) and weep (cf. v. 24). Likewise, they fast, but only "till evening", which was apparently David's usual practice in these types of situations (cf. 2 Sam. 3:35; contrast the week-long fast of the Jabeshites for Saul and his sons [cf. 1 Sam. 31:13]). Their sorrow extends to the "house of Israel" (v. 12), a reference to the people as a whole ("house" in the sense of "family", "community"; cf. 1 Sam. 7:2), since all Israel has suffered tragic and irreparable loss in the death of their King.[92]

Likewise, David fasts when Joab murders Abner, "Then they all came and urged David to eat something while it was still day; but David took an oath, saying, 'May God deal with me, be it ever so severely, if I taste bread or anything else before the sun sets!'" (2 Sam. 3:35). When David discovered that Joab had murdered Abner, he did not rejoice but rather uttered a curse on Joab and his offspring (3:29). Joab's murder of Abner had taken place in Hebron, which was a city of refuge (Jos. 21:13), where such revenge was not permitted (Num. 35:22-25). David proclaimed a public mourning (2 Sam. 3:31), honoured Abner by burying him at Hebron, and composed a lamentation, which spoke of the shameful

---

[90] אָלָה "426", In Gilbrant, ed., *The Complete Biblical Library Hebrew-English Dictionary, Aleph-Beth.*

[91] Walvoord and Zuck, eds., *The Bible Knowledge Commentary*, Vol. 1, 446.

[92] Frank E. Gaebelein, ed., *The Expositor's Bible Commentary, Volume 3: Deuteronomy, Joshua, Judges, Ruth, 1 & 2 Samuel* (Grand Rapids, MI: Zondervan Publishing House. Database © 2010 WORDsearch CROSS e-book, 1992), 807.

manner in which Abner had died (vv. 32-34). David's compassion and forgiving spirit are evident here, qualities which separated him from ordinary men.[93]

Moreover, Daniel records a fast that lasts the entire night,

> A stone was brought and placed over the mouth of the den, and the king sealed it with his own signet ring and with the rings of his nobles, so that Daniel's situation might not be changed. Then the king returned to his palace and spent the night without eating and without any entertainment being brought to him. And he could not sleep (Dan. 6:17-18).

The fast of Esther continued for three days, both day and night, which seems to have been a special case (Est. 4:16; Acts 9:9, 17-19). The only instance of a severer fast of three days, including both day and night, is also in Esther (4:16). Likewise, when Jesus saw the multitudes and that they had been without food for three days, He had compassion on them, "Jesus called his disciples to him and said, 'I have compassion for these people; they have already been with me three days and have nothing to eat. I do not want to send them away hungry, or they may collapse on the way'" (Mt. 15:32; cf. Mk. 8:2-3). Moreover, is the example of an Egyptian servant of an Amalekite who "had not eaten any food or drunk any water for three days and three nights" (1 Sam. 30:11-12).

A longer fast, of seven days is seen at the burial of King Saul, by the people of Jabesh-Gilead (1 Sam. 31:11-13; 1 Chr. 10:12). The seven day fast of 1 Samuel 31:13 (cf. 2 Sam. 3:35), involves fasting only during the day until sunset. A longer fast of fourteen days is seen in Acts

> Just before dawn Paul urged them all to eat. "For the last fourteen days", he said, "you have been in constant suspense and have gone without food—you haven't eaten anything. Now I urge you to take some food. You need it to survive. Not one of you will lose a single hair from his head" (Acts 27:33-34).

This third plot by "the Jews" against Paul (cf. 9:23, 29; 20:3, 19) is the most meticulously planned and elaborately described, included over forty conspirators (23:13, 21), a full-fast oath (vv. 12, 14, 21), conspiracy with the "chief priests and elders" (v. 14; 25:15; also 4:23; 22:30; 25:2), and repeated references to their determination to kill Paul (23:12, 14, 15, 21, 27).[94] Luke uses the verb ἀναθεματίζω *anathematizo*, which refers to an oath the Jews took against their own lives if they failed to kill the Apostle Paul (cf. Acts 23:12, 14, 21). The only other place this verb is used in the New Testament is Mark 14:71 where Peter denied Christ. The root word is ἀνάθεμα *anathema* meaning "accursed" or "dedicated to destruction", literally meant they "cursed themselves with a curse not to eat" and points to those upon whom the curse was laid (Rom. 9:3; 1 Cor. 12:3; 16:22; Gal. 1:8-9).[95]

---

[93] Walvoord and Zuck, eds., *The Bible Knowledge Commentary*, Vol. 1, 459.

[94] James Luther Mays, ed., *Harper's Bible Commentary* (San Francisco, CA: Harper & Row, 1988), 1111.

[95] ἀναθεματίζω *anathematizo* "330", In Gilbrant, ed., *The Complete Biblical Library Greek-English Dictionary, Alpha-Gamma*. ἀνάθεμα *anathema* "329", In Gilbrant, ed., *The Complete Biblical Library Greek-English Dictionary, Alpha-Gamma*.

Daniel 10:3-13 speaks of a twenty-one day fast and mourning, when he received the vision of a man, "At that time I, Daniel, mourned for three weeks. I ate no choice food; no meat or wine touched my lips; and I used no lotions at all until the three weeks were over" (Dan. 10:2-3). Daniel was so impressed by this vision that he resorted to three weeks of mourning. The Hebrew verb מִתְאַבֵּל *mit'abbēl* from the verb אָבַל *'āval* is used in connection with someone lamenting the death of a loved one. From verse 12, we can see that this mourning and the semi-fast that accompanied it (v. 3) marked a prolonged period of intense supplication and prayer.[96] The severity of fasting can be seen in Psalms 109:23-24

> I fade away like an evening shadow; I am shaken off like a locust. My knees give way from
> fasting; my body is thin and gaunt.[97]

The longest fasts mentioned in Scripture were the forty day fasts by Moses (Ex. 24:18; 34:28; Deut. 9:9, 18, 25-29; 10:10), Elijah (1 Kgs. 19:8), and Jesus (Mt. 4:2; Mk. 1:13; Lk. 4:2). Throughout Scripture, the number forty speaks of cleansing and purifying, which can be seen as God brought a flood that lasted forty days to purify the earth of wickedness (Gen. 6-8). Moses spent forty years in Egypt before he delivered the Israelites from Egyptian bondage and then spent forty years in the wilderness before they entered the Promised Land. While in the wilderness, he fasted forty days in preparation of receiving the Ten Commandments and then fasted and interceded another forty days after he saw their wickedness and building a golden calf (Deut. 9:9, 18). The Lord sends Jonah to Nineveh to proclaim "Forty more days and Nineveh will be overturned" (Jon. 3:4). After Elijah defeated the 450 prophets of Baal and ordered their execution, he escaped to the desert to avoid the death threats of Jezebel and was fed by an angel (1 Kgs. 18-19). Franklin states "There is a prophetic release that occurs in a church or an individual who fasts continually for forty days".[98] Walter T. P. Wolston offers a great study on the topic of forty days in Scripture, which can be seen in the following table. However, it should be noted that this study is not related to fasting but to the significance of forty days in Scripture.

Forty Days	Scripture References	Results
Noah's Forty Days	(Gen. 6:1-22; 7:1-24; 8:1-22)	Judgment and Salvation; or, The Flood and its Import
Joseph's Forty Days	(Gen. 49:33; 50:1-21)	The Effect of Death; or, Conscience and its Workings
Moses' First Forty Days	(Ex. 32:1-28; Deut. 9:8-17)	Law and the Curse; or, Man's Responsibility and Failure

---

[96] אָבַל *'āval* "57", In Gilbrant, ed., *The Complete Biblical Library Hebrew-English Dictionary, Aleph-Beth.* Gaebelein, ed., *The Expositor's Bible Commentary*, Vol. 7: *Daniel and the Minor Prophets* (Grand Rapids, MI: Zondervan Publishing House, 1985), WORDsearch CROSS e-book, 122.

[97] Kittel, Bromiley and Friedrich, eds., *Theological Dictionary of the New Testament*, Vol. 4, 928. Copeland, *Fasting: A Special Study*, <http://www.e-sword.net>. Accessed on June 12, 2014.

[98] Franklin, *Fasting*, 61.

Moses' Second Forty Days	(Ex. 32:30-35; 33:1-23; 34:1-9, 27-35; Deut. 9:25-29; 10:1-5)	Mercy and Blessing; or, God's Sovereignty and its Ways
Caleb's Forty Days	(Num. 13:1-33; 14:1-45)	Canaan and the Wilderness; or, Unbelief and its Results
Goliath's Forty Days	(1 Sam. 17:1-58; 1 Sam. 18:1-4)	Despair and Deliverance; or, The Challenge Accepted
Elijah's Forty Days	(1 Kgs. 17-19)	Dejection and Support; or, A Failing Servant and a Faithful Master
Ezekiel's Forty Days	(Eze. 4:1-11)	Israel's End; or Guilt, Grace, and Glory
Jonah's Forty Days	(Jon. 3:1-10; Mt. 12:38-41)	Faith and Repentance; or, God's Message and Nineveh's Response
Satan's Forty Days	(Mk. 1:12-13; Mt. 3:16-17; 4:1-11, 23-25; Lk. 4:1-15)	Temptation and Defeat; or, The Strong Man Bound and His Palace Spoiled
The Lord Jesus' Forty Days 1	(Jn. 20:1-18; Acts 1:1-3)	Resurrection Scenes: Mary Magdalene and her Message
The Lord Jesus' Forty Days 2	(Mt. 27:57-66; 28:1-20)	Resurrection Scenes: Mary's Friends and their Message
The Lord Jesus' Forty Days 3	(Lk. 24:13-35)	Resurrection Scenes: The journey to Emmaus
The Lord Jesus' Forty Days 4	(Jn. 20:19-25)	Resurrection Scenes: The Appearing in the Upper Room
The Lord Jesus' Forty Days 5	(Jn. 20:24-31; 21:1-25)	Resurrection Scenes: The Appearings to Thomas and the Seven
The Lord Jesus' Forty Days 6	(Lk. 24:44-53; Acts 1:9-11)	Resurrection Scenes: Galilee and Bethany.[99]

Categories of Fasting

There are various categories of fasting that can be seen in Scripture. Each category will be briefly discussed along with examples, which will be explained in greater detail at a later time within this study. It should be noted that the fasts described in this study fit within one or more of these categories. The first category is the partial fast or sometimes referred to as a restricted fast/diet. It generally refers to omitting a specific meal or refraining from certain types of foods. The partial fast consisted of certain foods or fasting for one meal per day, "So the guard took away their choice food and the wine they were to drink and gave them vegetables instead" (Dan. 1:16). Daniel 10:2-3 says, "At that time I, Daniel, mourned for three weeks. I ate no choice food; no meat or wine touched my lips; and I used no lotions at all until the three weeks were over".[100]

---

[99] Walter T. P. Wolston, *The "Forty Days" of Scripture*, Sixteen Addresses, Third edition, In Rick Meyers, e-Sword, Version 10.2.1, 2000-2012, <http://www.e-sword.net>.

[100] Part of this section on the categories of fasting has been taken from the following website, <http://www.all aboutprayer.org/types-of-fasting-faq.htm>, Accessed on September 3, 2013.

In Daniel 1:12, they restricted their diet to vegetables and water: "Please test your servants for ten days: Give us nothing but vegetables to eat and water to drink". We don't know exactly the reason why Daniel did not completely abstain from food like he appears to have done in chapter 9. However, he engaged in a partial fast to seek the Lord's wisdom. Another example of a partial fast is to give up food between meals or snacking like people do for Lent. However, since some food is eaten, some argue that this is not really a fast. However, the Daniel fast is one of the more popular practiced fasts.

The second category is the public fast which were called in times of special need and/or emergency. Almost all regular fasts were public fasts, but all public fasts are not necessarily regular fasts. For example, first, there was King Jehoshaphat when Judah was invaded,

> After this, the Moabites and Ammonites with some of the Meunites came to make war on Jehoshaphat. Some men came and told Jehoshaphat, "A vast army is coming against you from Edom, from the other side of the Sea. It is already in Hazazon Tamar" (that is, En Gedi). Alarmed, Jehoshaphat resolved to inquire of the LORD, and he proclaimed a fast for all Judah. The people of Judah came together to seek help from the LORD; indeed, they came from every town in Judah to seek him (2 Chr. 20:1-4).

Second, when Ezra returned with the exiles,

> There, by the Ahava Canal, I proclaimed a fast, so that we might humble ourselves before our God and ask him for a safe journey for us and our children, with all our possessions. I was ashamed to ask the king for soldiers and horsemen to protect us from enemies on the road, because we had told the king, "The gracious hand of our God is on everyone who looks to him, but his great anger is against all who forsake him". So we fasted and petitioned our God about this, and he answered our prayer (Ezra 8:21-23).

Third, when Nineveh repented as a result of Jonah's preaching,

> The Ninevites believed God. They declared a fast, and all of them, from the greatest to the least, put on sackcloth. . . . When God saw what they did and how they turned from their evil ways, he had compassion and did not bring upon them the destruction he had threatened (Jon. 3:5, 10).

Only one such fast is spoken of as having been instituted and commanded by the Law of Moses, that of the Day of Atonement and is called "the Fast" in Acts 27:9.[101] Four *annual* fasts were later observed by the Jews in commemoration of the dark days of Jerusalem: (a) the day of the beginning of Nebuchadnezzar's siege in the tenth month; (b) the day of the capture of the city in the fourth month; (c) the day of its destruction in the fifth month; and (d) the day of Gedaliah's murder in the seventh month.

---

[101] "Antiquities of the Jews", In Flavius Josephus, *The Works of Josephus: Complete and Unabridged* (Peabody, MA: Hendrickson Publishers, 1987), 14.4.3. Cf. "On the Life of Moses", In Philo of Alexandria and Charles Duke Yonge, *The Works of Philo: Complete and Unabridged* (Peabody, MA: Hendrickson Publishers, 1995), 493.

This is what the LORD Almighty says: "The fasts of the fourth, fifth, seventh and tenth months will become joyful and glad occasions and happy festivals for Judah. Therefore love truth and peace" (Zech. 8:19).

There is the text of Isaiah 58 which will be discussed later. However, Isaiah addresses the people whose fasting had reached a level of such formality that their ordinary selfish lives that there was no inner transformation. The greatest significance is that in God's view character grows bountiful and life joyful, not through fasts or formal observances, but through acts of unselfish service inspired by a heart of love. These fasts later fell into utter disuse, but they were revived after the destruction of Jerusalem by the Romans.

Occasional public fasts were proclaimed in Israel, as well as among other cultures, in times of famine or public calamity. It seems that according to Jewish accounts that it was customary to fast on the second and fifth days of the week, since it was believed that Moses ascended Mt. Sinai on the fifth day of the week (Thursday) and to have descended on the second day of the week (Monday).[102]

The third category is the private or personal fast. Besides public fasts, individuals would practice the discipline of fasting as the Apocryphal book of Judith states, "And she fasted all the days of her widowhood, save the eves of the sabbaths, and the sabbaths, and the eves of the new moons, and the new moons and the feasts and solemn days of the house of Israel" (Judith 8:6; cf. Lk. 2:37). Publius (or Gaius) Cornelius Tacitus (56-117 AD) alludes to the "frequent fasts" of the Jews in "*The Histories*" and Flavius Josephus speaks of the spread of fasting among the Gentiles. The New Testament speaks of fasting in relation to the disciples (cf. Mt. 9:14; Mk. 2:18; Lk. 5:33).[103] Even though Scripture does not mention fasting from activities such as, watching TV, movies, or other activities for a specified period of time, it does refer to fasting from entertainment as in the case of King Darius (Dan. 6:18). However, this does not mean that this is not a valid type of fasting.[104]

The fourth category is the regular fast which means to refrain from eating all food and observing an event or weekly fasts on a regular day. Most people still drink water or juice during a regular fast. When Jesus fasted for forty days in the desert, Scripture says, "After fasting forty days and forty nights, he was hungry" (Mt. 4:2), but there is no mention of Jesus being thirsty. For example: (a) Day of Atonement (Lev. 23:27; Ps. 35:13; Isa. 58:5); (b) a fast day (Jer. 36:6); (c) four separate festivals (Zech. 8:19); and (d) twice a week (Lk. 18:11-12). The fifth category is the radical fast, which includes two different methods. First of all, when no food or water is consumed like Jesus fasted for forty days in the

---

[102] *The Didache or The Teaching of the Twelve Apostles*, Tim Sauder, trans., <http://www.scrollpublishing.com/store/Didache-text.html>, 8. Accessed on September 3, 2013. *Apostolical Constitutions*, VIII, 23. "Abstinence", In James Orr, ed., *International Standard Bible Encyclopedia*, Rick Meyers, e-Sword, Version 10.2.1, 2000-2012, <http://www.e-sword.net>.

[103] Publius Cornelius Tacitus, *The Histories*, 109 ACE. Alfred John Church and William Jackson Brodribb, trans., <http://classics.mit.edu/Tacitus/histories.html>, Accessed on September 3, 2013. "Against Apion", In Flavius Josephus, *The Works of Josephus: Complete and Unabridged* (Peabody, MA: Hendrickson Publishers, 1987), 2.40. "Abstinence", In Orr, ed., *International Standard Bible Encyclopedia*, <http://www.e-sword.net>.

[104] <http://www.allaboutprayer.org/types-of-fasting-faq.htm>, Accessed on September 3, 2013.

wilderness. Second, when only water was allowed, but nothing else. For example: (a) David (2 Sam. 12:15-20); (b) Esther and her family (Est. 4:15-16); (c) Moses (Deut. 9:9-18); and (d) Jesus (Mt. 4:1-11).

The sixth category is the rotational fast which consists of eating or omitting certain families of foods for designated periods. For example, grains may be eaten only every fourth day. The various food families are rotated so that some food is available each day.[105] The last category is the supernatural fast which is described in Scripture in three separate instances. The first refers to two occurrences of Moses at Mount Horeb (Mt. Sinai; cf. Deut. 1:2). The supernatural fast requires God's supernatural intervention into the bodily processes, which are not repeatable apart from the Lord's specific calling and miraculous provision.

> When I went up on the mountain to receive the tablets of stone, the tablets of the covenant that the LORD had made with you, I stayed on the mountain forty days and forty nights; I ate no bread and drank no water. . . . Then once again I fell prostrate before the LORD for forty days and forty nights; I ate no bread and drank no water, because of all the sin you had committed, doing what was evil in the LORD's sight and so provoking him to anger. . . . I lay prostrate before the LORD those forty days and forty nights because the LORD had said he would destroy you (Deut. 9:9, 18, 25; cf. Deut. 10:10).

The second occurrence refers to Elijah who also in the vicinity of Mount Horeb (Mt. Sinai, cf. Ex. 3:1; 17:6; 33:6; Deut. 5:2; 1 Kgs. 8:9; Ps. 106:19; Mal. 4:4), the mountain of God, travelled the same desert for forty days and forty nights like the Israelites wandered for forty years.

> The angel of the LORD came back a second time and touched him and said, "Get up and eat, for the journey is too much for you". So he got up and ate and drank. Strengthened by that food, he traveled forty days and forty nights until he reached Horeb, the mountain of God (1 Kgs. 19:7-8).

Elijah was supernaturally sustained for forty days and forty nights by food given to him by an angel. If he had travelled on a direct route from Beersheba to Mount Horeb it would probably have taken him approximately fourteen days, since this distance was about 200 miles. This is the same location where God revealed Himself and made a covenant with His people.[106]

The third occurrence refers to Jesus,

> Then Jesus was led by the Spirit into the desert to be tempted by the devil. After fasting forty days and forty nights, he was hungry (Mt. 4:1-2).

Jesus being "led by the Spirit into the desert" immediately follows His baptism in water by John the Baptist stresses the connection between these two events. Matthew uses the noun ἔρημον *erēmon* from ἔρημος *erēmos* which is used 23 of 29 times in the Gospels and the Book of Acts and of these refers to the wilderness of Judea (Mt. 3:1-3) and also the wilderness of Sinai (Jn. 3:14-15; Acts 7:30-32).

---

[105] Towns, *Fasting for Spiritual Breakthrough*, 24.

[106] Walvoord and Zuck, eds., *The Bible Knowledge Commentary*, Vol. 1, 528.

51

In those days John the Baptist came, preaching in the wilderness of Judea and saying, "Repent, for the kingdom of heaven has come near". This is he who was spoken of through the prophet Isaiah: "A voice of one calling in the wilderness, "Prepare the way for the Lord, make straight paths for him" (Mt. 3:1-3).

Just as Moses lifted up the snake in the wilderness, so the Son of Man must be lifted up, that everyone who believes may have eternal life in him" (Jn. 3:14-15).

After forty years had passed, an angel appeared to Moses in the flames of a burning bush in the desert near Mount Sinai. When he saw this, he was amazed at the sight. As he went over to get a closer look, he heard the Lord say: "I am the God of your fathers, the God of Abraham, Isaac and Jacob". Moses trembled with fear and did not dare to look (Acts 7:30-32).

The wilderness is not only an area associated with demonic activity, but in reference to Deuteronomy 6-8, it was in the wilderness where Israel experienced their greatest testings.

But desert creatures will lie there, jackals will fill her houses; there the owls will dwell, and there the wild goats will leap about (Isa. 13:21).

Desert creatures will meet with hyenas, and wild goats will bleat to each other; there the night creatures will also lie down and find for themselves places of rest (Isa. 34:14).

"When an impure spirit comes out of a person, it goes through arid places seeking rest and does not find it. Then it says, 'I will return to the house I left'. When it arrives, it finds the house unoccupied, swept clean and put in order. Then it goes and takes with it seven other spirits more wicked than itself, and they go in and live there. And the final condition of that person is worse than the first. That is how it will be with this wicked generation" (Mt. 12:43-45).

With a mighty voice he shouted: "Fallen! Fallen is Babylon the Great!" She has become a dwelling for demons and a haunt for every impure spirit, a haunt for every unclean bird, a haunt for every unclean and detestable animal (Rev. 18:2).

Jesus' temptation and triumph in the wilderness was a prelude to the greatest triumph over the devil on the cross. It was at the end of these forty days that the devil came to test Jesus. This is typical of the enemy who attacks us at our weakest point. As the Old Covenant was connected by Moses' forty day fast, likewise, the inauguration of the New Covenant was connected to Jesus fasting in the wilderness.[107]

---

[107] Gilbrant, ed., *The Complete Biblical Library Commentary, Matthew*, 60-61. ἔρημος *erēmos* "2031", In Gilbrant, ed., *The Complete Biblical Library Greek-English Dictionary, Delta-Epsilon* (Springfield, MO: Complete Biblical Library, WORDsearch CROSS e-book, 1991). Frank E. Gaebelein, ed., *The Expositor's Bible Commentary, Volume 8: Matthew, Mark, Luke* (Grand Rapids, MI: Zondervan Publishing House. Database © 2010 WORDsearch CROSS e-book, 1984), 111-12.

Chapter 4: The Biblical Foundation to Fasting

The purpose of this chapter is to describe the origin of fasting that can be traced back to ancient times and the purpose for fasting along with a proper perspective of the key characteristics of what fasting is not and what fasting is within the Christian life. In order to build the necessary foundation on which to build upon, we must first of all, define fasting from its Hebrew and Greek roots.

In the Old Testament and Intertestamental books, fasting is a means of humbling oneself before God. The motive for such humbling may include confession, repentance, or petition. The act of abstention and the physical practices which accompany it indicate submission. Often, people tear their clothes and dress in sackcloth and ashes as they fast (2 Sam. 1:11-12; 1 Macc. 3:47; Dan. 9:3; Est. 4:3). Such activities physically mark the participants as being in a lowly state and indicate weakness. Fasting is a means of physically lowering oneself.

In the New Testament, sackcloth and ashes do not specifically accompany fasting and seems to be not limited to suffering or danger. Instead, it is the regular practice of John, his disciples, and the Pharisees (Mt. 9:14; Mk. 2:18; Lk. 5:22; 18:12). In Acts 13:2, worshiping and fasting seems to be common conjoined practices for the church at Antioch. As no sin, disaster, or mourning is specified, fasting is a regular religious practice in these cases.

The Gospel of Matthew contends that fasting should not be a means of public display of piety. In Matthew 4:2, Jesus fasts in the wilderness for forty days and nights. He tells the disciples to give alms, pray, and fast in ways which are visible only to the Lord—when they fast, they should not disfigure their faces or look gloomy, but they should wash their faces and put oil on their heads so that only God knows they are fasting (Mt. 6:16-18). This perspective contrasts Luke and Acts, which depict fasting as a part of worship (Lk. 2:37; Acts 14:23). It is also distinct from the Old Testament and Intertestamental Literature, which depict fasting as an outward display of penitence, grief, or supplication.

This contrast between Matthew and other texts shows that fasting took on different forms and meanings for different Jewish and Christian groups. For some, fasting was a regular practice of worship, often accompanied by prayer. For others, it was limited to times of grief. By the middle of the first millennium AD, fasting became part of the observance of Lent since Jesus fasted in the wilderness.[108]

The Origin of Fasting

The origin of fasting can be traced back to ancient times, possibly connected with the rites of mourning (1 Sam. 31:13; 2 Sam. 1:12; cf. 2 Sam. 12:20-23). Fasting was observed as a sign of penitence (1 Sam. 7:6; 1 Kgs. 21:27), an accompaniment to prayer (2 Sam. 12:16-17; Ps. 35:13), and preparation to receive divine revelation (Ex. 34:28; Deut. 9:9; Dan. 9:3; 10:3; cf. 1 Sam. 28:20; Mt. 4:2).

---

[108] "Fast", In Barry and Wentz, eds., *The Lexham Bible Dictionary*.

The practice of fasting, found in all religions, and used here in the specific sense of temporary abstention from all nourishment on religious grounds[109], is at first more common among the Greeks than the Romans, but then under foreign influences it spread across the whole of the ancient world. The original and most powerful motive for fasting in antiquity is to be found in the fear of demons who gained power over men through eating. Fasting was also an effective means of preparing for intercourse with the deity and for the reception of ecstatic or magical powers.[110]

Moreover, it is apparent that the rite of mourning and fasting had apotropaic implications. This is seen as the parents of the deceased fasted three days before the burial and also a person guarding a corpse must abstain from food and wine. It was believed that as long as the soul of the deceased was near that those near the corpse were vulnerable of demonic inflection through food and drinking.

Herodotus of Halicarnassus, the father of history, writes of Egyptian priests who observed fasts before they could enter the sanctuary, offer sacrifices, and perform their duties or rituals. Likewise, among the Greek and Roman cults, there was no parallel tradition. Through abstinence from food and drink they would become susceptible to euphoric revelations, divination and prophecy—an important role in antiquity. Graeco-Roman fasting was not asceticism, but a custom performed for the benefit of the spirits and the gods.[111]

The Purpose for Fasting

Before we discuss the purpose of fasting, we need to take a moment to briefly discuss what biblical fasting is not. Fasting is not a religious exercise to be taken and used for selfish motives. Likewise, fasting is a religious act that has been misunderstood, misused, and subsequently abused. Fasting is, first of all, not a physical or psychological discipline. We are not told in Scripture to fast as a physical discipline, i.e., dieting to achieve personal and physical benefits. It should be remembered that fasting and dieting are two different things—the former is spiritual and the latter is physical, which is also not found in Scripture. Fasting in Scripture is encouraged for spiritual reasons, which will be discussed throughout this study on fasting. However, we cannot deny the fact that there are physical and psychological benefits to fasting. Those who have fasted or live a lifestyle of constant fasting can testify that fasting has given them a greater degree of discipline in their lives.

Second, fasting is not or should not be used as a manipulative tool in an attempt to twist the arm of God, win His approval, or as an attempt for God to relent on what He has spoken. God, who is omniscient, and knows the motive behind the action and will not succumb to something, that results in selfish gain. For example, God spoke through Jeremiah, "Although they fast, I will not listen to their cry; though they offer burnt offerings and grain offerings, I will not accept them. Instead, I will destroy them with the sword, famine and plague" (Jer. 14:12). The result here is God's wrath being poured out.

---

[109] The temporary or permanent abstention from particular foods is a different phenomenon which is not considered here, though sometimes the motives and practice of this type of abstinence are much the same as those of true fasting. Kittel, Bromiley and Friedrich, eds., *Theological Dictionary of the New Testament*, Vol. 4, 926.

[110] Kittel, Bromiley and Friedrich, eds., *Theological Dictionary of the New Testament*, Vol. 4, 926.

[111] Kittel, Bromiley and Friedrich, eds., *Theological Dictionary of the New Testament*, Vol. 4, 924-35.

Moreover, in the Book of Acts, a group of Jews, attempted to manipulate God through fasting for the purpose of killing Paul.

> The next morning the Jews formed a conspiracy and bound themselves with an oath not to eat or drink until they had killed Paul. More than forty men were involved in this plot. They went to the chief priests and elders and said, "We have taken a solemn oath not to eat anything until we have killed Paul" (Acts 23:12-14).

Of course, God was not moved by their selfish motives. We must never think of fasting as a hunger strike to force God to respond by trying to backing Him into a corner and His only option is to relent. God cannot be manipulated.

Third, fasting is not a hypocritical religious exercise, which in Jesus' day had become a very important part of the Jewish everyday way of life. When we consider, Luke 18:12, "I fast twice a week and give a tenth of all I get" and that some strict Pharisees fasted two times a week—Monday and Thursday, which they adhered to since they believed that Moses ascended Mt. Sinai to receive the Ten Commandments on the fifth day and returned on the second day. A closer look at Jewish history reveals that a possible reason could be that in the City of Jerusalem, Market Day was held on the 2nd and 5th day of the week. On these days, everyone would enter Jerusalem and the Pharisees could demonstrate an outward show of spirituality without an inward repentance. Fasting served as an outward sign of inner sorrow. The purpose of fasting is about more than going without food—it is connecting with reality and noticing the suffering of your neighbour.[112]

The primary purpose of fasting is to strengthen one's reliance on Jesus Christ, "As a penitential practice, fasting is designed to strengthen the spiritual life by weakening the attractions of sensible pleasures. The early Church continued the Jewish custom of linking fasting and prayer, and in the lives of the saints the two almost always go together".[113]

The use of the phrase "afflict one's soul" suggests a purpose of fasting. David in Psalms 69 states,

> When I weep and fast, I must endure scorn; when I put on sackcloth, people make sport of me. Those who sit at the gate mock me, and I am the song of the drunkards (Ps. 69:10-12).

Fasting confirms our utter dependence upon God by finding in Him a source of sustenance beyond food. Through it, we learn by experience that God's Word to us is a life substance. Elmer L. Towns states,

---

[112] The Pharisees would walk through the streets of Jerusalem with messy hair, wear old clothes and cover themselves with dirt. They would cover their faces with white chalk in order to look pale, and cover themselves with ashes as a sign of their humility!! Fasting had become a "look-at-how-spiritual-I-am" exercise. It was a hypocrisy. "Fasting", In D. R. W. Wood and I. Howard Marshall, eds., *New Bible Dictionary*, 3rd ed (Downers Grove, IL: InterVarsity Press, 1996), 364. νηστεύω *nēsteuō* "3384", In Gilbrant, ed., *The Complete Biblical Library Greek-English Dictionary, Lambda-Omicron*. Robert James Utley, *The First Christian Primer: Matthew*, Study Guide Commentary Series, Vol. 9 (Marshall, TX: Bible Lessons International, 2000), 55.

[113] F. L. Cross and Elizabeth A. Livingstone, *The Oxford Dictionary of the Christian Church*, 3rd revised edition (New York: Oxford University Press, 2005), 603.

Fasting is not an end in itself; it is a means by which we can worship the Lord and submit ourselves in humility to him. We don't make God love us any more than He already does if we fast, or if we fast longer. As Galatians states, "It is for freedom that Christ has set us free. Stand firm, then, and do not let yourselves be burdened again by a yoke of slavery" (5:1). The goal of any discipline is freedom. If the result is not greater freedom, something is wrong.[114]

The fast or fasting alone has no intrinsic value (Mt. 6:16; 9:14), but was probably initiated by a person who felt that they needed to express their seriousness over a particular situation or because circumstances diminished the desire for normal daily living. The subject of freedom was a common theme in the Epistles of Paul.

You, my brothers and sisters, were called to be free. But do not use your freedom to indulge the flesh; rather, serve one another humbly in love. For the entire law is fulfilled in keeping this one command: "Love your neighbor as yourself". If you bite and devour each other, watch out or you will be destroyed by each other. You, my brothers, were called to be free. But do not use your freedom to indulge the sinful nature; rather, serve one another in love (Gal. 5:13-15).

In the Christian life, repentance is more than atoning for our sins since we have already been acquitted from all charges through Christ's work on the cross. Moreover, we too often think that God will love us more if we were only perfect. However, God loves us in order that our lives can be transformed through the Holy Spirit. As we practice the Christian disciplines and "continue to work out your salvation with fear and trembling" (Phil. 2:12) these disciplines will enable us to live out the freedom given through grace.[115]

We put no stumbling block in anyone's path, so that our ministry will not be discredited. Rather, as servants of God we commend ourselves in every way: in great endurance; in troubles, hardships and distresses; in beatings, imprisonments and riots; in hard work, sleepless nights and hunger; . . . I have labored and toiled and have often gone without sleep; I have known hunger and thirst and have often gone without food; I have been cold and naked (2 Cor. 6:3-5; 11:27).

In the Old Testament and Judaism, fasting replaced sacrifice and was seen as being greater alms, since it included more than just money—it included the body. Fasting brought about and assured the person fasting a divine answer. However, when a person prayed and the prayer was not answered, they were to fast: "He who prays and is not answered must fast". When a person fasted and wore sackcloth they were not to remove the sackcloth until their prayer was answered,

He who puts on sackcloth and fasts, let him not lay it off until what he prays for takes place, . . . Fasting makes a saint, . . . The point of fasting is not just to expiate sin, to avert calamity or to attain the fulfilment of a desire. Fasting is for its own sake. Its self-evident character can be understood only in terms of the conviction that God recognises the achievement as such. There is

---

[114] Towns, *Fasting for Spiritual Breakthrough*, 17. צוּם *tsûm* "6947", In Gilbrant, ed., *The Complete Biblical Library Hebrew-English Dictionary, Pe-Resh.*

[115] Thomas Ryan, *Fasting: A Fresh Look*, <http://americamagazine.org/issue/563/article/fasting-fresh-look>, Accessed on June 13, 2013.

lively recollection of Isaiah 58:3ff., . . . where in a sermon on fasting we are told that the power lies, not in the sackcloth and fasting, but in penitence and good works. . . . The individual fasts representatively. His exercise in piety is for the salvation of the whole body. In this light one can understand the concern of the Pharisee in Lk. 18:12: He stands before God as one who in fasting and prayer bears on his heart the weal and woe of the people. He thus thinks that he should be seen before God".[116]

According to John Calvin, the purpose of fasting, generally accepted by the Reformed Churches, was threefold: (a) a restraint of the flesh, to preserve it from licentiousness—not considered in public fasting, since each individual has a different bodily health—therefore it is more appropriate in private fasting; (b) as a preparation for prayers or pious meditations was necessary for the whole Church and every individual of the faith; and (c) as a testimony of our humiliation in the presence of God, since God may inflict an entire nation with war, pestilence, or other calamity and therefore is applicable to all people to confess their sin.[117]

Reasons given for fasting are to strengthen prayer, to prepare for revelation, to express sorrow, to help the poor with food, and to reconcile penitents with God. Criticisms of fasting are based on the Old Testament prophets[118], and there is a tendency to subordinate the rite to inwardness and to the ethical.[119] But the early church shows little awareness of Jesus' distinctive approach to fasting.[120] It helps discipline our spirit:

1. "These disciplines train our body and personality to be able to want something and not get it". Dallas Willard
2. "Fasting transforms us to transform the world". Dr. Bill Bright
3. "Fasting can be God's catalyst to thrust us into a whole new world". Don DeWelt

In biblical times, it wasn't unusual for people to fast. The practice crossed cultures and classes in ancient times. In the Old and New Testaments, believers fasted periodically for reasons such as:

1. spiritual purification;
2. penitence;
3. deliverance;
4. preparation to unite with God.

---

[116] Kittel, Bromiley and Friedrich, eds., *Theological Dictionary of the New Testament*, Vol. 4, 930-31.

[117] "Fasting in the Christian Church", In John M'Clintock and James Strong, eds., *Cyclopedia of Biblical and Ecclesiastical Literature*, 12 Vols (New York: Harper & Brothers, Publishers, 1895), Rick Meyers, e-Sword, Version 10.2.1, 2000-2012, <http://www.e-sword.net>.

[118] Marcus Dods and G. Reith, trans. *Epistle of Barnabas* 3.1ff., In Rick Meyers, e-Sword, Version 10.2.1, 2000-2012, <http://www.e-sword.net>.

[119] Shepherd of Hermas, *Similitudes* 5.3.5ff., In Rick Meyers, e-Sword, Version 10.2.1, 2000-2012, <http://www.e-sword.net>.

[120] Gerhard Kittel, Gerhard Friedrich and Geoffrey W. Bromiley, eds. *Theological Dictionary of the New Testament: Abridged in One Volume* (Grand Rapids, MI: William B. Eerdmans Publishing Company, 1985), 633. Copeland, *Fasting: A Special Study*, <http://www.e-sword.net>. Accessed on June 12, 2014.

The purpose of fasting was to:

1. To afflict the soul

The LORD said to Moses, The tenth day of this seventh month is the Day of Atonement. Hold a sacred assembly and deny yourselves, and present an offering made to the LORD by fire. Do no work on that day, because it is the Day of Atonement, when atonement is made for you before the LORD your God. Anyone who does not deny himself on that day must be cut off from his people. I will destroy from among his people anyone who does any work on that day. You shall do no work at all. This is to be a lasting ordinance for the generations to come, wherever you live. It is a sabbath of rest for you, and you must deny yourselves. From the evening of the ninth day of the month until the following evening you are to observe your sabbath (Lev. 23:26-32).

2. To chasten the soul

When I weep and fast, I must endure scorn (Ps. 69:10).

3. To humble the soul

There, by the Ahava Canal, I proclaimed a fast, so that we might humble ourselves before our God and ask him for a safe journey for us and our children, with all our possessions. I was ashamed to ask the king for soldiers and horsemen to protect us from enemies on the road, because we had told the king, "The gracious hand of our God is on everyone who looks to him, but his great anger is against all who forsake him". So we fasted and petitioned our God about this, and he answered our prayer (Ezra 8:21-23).

Yet when they were ill, I put on sackcloth and humbled myself with fasting (Ps. 35:13).

4. To seek the Lord

Alarmed, Jehoshaphat resolved to inquire of the LORD, and he proclaimed a fast for all Judah. The people of Judah came together to seek help from the LORD; indeed, they came from every town in Judah to seek him (2 Chr. 20:3-4).

5. To prepare for spiritual warfare

But this kind does not go out except by prayer and fasting (Mt. 17:21; some manuscripts do not contain this verse.).

Therefore, the purpose of fasting was observed for:

1. forgiveness for sin (Moses, Ahab, and Daniel);
2. their loved ones restored to health (David);
3. protection from danger (Ezra);
4. deliverance from their enemies (the Israelites).[121]

---

[121] Towns, *Fasting for Spiritual Breakthrough*, 224.

The Biblical Definition of Fasting

Fasting is the laying aside of food for a period of time when the believer is seeking to know God in a deeper experience (Isa. 58; Zech. 7:5). It also means "one who has not eaten, who is empty".[122] It is to be done as an act before God in the privacy of one's own pursuit of God (Ex. 34:28; 1 Sam. 7:6; 1 Kgs. 19:8; Mt. 6:17). Fasting relates to a time of confession (Ps. 69:10) and can be a time of seeking a deeper prayer experience and drawing near to God in prevailing prayer (Ezra 8:23; Joel 2:12). The early church often fasted in seeking God's will for leadership in the local church (Acts 13:2). When the early church wanted to know the mind of God, there was a time of prayer and fasting.[123] John Calvin, in his *Institutes of the Christian Religion* defines fasting as:

> But that there maybe no error in the name, let us define what fasting is; for we do not understand by it simply a restrained and sparing use of food, but something else. The life of the pious should be tempered with frugality and sobriety, so as to exhibit, as much as may be, a kind of fasting during the whole course of life. But there is another temporary fast, when we retrench somewhat from our accustomed mode of living, either for one day or a certain period, and prescribe to ourselves a stricter and severer restraint in the use of that ordinary food. This consists in three things—viz. the time, the quality of food, and the sparing use of it. By the time I mean, that while fasting we are to perform those actions for the sake of which the fast is instituted. For example, when a man fasts because of solemn prayer, he should engage in it without having taken food. The quality consists in putting all luxury aside, and, being contented with common and meaner food, so as not to excite our palate by dainties. In regard to quantity, we must eat more lightly and sparingly, only for necessity and not for pleasure.[124]

Martyn Lloyd-Jones, in *Studies in the Sermon on the Mount* states,

> fasting, if we conceive of it truly, must not only be confined to the question of food and drink; fasting should really be made to include abstinence from anything which is legitimate in an[d] of itself for the sake of some special spiritual purpose. There are many bodily functions which are right and normal and perfectly legitimate, but which for special peculiar reasons in certain circumstances should be controlled. That is fasting. There, I suggest, is a kind of general definition of what is meant by fasting.[125]

Likewise, Ian Newberry in *Available for God: A Biblical and Practical Approach to Fasting* states, that fasting is,

> an outward sign of an inward attitude. It denotes an attitude of humility, of dependance and of complete surrender to God. Fasting expresses a desire to break momentarily with our habitual

---

[122] Kittel, Bromiley and Friedrich, eds., *Theological Dictionary of the New Testament*, electronic ed., Vol. 4, 926.

[123] Brand, Draper, England, *Holman Illustrated Bible Dictionary*, 560. "Fast, Fasting", In David Noel Freedman, ed., *The Anchor Yale Bible Dictionary*, Vol. 2 (New York: Doubleday, 1992), 773. Cf., <http://www.centerpointechristian.org/Ministries/Adults/Fasting.aspx>, Accessed on September 3, 2013.

[124] John Calvin, *Institutes of the Christian Religion* (Bellingham, WA: Logos Bible Software, 1997), IV, 12, 18.

[125] Lloyd-Jones, *Studies in the Sermon on the Mount*, Vol. 2, 38.

behaviour, for example eating, and to replace it with something even better and even more important: the presence of God, the Word of God.[126]

Broadbent III states "Fasting is a voluntary act that reveals an inward reality of a humble, dependent heart that desires to completely surrender to God motivated by special times of testing, trials, or struggles".[127] Therefore, as we can see that fasting is a spiritual discipline and as such usually extends longer than our time alone with the Lord in prayer. As a spiritual discipline it enhances our spiritual sensitivity by partially or completely abstaining from food for the purpose of seeking God. Fasting can be seen throughout all of Scripture, and as will be seen throughout this study that there are many references to this subject. It almost seems as though there are as many references to fasting as repentance and confession. Charles M. Murphy defines religious fasting as

> an act of humility before God, a penitential expression of our need for conversion from sin and selfishness. Its aim is nothing less than helping us to become more loving persons, loving God above all and our neighbor as ourselves. Its purpose therefore is the transformation of our total being—mind, body, and spirit. Fasting cannot achieve these aims unless its focus is on God in prayer and not on ourselves. . . . Fasting finds its most powerful expression as a corporate exercise within the Body of Christ.[128]

Some of the ways fasting is referred to include: first of all, fasting is used in desperate circumstances: (a) David fasted when he sought God for the life of his dying child (2 Sam. 12:16-23); (b) when Judah was invaded by an overwhelming army, King Jehoshaphat called a national fast (2 Chr. 20:3); and (c) when the Jews of Persia were to be massacred, Mordecai and Esther called a fast to seek God for deliverance (Est. 4:16). Second, fasting expresses repentance: (a) when the exiled Jewish nation returned to the Promised Land under Ezra and Nehemiah (Neh. 9:1); and (b) as Ezra read the Law, the exiles discovered how far they had departed from the ways of God. Fasting was their repentant response. Third, fasting is used as a means of dedication and preparation: (a) Jesus fasted for forty days in the wilderness prior to the beginning of his ministry (Mt. 4:2); and (b) Paul and Barnabas fasted prior to their missionary journeys (Acts 13:1-3). Fourth, fasting is a symbol of tremendous significance: (a) in its highest form it epitomizes an inward act of supreme self-abnegation; and (b) it involves the entire person—energies and interests—so that they can concentrate upon a single task.

Fifth, fasting represents an attitude of detachment from the things of time and sense: (a) this includes food, pleasure, or ambition; (b) prayer is an interdependent attitude towards the things of God and the spiritual world; (c) the Puritans believed in the relationship between physical food and spiritual blessings; (d) fasting focuses our attention not upon food, dress, books, recreation, friendship, ambition, but gives us the unwavering determination to rise above them so that the spiritual may rule everything; (e) the true idea of fasting is found in Paul's statement "I have the right to do anything", you say—but not everything

---

[126] Ian Newberry. *Available for God: A Biblical and Practical Approach to Fasting*. Trans. by Peter Coleman (Carlisle, UK: OM Publishing, 1996), 15.

[127] Broadbent III, *A Call to Biblical Fasting*, 7.

[128] Murphy, *The Spirituality of Fasting*, x.

is beneficial. "I have the right to do anything"—but I will not be mastered by anything. You say, "Food for the stomach and the stomach for food, and God will destroy them both" (1 Cor. 6:12); and (f) it is through fasting that we detach ourselves from earthly things so that we can attach ourselves to God through prayer.[129]

The Hebrew Definition of Fasting

In the Old Testament, the usual Hebrew noun used for "to fast" "fasting" is צוֹם *tsôm* and the verb צוּם *tsûm*. The verb used here *tsûm* literally means "the mouth being shut or covered". This noun and verb occur 14 and 20 times respectively in the Hebrew Scriptures. The concept of fasting was practiced throughout the nations of the world in connection with humbling the soul, self-mortification, mourning, sorrow, affliction, and repentance.[130] The following quote is wonderful summation of how fasting expresses submission to God.

> With צוּם, the Old Testament also uses for fasting עִנָּה נֶפֶשׁ, "to humble the soul," "to mortify oneself," (Lev. 16:29, 31; 23:27, 32; Num. 29:7; Isa. 58:3); pleonastically Ps. 35:13 בְּצוֹם נַפְשׁוֹ עִנָּה (originally Ps. 69:10). In Ezra 8:21 הִתְעַנָּה too means "to fast," and then in Rabbical writings, where צוּם and הִתְעַנָּה are used synonymously תַּעֲנִית, "self-mortification" in the sense of fasting, occurs in the Masora only in Ezra 9:5; it is a *terminus technicus* in Rabbical Hebrew. Many aspects of Old Testament fasting are the same as in other religions. Fasting in case of death has its roots here too in belief in demons, though in the historical period it has the character of a mourning custom expressing sorrow for the deceased, 1 Sam. 31:13 (1 Chr. 10:12); 2 Sam. 1:12; 3:35; 12:21. . . . The most prominent feature, and one which is singular to the Old Testament, is, however, the fact that fasting expresses submission to God, as the phrase עִנָּה נֶפֶשׁ shows. The fast is an act of self-renunciation and self-discipline which is designed to make an impression on God, to mollify His wrath and to move Him to grant what man desires. [131]

The primary meaning behind the Old Testament concept of fasting can be seen in the verb צוּם *tsûm* which refers to depriving the body of nourishment as a sign that one is experiencing great sorrow. Moreover, the idea expressed by צוּם *tsûm* refers to the mouth being shut or covered. Mourning is further expressed in weeping and lamentation and in putting on sackcloth and ashes (Est. 4:3). He who fasts claims to afflict himself or his soul, i.e. his inner person. In the Old Testament, a person could fast in proxy, e.g., the Psalmist fasted for his enemies during their illness (Ps. 35:13), which usually lasted from sunrise to sunset (2 Sam. 1:12). It could also be complete or partial abstinence (Ps. 35:13; Dan. 10:3).

---

[129] James Hastings, *The Christian Doctrine of Prayer* (Edinburgh, UK: T & T Clark, 1915), 200-01. "Fasting", In Stephen D. Eyre, *Drawing Close to God: The Essentials of a Dynamic Quiet Time: A Lifeguide Resource* (Downers Grove, IL: InterVarsity Press, 1995).

[130] צוֹם, *tsôm* "6948", and צוּם *tsûm* "6947", In Gilbrant, ed., *The Complete Biblical Library Hebrew-English Dictionary, Pe-Resh*. "Fast, Fasting", In Freedman, ed., *The Anchor Yale Bible Dictionary*, Vol. 2, 773.

[131] Kittel, Bromiley and Friedrich, eds., *Theological Dictionary of the New Testament*, electronic ed., Vol. 4, 927-28. "Antiquities of the Jews", In Josephus, *The Works of Josephus*, 14.4.3. "On the Life of Moses, II", In Philo of Alexandria and Yonge, *The Works of Philo*, 493.

Fasting was also adhered to for mourning for the dead, and in cases of severe grief it could last seven days (1 Sam. 31:13). A person could also fast to call upon God to listen to their pain, suffering, and sickness. When David's illegitimate son with Bathsheba became critically sick, he fasted and mourned for many days (2 Sam. 12:16ff.). On the seventh day his child died and David then arose, cleaned and anointed himself, and changed his clothing, since he recognized that he could not accomplish anything now that his son was dead (2 Sam. 12:20-23).

Fasting, in the Old Testament, was also practiced when a vital decision needed to be made or following a dangerous course of action. For example, Esther in seeking the king's favour placed herself at his mercy and possibly losing her life she requested that all Jews fast and plead for God's favour in her mission on behalf of the Jews (Est. 4:16). When Nehemiah heard of the destruction of Jerusalem, he fasted, "When I heard these things, I sat down and wept. For some days I mourned and fasted and prayed before the God of heaven" (Neh. 1:4).

He did not stop here; he sought the Lord for a plan to restore the walls of Jerusalem. Moreover, it seems as though before a person was stoned for blasphemy, the people mourned the sin and coming execution with fasting. Jezebel proclaimed such a fast for Naboth (1 Kgs. 21:9, 12) and a person who became aware of their sin would fast. When Elijah condemned Ahab for Naboth's death, he mourned in sackcloth and fasted. God showed mercy on him and delayed the punishment on his house (1 Kgs. 21:27ff.).

A person could pray, intercede, and fast for an entire nation, like Daniel as he confessed his sin and the sins of his people that had led them into captivity (Dan. 9:3-19). Gabriel answered his prayer, assured him of the ending of the captivity, and promised the establishing of a new covenant (Dan. 9:22-27). A time of national fasting was called during a crisis such as a plague, a military threat, or the death of a king. Jehoshaphat announced a fast because the kings of Moab and Ammon had planned an attack upon Judah. Jehoshaphat had the people gather together in Jerusalem and he led the entire assembly in prayer. Later, the Levite Jahaziel, inspired by the Lord's Spirit, declared that an assurance of salvation was coming. Later Jehoshaphat led the army to war, but Yahweh had already humiliated the enemies, which the army only needed to collect the spoil (2 Chr. 20:1-29).

In 604 BC, when the Babylonian army was camped three days march from Jerusalem, King Jehoiakim proclaimed a fast. Jeremiah used this occasion to have Baruch read his prophecies from a scroll to the people near the New Gate of the temple (Jer. 36:1-10). Jeremiah desired that the people come to true repentance instead of demonstrating an outward show of contrition as was their custom. Likewise, Joel prophesied the coming of the Day of Yahweh and exhorted the people to sanctify a fast and call a solemn assembly (Joel 1:14; 2:15). He declared that if the people would truly "return to me with all your heart, with fasting and weeping and mourning" (Joel 2:12), then he would be "gracious and compassionate, slow to anger and abounding in love" and delay His judgment (Joel 2:13). God extending mercy and not judgment can be seen in the Book of Jonah as he is sent to Nineveh to proclaim judgment. The Ninevites respond with fasting and judgment is averted (Jon. 3:5-10).

In the Old Testament, fasting alone did not cause Yahweh to turn and listen to His people. He did not succumb to those who afflicted their body. The type of fast that the Lord turned and listen to His people was a fast where people demonstrated a true seeking after righteousness, which included taking care of the poor and needy (Isa. 58; cf. Jer. 14:12; Zech. 7:5). Fasting is to be done with the object of seeking to know God in a deeper experience. However, when the Lord brings final salvation to His people, the months of fasting will be turned into feasts of joy and gladness (Zech. 8:19).[132]

The Greek Definition of Fasting

The primary meaning behind the New Testament concept of fasting can be seen in the adjective νῆστις *nēstis* meaning "one who has not eaten, who is empty". The verb νηστεύω *nēsteuō* meaning "to be hungry, without food" usually means "to fast" in a religious and ritual sense, and the noun νηστεία *nēsteia* means "not having eaten" "being without nourishment", or "suffering hunger".[133] These Greek words convey the idea of complete abstinence from food, whether by choice or by obligation. In a metaphorical sense, it could mean "to hold back from evil or pollution" or "fasting from the world". The word νηστεία *nēsteia* comes from *nē*, a negative prefix, and *esthiō*, to eat.

In the pagan religions of the Hellenistic world, fasting revealed one's fear of evil spirits. It also prepared a person to approach a deity. The connection between fear and preparation for a meeting with a god, therefore, is direct. Fasting was also practiced widely in conjunction with death. It was believed that eating and drinking while the soul of the dead person was still near brought the risk of demonic infection. The verb *nēsteuō* is used in the Septuagint 18 out of 21 times to translate the Hebrew term *tsûm*, "fasting". A fast might be total (both food and drink) or partial (perhaps only food). A total fast might last only a day (cf. 2 Sam. 1:12 [LXX, 2 Kings 1:12]). If the period extended into several days it was usually only a partial fast (cf. Est. 4:16). During the time of Jesus, fasting was a typical rite practiced by pious Judaism. Both public and private fasting was common. The Law prescribed only one national fast per year in connection with the Day of Atonement (cf. Lev. 16:29).

In New Testament, the verb νηστεύω *nēsteuō* is used 21 times which only occurs in the Gospels and the Book of Acts and translated to fast". John the Baptist taught his disciples to fast (Mk. 2:18), but Jesus was questioned because His disciples did not. "Jesus answered, 'How can the guests of the bridegroom mourn while he is with them? The time will come when the bridegroom will be taken from them; then they will fast'" (Mt. 9:15). This same passage records the comment made by John's disciples concerning the Pharisees' fasting (Mt. 9:14). According to tradition the Pharisees fasted twice a week, Mondays and Thursdays. Jesus condemned their hypocritical attitude of fasting for the sake of being seen by others. The purpose of the fast was not to be seen by men but by God—in secret. Therefore, Jesus advised that those who fast anoint themselves and bathe and not give the appearance of fasting. A fast is not a public performance; rather, it is a private act of divine worship.

---

[132] צוֹם *tsûm* "6947", In Gilbrant, ed., *The Complete Biblical Library Hebrew-English Dictionary, Pe-Resh.* צוּם *ṣûm* "1890", In Harris, Archer, Jr., and Waltke, eds., *Theological Wordbook of the Old Testament*, 758-59. "Fasting", In Brand, Draper, England, *Holman Illustrated Bible Dictionary*, 560.

[133] "νῆστις, νηστεύω, νηστεία", In Kittel, Bromiley and Friedrich, eds., *Theological Dictionary of the New Testament*, electronic ed., Vol. 4, 925.

Jesus began His own public ministry with a forty day "fast" in the desert (Mt. 4:2). The Early Church associated "fasting" with prayer (Acts 13:3). This was especially true prior to the selection and sending of missionaries and with the appointment of "elders in every church" (Acts 14:23). A fast in keeping with Biblical guidelines always involves prayer. The aged widow Anna "never left the temple but worshiped night and day, fasting and praying" (Lk. 2:37). Following his conversion Paul (Saul) fasted and prayed after being led to Damascus (Acts 9:9, 11).[134]

---

[134] νηστεία *nēsteia* "3383", νηστεύω *nēsteuō* "3384", νῆστις *nēstis* "3385", In Gilbrant, ed., *The Complete Biblical Library Greek-English Dictionary, Lambda-Omicron*. Kittel, Bromiley and Friedrich, eds., *Theological Dictionary of the New Testament*, electronic ed., Vol. 4, 924-35.

Chapter 5: Fasting in the Old Testament

The purpose of this chapter is to describe the foundation for fasting in the Old Testament, which was commanded by Moses on the Day of Atonement and was to be observed "for the generations to come, wherever you live" (Lev. 23:26-32). Included in this fast was a strict warning for those who failed to observe, or observed for selfish reasons. It also provides the Old Testament foundation from ancient cultures, and the use of sackcloth and ashes in fasting.

Fasting occurs in the entire canon of scripture and is frequently practiced along with mourning, lamentation or penitence, special occasions and calendrical days, and sackcloth and ashes. At times, it also functions apotropaically—as a preventative measure—prior to engaging in dangerous activity, such as a journey or battle. It parallels the practice of prayer; the two are often conjoined.[135]

The Day of Atonement (*Yom Kippur*)

The exclusive fast commanded by the Mosaic Law was the fast observed on the Day of Atonement (*Yom Kippur*, יוֹם *yôm*, כִּפֻּרִים *kippurîm*). This fast was "to be a lasting ordinance" and is referred to in the Book of Acts as "the fast" (27:9),

> The LORD said to Moses, "The tenth day of this seventh month is the Day of Atonement. Hold a sacred assembly and deny yourselves, and present a food offering to the LORD. Do not do any work on that day, because it is the Day of Atonement, when atonement is made for you before the LORD your God. Those who do not deny themselves on that day must be cut off from their people. I will destroy from among their people anyone who does any work on that day. You shall do no work at all. This is to be a lasting ordinance for the generations to come, wherever you live. It is a day of sabbath rest for you, and you must deny yourselves. From the evening of the ninth day of the month until the following evening you are to observe your sabbath" (Lev. 23:26-32; cf. 16:29-31; 25:9; Num. 29:7-11).

Moses, in the above reference, gives a stern warning to those who do not observe fasting and working on the Day of Atonement, "Those who do not deny themselves on that day must be cut off from their people. I will destroy from among their people anyone who does any work on that day". Moses uses the verb כָּרַת *kārath* meaning "to cut off", "to cut down", "to exterminate". Even though death is not explicitly stated for disobeying God's command, some scholars have suggested that those guilty of such an offense would be excommunicated from the community of Israel. Some of the passages that associate being cut off with destruction probably refer to death as the ultimate punishment for disobedience (Ex. 31:14).[136]

---

[135] "Fast", In Barry and Wentz, eds., *The Lexham Bible Dictionary*. "Fast, Fasting", In Freedman, ed., *The Anchor Yale Bible Dictionary*, Vol. 2, 773. Edward Burnett Tylor, *Primitive Culture*, Vol. 2 (Boston, MA: Estes and Lauriat, 1871), 410.

[136] כָּרַת *kārath*, "3901", In Gilbrant, ed., *The Complete Biblical Library Hebrew-English Dictionary, Kaph-Mem*.

This was a day set apart for the Israelites to humble themselves or "deny themselves". Even though the Hebrew root word is not used, the verb עָנָה, *ānāh* meaning "to answer, to respond, to be afflicted"[137], is connected with נֶפֶשׁ, *nephesh* meaning "soul, breath, life".

> The *nephesh*, then, is used to personify the basic desires so that just as the stomach is said to hunger for food, the *nephesh*—the throat, the organ or passageway of the needs of life and thus the organ associated with what it means to be a living being—hungers and thirsts both for physical appetites and for emotional and spiritual fulfillment (Ps. 42:1f.; 107:9; Pr. 2:10; 13:4; 21:10; Isa. 26:8). The *nephesh*, as personifying inner needs and desires, is therefore extended to refer to various feelings, emotions and thoughts.[138]

It indirectly refers to fasting and understood as so in the postexilic period and later in extra biblical Hebrew and Aramaic texts, which include the Dead Sea Scrolls, the Midrashim, and the Talmud. *Yom Kippur* is prescribed in Leviticus and states that the 10th day of the seventh month is as the Day of Atonement (Lev. 23:27-28; 25:9). On that day, the Israelites are to humble themselves and present an offering by fire

> The tenth day of this seventh month is the Day of Atonement. Hold a sacred assembly and deny yourselves, and present a food offering to the LORD (Lev. 23:27).

The primary Hebrew root for fasting is not mentioned, but a verb which generally means to humiliate or injure is used (עַנה *'nh*). This verb does not specifically refer to fasting, but was probably understood in that regard in the postexilic period and later. This same root appears in later extra biblical Hebrew and Aramaic texts—including the Dead Sea Scrolls, the Midrashim, and the Talmud—in reference to fasting. These texts refer to fasting with the noun תַּעֲנִית *ta'anith*[139], which is related to the verb in Leviticus. The only appearance of this noun in the Old Testament is in Ezra where it is accompanied by the practices of tearing clothes and praying to God, "Then, at the evening sacrifice, I rose from my self-abasement, with my tunic and cloak torn, and fell on my knees with my hands spread out to the Lord my God" (Ezra 9:5).

---

[137] It typically means a verbal response to something that has been said, whether a question or statement (e.g., Jdg. 8:8; 1 Sam. 4:20; Job 9:15). The word usually refers to human conversation, literally to cry out in expectation of a response, and is often followed by an identification of the person to whom the reply is made (Gen. 45:3; Jdg. 5:29; 2 Kgs. 18:36). עָנָה, *ānāh* "6257", In Gilbrant, ed., *The Complete Biblical Library Hebrew-English Dictionary, Nun-Ayin*.

[138] נֶפֶשׁ, *nephesh* "5497", In Gilbrant, ed., *The Complete Biblical Library Hebrew-English Dictionary, Nun-Ayin*.

[139] Derived from the root verb עָנָה, *'ānāh*, meaning "to afflict" "to oppress" "to humble" *ta'ănîth* means "mortification" "penance". תַּעֲנִית, *ta'ănîth* "8922", In Gilbrant, ed., *The Complete Biblical Library Hebrew-English Dictionary, Sin-Taw*.

Given that Ezra is a postexilic book, this particular noun probably came to refer to fasting later. Although Leviticus calls for humbling of oneself or self-affliction, the verb (עָנָה *'nh*) and *Yom Kippur* eventually came to be associated with fasting. Fasting was probably obligatory only on *Yom Kippur*.[140]

Throughout the Hebrew Scriptures other alternatives to fasting are used, such as: (a) "ate no bread and drank no water" (Deut. 9:9, 18; cf. 1 Sam. 28:20; Lk. 7:33; NIV); (b) "deny yourself(ves)" (Lev. 16:29, 31; 23:27, 32; Num. 29:7; NIV, NRSV); (c) "afflict your souls" or "afflict yourselves" (Lev. 16:29, 31; 23:27, 32; Num. 29:7, KJV, NKJV, ASV, RSV); (d) "self-denial" (HCSB); "humble your souls" or "humble yourselves" (NASB, the Net Bible); (e) "fast, solemn fast, humble yourselves" (The Message); and (f) "to afflict oneself" or "to afflict the soul" (*'innah nepēš*), a technical term used in the Priestly Code.[141]

The remnant upon returning from the Exile, observed four other annual fasts,

> This is what the LORD Almighty says: "The fasts of the fourth, fifth, seventh and tenth months will become joyful and glad occasions and happy festivals for Judah. Therefore love truth and peace" (Zech. 8:19).

These fasts are seen as disasters in Jewish history and will be discussed later under the heading of The Fasts of Jewish Captivity, (Zech. 7:1-7; 8:19). Esther 9:30-31, can be interpreted as implying the establishment of yet another regular fast. This fast in Esther will be discussed under The Esther Fast (Est. 4:3, 12-17; 9:30-31).

> And Mordecai sent letters to all the Jews in the 127 provinces of Xerxes' kingdom—words of goodwill and assurance—to establish these days of Purim at their designated times, as Mordecai the Jew and Queen Esther had decreed for them, and as they had established for themselves and their descendants in regard to their times of fasting and lamentation (Est. 9:30-31).

The following table shows the types of fasting, references, the participants, and associated ritual actions in the Old Testament.

Types of Fasting	References	Participants	Ritual Actions
Day of Atonement	Leviticus 16:29, 31; Leviticus 23:27-32	Public / Public	"Do no work"; "Offer an offering made by fire unto the LORD"; "do not work"
	Numbers 29:7-10	Public	No work, sacrificial offering
	Isaiah 58:3, 5, 10	Public	
Following a Death	1 Samuel 31:13; 2 Samuel 1:12	Public and Individual	"Fasting seven days"; Rent clothes, mourned, wept
	2 Samuel 3:35; 1 Chronicles 10:12	Individual and Public	

---

[140] "Fast", In Barry and Wentz, eds., *Lexham Bible Dictionary*.
[141] "Fast, Fasting", In Freedman, ed., *The Anchor Yale Bible Dictionary*, Vol. 2, 773.

Petitionary Fasting	Judges 20:26	Public	Offered peace offerings and burnt offerings
	2 Samuel 12:16, 21-23	Individual	
	2 Chronicles 20:3	Public	
	Ezra 8:21, 23	Public	
	Nehemiah 1:4	Individual	Wept, mourned, prayed
	Esther 4:16	Communal	
	Psalms 35:13	Individual	"My clothing was sackcloth"
	Psalms 109:24	Individual	
	Jeremiah 14:12	Public	Crying out to the Lord
	Jeremiah 36:6, 9	Public	
	Daniel 6:18	Individual	
	Daniel 9:3	Individual	Prayer, supplication, sackcloth, ashes
Preparatory	Exodus 34:28	Individual	
	Deuteronomy 9:9	Individual	
	1 Samuel 28:20	Individual	
	1 Kings 21:9, 12	Public	
Penitential	Deuteronomy 9:18	Individual	
	1 Samuel 7:6	Public	Drew water and poured it out before the Lord
	1 Kings 21:7	Individual	Put on sackcloth
	Ezra 10:6	Individual	
	Nehemiah 9:1	Public	"Sackclothes and earth upon them"
	Joel 1:14	Public	"Call a solemn assembly"
	Joel 2:12-17	Public	Weeping, mourning, solemn assembly
	Jonah 3:5-9	Public	Sackcloth and ashes
Following Misfortune Besides Death	Joshua 7:6	Private	"Joshua rent his clothes, and fell to the earth. . . and put dust upon [his head]".
	1 Samuel 1:7	Individual	
	1 Samuel 20:34	Individual	
	1 Kings 21:4	Individual	
	Esther 4:1, 3	Individual	Tore clothes, sackcloth, ashes; cried out
War	1 Samuel 14:24	Public	
Zechariah	Zechariah 7:3, 5; 8:19	Public	

Fasting On Special Occasions

Likewise, there were also occasional fasts, individual (*e.g.*, 2 Sam. 12:22) and corporate (*e.g.*, Jdg. 20:26; Joel 1:14). Fasting conveyed grief (1 Sam. 31:13; 2 Sam. 1:12; 3:35; Neh. 1:4; Est. 4:3; Ps. 35:13-14) and penitence (1 Sam. 7:6; 1 Kgs. 21:27; Neh. 9:1-2; Dan. 9:3-4; Jon. 3:5-8). It was a means where men and women might humble or deny themselves (Ezra 8:21; Ps. 69:10). At times, fasting was seen as a self-inflicted punishment (cf. "to afflict the soul"). Sometimes fasting was directed towards capturing the guidance, direction, and assistance of God

> Moses was there with the LORD forty days and forty nights without eating bread or drinking water. And he wrote on the tablets the words of the covenant—the Ten Commandments (Ex. 34:28; Deut. 9:9; 2 Sam. 12:16-23; 2 Chr. 20:3-4; Ezra 8:21-23).

Fasting can be seen as being vicarious (Ezra 10:6; Est. 4:15-17). Some believe that fasting would automatically acquire a hearing with God (Isa. 58:3-4). Against this the prophets declared that without right conduct fasting was in vain (Isa. 58:5-12; Jer. 14:11-12; Zech. 7).[142] Fasting in itself did not cause Yahweh to turn to His people. He did not succumb merely to the afflictions of the body. A true fast indicated that the people were intent on seeking righteousness, which included taking care of the poor and needy (Isa. 58; cf. Jer. 14:12; Zech. 7:5). However, when the Lord brings final salvation to His people, the months of fasting will be turned into feasts of joy and gladness (Zech. 8:19).[143]

Fasting is a response to an immediate or impending situation which calls for repentance, protection, or mourning. Subsequently, fasting is clearly prescribed in observance of *Yom Kippur* and Purim in the Old Testament, and occasional fasts are the only type clearly depicted in the Old Testament. The first type of infrequent fasting is associated with repentance and confession. Some biblical examples include: (a) the Israelites fasted as a way of turning away from foreign gods and back to the Lord (1 Sam. 7:6); (b) the Ninevites fasted when they learn that the city will be overturned in forty days (Jon. 3:4-9); and (c) the Israelites fasted and confessed their sins once all the foreigners were removed from their community (Neh. 9:1-2).[144]

A second type of infrequent fasting was practiced proceeding or in the midst of a dangerous event, such as military battles. It is a means of seeking God's protection in a dangerous situation. Some biblical examples include: (a) the Israelites fight the tribe of Benjamin. Despite having more soldiers, they were losing the battle and returned to their camp to fast and weep. This resulted in the Lord defeating the Benjaminites (Jdg. 20:26, 35); (b) when the Moabites and Ammonites confront Jehoshaphat in battle, he proclaims a fast in Judah and the Lord brings victory (2 Chr. 20:1-3, 22); (c) Ezra proclaims a fast prior to the Jews returning to Judaea (Ezra 8:21-23); (d) the Jews lives are in danger because Haman has decreed that they all be put to death, since Mordecai refused to bow to him. Esther responds by proclaiming a

---

[142] Wood and Marshall, *New Bible Dictionary*, 364.

[143] צוּם "1890", In Harris, Archer, Jr., and Waltke, eds., *Theological Wordbook of the Old Testament*, 759. Kittel, Bromiley and Friedrich, eds., *Theological Dictionary of the New Testament*, electronic ed., Vol. 4, 927-30.

[144] "Fasting", In Barry and Wentz, eds., *The Lexham Bible Dictionary*.

three-day fast for all the Jews in Susa before seeking an unannounced meeting with the King (Est. 4:16); and (e) Joel prophesies the day of the Lord which will bring destruction. The Jews are told to lament and sanctify a fast (Joel 1:13-15).

A third type of infrequent fasting occurs in times of mourning and also when a person is on the brink of death. Some biblical examples include: (a) the men of Jabesh-Gilead fast when Saul and his sons are killed in battle (1 Sam. 31:12); (b) David and his men fast when they learn of the death of Saul and Jonathan (2 Sam. 1:12); (c) Nehemiah proclaims a fast when he hears that the gates of Jerusalem have been destroyed and his people are in danger (Neh. 1:4); and (d) Similarly, when the Jews in every province receive notice that Haman has decreed that all Jews be killed, they respond with mourning and fasting (Est. 4:3).

Fasting Based Upon Calendar Days

Leviticus and Esther are the only Old Testament books which mention calendrical days related to fasting. As the Pentateuch does not prescribe or proscribe fasting, or even mention the primary word for fasting—fasting was treated differently among ancient communities. The most strident groups seem to have fasted only on holy days such as *Yom Kippur*, when a communal fast was a petition for atonement of the previous year's sins. However, in the Old Testament, fasting is practiced on a number of important occasions besides *Yom Kippur*.

In conjunction with the Book of Esther, fasting became part of the observance of Purim, which was a two-day festival to celebrate the Jews' deliverance from destruction and their victory over their enemies. Both feasting and fasting are mentioned as observances in Esther 9:25-32. Esther has often been described as an etiology for Purim, which was celebrated with a fast followed by a feast. The earliest reference to the Fast of Purim is found in the Talmud, which is dated to the fifth century AD. The Book of Esther simply mentions feasting and fasting as two Jewish observances. At some point in late antiquity, they became connected with Purim. The extent to which other days are observed with fasting varied among the Jews in antiquity. In the Talmud, fasting varied among Jews. Commemorative days that may include fasting include the day of the destruction of Solomon's temple and the deaths of important leaders, such as Joshua, Miriam, and Eli and his sons.[145]

Fasting in Ancient Israel

As previously discussed, the only required fast was the Day of Atonement (Lev. 16:29-31; 23:27), prescribed in Old Testament Law. In ancient Israel, this was a universal fast emphasized by the phrase "self-affliction" or "afflict your soul" (Lev. 16:29, 31; 23:27, 32; Num. 29:7). Other fasts that were voluntary included liturgical fasts (cf. Jer. 36:6) and a public fast observed at times of contrition (1 Sam.

---

[145] "Fast", In Barry and Wentz, eds., *The Lexham Bible Dictionary*.

14:24). Moreover, there are pre-exilic references to fasting that include smaller groups or individuals relating to a mourning rite[146], personal repentance, and prayer (e.g., Ps. 35:13; 1 Kgs. 21:27; Num. 30:13).

In the post-exilic period, public fasts increased (cf. Ezra 8:21-23; Neh. 9:1) and in Zechariah 8:19, four days are highlighted, which were established while the Israelites were in exile. Zechariah advocates for the continuation of these four days of fasting as they are "joyful and glad occasions and happy festivals for Judah". The prophetic of this time, fasting in sincerity, and charity of heart was stressed (e.g., Isa. 58:3-9; Joel *passim*, e.g., 2:12-13). Likewise, may have been used as a method of divination as seen in Moses' forty-day fast on Mt. Sinai interpreted by the rabbis, even though the dominant thought was of miraculous provision.

> When I went up on the mountain to receive the tablets of stone, the tablets of the covenant that the LORD had made with you, I stayed on the mountain forty days and forty nights; I ate no bread and drank no water. The LORD gave me two stone tablets inscribed by the finger of God. On them were all the commandments the LORD proclaimed to you on the mountain out of the fire, on the day of the assembly; (Deut. 9:9-10; cf. Ex. 24:18; 1 Kgs. 19:8).

In later apocalyptic literature, fasting as a method of becoming more receptive to divine revelation becomes more prominent and at the same time remorse becomes the incentive to fasting in Daniel 9:3. Fasting utilized as preparing to receive visions cannot be seen as a subordinate idea (cf. Dan. 10:3), primarily since there are various Intertestamental references to this existence (e.g., 2 Esdras 5:13; 2 Baruch 5:7f.; Ascension of Isaiah 2:7).[147]

In Mesopotamia, fasting was an integral part of the mourning rite—seen as a public display on grief juxtaposed with celebration. In the ancient Near East, fasting held social significance similar to feasting. Both could create or renew a social bond and displayed the current state of both individuals and/or groups. While feasting was often a public display of wealth and success, fasting was a display of humility and grief.[148]

Fasting in Sackcloth and Ashes

The Hebrew word used for sackcloth is שַׂק *saq*, and symbolized a person's passionate desire for mercy from God (Dan. 9:3).[149] Sackcloth in the New Testament symbolically illustrates grief and

---

[146] Of special note is the mourning rite associated with David who fasted subsequent to the deaths of Saul, Jonathan and Abner (2 Sam. 1:12; 3:36) which are associated with his approval. However, David fasted as long as his son with Bathsheba lived and when he died David stopped the fast, which suggests that the death of his son was accepted as an atonement for his sin of adultery and the mourning rite was irrelevant (Mk. 2:18-22; 2:23-28).

[147] "Fast, Fasting", In Freedman, ed., *The Anchor Yale Bible Dictionary*, Vol. 2, 773-74. For a further discussion on asceticism and ancient Israel, see E. G. Hirsch, ed., *The Jewish Encyclopaedia*, 12 Vols (New York: Funk & Wagnalls Company, 1901).

[148] "Fast", In Barry and Wentz, eds., *The Lexham Bible Dictionary*. See Susan Pollock, "Feasts, Funerals and Fast Food in Early Mesopotamian States", Tamara L. Bray, ed., *The Archaeology and Politics of Food and Feasting in Early States and Empires* New York: Kluwer Academic Publishers, 2002), 17-38.

[149] שַׂק *saq* "8012", In Gilbrant, ed., *The Complete Biblical Library Hebrew-English Dictionary, Sin-Taw*.

repentance—the primary purpose in the Old Testament and the only purpose in the New Testament.[150] Sackcloth was a coarse cloth (Zech. 13:4; Mt. 3:4) usually made from goat's hair, and black in colour (Isa. 50:3; Rev. 6:12). The symbolic value of sackcloth was not based upon any discomfort in wearing it, but from its association with poverty, hence it was the typical clothing worn by the poor. It was worn during time of mourning the dead (Gen. 37:34; 2 Sam. 3:31; Joel 1:8), mourning because of personal or corporate disaster (Job 16:15; Lam. 2:10; Est. 4:1), repentance of sins (1 Kgs. 21:27; Neh. 9:1; Jon. 3:5; Mt. 11:21), special prayer for deliverance (2 Kgs. 19:1-2; Dan. 9:3), and by captives (1 Kgs. 20:31-32; Isa. 3:24). Sackcloth often had a band tied around the waist (1 Kgs. 20:31-32; Isa. 3:24; 20:2) and usually worn next to the skin (2 Kgs. 6:30; Job 16:15), and sometimes worn while sleeping (1 Kgs. 21:27; Joel 1:13). In one case the King of Nineveh wore sackcloth instead of a royal robe (Jon. 3:6), and used to lie upon (2 Sam. 21:10; Isa. 58:5). However, no one clothed in sackcloth could enter a King's palace (Est. 4:2).

Sackcloth was also worn by Palestinian shepherds because it was economical and durable[151], and prophets wore it because it was symbolic of repentance and the message in which they preached (Isa. 20:2; Rev. 11:3). Sometimes animals were covered in sackcloth demonstrating corporate repentance and prayer (Jon. 3:8). The custom of wearing sackcloth for mourning and repentance was not limited to Israel, but also in Damascus (1 Kgs. 20:31), Moab (Isa. 15:3), Ammon (Jer. 49:3), Tyre (Eze. 27:31), and Nineveh (Jon. 3:5). Sackcloth is used symbolically, "I clothe the heavens with darkness and make sackcloth its covering" (Isa. 50:3). The two witnesses of Revelation 11:3, "prophesy for 1,260 days, clothed in sackcloth" symbolizing coming trouble. It was a common practice among the Canaanites while mourning to cut oneself, which was a prohibited practice for an Israelite (Deut. 14:1). To put it off or have it removed demonstrated joy in relief from sorrow (Ps. 30:11). In Isaiah 20:2, the Lord commanded Isaiah to put off the outer garment of sackcloth was a sign that Egypt would be stripped of its possessions, and to give a silent exhortation as to the need of repentance.[152]

The wearing of sackcloth was often accompanied by being covered in ashes in times of mourning, personal and corporate repentance, corporate disaster, and prayer (Est. 4:1, 3; Isa. 58:5; Dan. 9:3; Mt. 11:21; Lk. 10:13). The Hebrew noun used for ashes is אֵפֶר *'fpher* meaning "ground", "earth", "soil", "dust", and "ashes". The key usage of *'fpher* is in the practice of mourning—a position of humiliation, disgrace, and shame— symbolic of worthlessness (2 Sam. 13:19; Dan. 9:3). Abraham is a good example of this in speaking of the coming destruction of Sodom and Gomorrah says that "though I am nothing but dust and ashes" (Gen. 18:16-33).

---

[150] σάκκος *sakkos* "4383", In Gilbrant, ed., *The Complete Biblical Library Greek-English Dictionary, Sigma-Omega*.

[151] H. Freedman, ed., Babylonian Talmud: *Tractate Shabbath, Folio 64a*, <http://halakhah.com/shabbath/ shabbath_64.html>. Accessed on December 4, 2013.

[152] Wood and Marshall, *New Bible Dictionary*, 1032-34. Myers, *The Eerdmans Bible Dictionary*, 899. Achtemeier, ed. *Harper's Bible Dictionary*, 890. "Sackcloth", In Easton, *Easton's Bible Dictionary*. אֵפֶר *'fpher*, "684", In Gilbrant, ed., *The Complete Biblical Library Hebrew-English Dictionary, Aleph-Beth*. "Sackcloth", In W. E. Vine and F. F. Bruce, *Vine's Expository Dictionary of Old and New Testament Words*, Vol. 1 (Grand Rapids, MI: Fleming H. Revell, 1981), 120.

Likewise, Isaiah prophesies that God will "bestow on them a crown of beauty instead of ashes, the oil of joy instead of mourning, and a garment of praise instead of a spirit of despair" (61:3), Job notes, "He throws me into the mud, and I am reduced to dust and ashes" (30:19), and Ezekiel states the same fate of the King of Tyre "I reduced you to ashes on the ground in the sight of all who were watching" (28:18).[153]

There are no Old Testament examples of non-Israelites placing ashes upon their heads, which could possibly be because there are only a few examples of mourning among non-Israelites. Some of these examples include the King of Nineveh "covered himself with sackcloth and sat down in the dust" (Jon. 3:6). Likewise, Job "took a piece of broken pottery and scraped himself with it as he sat among the ashes" (Job 2:8), and Ben-hadad's officials advised him to go to Ahab in sackcloth and with a rope around his head (1 Kgs. 20:31).

Please refer to *Fasting: Unlocking Spiritual Power and Breakthrough, Personal Reflections* under the heading "Personal Reflections from the Old Testament" to conclude this section of this study.

---

[153] אֵפֶר *'fipher* "684", In Gilbrant, ed., *The Complete Biblical Library Hebrew-English Dictionary, Aleph-Beth.*

Chapter 6: The Fasts of the Pentateuch, Historical Books, and Psalms

The purpose of this chapter is to describe the various fasts of biblical characters found within the Pentateuch, Historical Books, and Psalms. Each fast presents the context and purpose in which the fasting occurs. Fasting in Scripture was not only practiced corporately but also by individuals. Each fast concludes by completing the relevant "Personal Reflections" sections.

The Moses Fast

Moses had already been on Mt. Sinai two times (Ex. 19:3, 20). The first time was the establishment of the covenant between God and Israel (Ex. 19:3-9). The second time Moses received various ordinances (Ex. 19:20-23:33). Then the Lord called Moses a third time to ascend Mt. Sinai (Ex. 24). Nadab, Abinhu and seventy elders were allowed to witness God's glory from somewhere below the pinnacle "they stood at the foot of the mountain", where they ate and drank (Ex. 19). The two contexts below describe Moses fasting on two separate occasions: (a) he fasted "forty days and forty nights" on Mt. Sinai and received divine direction (The Ten Commandments); and (b) he fasted "forty days and forty nights" over the evil that the Israelites committed before the Lord, which aroused His anger.

> When I went up on the mountain to receive the tablets of stone, the tablets of the covenant that the LORD had made with you, I stayed on the mountain forty days and forty nights; I ate no bread and drank no water. The LORD gave me two stone tablets inscribed by the finger of God. On them were all the commandments the LORD proclaimed to you on the mountain out of the fire, on the day of the assembly (Deut. 9:9-10).

> So I turned and went down from the mountain while it was ablaze with fire. And the two tablets of the covenant were in my hands. When I looked, I saw that you had sinned against the LORD your God; you had made for yourselves an idol cast in the shape of a calf. You had turned aside quickly from the way that the LORD had commanded you. So I took the two tablets and threw them out of my hands, breaking them to pieces before your eyes. Then once again I fell prostrate before the LORD for forty days and forty nights; I ate no bread and drank no water, because of all the sin you had committed, doing what was evil in the LORD's sight and so arousing his anger. I feared the anger and wrath of the LORD, for he was angry enough with you to destroy you. But again the LORD listened to me (Deut. 9:15-19).

Moses in the first fast on Mt. Sinai received "the tablets of the covenant" and "ate no bread and drank no water". This fast is referred to as an "Absolute Fast", "Radical Fast", or "Supernatural Fast" since Moses abstains from eating food and drinking water for "forty days and forty nights".

This is a rare fast and normally should not last for more than three (3) days. It is recommended that this type of fast be done with extreme caution, not for extended periods of time, and only if you have a clear directive from the Lord and are in good health. It is only mentioned a few times in the Bible, both in reference to Israel. "Then Ezra withdrew from before the house of God and went to the room of Jehohanan son of Eliashib. While he was there, he ate no food and drank no water, because he continued to mourn over the unfaithfulness of the exiles" (Ezra 10:6); "Then Esther sent this reply to Mordecai: 'Go, gather together all the Jews who are in Susa, and fast for me. Do not eat or drink for three days, night or day. I and my attendants will fast as you do. When this is done, I will go to the king, even though it is against the law. And if I perish, I perish'" (Est. 4:15-16). Likewise, the Apostle Paul following his encounter with Jesus on the road to Damascus (Acts 9:9; cf. Acts 27:33).

The purpose of the Moses Fast is to receive divine direction from the Lord as Moses did on Mt. Sinai and also when he saw the sin that the Israelites had committed and "feared the anger and wrath of the Lord, for he was angry enough with you to destroy you" (Deut. 9:19). Moses realized the seriousness of the Israelites having broken their covenant relationship with God that he fasted another "forty days and forty nights". Moses intercedes for the Israelites as a whole and for Aaron and destroys the calf, "Also I took that sinful thing of yours, the calf you had made, and burned it in the fire. Then I crushed it and ground it to powder as fine as dust and threw the dust into a stream that flowed down the mountain" (Deut. 9:21). Moses' prayer is one of the most critical intervention and intercessory prayers in the history of Israel (Ex. 32:9-14). Samuel's prayer at Mizpah (1 Sam. 7:5, 8-9) and the Lord reminded Jeremiah of this type of prayer when He told him that his heart would not go out to Judah in the last days of the empire (Jer. 15:1).[154]

The major issue that the Lord has with the golden calf is that it contrasts the Lord Himself as the Almighty Creator and could have possibly been an attempt to syncretize worship of the Lord with Egyptian Canaanite calf worship (Ex. 32:4, 8). The Lord's response would always be that other gods would never be tolerated (Deut. 5:6-8; 6:4-5). Moses then makes the Israelites drink the water from where the crushed idol was thrown, "And he took the calf the people had made and burned it in the fire; then he ground it to powder, scattered it on the water and made the Israelites drink it" (Ex. 32:20), which is a suitable conclusion to the shameful act of the Israelites. Jeroboam's altar at Bethel was to suffer a similar fate, "Even the altar at Bethel, the high place made by Jeroboam son of Nebat, who had caused Israel to sin—even that altar and high place he demolished. He burned the high place and ground it to powder, and burned the Asherah pole also" (2 Kgs. 23:15).

Please refer to *Fasting: Unlocking Spiritual Power and Breakthrough, Personal Reflections* under the heading "The Moses Fast" to complete the Personal Reflections section of this study.

The Jewish Fast

Then all the Israelites, the whole army, went up to Bethel, and there they sat weeping before the LORD. They fasted that day until evening and presented burnt offerings and fellowship offerings to the LORD (Jdg. 20:26).

"So I stood beside him and killed him, because I knew that after he had fallen he could not survive. And I took the crown that was on his head and the band on his arm and have brought them here to my lord". Then David and all the men with him took hold of their clothes and tore

---

[154] "Deuteronomy 9:18-19", In Gilbrant, ed., *The Complete Biblical Library Commentary, Deuteronomy* (Springfield, IL: World Library Press, Inc., WORDsearch CROSS e-book, 1996). Gaebelein, ed., *The Expositor's Bible Commentary, Volume 3*, 80-81. Gaebelein, ed., *The Expositor's Bible Commentary, Volume 2*, 479.

them. They mourned and wept and fasted till evening for Saul and his son Jonathan, and for the army of the LORD and for the nation of Israel, because they had fallen by the sword (2 Sam. 1:10-12).

In the Jewish Fast, which occurred during the dry season, many devout Jews fasted without drinking any water, two days per week. The Jewish Fast can also be referred to as a "normal fast", which would last for a full day from sunset of one day to the sunset of the next day. This type of fasting was seen as being meritorious, even though ascetic fasting was prohibited. Anyone who participated in a Jewish fast was required to abstain from eating food and pleasures which included the common practice of anointing one's head to prevent dry skin and deny oneself of anything that would bring attention to themselves. Among the Greeks, they would rub their body with oil before exercising and then used a strigil[155] to scrape off dirt, sweat, or anything that had accumulated on their skin. The Jews were forbidden from this practice. The true fast from God was not external appearance but the internal attitude of the heart in relation to Him (Mt. 6:16-18; Isa. 58:3-12; Jer. 36:9).[156]

The Jewish fast was also announced corporately as in the case of a war (Jdg. 20:26; 2 Chr. 20:3) or pestilence (Joel 1:13f.). In the Book of Judges, the Israelites became very discouraged and retreated north to Bethel and began weeping and fasting which revealed their desperation for it seemed that the Lord was silent and ignored their just cause. The combination of burnt offerings and fellowship offerings was usually an expression of devotion and commitment. Solomon offered both kinds of sacrifices at the dedication of the temple (1 Kgs. 8:64), and Joshua had built an altar on Mount Ebal as the nation renewed its allegiance to the Lord (Jos. 8:31). The absence of a sin offering implies that the people were innocent of wrongdoing. Later David mourned, wept, and fasted as he petitioned the Lord to save his child with Bathsheba (2 Sam. 12:21-22). Fasting as a means of seeking divine favor, guidance and protection, naturally became associated with confession of sin, as indisputable evidence of penitence or sorrow for sin. The principle of the Jewish Fast is seen as the Israelites sought God's guidance with increasing earnestness—repentance with weeping, fasting for grief, and sacrifices for forgiveness and peace.

The Jews also instituted particular days of humiliation, which were known as the fasts of the congregation. These fasts were observed on the second and fifth days of the week beginning at sunset and lasted until midnight of the following day. During this time they wore sackcloth against their skin, tore their clothes, threw ashes upon themselves, did not wash their hands, or anoint their heads with oil. They made supplication in the synagogues, prayed long and mournful prayers, and had the appearance of sorrow and repentance, which was contrary to what Jesus taught.[157]

---

[155] In ancient Greece and Rome, a strigil was an instrument with a curved blade used to scrape dirt and sweat from the skin after bathing or exercising. "Strigil", In Inc Merriam-Webster, *Merriam-Webster's Collegiate Dictionary*, Eleventh ed. (Springfield, MA: Merriam-Webster, Inc., 2003).

[156] "Matthew 6:16-18", In Craig S. Keener, *The IVP Bible Background Commentary, New Testament* (Downers Grove, IL: InterVarsity Press, 1993), WORD*search* CROSS e-book.

[157] Gaebelein, ed., *The Expositor's Bible Commentary, Volume 3*, 498-99. Andrew Knowles, *The Bible Guide*, 1st Augsburg books ed. (Minneapolis, MN: Augsburg, 2001), 127. "Fasting", In Richard Watson, *A Biblical and Theological Dictionary* (New York: Lane & Scott, 1849).

When you fast, do not look somber as the hypocrites do, for they disfigure their faces to show men they are fasting. I tell you the truth, they have received their reward in full. But when you fast, put oil on your head and wash your face, so that it will not be obvious to men that you are fasting, but only to your Father, who is unseen; and your Father, who sees what is done in secret, will reward you (Mt. 6:16-18).

Please refer to *Fasting: Unlocking Spiritual Power and Breakthrough, Personal Reflections* under the heading "The Jewish Fast" to complete the Personal Reflections section of this study.

The Hannah Fast

But to Hannah he gave a double portion because he loved her, and the LORD had closed her womb. And because the LORD had closed her womb, her rival kept provoking her in order to irritate her. This went on year after year. Whenever Hannah went up to the house of the LORD, her rival provoked her till she wept and would not eat. Elkanah her husband would say to her, "Hannah, why are you weeping? Why don't you eat? Why are you downhearted? Don't I mean more to you than ten sons?" Once when they had finished eating and drinking in Shiloh, Hannah stood up. Now Eli the priest was sitting on a chair by the doorpost of the LORD's temple. In bitterness of soul Hannah wept much and prayed to the LORD. And she made a vow, saying, "O LORD Almighty, if you will only look upon your servant's misery and remember me, and not forget your servant but give her a son, then I will give him to the LORD for all the days of his life, and no razor will ever be used on his head". . . . She said, "May your servant find favor in your eyes". Then she went her way and ate something, and her face was no longer downcast. Early the next morning they arose and worshiped before the LORD and then went back to their home at Ramah. Elkanah lay with Hannah his wife, and the LORD remembered her. So in the course of time Hannah conceived and gave birth to a son. She named him Samuel, saying, "Because I asked the LORD for him" (1 Sam. 1:5-11, 18-20).

The Hannah fast is a fast to receive healing. This is a great example as the Lord opened up Hannah's womb so that she could conceive. In Hannah's case, because of being greatly distressed she became barren and

Because the LORD had closed Hannah's womb, her rival kept provoking her in order to irritate her. This went on year after year. Whenever Hannah went up to the house of the Lord, her rival provoked her till she wept and would not eat (1 Sam. 1:6-7).

It is a matter of common sense that when a person experiences a deep level of distress that they often lose their appetite.[158]

In Hebrew culture, a man's posterity was bound up in having a son to perpetuate his lineage and if his wife was unable to conceive a son it was regarded as a curse from God.

He will love you and bless you and increase your numbers. He will bless the fruit of your womb, the crops of your land—your grain, new wine and oil—the calves of your herds and the lambs of your flocks in the land that he swore to your forefathers to give you. You will be blessed more

---

[158] Gaebelein, ed., *The Expositor's Bible Commentary, Volume 3*, 571.

than any other people; none of your men or women will be childless, nor any of your livestock without young (Deut. 7:13-14).

Even though Hannah could not conceive, Elkanah's love did not grow cold but increased as he gave her "a double portion" of what he gave his other wife Peninnah (Jos. 18:1). This provoked and irritated Peninnah until Hannah "wept and would not eat" (1 Sam. 1:7). This reminds us of the jealousy which Jacob's bigamy wrought in Rachel's heart (Gen. 30:1). None of Elkanah's assurances of devotion had any beneficial effect upon Hannah and her sorrow (1 Sam. 1:8). Her only resort was to cast herself entirely on the mercies of God.

The law required all adult Hebrew males to appear at the temple for the three major festivals of the year—the Feast of Unleavened Bread, the Feast of Harvest, and the Feast of Ingathering (Ex. 23:14-17). Therefore, Elkanah would attend these festivals year after year with his wives, and Hannah would pour out her soul to God to conceive a son for Elkanah (1 Sam. 1:15). The book of Samuel uses the verb שָׁפַךְ *shāphakh*[159] which occurs 113 times meaning "pouring a liquid", such as water (Ex. 4:9) or broth (Jdg. 6:20) or "the emptying of a container". The majority of its usage involves sacrificial blood (Ex. 29:12), and drink offerings (Isa. 57:6). The verb also applies to the emptying of a vessel filled with dust (Lev. 14:41), ashes (1 Kgs. 13:3) or dirt for siege mounds (Eze. 4:2).[160] Therefore, as Hannah cried out to the Lord, she was literally emptying everything she had, which demonstrates the depth of her soul in conceiving a son.

She vowed, "O LORD Almighty, if you will only look upon your servant's misery and remember me, and not forget your servant but give her a son, then I will give him to the Lord for all the days of his life, and no razor will ever be used on his head" (1 Sam. 1:11). This dedication of her son demonstrated her commitment to the Nazirite Vow[161] (Num. 6:1-8), the same vow of Samson's parents under nearly identical circumstances (Jdg. 13:2-5). Hannah's prayer was so intense that Eli the Priest thought that she was drunk with wine or beer. However, when he learned of her true dilemma, he assured her that God would answer her prayer.

Shortly after Elkanah and Hannah returned to Ramah, she conceived and had a son whom she named Samuel meaning "heard or asked of God", who was born between the judges and the kings of the

---

[159] The verb שָׁפַךְ *shāphakh* is used symbolically or metaphorically. Murder is referred to as the pouring out of a person's blood (Lev. 17:4), which constitutes the single most frequent use of the verb. David referred to passionate prayer as pouring out his soul (Ps. 42:4). Joel promised that one day God's Spirit would be poured out upon people (Joel 2:28f.). Zechariah saw a pouring out of God's grace and supplication in the time of the Messiah's appearing (Zech. 12:10). The most common metaphorical usage is that of God's anger being poured out upon his rebellious people (e.g., Jer. 6:11). שָׁפַךְ *shāphakh* "8581", In Gilbrant, ed., *The Complete Biblical Library Hebrew-English Dictionary, Sin-Taw.* שָׁפַךְ "2444", In Harris, Archer, Jr., and Waltke, eds., *Theological Wordbook of the Old Testament*, 950.

[160] שָׁפַךְ *shāphakh* "8581", In Gilbrant, ed., *The Complete Biblical Library Hebrew-English Dictionary, Sin-Taw.*

[161] The Nazirite vow included (a) abstaining from the use of grapes in any form; (b) not shaving the hair on one's head; and (c) avoiding dead bodies (Num. 6:3-7). Gaebelein, ed., *The Expositor's Bible Commentary, Volume 3*, 572.

undivided nation (Saul, David, Solomon). Samuel, like Moses served as a priest, judge, leader and prophet. His parents, Elkanah and Hannah, from the territory of Ephraim, were Levites of the family of Kohath (1 Sam. 1:1f.; 1 Chr. 6:22-28). Samuel's sons were named Joel and Abijah (1 Sam. 8:2).[162]

After the birth of Samuel, Elkanah attended the next festival in Shiloh, but this time, besides offering his sacrifice to the Lord, he paid his vow of offering Samuel whom Hannah and himself had vowed if the Lord blessed them with a son (cf. Lev. 27:1-8; Num. 30:1-8). However, Hannah and Samuel did not go with Elkanah to the temple since Samuel was only a baby and remained at home. Fearful of not presenting Samuel to the Lord, Hannah prayed "only may the Lord make good his word". When Samuel had been weaned, she took him "with a three-year-old bull, an ephah of flour and a skin of wine" to the house of the Lord in Shiloh and dedicated his life to the service of the Lord (1 Sam. 1:24).[163]

Moreover, fierce anger can produce the same effect as Hannah,

> Jonathan got up from the table in fierce anger; on that second day of the month he did not eat, because he was grieved at his father's shameful treatment of David (1 Sam. 20:34).

The Hebrew word אַף־חֳרִי for "fierce anger" here describes the highest levels of disappointed human fury (cf. Ex. 11:8; 2 Chr. 25:10; Isa. 7:4). Jonathan grieves that his father King Saul attempts to mistreat and kill his best friend David, who had known of this; "Jonathan must not know this or he will be grieved" (1 Sam. 20:3). On the second day of the New Moon festival, neither David (v. 27) nor Jonathan (v. 34) ate at the king's table (1 Sam. 20:29, 34).[164]

Please refer to *Fasting: Unlocking Spiritual Power and Breakthrough, Personal Reflections* under the heading "The Hannah Fast" to complete the Personal Reflections section of this study.

The King Saul Fast

> Samuel said, "Why do you consult me, now that the LORD has turned away from you and become your enemy? The LORD has done what he predicted through me. The LORD has torn the kingdom out of your hands and given it to one of your neighbors—to David. Because you did not obey the LORD or carry out his fierce wrath against the Amalekites, the LORD has done this to you today. The LORD will hand over both Israel and you to the Philistines, and tomorrow you and your sons will be with me. The LORD will also hand over the army of Israel to the Philistines". Immediately Saul fell full length on the ground, filled with fear because of Samuel's words. His strength was gone, for he had eaten nothing all that day and night (1 Sam. 28:16-20).

The Law of Moses specifically stated that no Israelite should ever try to gather information from the dead through a witch, wizard, or medium since those things that are hidden belong to God and

---

[162] שְׁמוּאֵל *shemû 'fil* "8442", In Gilbrant, ed., *The Complete Biblical Library Hebrew-English Dictionary, Sin-Taw*.

[163] Walvoord and Zuck, eds., *The Bible Knowledge Commentary*, Vol. 1, 433.

[164] Gaebelein, ed., *The Expositor's Bible Commentary, Volume 3*, 724.

information revealed to His people. He will reveal the things that need to be revealed and what He does not reveal must be left hidden.

> When you enter the land the LORD your God is giving you, do not learn to imitate the detestable ways of the nations there. Let no one be found among you who sacrifices his son or daughter in the fire, who practices divination or sorcery, interprets omens, engages in witchcraft, or casts spells, or who is a medium or spiritist or who consults the dead. Anyone who does these things is detestable to the LORD, and because of these detestable practices the LORD your God will drive out those nations before you. You must be blameless before the LORD your God (Deut. 18:9-13).

The prophet Isaiah speaks directly to those who consult mediums and spiritists,

> When men tell you to consult mediums and spiritists, who whisper and mutter, should not a people inquire of their God? Why consult the dead on behalf of the living? (Isa. 8:19).

However, as the Philistines threatened war in the Jezreel Valley, King Saul seeks divine direction from the Lord, who does not answer him. Ironically, Saul had earlier despised the Lord's will (1 Sam. 15:26) and now seeks the Lord to speak to him when he desperately needed to hear from the Lord. God refuses to answer him and King Saul seeks out the witch of Endor. When Samuel appears to Saul, he tells him

> Why do you consult me, now that the LORD has turned away from you and become your enemy? The LORD has done what he predicted through me. The LORD has torn the kingdom out of your hands and given it to one of your neighbors—to David. Because you did not obey the LORD or carry out his fierce wrath against the Amalekites, the LORD has done this to you today. The LORD will hand over both Israel and you to the Philistines, and tomorrow you and your sons will be with me. The LORD will also hand over the army of Israel to the Philistines (1 Sam. 28:16-19).

Saul becomes greatly distressed at the word that Samuel speaks to him. Samuel uses the adjective צַר־לִי ṣar-lî meaning "adversity to me" and may refer to the strong emotional response experienced when a person is externally pursued by enemies or internally by wrong decisions or passions. For example, when Jacob confronts Esau, "In great fear and distress Jacob divided the people who were with him into two groups, and the flocks and herds and camels as well". He thought, "If Esau comes and attacks one group, the group that is left may escape" (Gen. 32:7-8).[165]

After King Saul hears of his fate from Samuel for not obeying the Lord, and being physically hungry, he is now crushed spiritually. He falls "full length on the ground" מְלֹא־קוֹמָתוֹ mĕlō'-qômātô meaning that he fell completely prostrate, demonstrating his kingship among the Israelites, but not in the eyes of God (1 Sam. 16:7; cf. 10:23-24).[166] Saul prostrates himself, partially from mental distress and partially from bodily exhaustion. It was this strong and unrelenting emotion of feeling that had driven Saul to contact the witch of Endor. It was this one day fast, and the distress of mind, which was the worst possible

---

[165] Harris, Archer, Jr., and Waltke, eds., *Theological Wordbook of the Old Testament*, 778.
[166] קוֹמָה qômāh "7253", In Gilbrant, ed., *The Complete Biblical Library Hebrew-English Dictionary, Pe-Resh.*

preparation for a visit to one used to persuade her victims by pretended magical arts, and gifted, as people of her class usually are, with great shrewdness.

Saul's loss of strength "for he had eaten nothing all that day and night" could be seen as a ritualistic act (1 Sam. 28:20; cf. Ezra 10:6) and possibly a requirement of a necromantic ritual.[167] Robert Polzin highlights the contrast in the use food at the beginning and end of the Book of 1 Samuel. In the first chapter of First Samuel, Hannah "would not eat" (1:7) and then when Samuel tells Saul that he and his sons will soon die, he will not eat. Likewise, when David hears of his first son with Bathsheba has become very ill, he does not eat and only starts to eat after the death of his son (2 Sam. 12:15-23).[168] Then Saul's men and the witch of Endor encourage him to eat and he agrees. She butchers a fattened calf and makes unleavened bread and offers it to Saul and his men. A "fattened calf" was a delicacy (cf. Jer. 46:21; Mal. 4:2), which only those who were wealthy could afford (Am. 6:4; cf. Lk. 15:22-30). Archaeological evidence supports the fact that domestic stables were probably located within a person's home, which is seen in the phrase "at the house".[169] Samuel tells Saul,

> The LORD will hand over both Israel and you to the Philistines, and tomorrow you and your sons will be with me. The LORD will also hand over the army of Israel to the Philistines (1 Sam. 28:19).

Walter Brueggemann summarizes this verse, "read at its best, this meal is a kind of last supper, one final meal for a king (cf. 1 Sam. 25:36) who will not be a king much longer. It is as though the woman wants one last regal gesture for Saul when no one else will give it (cf. Mk. 14:3-9)".[170] Therefore, after Saul's one day fast and eating a delicacy which could be his last meal, Saul and his men go out into the night—"that same night" (v. 25) in which Samuel's words have sealed the fate of a doomed king.[171]

Please refer to *Fasting: Unlocking Spiritual Power and Breakthrough, Personal Reflections* under the heading "The King Saul Fast" to complete the Personal Reflections section of this study.

---

[167] Theodore J. Lewis, *Cults of the Dead in Ancient Israel and Ugarit* (Harvard Semitic Monograph, 39. Atlanta, GA: Scholars Press, 1989), 114.

[168] Robert Polzin, *Samuel and the Deuteronomist* (San Francisco, CA: Harper, 1989), 271, note 10.

[169] Philip J. King, *Amos, Hosea, Micah—An Archaeological Commentary* (Philadelphia, PA: Westminster John Knox Press, 1988), 149-51.

[170] Walter Brueggemann, *First and Second Samuel. Interpretation: A Bible Commentary for Teaching and Preaching* (Louisville, KY: John Knox Press, 1990), 196.

[171] "1 Samuel 28:20-25", In Thoralf Gilbrant, ed., *The Complete Biblical Library Commentary, Samuel* (Springfield, IL: World Library Press, Inc., WORDsearch CROSS e-book, 1996). Gaebelein, ed., *The Expositor's Bible Commentary, Volume 3*, 783-784. Lawrence O. Richards, *The Bible Reader's Companion*, electronic ed (Wheaton, IL: Victor Books, 1991), 198. Mays, ed., *Harper's Bible Commentary*, 285. David S. Dockery, ed., *Holman Concise Bible Commentary: Simple, Straightforward Commentary on Every Book of the Bible* (Nashville, TN: Broadman & Holman Publishers, 1998), 118-19. B. H. Carroll, *An interpretation of the English Bible*, In Rick Meyers, e-Sword, Version 10.2.1, 2000-2012, <http://www.e-sword.net>. Harris, Archer, Jr., and Waltke, eds., *Theological Wordbook of the Old Testament*, 778.

The Egyptian Servant Fast

They found an Egyptian in a field and brought him to David. They gave him water to drink and food to eat—part of a cake of pressed figs and two cakes of raisins. He ate and was revived, for he had not eaten any food or drunk any water for three days and three nights (1 Sam. 30:11-12).

In Egyptian culture, old or Egyptian born slaves were customarily treated with kindness and respect. However, a slave who was purchased or captured was not given any special treatment and if they became sick or needed the help of another, their master would abandon them, rather than become a burden. As David and his 400 men pursued their enemy, they found an Egyptian who had been without food and water for three days, was revived with nourishment and identified himself as an Egyptian slave abandoned by the Amalekites due to sickness (1 Sam. 30:13; cf. Jdg. 15:19). David could have killed the Egyptian who had taken part in kidnapping two of his wives, but instead he uses this opportunity to question the Egyptian (v. 13; 1 Sam. 25:10-11; cf. Jon. 1:8), who then gives David the details of the Amalekites siege of the "the Negev and Ziklag" (1 Sam. 30:1). The Egyptian had David swear "before God that you will not kill me or hand me over to my master, and I will take you down to them" (1 Sam. 30:15).

There is poignancy in his speech since it speaks of both Saul's earlier request for David not to kill him (1 Sam. 24:22) and Saul's subsequent death on Mt. Gilboa. He then leads David and the 400 men to the raiding party (1 Sam. 25:13)[172] who were "scattered over the countryside, eating, drinking and reveling because of the great amount of plunder they had taken from the land of the Philistines and from Judah" (1 Sam. 30:16).[173] The fact that these Amalekites were "eating, drinking and reveling" was characteristic of "a degenerate people who practice excessive self-indulgence".[174] This is contrasted with the Egyptian who the Amalekites had left behind because he had become ill.

Please refer to *Fasting: Unlocking Spiritual Power and Breakthrough, Personal Reflections* under the heading "The Egyptian Servant Fast" to complete the Personal Reflections section of this study.

The Uriah Fast

Uriah said to David, "The ark and Israel and Judah are staying in tents, and my master Joab and my LORD's men are camped in the open fields. How could I go to my house to eat and drink and lie with my wife? As surely as you live, I will not do such a thing!" Then David said to him, "Stay here one more day, and tomorrow I will send you back". So Uriah remained in Jerusalem that day and the next. At David's invitation, he ate and drank with him, and David made him drunk. But in the evening Uriah went out to sleep on his mat among his master's servants; he did not go home. In the morning David wrote a letter to Joab and sent it with Uriah. In it he wrote,

---

[172] Here David and only 400 men continue the pursuit, while 200 were too exhausted to continue (1 Sam. 30:10) and earlier 400 men continued the pursuit, while 200 men stayed with the supplies (1 Sam. 25:13).

[173] "1 Samuel 30", In Jamieson, Fausset, and Brown, *Commentary Critical and Explanatory on the Whole Bible*. "1 Samuel 30", In Gilbrant, ed., *The Complete Biblical Library Commentary, Samuel*.

[174] Brueggemann, *First and Second Samuel. Interpretation*, 202-03. Gaebelein, ed., *The Expositor's Bible Commentary, Volume 3*, 792-794.

"Put Uriah in the front line where the fighting is fiercest. Then withdraw from him so he will be struck down and die". So while Joab had the city under siege, he put Uriah at a place where he knew the strongest defenders were. When the men of the city came out and fought against Joab, some of the men in David's army fell; moreover, Uriah the Hittite died (2 Sam. 11:11-17).

Uriah the Hittite, a resident alien in Israel, was probably a professional soldier who had married Bathsheba, a Jewess and faithfully served David and the Israelite army. According to Old Testament Law, a resident alien was given most of the rights and obligations of a Hebrew (Ex. 23-24) and David was both legally and morally obligated by the Law to treat him as he would treat any Hebrew, but this not the case with Uriah. It was at the height of David's success that a weakness in his character was exposed. The ancient law of the Hebrews was quite strict when it came to the punishment of adultery and murder which David was both guilty of committing. The avenging of murder was the responsibility of their next of kin or kinsmen. However, the person who has committed adultery was guilty of an unpardonable sin against society, and as such, Hebrew law stated that they were to be stoned to death by the community. Therefore, the punishment levied upon the person committing an act of sexual immorality was more severe than the person who committed murder and David should have faced both. However, the hand of the Lord was upon him and his life was spared.[175]

David tried to cover up his adultery on two occasions by tempting Uriah to sleep with his wife Bathsheba to make it look like he had made her pregnant. The first scheme was quite subtle as David tells Uriah to "go down to your house and wash your feet" where he would see Bathsheba and possibly sleep with her since he had not seen her for a while. Uriah, instead of returning home, sleeps in the porch area which was customary for both servants and guards. When asked, Uriah responds to David by refusing to return home when his friends in combat were deprived of these comforts. His high and honourable sense of military duty and loyalty to his fellow soldiers prevailed over his desire to spend a short time of intimacy with his wife.[176]

It is interesting that Uriah's statement "as surely as you live, I will not do such a thing!" in Hebrew literally means taking an oath "by your life, and by the life of your soul" (2 Sam. 11:11), both emphatically rejects David's offer (2 Sam. 14:19; cf. 15:21). In this context, we find an orthodox Israelite respecting the soldier's code of conduct in battle against marital relations, which was customary for soldiers not to sleep with their wives during a military campaign,

"I don't have any ordinary bread on hand; however, there is some consecrated bread here—provided the men have kept themselves from women". David replied, "Indeed women have been kept from us, as usual whenever I set out. The men's things are holy even on missions that are not holy. How much more so today!" So the priest gave him the consecrated bread, since there was

---

[175] Charles Foster Kent, *The Founders and Rulers of United Israel: From the Death of Moses to the Division of the Hebrew Kingdom*, The Historical Bible (New York: Charles Scribner's Sons, 1908), 151. Richards, *The Bible Reader's Companion*, 210.

[176] "2 Samuel 11:9", In Jamieson, Fausset, and Brown, *Commentary Critical and Explanatory on the Whole Bible.*

no bread there except the bread of the Presence that had been removed from before the LORD and replaced by hot bread on the day it was taken away (1 Sam. 21:4-6).

David, in the second scheme, invited Uriah to eat and drink until he was drunk. He assumes that since he was drunk that he would lose his inhibitions, sleep with Bathsheba, and therefore cover-up his adultery with her (Hab. 2:15). However, David's plan for Uriah to return home and sleep with his wife backfires.

> Then David said to him, "Stay here one more day, and tomorrow I will send you back." So Uriah remained in Jerusalem that day and the next. At David's invitation, he ate and drank with him, and David made him drunk. But in the evening Uriah went out to sleep on his mat among his master's servants; he did not go home (2 Sam. 11:12-13).

David was trying to get Uriah to disobey the soldier's code of conduct in battle.[177] Therefore, after these two failed attempts, David then resorts to his last and only option, "Put Uriah in the front line where the fighting is fiercest. Then withdraw from him so he will be struck down and die" (2 Sam. 11:15). David involves Joab in his conspiracy to cover-up his adulterous relationship with Bathsheba.

When we compare the contents of the narrative of David and Bathsheba with the infamous letters of Jezebel concerning Naboth (cf. 1 Kgs. 21:9-11), there is not a lot of difference. In both cases, an innocent man is executed at the impulse of an Israelite monarch. David in sending orders to Joab to place Uriah "where the fighting is fiercest" (2 Sam. 11:15) brings to remembrance the same Hebrew expression as seen "all the days of Saul there was bitter war with the Philistines" (1 Sam. 14:52).

The phrase "he will be struck down" is the Hebrew verb וְנִכָּה *wĕnikkâ* from the verb נָכָה *nākhāh*, which alludes to the Levites pronouncing curses from Mount Ebal on all Israelites who commit any of these acts (Deut. 27:9-26). This specifically refers to the verse "cursed is the man who kills his neighbor secretly" (Deut. 27:24). This verb is used about 500 times and refers to someone "striking" a person (Ex. 21:26; Ps. 3:7; Lam. 3:30), an animal (Num. 22:23, 25, 27), a river (Ex. 7:17), the dust (Ex. 8:16, 17); and a rock (Ex. 17:6).[178] David "struck down" (נָכָה *nākhāh*) Uriah and took his wife (2 Sam. 12:9), and these things were done "in secret" (בַּסָּתֶר *bassāter*, 2 Sam. 12:12). David's wicked behaviour is punishable under the divine curse.[179]

An interesting observation is that when Joab receives the letter from David to place Uriah "where the fighting is fiercest", he realizes that if Uriah was the only casualty at this time of the war, it would raise suspicion as to David's motives. Therefore, he "makes improvements on the plan, implementing it in spirit rather than to the letter. . . . He realized that the saving in casualties, however desirable in itself, is

---

[177] "2 Samuel 11", In Jamieson, Fausset, and Brown, *Commentary Critical and Explanatory on the Whole Bible.* Walvoord and Zuck, eds., *The Bible Knowledge Commentary*, Vol. 1, 467. "2 Samuel 11:6-13", In Henry, *Matthew Henry's Commentary on the Whole Bible.*

[178] נָכָה "1364", In Harris, Archer, Jr., and Waltke, eds., *Theological Wordbook of the Old Testament*, 578.

[179] נָכָה *nākhāh* "5409", In Gilbrant, ed., *The Complete Biblical Library Hebrew-English Dictionary, Nun-Ayin.* R. A. Carlson, *David the Chosen King: A Traditio-Historical Approach to the Second Book of Samuel* (Stockholm, Sweden: Almqvist and Wiksell, 1964), 141.

also the weak spot in the king's plan. It is better for many to fall, he decides, than for the conspiracy to stand revealed".[180] The author of Samuel uses the noun מִן־הָעָם *min-hā 'ām* from the noun עַם *'am* for "some of the men" (2 Sam. 11:17) which was a frequent expression for soldiers in a military context.[181]

Please refer to *Fasting: Unlocking Spiritual Power and Breakthrough, Personal Reflections* under the heading "The Uriah Fast" to complete the Personal Reflections section of this study.

The Man of God Fast

> The king said to the man of God, "Come home with me for a meal, and I will give you a gift". But the man of God answered the king, "Even if you were to give me half your possessions, I would not go with you, nor would I eat bread or drink water here. For I was commanded by the word of the LORD: 'You must not eat bread or drink water or return by the way you came'". So he took another road and did not return by the way he had come to Bethel (1 Kgs. 13:7-10).

In the preceding context, Rehoboam had succeeded his father Solomon as King (1 Kgs. 11:41-43) and Jeroboam had gathered together "the whole assembly of Israel" and goes to Rehoboam to protest against the high taxes instituted under King Solomon, "Your father put a heavy yoke on us, but now lighten the harsh labor and the heavy yoke he put on us, and we will serve you" (1 Kgs. 12:4). Samuel uses the noun עֹל *'ōl* for yoke from the verb עָלַל *'ālal* meaning "to abuse, to glean, to do repeatedly" and is "frequently used of relationships in which one party exercises power over another, generally to maltreat or ridicule".[182] Solomon had placed a heavy yoke upon the Israelites—a weight of the stress or burden of circumstances, or oppression. Rehoboam after consulting his elders foolishly responds to Jeroboam's request to lighten the yoke by saying "My father laid on you a heavy yoke; I will make it even heavier. My father scourged you with whips; I will scourge you with scorpions" (1 Kgs. 12:11).

Since Rehoboam refused to lighten the yoke established by his father King Solomon, the ten tribes of northern Israel separate from Judah and make Jeroboam their King who had been in charge of the labour force under the leadership of King Solomon. He had turned to worship the idols of his foreign wives and willfully disobeys the Lord's promise years earlier and institutes a system of worship that mimics the pattern given to Moses.

> If you do whatever I command you and walk in obedience to me and do what is right in my eyes by obeying my decrees and commands, as David my servant did, I will be with you. I will build you a dynasty as enduring as the one I built for David and will give Israel to you (1 Kgs. 11:38).

---

[180] Meir Sternberg, *The Poetics of Biblical Narrative: Ideological Literature and the Drama of Reading* (Bloomington, IN: Indiana University Press, 1987), 214.

[181] עַם *'am* "6194", In Gilbrant, ed., *The Complete Biblical Library Hebrew-English Dictionary, Nun-Ayin*. Gaebelein, ed., *The Expositor's Bible Commentary, Volume 3*, 933-935.

[182] עָלַל *'ālal* "6177", In Gilbrant, ed., *The Complete Biblical Library Hebrew-English Dictionary, Nun-Ayin*. עֹל *'ōl* "6144", In Gilbrant, ed., *The Complete Biblical Library Hebrew-English Dictionary, Nun-Ayin*.

This system was an apostate and/or counterfeit system to the Day of Atonement, which included an illegitimate priesthood, illicit sacrifices and festivals, and images of bulls. This system was adhered to by every successive northern king and had caused Israel to follow a system built upon a counterfeit Day of Atonement for centuries.

Jeroboam sought to make Israel's festival just as good as if not "better" than Judah's. Israel's festivals were designed by Jeroboam whereas Judah's feasts had been decreed by God. Upon the death of Solomon, stress and rivalries began to develop which not only divided the tribes of Israel, but within a few hundred years the divided northern and southern kingdoms were devastated and dispersed to foreign lands. In 730 BC, the Hebrew people were divided into the ten tribes of Israel known as the Northern Kingdom of Israel and the two tribes of Judah known as the Southern Kingdom of Judah.[183]

There is some speculation as to the name of "the man of God". Flavius Josephus, in *The Antiquities of the Jews*, calls him Jadon, who had come from Judah to Bethel to atone for the silence of Israel and to put an end to Jeroboam's institution of a new festival—designed to be as good if not better than Judah's festivals, decreed by God Himself.[184] Epiphanius refers to the man of God as Joas, and Sameas by Tertullian; but these names along with the assumption that he was identical with Iddo the seer, or Shemaiah, have grown out of mere speculation.[185] In regards to "the man of God", Josephus states,

> So the king understood that he was a man of veracity, and had a divine foreknowledge; and entreated him to pray to God that he would restore his right hand. Accordingly the prophet did pray to God to grant him that request. So the king having his hand recovered to its natural state, rejoiced at it, and invited the prophet to sup with him; but Jadon said, that he could not endure to come into his house, nor to taste of bread or water in this city, for that was a thing God had forbidden him to do; as also to go back by the same way which he came; but he said he was to return by another way. So the king wondered at the abstinence of the man; but was himself in fear, as suspecting a change of his affairs for the worse, from what had been said to him.[186]

The Lord sends the "man of God" a prophet from Judah to Bethel and as Jeroboam presents an offering on the altar, the "man of God" loudly condemns the offering, the altar, and announces the coming destruction,

> He cried out against the altar by the word of the LORD: "O altar, altar! This is what the LORD says: 'A son named Josiah will be born to the house of David. On you he will sacrifice the priests of the high places who now make offerings here, and human bones will be burned on you'". That same day the man of God gave a sign: "This is the sign the LORD has declared: The altar will be split apart and the ashes on it will be poured out". When King Jeroboam heard what the man of

---

[183] Richards, *The Bible Reader's Companion*, 218, 230. Walvoord and Zuck, eds., *The Bible Knowledge Commentary*, Vol. 1, 513.

[184] Walvoord and Zuck, eds., *The Bible Knowledge Commentary*, Vol. 1, 513. "1 Kings 13", In Thoralf Gilbrant, ed., *The Complete Biblical Library Commentary, Kings* (Springfield, IL: World Library Press, Inc., WORDsearch CROSS e-book, 1996).

[185] "1 Kings 13:1", In Wheddon, *Whedon's Commentary on the Old and New Testaments*, <http://www.e-sword.net>.

[186] "Antiquities of the Jews", In Josephus, *The Works of Josephus*, 8.234-35.

God cried out against the altar at Bethel, he stretched out his hand from the altar and said, "Seize him!" But the hand he stretched out toward the man shriveled up, so that he could not pull it back. Also, the altar was split apart and its ashes poured out according to the sign given by the man of God by the word of the LORD. Then the king said to the man of God, "Intercede with the LORD your God and pray for me that my hand may be restored". So the man of God interceded with the LORD, and the king's hand was restored and became as it was before (1 Kgs. 13:2-6).

The man of God's prophecy has been referred to as one of the most astonishing prophetic words spoken since it states the reign and action of the future King Josiah (640-609 BC) who would not appear for 290 years (2 Kgs. 23:15-20). As Jeroboam becomes enraged at the prophecy and stretches out his hand to condemn the "man of God" and have him arrested, his hand "shriveled up" illustrating God's authority is more powerful than Jeroboam's. Likewise, the altar split in two and the ashes poured out as the "man of God" had spoken.[187] Jeroboam had built two golden calves in Bethel and Dan on the same place (Bethel) where Abram had built the first altar to God (1 Kgs. 12:29; cf. Gen. 12:8). He had built these two calves under the pretense that it is for the people's good; but the end result was that it led to wickedness and idolatry.[188]

It is interesting that Jeroboam refers to Yahweh as "your God" which emphasizes his own idolatry. After, he pleads with the "man of God" to restore his hand, the Lord heals his hand, and he offers shelter in the royal palace, a meal, and a gift (1 Kgs. 13:7). In the ancient Near East, showing hospitality was a sacred custom and to share a meal with someone was a promise of personal protection. However, the "man of God" was divinely "commanded by the word of the Lord: 'You must not eat bread or drink water or return by the way you came'" (1 Kgs. 13:9), since this would have placed him in Jeroboam's debt. God had forbidden the prophet to eat and drink and return home via the way in which he had come to Bethel

> to manifest His detestation of idolatry, and to show by that fact that the Bethelites were so detestable, and as it were excommunicated by God, that He wished none of the faithful to join with them in eating and drinking. He was not to return by the way by which he came, that no one might look out for him, and force him to a delay which was irreconcilable with his commission, or lest by chance being brought back by Jeroboam, he should do anything to please him which was unworthy of a prophet, or from which it might be inferred that idolaters might hope for some favour from the Deity.[189]

The prophet had been faithful to obey the commands of God up to this point, even taking another route back to Judah (1 Kgs. 13:10). However, he now violates the Lord's commands as he listens and

---

[187] Gaebelein, *The Expositor's Bible Commentary, Volume 4: 1 & 2 Kings, 1 & 2 Chronicles, Ezra, Nehemiah, Esther, Job* (Grand Rapids, MI: Zondervan Publishing House. Database © 2010 WORDsearch CROSS e-book, 1988), 119. Walvoord and Zuck, eds., *The Bible Knowledge Commentary*, Vol. 1, 514.

[188] Richards, *The Bible Reader's Companion*, electronic ed., 231. "1 Kings 13:7-32", In *Life Application Study Bible* (Carol Stream, IL: Tyndale House Publishers Inc., 2004), Rick Meyers, e-Sword, Version 10.2.1, 2000-2012, <http://www.e-sword.net>. Keith Brooks, *Summarized Bible: Complete Summary of the Old Testament* (Bellingham, WA: Logos Bible Software, 2009), 72.

[189] "1 Kings 13:1-10", In Johann C. F. Keil & Franz Delitzsch, *Keil & Delitzsch Commentary on the Old Testament* (Peabody, MA: Hendrickson Publishers, 1996), Rick Meyers, e-Sword, Version 10.2.1, 2000-2012, <http://www.e-sword.net>.

obeys a false prophet from Bethel who he met on his way home. This false prophet upon meeting the "man of God" sitting under an oak tree told him that an angel had spoken to him to "bring him back with you to your house so that he may eat bread and drink water". The "man of God" returns and has shares a meal with the old prophet in his home (1 Kgs. 13:19). However, as they were fellowshipping together, the Lord spoke through the old prophet once again—the first time was a deception and the second time was the Lord's judgment,

> While they were sitting at the table, the word of the LORD came to the old prophet who had brought him back. He cried out to the man of God who had come from Judah, "This is what the LORD says: 'You have defied the word of the LORD and have not kept the command the LORD your God gave you. You came back and ate bread and drank water in the place where he told you not to eat or drink. Therefore your body will not be buried in the tomb of your ancestors'" (1 Kgs. 13:20-22)

The "man of God" on his way home encounters a lion that kills him and his body is left on the road for everyone to see. In ancient Israel, lions were not commonly seen on a road, but seldomly would kill people. It seems as though this lion was divinely sent as judgment to the "man of God" since the lion only mauled and killed him, yet did not devour him or his donkey. The old prophet, out of reverence to the "man of God" finds the body and brings him back to Bethel, mourned for him, buried him, and placed him in his own tomb (1 Kgs. 13:29-30). Josephus recounts the words spoken through the old prophet concerning his destiny for disobeying the Word of the Lord,

> Now Jadon gave credit to this lying prophet, and returned back with him. But when they were at dinner, and merry together, God appeared to Jadon, and said, that he should suffer punishment for transgressing his commands,—and he told him what that punishment should be: for he said that he should meet with a lion as he was going on his way, by which lion he should be torn in pieces, and be deprived of burial in the sepulchres of his fathers:—which things came to pass, as I suppose, according to the will of God, that so Jeroboam might not give heed to the words of Jadon, as of one that had been convicted of lying. However, as Jadon was again going to Jerusalem a lion assaulted him, and pulled him off the beast he rode on, and slew him; yet did he not at all hurt the ass, but sat by him, and kept him, as also the prophet's body. This continued till some travellers that saw it came and told it in the city to the false prophet, who sent his sons and brought the body into the city, and made a funeral for him at great expense.[190]

The Man of God Fast clarifies the importance of consistent and complete obedience to the Word of God—the lesson God was seeking to impress upon Jeroboam and His people at that time. It also illustrates that added privilege brings increased responsibility; God dealt with the prophet who had the greater responsibility more severely than he did with the man who had less. The effects of spiritual apostasy even on God's servants can be seen too, especially in the behavior of the old prophet.[191]

Please refer to *Fasting: Unlocking Spiritual Power and Breakthrough, Personal Reflections* under the heading "The Man of God Fast" to complete the Personal Reflections section of this study.

---

[190] "Antiquities of the Jews", In Josephus, *The Works of Josephus*, 8.240-42.

[191] Walvoord and Zuck, eds., *The Bible Knowledge Commentary*, Vol. 1, 515. Brooks, *Summarized Bible*, 72.

The Jehoshaphat Fast

> After this, the Moabites and Ammonites with some of the Meunites came to wage war against Jehoshaphat. Some people came and told Jehoshaphat, "A vast army is coming against you from Edom, from the other side of the Dead Sea. It is already in Hazezon Tamar" (that is, En Gedi). Alarmed, Jehoshaphat resolved to inquire of the LORD, and he proclaimed a fast for all Judah. The people of Judah came together to seek help from the LORD; indeed, they came from every town in Judah to seek him (2 Chr. 20:1-4).

After Jehoshaphat's devastating campaign with Ahab (2 Chr. 18) he accepts the rebuke of the prophet Jehu (2 Chr. 19:1-3) and remains faithful to the Lord and appoints Judges to oversee the administration of the Law of Moses throughout Judah (2 Chr. 19:4-11). When Jehoshaphat is about to be attacked by "the Moabites and Ammonites with some of the Meunites", he "resolved to inquire of the Lord, and he proclaimed a fast for all Judah" who "came from every town in Judah to seek him". He leads the Judean assembly in prayer (2 Chr. 19:5-13), which the Lord answers through the prophet Jahaziel (2 Chr. 19:14) who prophesies a victory not through a battle but by the Lord Himself (2 Chr. 19:15-17).

Jehoshaphat "proclaimed a fast" (2 Chr. 20:3) to emphasize in the presence of the "Lord" (v. 4) and Judah's distress (cf. Jdg. 20:26). Fasting did not exist as an official part of pre-exilic Hebrew religion, unless it is implied in Leviticus 16:29-31; but from the time of Samuel onward, it had been employed to stress the sincerity of the prayers of God's people when they were facing special needs (1 Sam. 7:6; cf. Acts 13:2-3). Occasionally fasting was proclaimed on a national scale, war (Jdg. 20:26; 2 Chr. 20:3) or pestilence (Joel 1:13f.). Fasting having thus become a recognized mode of seeking Divine favor and protection, it was natural that it should be associated with confession of sin, as indisputable evidence of penitence or sorrow for sin.

Jehoshaphat "bowed down with his face to the ground" followed by "all the people of Judah and Jerusalem" and the next morning Judah's army marches into battle singing hymns of praise (2 Chr. 20:18-22). As the Jews approach, the Ammonites and Moabites fight the men from Mt. Seir and then begin to fight each other (20:23). Judah, upon arriving on the scene of this battle, collect the plunder which took three days to collect (20:25) and they return home to Jerusalem rejoicing in the victory the Lord had brought them (20:24-30). King Jehoshaphat sought the Lord by proclaiming a fast throughout all the land. He understood that fasting was the way to get God's attention during times of distress. It was through fasting that God dramatically and supernaturally rescued His people from their enemies.

Despite Jehoshaphat's efforts and the evidence of God's love and power, his reformation is not successful. The people as a whole have "not set their hearts on the God of their ancestors" (2 Chr. 20:31-33) and Jehoshaphat allies himself with wicked Ahaziah King of Israel "to construct a fleet of trading ships", and is once again rebuked by the prophet Eliezer son of Dodavahu of Mareshah (20:34-36). This alliance fails when God brings a storm that sinks the ships (v. 37) and Jehoshaphat later dies a godly man.

> Then Jehoshaphat rested with his ancestors and was buried with them in the City of David. And Jehoram his son succeeded him as king. Jehoram's brothers, the sons of Jehoshaphat, were

Azariah, Jehiel, Zechariah, Azariahu, Michael and Shephatiah. All these were sons of Jehoshaphat king of Israel (2 Chr. 21:1-2).[192]

Please refer to *Fasting: Unlocking Spiritual Power and Breakthrough, Personal Reflections* under the heading "The Jehoshaphat Fast" to complete the Personal Reflections section of this study.

The Nehemiah Fast

When I heard these things, I sat down and wept. For some days I mourned and fasted and prayed before the God of heaven. Then I said: "O LORD, God of heaven, the great and awesome God, who keeps his covenant of love with those who love him and obey his commands, let your ear be attentive and your eyes open to hear the prayer your servant is praying before you day and night for your servants, the people of Israel. I confess the sins we Israelites, including myself and my father's house, have committed against you. We have acted very wickedly toward you. We have not obeyed the commands, decrees and laws you gave your servant Moses. "Remember the instruction you gave your servant Moses, saying, 'If you are unfaithful, I will scatter you among the nations, but if you return to me and obey my commands, then even if your exiled people are at the farthest horizon, I will gather them from there and bring them to the place I have chosen as a dwelling for my Name'" (Neh. 1:4-9).

Nehemiah, who lived in Susa, received a discouraging report from his brother Hanani concerning the "great trouble and disgrace" of the Jewish remnant and "the wall of Jerusalem is broken down, and its gates have been burned with fire" by Nebuchadnezzar (Neh. 1:3). Despite attempts to rebuild (Ezra 4:6-23) it remained in ruins for approximately a century and a half and had made Jerusalem vulnerable to attack by numerous enemies. The Jews, due to apathy and fear, had not been successful in rebuilding and needed a dynamic catalyst like Nehemiah to protect the Jews and the city of Jerusalem by rebuilding its walls.

Nehemiah, first of all, questioned his brother Hanani and the other men concerning "the Jewish remnant that had survived the exile, and also about Jerusalem" (Neh. 1:2). He responds with the same attitude and response as Jesus taught in the Parable of the Good Samaritan (Lk. 10:25-37). He demonstrates the type of person who cares about the tradition of the past, the needs of the current situation, the hopes for the future, his heritage, ancestral city, and the glory of his God.

Nehemiah demonstrated the spiritual maturity of a leader by responding to the state of the walls of Jerusalem by: (a) "I sat down"; (b) "wept"; (c) "I mourned"; (d) "fasted"; and (e) "prayed". It is interesting that Nehemiah did not immediately respond with human help, or the help of King Artaxerxes, since responding to such a need was more than a humanitarian effort—it first of all needed to be a heavenly response. Nehemiah's focus in his response was directed towards "the God of heaven", which illustrates his intimate relationship with God—the focus in everything we do (Neh. 1:4ff.; cf. 2:4, 20;

---

[192] Richards, *The Bible Reader's Companion*, 293. Gaebelein, *The Expositor's Bible Commentary, Volume 4*, 501-02. "2 Chronicles 20", In Thoralf Gilbrant, ed., *The Complete Biblical Library Commentary, Chronicles* (Springfield, IL: World Library Press, Inc., WORDsearch CROSS e-book, 1996). צוֹם "1890", In Harris, Archer, Jr., and Waltke, eds., *Theological Wordbook of the Old Testament*, 759.

Ezra 1:2; 5:11-12; 6:9-10; 7:12, 21, 23; Dan. 2:18f., 28, 37). During this Persian imperialism, God was sovereign over all things.

Upon hearing this report, he "sat" (יָשַׁב yāshav) meaning "causing to set up home", "to inhabit" or "to dwell".[193] Nehemiah was so overwhelmed with the walls of Jerusalem that he made Jerusalem his place of dwelling. Next, he "wept" (בָּכָה bākhāh) can refer to weeping, whether in grief, joy, or humiliation (cf. Gen. 42:24; 43:30; Jer. 41:6). This weeping is frequently associated with distress or sorrow, and also a sign of joy and rejoicing. It refers to mourning over death, pleading or complaint, remorse, sorrow for punishment, and repentance.[194]

Nehemiah then uses the verb אָבַל ’āval for mourning, which in this context emphasizes the outward behavior contrasted with inner feelings (cf. Gen. 37:34; 1 Sam. 16:1; 2 Sam. 13:31-37; 14:2; Dan. 10:2). Such explicit expressions include the shedding of tears, wearing sackcloth and ashes, lying on the ground and shaving one's head and beard.[195] The verb צוּם tsûm for "fasted" referred to here is connected to a various circumstances related to personal or family incidents (cf. 1 Sam. 1:7; 20:34; 1 Kgs. 21:9; Ezra 10:6). Fasting in and of itself merited no particular worth, but Nehemiah had a specific purpose for fasting, which was to provide protection for his people and their ancestral city of Jerusalem.[196] Lastly, Nehemiah "prayed" (פָּלַל pālal) meaning to judge, to decide, to expect, to intercede, and to pray, which refers to his reverential frame of mind.[197]

Nehemiah's model prayer is one of theological propriety as he acknowledges God's sovereignty, "covenant of love" and faithfulness (Neh. 1:5) and then appeals to the Lord to hear their confession or national and personal sins (Neh. 1:6), covenant violations (Neh. 1:7), resulting in the dispersion of the Jews to "among the nations" (Neh. 1:8; Lev. 26:27-33; Deut. 28:25, 36, 47-57). Nehemiah's confession and sincere repentance prompted the Lord to forgive and restore His remnant to their land once again (cf. Deut. 30:1-10).

Nehemiah reminded the Lord that His suffering remnant, "They are your servants and your people, whom you redeemed by your great strength and your mighty hand" (Neh. 1:10), and prays that the Lord would be attentive to his prayer and give him favour before King Artaxerxes (Neh. 1:11; cf. 2:5). His role as the cupbearer was a significant position in the royal court, but it also illustrates his indispensability. Therefore, he prays for divine intervention.[198]

---

[193] יָשַׁב yāshav "3553", In Gilbrant, ed., *The Complete Biblical Library Hebrew-English Dictionary, Heth-Yodh.*

[194] בָּכָה bākhāh "1098", In Gilbrant, ed., *The Complete Biblical Library Hebrew-English Dictionary, Aleph-Beth.* "בָּכָה 243", In Harris, Archer, Jr., and Waltke, eds., *Theological Wordbook of the Old Testament*, 108.

[195] אָבַל ’āval "57", In Gilbrant, ed., *The Complete Biblical Library Hebrew-English Dictionary, Aleph-Beth.*

[196] צוּם tsûm "6947", In Gilbrant, ed., *The Complete Biblical Library Hebrew-English Dictionary, Pe-Resh.*

[197] פָּלַל pālal "6663", In Gilbrant, ed., *The Complete Biblical Library Hebrew-English Dictionary, Pe-Resh.*

[198] "Nehemiah 1:4", In Thoralf Gilbrant, ed., *The Complete Biblical Library Commentary, Ezra-Job* (Springfield, IL: World Library Press, Inc., WORDsearch CROSS e-book, 1996). Gaebelein, *The Expositor's Bible*

The next context of fasting in Nehemiah (9:1-3) refers to the time of the celebration of the Feast of Tabernacles which concluded on the twenty-second day of the month of Tishri—a month dedicated to fasting (cf. Zech. 7:5; Ezra 8:1; 10:6).

On the twenty-fourth day of the same month, the Israelites gathered together, fasting and wearing sackcloth and having dust on their heads. Those of Israelite descent had separated themselves from all foreigners. They stood in their places and confessed their sins and the wickedness of their fathers. They stood where they were and read from the Book of the Law of the LORD their God for a quarter of the day, and spent another quarter in confession and in worshiping the LORD their God. Standing on the stairs of the Levites were Jeshua, Bani, Kadmiel, Shebaniah, Bunni, Sherebiah, Bani and Kenani. They cried out with loud voices to the LORD their God. And the Levites—Jeshua, Kadmiel, Bani, Hashabneiah, Sherebiah, Hodiah, Shebaniah and Pethahiah—said: "Stand up and praise the LORD your God, who is from everlasting to everlasting (Neh. 9:1-5).

It is interesting, that the ninth chapters of Ezra, Nehemiah, and Daniel are each devoted to confessions of national sin and prayers for God's grace.[199] During the Feast of Tabernacles, "from the first day to the last, Ezra read from the Book of the Law of God" (Neh. 8:18) and many were convicted of their sin. They spent a "quarter of the day" studying the Law, and a "quarter of the day" confessing their sins and worship of God (Neh. 9:1-5). According to Jewish custom, a day consisted of twelve hours and therefore, the phrase "quarter of the day" meant that the Jews spent three hours studying the Torah and three hours in a state of contrition (cf. Jn. 11:9).

Nehemiah, in the rest of the chapter, records a prayer that expresses: (a) their transformed reverence for God (Neh. 9:6); (b) their history of rebellion (Neh. 9:16-18); (c) Yahweh's compassion (Neh. 9:13-31); and (d) a fervent petition for deliverance (Neh. 9:32-37). Their commitment to the Lord through Rosh Hashanah, the Day of Atonement, and the Feast of Tabernacles—had so stirred their hearts that they corporately resolved to renew their covenant commitment to the Lord. Nehemiah prayer concludes, "In view of all this, we are making a binding agreement, putting it in writing, and our leaders, our Levites and our priests are affixing their seals to it" (Neh. 9:38).

This was one of the most sacred months in the Jewish calendar and in today's calendar would be New Year's Day. It was after hearing the Law that the elders urged Ezra to call an assembly for all Jews to observe the Feast of Booths or Tabernacles, which was a traditional celebration lasting seven days at the time of harvest ingathering (Ex. 34:22). This feast commemorated God's provision in the wilderness when Israel lived in temporary shelters or booths (cf. Lev. 23:33-43). This feast was a remembrance as a second "Exodus" from Babylon and had not been celebrated in this way since the time of Joshua. The Jews set apart the eighth day (Lev. 23:36; cf. Lev. 23:24-36) for special assembly (Neh. 8:13-18).[200]

Commentary, Vol. 4, 680. "Nehemiah 1:1-11", In Mays, ed., *Harper's Bible Commentary*. Warren W. Wiersbe, *Be Determined*, "Be" Commentary Series (Wheaton, IL: Victor Books, 1996), 12-13.

[199] Gaebelein, *The Expositor's Bible Commentary, Volume 4*, 729.

[200] David S. Dockery, Trent C. Butler, Christopher L. Church et al., *Holman Bible Handbook* (Nashville, TN: Holman Bible Publishers, 1992), 297.

This was the opportune time for the Jews to recommit their lives to the Lord. It is interesting that "When the seventh month came and the Israelites had settled in their towns, all the people assembled as one man in the square before the Water Gate. They told Ezra the scribe to bring out the Book of the Law of Moses, which the Lord had commanded for Israel" (Neh. 7:73-8:1). Nehemiah chapter 8 is a significant chapter since it records a revival of the Jews through the reading of the Law.[201]

The phrase "assembled as one man" is quite significant since it was, first of all, used by Ezra (3:1; cf. vv. 1-13) and speaks of unity of purpose and the restoration of the altar of burnt offerings and sacrificial worship. This phrase is a Semitic idiom indicating that they were present in agreement and purpose about what was to be done.[202] It is the assembled Jews who desire that the Law be read as a way of showing thanks for the Lord's protection during the building of the wall of Jerusalem. They also committed themselves to following God's Law and walking in His ways and not their own. This assembly "was made up of men and women and all who were able to understand" (Neh. 8:2) אִישׁ וְעַד אִשָּׁה (cf. Jos. 6:21; 8:25; 1 Sam. 22:19; 1 Chr. 16:3), and also כֹּל מֵבִין לִשְׁמֹעַ included older children. The Water Gate suggests cleansing, a time of refreshing, and the reviving power of God's Law.[203]

This fast appears to have been selected with a view to call out to God for His pardon for their intermarriage with the idolatrous nations around them. The phrase "those of Israelite descent" literally meant "the seed of Israel" (cf. Ezra 9:2) and pointed to the promised seed of Jesus who would come from the Jews. Therefore, this fast must be considered more particularly as a solemn ordinance of faith.[204] The blending of the remnant with pagan elements had corrupted God's holy seed (Ezra 9:4; cf. Ex. 19:5f.; Hag. 2:10-14) and Ezra and the leaders saw how this blending could eradicate the holy seed—the remnant (Ezra 9:8, 13f.)—if the process of apostasy was not stopped. They were a remnant only because of God's grace, but His grace was becoming quite thin since they had repeated the sins of their fathers. Isaiah speaks of the remnant as a "holy seed" that would remain after He had completed His devastating acts of judgment (6:11f.). This remnant was to remain pure and holy before the Lord and not blending their bodies and spirits with pagan gods (Mal. 2:15). Solomon's love for foreign women and his intermarriage with them resulted in his heart being turned toward other gods and not being fully devoted to the Lord his God like his father David (1 Kgs. 11:1-11).[205]

The day following the feast, the twenty-third, was probably focused upon separating the disobedient from their foreign wives. Ezra was informed of how "the seed of Israel" had been contaminated shortly after the fifth month of their arrival in Jerusalem (7:8f., 25; 8:31f.) and before the tenth month (8:32;

---

[201] Wiersbe, *Be Determined*, 96.

[202] Similar expressions of the unity of Israel are found in Numbers 14:15; Judges 6:16; 20:1, 8, 11; 1 Samuel 11:7; 2 Samuel 19:14. Gaebelein, *The Expositor's Bible Commentary, Volume 4*, 622, 723, 729. "Ezra 3", In Gilbrant, ed., *The Complete Biblical Library Commentary, Ezra-Job*.

[203] "Nehemiah 9", In Gilbrant, ed., *The Complete Biblical Library Commentary, Ezra-Job*. Walvoord and Zuck, eds., *The Bible Knowledge Commentary*, Vol. 1, 690. "Nehemiah 9", In Robert Hawker, *The Poor Man's Commentary on the Whole Bible* (Birmingham, AL: Solid Ground Christian Books).

[204] "Nehemiah 9", In Hawker, *The Poor Man's Commentary on the Whole Bible*.

[205] "Ezra 9:1-5", In Gilbrant, ed., *The Complete Biblical Library Commentary, Ezra-Job*.

93

10:16). The process of cleansing "the seed of Israel" began five months after their arrival and was completed within three months—the first day of the first month of the next year (cf. Ezra 7:8-9).[206]

The leaders probably setup a system or laws to guard against their idolatrous practices of marrying foreign wives. Even though this reformation had been initiated by Ezra (10:1-17), and somewhat successful, it appears as though this reformation was only partial and defective. Yet there still existed those who contacted their former forbidden relatives, resulting in Nehemiah's proactive measures and removal of the social evil, rebellion, or sin which jeopardized the character and prosperity of the chosen people. This resulted in an official fast to observe the contrite and mournful feelings, which the reading of the law had produced. These feelings that had been suppressed in the midst of the celebration and the genuineness of their repentance was manifested through correcting the existing abuses in the intermarriage with foreign wives.[207]

Please refer to *Fasting: Unlocking Spiritual Power and Breakthrough, Personal Reflections* under the heading "The Nehemiah Fast" to complete the Personal Reflections section of this study.

The Davidic Fast

> Yet when they were ill, I put on sackcloth and humbled myself with fasting. When my prayers returned to me unanswered, I went about mourning as though for my friend or brother. I bowed my head in grief as though weeping for my mother (Ps. 35:13-14).

> When I weep and fast, I must endure scorn; when I put on sackcloth, people make sport of me (Ps. 69:10-11).

> My knees give way from fasting; my body is thin and gaunt. I am an object of scorn to my accusers; when they see me, they shake their heads (Ps. 109:24-25).

In Scripture, there are many examples of a Davidic Fast. First, David was known to have all types of enemies, which are illustrated in Psalms 35 as a lament over unjust hatred and unjustly accused. David's prayer in verse 1a uses the same word and metaphor as he does in his argument with Saul, "Contend, O LORD, with those who contend with me; fight against those who fight against me" (Ps. 35:1; cf. 1 Sam. 24:15). His prayer in verse 1, includes false witnesses (vv. 11, 21), opponents in a battle (vv. 1-4), hunters trying to trap him like an animal (vv. 7-8), mockers (vv. 15-16), and as wild beasts (v. 17). However, David sees the Lord God as his last defense (vv. 1-10), prays that God will publicly announce his innocence (vv. 11-25) and be divinely vindicated, enemies chastised, and friends rewarded (vv. 26-28).[208]

Second, David and the Israelites fasted at the death of Saul and Jonathan during the day for seven days (1 Sam. 31:13; 2 Sam. 1:12; 3:35; 1 Chr. 10:11-12).

---

[206] "Ezra 9:1-5", In Gilbrant, ed., *The Complete Biblical Library Commentary, Ezra-Job.*

[207] "Nehemiah 9", In Jamieson, Fausset, and Brown, *Commentary Critical and Explanatory on the Whole Bible.*

[208] Franklin H. Paschall and Herschel H. Hobbs, eds., *The Teacher's Bible Commentary* (Nashville, TN: Broadman and Holman Publishers, 1972), 307. "Psalms 35", In Thoralf Gilbrant, ed., *The Complete Biblical Library Commentary, Psalms* (Springfield, IL: World Library Press, Inc., WORDsearch CROSS e-book, 1996).

Then David and all the men with him took hold of their clothes and tore them. They mourned and wept and fasted till evening for Saul and his son Jonathan, and for the army of the LORD and for the nation of Israel, because they had fallen by the sword (2 Sam. 1:11-12).

King Saul and his son Jonathan were both killed in battle on Mount Gilboa, which is known as a place of honour for their lives. David pays tribute to them by ordering the people of Judah to learn the "lament of the bow" (2 Sam. 1:18, cf. 1:19-27). In this setting, David as a valued member of King Saul's court recognizes King Saul's crown and armlet in the hands of the young Amalekite. This young man thinking that he would be honoured for his act could not have been prepared for David's response. David was so enraged and his grief somewhat alleviated that he commanded the Amalekite to be executed because he was not "afraid to lift your hand to destroy the LORD's anointed?" (2 Sam. 1:11-15; cf. 1 Sam. 24:6; 26:23). David had every reason to raise his hand against the Lord's anointed, but he never did. However, since this Amalekite did not respect the Lord's anointed, David had his men execute him. It is interesting that King Saul had lost his kingdom because he had failed to annihilate the Amalekites, and now one who said he was an Amalekite died because he claimed to have destroyed Saul.

David demonstrated genuine and profound expressions of grief over the death of King Saul and Jonathan (cf. 2 Sam. 1:17-27) and all Israelite soldiers. David along with his men mourn (v. 12; 11:26; 1 Sam. 25:1; 28:3) and weep (cf. v. 24). The fast spoken of here is David's usual practice of fasting "before the sun sets" (cf. 3:35). This is contrasted with the seven day fast of the Jabeshites for Saul and Jonathan (1 Sam. 31:13). Their grief, mourning, and sorrow extended as "They mourned and wept and fasted till evening for Saul and his son Jonathan, and for the army of the LORD and for the nation of Israel, because they had fallen by the sword" (2 Sam. 1:12) since all of Israel had suffered the tragic loss in the death of their King Saul.[209]

Third, David fasted and showed his grief at the murder of Abner (2 Sam. 3:31, 35; Ps. 35:13).

Then David said to Joab and all the people with him, "Tear your clothes and put on sackcloth and walk in mourning in front of Abner". King David himself walked behind the bier. . . . Then they all came and urged David to eat something while it was still day; but David took an oath, saying, "May God deal with me, be it ever so severely, if I taste bread or anything else before the sun sets!" (2 Sam. 3:31, 35).

Abner was the cousin of King Saul and the commander of his army and one of the few state officials mentioned in connection with the reign of King Saul (1 Sam. 14:50). David, in honouring Abner, demonstrated his grief in a threefold manner. He, first of all, had him buried in Hebron, which is the tomb where the patriarchs are buried. Second, David commanded the Israelites "tear your clothes and put on sackcloth and walk in mourning in front of Abner". David's response— "tear your clothes" "put on sackcloth" "walk in mourning"—illustrates his close relationship with Abner as a family member,

---

[209] Gaebelein, ed., *The Expositor's Bible Commentary, Volume 3*, 807. Knowles, *The Bible Guide*, 141. "2 Samuel 1:11-16", In Gilbrant, ed., *The Complete Biblical Library Commentary, Samuel*. Walvoord and Zuck, eds., *The Bible Knowledge Commentary*, Vol. 1, 457-58. "2 Samuel 1:1-27", In Dockery, ed., In *Holman Concise Bible Commentary*, 122.

comrade, and friend and discloses his tender heart (cf. 2 Sam. 1:12; 13:36-37; 18:33; 19:1-4). When David found out that Joab had murdered Abner to avenge Abner's murder of Joab's brother Asahel (2 Sam. 3:27, 30; 2:23) he cursed Joab and his offspring (3:29).

King David spoke an elegy over him, which was short and expressed the unworthy death of such a great man, "Do you not realize that a prince and a great man has fallen in Israel this day?" (2 Sam. 3:38). David fasts for Abner as he fasted for the deaths of Saul and Jonathan. Even though David grieves deeply for Abner, his most powerful rival for control, his emotions are genuine. As David protected King Saul—the Lord's anointed—likewise the Lord protected David as the His anointed one.[210]

Fourth, David fasts as he laments over the sickness and subsequent death of his first child with Bathsheba (2 Sam. 12:13-23). David fasted in an attempt to show his remorse for his sin and that his son with Bathsheba would live (receive healing), however, he died (2 Sam. 12:15-16, 22-23). This context suggests a twofold significance of fasting as a religious act or a mode of appealing to the Deity and as a funeral custom. David believed that through his fasting that his prayers for his son would be heard and receive healing (live; cf. 1 Kgs. 21:27; Ezra 8:21; Est. 4:16). When David received the news on the seventh day that his son had died and that he could accomplish nothing now, he "got up from the ground. After he had washed, put on lotions and changed his clothes, he went into the house of the Lord and worshiped. Then he went to his own house, and at his request they served him food, and he ate" (2 Sam. 12:20; cf. 12:20-23).[211] Some scholars suggest that the baby's death was accepted as atonement for the sin of adultery, so that the usual mourning customs were inapplicable.[212] John MacArthur, Jr., summaries those like David and Hannah who desire to help people fasting in times of sorrow,

> On such occasions of deep grief, fasting is a natural human response. Most people do not then feel like eating. Their appetite is gone, and food is the last thing they are concerned about. Unless a person is getting seriously weak from hunger or has some specific medical reason for needing to eat, we do them no favor by insisting that they eat.[213]

We need to remember that when a person is in mourning they need to connect with the Lord more than with food and/or drink. In the midst of their grief, mourning, and suffering of the loss of a loved one that God is sufficient—all that they need during this difficult time.

Please refer to *Fasting: Unlocking Spiritual Power and Breakthrough, Personal Reflections* under the heading "The Davidic Fast" to complete the Personal Reflections section of this study.

---

[210] "Abner", In Wood and Marshall, *New Bible Dictionary*, 4. Gaebelein, ed., *The Expositor's Bible Commentary, Volume 3*, 840-841. "2 Samuel 3:31-29", In Gilbrant, ed., *The Complete Biblical Library Commentary, Samuel*. Brueggemann, *First and Second Samuel. Interpretation*, 230. Walvoord and Zuck, eds., *The Bible Knowledge Commentary*, Vol. 1, 459-60.

[211] צוּם "1890", In Harris, Archer, Jr., and Waltke, eds., *Theological Wordbook of the Old Testament*, 758. Kittel, Friedrich and Bromiley, eds., *Theological Dictionary of the New Testament: Abridged in One Volume*, 632. Raymond Edward Brown, Joseph A. Fitzmyer, and Roland Edmund Murphy, *The Jerome Biblical Commentary*, Vol. 1 (Englewood Cliffs, NJ: Prentice-Hall, 1996), 582.

[212] "Fast, Fasting", In Freedman, ed., *The Anchor Yale Bible Dictionary*, Vol. 2, 774.

[213] "Matthew", In MacArthur, Jr., *The MacArthur New Testament Commentary*, Vol. 1, 402.

Chapter 7: The Fasts of Isaiah 58

The purpose of this chapter is to describe the various fasts that are included in Isaiah 58. Each fast presents the context and purpose in which the fasting occurs. These ten specific fasts focus on different types of chains or bondage in our lives and how to break these chains and live a life of freedom. Each fast concludes by completing the relevant "Personal Reflections" section.

In the beginning of Isaiah (chapter 1), the prophet had exposed the meaningless practice of the people of Judah and Jerusalem. In this section (Isaiah 56:9-59:21), Isaiah describes a sequence of indictments against a disobedient and rebellious nation of people. He addresses the leaders (56:9-57:2), the idolaters (57:3-13), the proud and greedy (57:14-21), the hypocritical worshipers (58:1-14), and those responsible for injustice in the land (59:1-21). However, even though God's wrath could be poured out upon His people, He remembers mercy (cf. Hab. 3:2) and He appeals for His people to humble and submit themselves wholeheartedly to Him.

Introduction to the Fasts of Isaiah 58

The context that involves chapter 58 begins in chapter 56, which speaks about the new community consisting of the descendants of Abraham and Jacob who seek the Lord, the kingdom of God, and the full deliverance ("righteousness") that only He can provide. Yahweh challenges them to practice their faith and bring in the kingdom of God through kingly leadership and responsible living. The prophet Isaiah states, "Maintain justice and do what is right, for my salvation is close at hand and my righteousness will soon be revealed" (Isa. 56:1). This type of practical faith manifests itself in observance of the Sabbath—a symbol of the Mosaic covenant (Ex. 31:13-17), expressed submission to the will of God. The Sabbath is highlighted as an expression of loyalty and those who are faithful will be divinely rewarded.

> And foreigners who bind themselves to the LORD to minister to him, to love the name of the LORD, and to be his servants, all who keep the Sabbath without desecrating it and who hold fast to my covenant—these I will bring to my holy mountain and give them joy in my house of prayer. Their burnt offerings and sacrifices will be accepted on my altar; for my house will be called a house of prayer for all nations. The Sovereign LORD declares—he who gathers the exiles of Israel: "I will gather still others to them besides those already gathered" (Isa. 56:6-8).

Blessed are those who submit to God's rule and become a part of this new community (Isa. 56:2-11). The Gentiles are also included as long as they submit themselves to God's rule (vv. 6-7). Moreover, God will judge everyone who attempts to destroy, corrupt, or bring this new community to ruin. The watchmen are blind (v. 10), obstructed God's kingdom, and were bound by religiosity. Their practices were lewd, idolatrous, and involved magic and powers of divination or prophecy (vv. 3-11).

The end result of their practices was that God's wrath would be poured out upon them in judgment and He would not hear their cries for mercy and will never enter into God's "peace", "There is no peace", says my God, "for the wicked" (Isa. 57:21). God had compassion on the faithful remnant (57:13), blessed and allowed them to share in His redemption, restoration, and the establishment of His kingdom and live in His presence. Isaiah emphasized that true godliness is expressed in right practices. Theocentric ethics includes being concerned with God's creation, justice, compassion and mercy. Those who practice theocentric ethics will receive His blessing (56:2), His communion (58:9), and those who observe the pious practice of prayer and fasting for one's own benefit will never enter into God's kingdom of peace "When you cry out for help, let your collection of idols save you! The wind will carry all of them off, a mere breath will blow them away. But the man who makes me his refuge will inherit the land and possess my holy mountain" (Isa. 57:13; cf. 1:10-17; 58:1-6). The teaching of Isaiah is identical to Jesus' teaching in the Sermon on the Mount. The presence and reality of the kingdom of God depends upon the response of the individuals (58:10-13).[214]

There are two classes of people whose practices were not accepted and blessed—those who do not observe it at all, and those who, while they observe it with outward formalities and even with strictness, yet do not keep it in the spirit of true penitence. The Lord denounced the people's hypocritical claims of loyalty and their empty expressions of repentance. Their unjust and violent deeds made their fasts unacceptable. The Lord demanded righteous living, not meaningless ritual. They were to free the oppressed, feed the hungry, give shelter to the homeless, and clothe the naked. In addition to caring for the needs of others, they also were to demonstrate true devotion to God by honouring His Sabbath Day. Then they would experience the Lord's protective presence, enjoy His blessings, and witness the rebuilding of the land. Proper fasting is not mere refraining from food, but a commitment to justice and the poor. This is where God's people will find life. Isaiah, like Amos and Micah, demands God's supreme concern for justice, mercy, and humility rather than obligatory religious acts.[215] Fasting is not simply a ritual exercise done by an individual for his or her own benefit; by freeing the worshiper from concern for the self, fasting partakes of God's mission of justice and liberation for all people, thus making new both giver and recipient.[216]

> Shout it aloud, do not hold back. Raise your voice like a trumpet. Declare to my people their rebellion and to the descendants of Jacob their sins (Isa. 58:1).

Now in chapter 58, Isaiah focuses on the religious activity of fasting and exposes the shallow worship of His people. The Word of the Lord to Isaiah was for him to shout like a trumpet the sins, disobedience, and rebellion of the descendants of Jacob. The people need to hear God's declaration of their rebellion and be convicted of their sins. The people are seen going to the temple, obeying God's laws, fasting, and

---

[214] Willem A. VanGemeren, *Interpreting the Prophetic Word: An Introduction to the Prophetic Literature of the Old Testament* (Grand Rapids, MI: Zondervan Publishing House, 1990), 281-282.

[215] Paschall and Hobbs, eds., *The Teacher's Bible Commentary*, 424. Warren W. Wiersbe, *Be Comforted*, "Be" Commentary Series (Wheaton, IL: Victor Books, 1996), 148. "Isaiah 58:1-14", In George A. Smith, *The Expositor's Bible Commentary: The Book of Isaiah*, Vol. 2 (London: Hodder and Stoughton, 1889-90), Rick Meyers, e-Sword, Version 10.2.1, 2000-2012, <http://www. e-sword.net>. "Isaiah 58:3", In Mays, ed., *Harper's Bible Commentary*. "The Major Prophets", In Dockery, ed., In *Holman Concise Bible Commentary*, 288. "Isaiah 58:1-14", In W. Robertson Nicoll, Jane T. Stoddart, and James Moffatt, ed., *The Expositor's Dictionary of Texts*, Rick Meyers, e-Sword, Version 10.2.1, 2000-2012, <http://www.e-sword.net>.

[216] <http://www.enterthebible.org/resourcelink.aspx?rid=477>, Accessed on September 3, 2013.

appear to eagerly seek the Lord, yet their worship was only an outward show—their hearts were strangers to God (1:10-15; 29:13; Mt. 15:8-9). Their worship had become ritualistic, religious, and hypocritical.[217]

Isaiah uses the verb קָרָא *qŏrā'* meaning "to summon" "to proclaim", "the act of making a vocal sound to establish contact with someone".[218] His voice like a trumpet was bold, clear, authoritative, and unambiguous (cf. 1 Cor. 14:8), so that the people would not misinterpret the message and awakened them to action. He was not to hold back anything, or water down the prophetic Word of the Lord. The eighth century Jews were more zealous for externals than for inward holiness and practiced their rituals to obtain God's favour and freedom. The statement "Declare to my people their rebellion" literally means "show them how they are especially offending me at this time". [219]

> But as for me, I am filled with power, with the Spirit of the LORD, and with justice and might, to declare to Jacob his transgression, to Israel his sin (Mic. 3:8).

> For day after day they seek me out; they seem eager to know my ways, as if they were a nation that does what is right and has not forsaken the commands of its God. They ask me for just decisions and seem eager for God to come near them (Isa. 58:2).

Isaiah, in verse 2, acknowledges that the religious practices of the people were commendable, demonstrating external evidence of following God's way—probably though consulting priest and prophets. They sought the Lord and delighted in His ways. However, when the prophet Isaiah revealed to them their transgressions they defended their behaviour and that they were not guilty of any wrongdoings. They believed that they were diligent and relentless in following the established patterns of worship of God—what more could be asked of them. However, like many people, they had confused rituals with relationship, and external acts with internal obedience.[220]

> "Why have we fasted", they say, "and you have not seen it? Why have we humbled ourselves, and you have not noticed?" "Yet on the day of your fasting, you do as you please and exploit all your workers" (Isa. 58:3).

Isaiah, now exposes their hypocrisy since their fast was not spiritually motivated—the shallow worship of His people (vv. 3-5). Moses had commanded the Jews to observe only one fast on the annual Day of Atonement (Lev. 16:29-31), but they were permitted to fast personally if they wished. The prophet

---

[217] Wiersbe, *Be Comforted*, 150-51. "Isaiah 58:1", In Thoralf Gilbrant, ed., *The Complete Biblical Library Commentary, Isaiah* (Springfield, IL: World Library Press, Inc., WORDsearch CROSS e-book, 1996).

[218] Some examples of this usage include: Pharaoh called to Abram (i.e., "summoned") to talk to him about Sarai (Gen. 12:18). On his deathbed, Isaac called for Esau (27:1). Occasionally, one might "call with a loud voice" (i.e., "shout", 39:14; Eze. 8:18). קָרָא *qārā'* "7410", In Gilbrant, ed., *The Complete Biblical Library Hebrew-English Dictionary, Pe-Resh.*

[219] "Isaiah 58:1", In Jamieson, Fausset, and Brown, *Commentary Critical and Explanatory on the Whole Bible.* "Isaiah 58:3", In Mays, ed., *Harper's Bible Commentary.*

[220] "Isaiah 58:1-2", In Henry, *Matthew Henry's Commentary on the Whole Bible.* "Isaiah 58", In Gilbrant, ed., *The Complete Biblical Library Commentary, Isaiah.* Gaebelein, ed., *The Expositor's Bible Commentary, Volume 6,* 321.

confronts their apathy and obligating their laborers to work extra hard. This type of fast, according to Isaiah, carried out as a duty can only produce a stressed out, irritable group of people, especially during strenuous climatic conditions, which is reflected in verse 4. They foolishly attempted to deceive God— "not seen it . . . not noticed"—into believing that an outward display of enduring the inconvenience of fasting that God would bless them. The people thought that they could maintain their disobedient and rebellious lifestyle, which was contrasted with the moral demands of God. The prophet Isaiah had earlier addressed their rebellion:

> Hear me, you heavens! Listen, earth! For the LORD has spoken: "I reared children and brought them up, but they have rebelled against me. The ox knows its master, the donkey its owner's manger, but Israel does not know, my people do not understand". Woe to the sinful nation, a people whose guilt is great, a brood of evildoers, children given to corruption! They have forsaken the LORD; they have spurned the Holy One of Israel and turned their backs on him. Why should you be beaten anymore? Why do you persist in rebellion? Your whole head is injured, your whole heart afflicted (Isa. 1:2-5).

The people needed to learn that worshiping God involves more than observing an external ritual, but that there must be an internal obedience and submission to the Lord (Mt. 6:16-18). The goal of true fasting will result in a healthy humility before God and ministry to others. It involves depriving and humbling ourselves in order that we might share with others for God's glory and not our own. The verb עָנָה ʾānāh meaning "to be afflicted in your soul" used here for humbling is often connected with קָרָא qārāʾ meaning "to summon" "to proclaim" or "to cry out for help", occurs frequently as a lament and the psalmist cries, "answer me", which is an appeal for God to show His grace.

> Answer me when I call to you, my righteous God. Give me relief from my distress; have mercy on me and hear my prayer (Ps. 4:1; cf. Ps. 13:2).

They wanted God to show His grace without paying the price. When we fast for selfish reasons, instead of maturing for the benefit of others, we have missed the meaning of worship. It delights the Lord when we delight in the Lord.[221]

> Your fasting ends in quarreling and strife, and in striking each other with wicked fists. You cannot fast as you do today and expect your voice to be heard on high (Isa. 58:4).

The noun used here for quarreling is רִיב rîv meaning "lawsuit, contention" and refers to a variety of conflicts among people (Pr. 20:3). David uses this noun in reference to personal attacks (Ps. 55:9) and in the Book of Judges it describes Jephthah and the Ephraimites at war against the Ammonites (Jdg. 12:2). Likewise, quarreling among herdsmen (Gen. 13:7) and can be compared to violence (Ps. 55:9). Even though it can refer to complaining and arguing between people (Ex. 17:7), it usually describes a legal

---

[221] Gaebelein, ed., *The Expositor's Bible Commentary, Volume 6*, 321. Knowles, *The Bible Guide*, 292. Walvoord and Zuck, eds., *The Bible Knowledge Commentary*, Vol. 1, 1113-14. Wiersbe, *Be Comforted*, 151.

argument. Moreover, God brings covenant lawsuits against His people, Israel (Hos. 12:2; Mic. 6:2) and in His mercy He defends Israel (Isa. 34:8), the helpless (Pr. 23:11), and David calls upon the Lord to come to his defense (Ps. 35:23). The people had become divided in parties and factions which probably made their fasting an occasion for quarreling and strife, which is why God rejected their fasting.[222]

In conjunction with quarreling, Isaiah uses the noun מַצָּה *matstsāh* derived from נָצָה *nātsāh*, meaning "to flee" "to struggle" "to fall in ruins". Proverbs says,

Where there is strife, there is pride, but wisdom is found in those who take advice (13:10).

Whoever loves a quarrel loves sin; whoever builds a high gate invites destruction (17:19).

The prophet Isaiah describes the pattern and goal of true fasting and then juxtaposes the kind of fasting that Israel practiced (Isa. 58). Therefore, their fasting was focused upon selfish motives, which was leading them into ruins.[223]

Isaiah continues his description of their fasting by using the verb נָכָה *nākhāh*, used over 500 times in the Old Testament meaning "to smite", "to strike (with a nonfatal blow)", "to hit", "to strike dead". This usage refers to striking an animal (Num. 22:23; 1 Sam. 17:35a), a person (Ex. 21:15; Job 16:10; Ex. 21:26), inanimate objects (Ex. 7:17; 17:6; 2 Kgs. 2:8, 14; Num. 20:11; Am. 9:1), one object striking another (Dan. 8:7; Jdg. 7:13; 1 Sam. 2:14; Isa. 49:10; Ps. 121:6; Jon. 4:8), God Himself striking the Euphrates River (Isa. 11:15), weapons (2 Kgs. 13:18; 1 Sam. 17:49; 19:10), and a person may be conscience-stricken (1 Sam. 24:5). People are often the object of beating (Ex. 2:11, 13; Neh. 13:25) and the verb *nākhāh* is frequently used in contexts related to punishment (Jer. 20:2; 37:15).

God's punishing strike on the wicked is also apparent in the Flood (Gen. 8:21), crops (Am. 4:9; Hag. 2:17), striking disobedient and rebellious people "seven times" (Lev. 26:24), and the guilty (Deut. 25:2f.). In Scripture, punishment or discipline is not simply retribution, but for the restoration of the trespasser (Pr. 23:13f.). The reference of striking referred to inflicting pain not only upon one another, but also exploiting their servants or debtors (v. 3). Their fasting, which meant to draw them close to God, had caused them to become divided and violent towards one another, which infuriated God.[224]

The noun אֶגְרֹף *'eghrōph* used for "fists" is used only in two places in the Old Testament and both contain the imagery of the "clenched human hand". The first reference, Exodus 21:18, states the penalty for such behaviour depends upon the extent of the injury. In the case of a non-fatal wound, the perpetrator

---

[222] רִיב *rîv* "7663", In Gilbrant, ed., *The Complete Biblical Library Hebrew-English Dictionary, Pe-Resh.* רִיב "2159", In Harris, Archer, Jr., and Waltke, eds., *Theological Wordbook of the Old Testament*, 845. "Isaiah 58:4", In Albert Barnes, *Albert Barnes' Notes on the Bible*, Rick Meyers, e-Sword, Version 10.2.1, 2000-2012, <http://www.e-sword.net>.

[223] מַצָּה *matstsāh* "4844", In Gilbrant, ed., *The Complete Biblical Library Hebrew-English Dictionary, Kaph-Mem.* "נָצָה 1402", In Harris, Archer, Jr., and Waltke, eds., *Theological Wordbook of the Old Testament*, 593.

[224] נָכָה *nākhāh* "5409", In Gilbrant, ed., *The Complete Biblical Library Hebrew-English Dictionary, Nun-Ayin.* נָכָה "1364", In Harris, Archer, Jr., and Waltke, eds., *Theological Wordbook of the Old Testament*, 578.

is required to pay the victim for any lost wages until he is able to return to work. The second reference, Isaiah 58:4, the prophet condemns those who participate in a religious ceremony, especially fasting, while continuing in a sinful behaviour that inflicts pain upon their fellow man using their fist. Isaiah emphasizes that fasting undertaken as an obligation will often produce a rebellious and agitated community especially during stressful conditions. It also refers to people who even though they are wrong, use their "fist of wickedness" to get their own way.[225]

The noun רָשָׁע *rāshā* used for "wicked" means "guilty", "evildoer", "impious person" often refers to being guilty of wrongdoing—especially against another person (Ex. 2:13; Num. 35:31) and used as the opposite of being righteous (cf. Ps. 1:1, 4ff.). Those who are "wicked" do not seek God (Ps. 10:4); forsake God's instruction (Ps. 119:53); are cruel (Pr. 12:10); pour out evil from within them (15:28); crave evil with their whole person (21:10); they are rejected by the Lord and will be cut off and perish (2:22; 21:27); and they have no peace (Isa. 48:22). Observing a fast was supposed to humble them before God. However, it made them bad-tempered and violent towards each other (58:4-5), as God had warned them earlier (Isa. 57:13). Isaiah's point is that fasting as an expression of piety is of far less concern to God than a righteous lifestyle. Spirituality is shown by the loving quality of our personal relationships (Isa. 58:4), by our commitment to social justice, and to helping the poor and oppressed (Isa. 58:6-7).[226]

> Is this the kind of fast I have chosen, only a day for people to humble themselves? Is it only for bowing one's head like a reed and for lying in sackcloth and ashes? Is that what you call a fast, a day acceptable to the LORD? (Isa. 58:5).

The people were conducting their fast based upon their own interpretation and not wholeheartedly as the Lord required. The Law never commanded one to fast in sackcloth and ashes. It was the way they expressed humility before the Lord, but it had degenerated into putting on an act. Their modified fast—worldly, selfish, perverted from the divine worship and absorption in the spiritual character of the day to the most thoroughly selfish purposes—left them expecting some divine worth and meriting some reward. This work-holy delusion, behind which self-righteousness and unrighteousness were concealed, is met thus by Jehovah through His prophet "Is this the kind of fast I have chosen". Isaiah contrasts true worship—works of mercy, compassion, and love towards our fellow man with the false worship that was being committed.[227] Matthew Henry states,

---

[225] אֶגְרֹף *'eghrōph* "103", In Gilbrant, ed., *The Complete Biblical Library Hebrew-English Dictionary, Aleph-Beth*. אֶגְרֹף *'egrōp* "388", In Harris, Archer, Jr., and Waltke, eds., *Theological Wordbook of the Old Testament*, 173. Gaebelein, ed., *The Expositor's Bible Commentary*, Vol. 6, 321. "Isaiah 58:4", In Gilbrant, ed., *The Complete Biblical Library Commentary, Isaiah*.

[226] רָשָׁע *rāshā* "7857", In Gilbrant, ed., *The Complete Biblical Library Hebrew-English Dictionary, Pe-Resh*. רָשָׁע *rāshā* "2222", In Harris, Archer, Jr., and Waltke, eds., *Theological Wordbook of the Old Testament*, 863. Knowles, *The Bible Guide*, 292. Gaebelein, ed., *The Expositor's Bible Commentary, Volume 6*, 321. Richards, *The Bible Reader's Companion*, 442.

[227] "Isaiah 58:5-7", In Albert Barnes, *Albert Barnes' Notes on the Bible*, <http://www.e-sword.net>.

If the solemnities of our fasting, though frequent, long, and severe, do not serve to put an edge upon devout affections, to quicken prayer, to increase godly sorrow, and to alter the temper of our minds and the course of our lives for the better, they do not at all answer the intention, and God will not accept them as performed to him, even to him.[228]

It is a common characteristic for hypocrites at heart to be vociferous to be seen by others, and then complain to God for not adequately rewarding their zeal. Isaiah 58 shares the condemnation of hypocritical worship practices found so often in the prophets (i.e., Isa. 1:12-17; Am. 5:21-24; Mic. 6:6-8). These people had the same issues as the Pharisees of Jesus' day in trusting in an empty ritual without spiritual reality. Jesus criticized fasting for external reward (cf. Mt. 6:16-18; 23:23; Lk. 18:9-14). In the midst of their hypocritical zeal, they were insincere in heart—outwardly going through the motions. The motive for their fast proceeded from a principle of pride, which was a cover-up for their hidden abominations. God abhorred their open display of vile hypocrisy—hollow and empty without any spiritual substance. Isaiah was commanded to confront such detestable behaviour and then describes a true fast that is accepted and approved by God. True fasting which leads to salvation is a real bowing of the soul (v. 5) in moral action, in loving service to the poor and unfortunate among the people (cf. Zech. 7:5ff.; 8:16-19; Joel 2:13.[229] The remaining verses of Isaiah 58 will be discussed following the ten fasts of Isaiah 58.

The Disciple's Fast

When they came to the crowd, a man approached Jesus and knelt before him. "Lord, have mercy on my son", he said. "He has seizures and is suffering greatly. He often falls into the fire or into the water. I brought him to your disciples, but they could not heal him". "You unbelieving and perverse generation", Jesus replied, "how long shall I stay with you? How long shall I put up with you? Bring the boy here to me". Jesus rebuked the demon, and it came out of the boy, and he was healed at that moment. Then the disciples came to Jesus in private and asked, "Why couldn't we drive it out?" He replied, "Because you have so little faith. Truly I tell you, if you have faith as small as a mustard seed, you can say to this mountain, 'Move from here to there', and it will move. Nothing will be impossible for you. But this kind does not go out except by prayer and fasting" (Mt. 17:14-21).

The first fast in Isaiah 58 is in verse 6, "to loose the chains of injustice" referred to as the Disciple's Fast (Mk. 9:14-29).[230] The purpose of this fast is to free ourselves and others from addictions to sin.

---

[228] "Zechariah 7:1-7", In Henry, *Matthew Henry's Commentary on the Whole Bible*.

[229] "Isaiah 58:5-11, Discourse 993", Charles Simeon, In *Horae Homileticae or Discourses* (London: Samuel Holdsworth, Amen Corner, Paternoster Row, 1836). "Isaiah 58:1-14", In David Guzik, *Guzik Commentary on OT and NT*, Rick Meyers, e-Sword, Version 10.2.1, 2000-2012, <http://www.e-sword.net>. "Isaiah 58", In Gilbrant, ed., *The Complete Biblical Library Commentary, Isaiah.* Walvoord and Zuck, eds., *The Bible Knowledge Commentary*, Vol. 1, 1113-14. Kittel, Bromiley and Friedrich, eds., *Theological Dictionary of the New Testament*, electronic ed., Vol. 4, 928.

[230] "Nearly all major ancient Greek manuscripts have "prayer and fasting" at the end of 9:29 (NIV marg.). Perhaps the words were added early by some scribes to the textual tradition to support asceticism. But the words, if

Today, as disciples of Jesus Christ, we do not take too seriously these types of sin that gain a stronghold in our lives and start the downward spiraling effect leading to death. The Apostle John states,

> The thief comes only to steal and kill and destroy; I have come that they may have life, and have it to the full (Jn. 10:10).

Jesus admonished His disciples who could not cast a "deaf and mute spirit" out of a boy who had been "possessed by a spirit" from childhood. The Disciple's Fast was prominent in the New Testament and Jesus uses this situation to teach the disciples that to accomplish certain types of ministry requires the regular ascetic practice of prayer and fasting. Too many Christians today have been content with living with these types of strongholds in their lives when they could have power, victory, and deliverance like this boy if they would have spent time in fasting and prayer.[231]

Jesus responds to the disciple's question "Why couldn't we drive it out?" in private. First, "this kind" of demon, referred to levels among evil spirits—some more powerful and more malicious than others.[232] The evil spirit that was afflicting the boy could only be expelled through persevering prayer and fasting. The failure of the disciples was because they had not depended upon God's power and had deceptively trusted in their past successes (Mk. 6:7, 13).[233]

In the Disciple's Fast, we seek the Lord for a breakthrough—"to loose the chains of injustice", wickedness and sin that has become a bondage in our lives. This type of fasting, gives us the strength to confront and receive God's deliverance, liberating us from strongholds, and living a life of freedom in Jesus Christ. Prayer combined with fasting adds spiritual strength to destroying Satan's influence over our lives. Matthew Henry, in his commentary states,

> Fasting and prayer are proper means for the bringing down of Satan's power against us, and the fetching in of divine power to our assistance. Fasting is of use to put an edge upon prayer; it is an evidence and instance of humiliation which is necessary in prayer, and is a means of mortifying some corrupt habits, and of disposing the body to serve the soul in prayer. When the devil's interest in the soul is confirmed by the temper and constitution of the body, fasting must be joined with prayer, to keep under the body.[234]

It is interesting that after Jesus rebukes the unclean, "deaf and mute spirit" and the boy is delivered, He has compassion on him as he lays prostrate on the ground. It was Jesus' custom to have compassion on people and in this case, He raises the boy up. "Immediately Jesus reached out his hand and caught him. 'You of little faith,' he said, 'why did you doubt?'" (Mt. 14:31). "So he went to her, took her hand and

---

original, refer to a practical means of focusing one's attention more fully on God for a specific purpose, for a limited period of time". Walvoord and Zuck, eds., *The Bible Knowledge Commentary*, Vol. 2, 145.

[231] Walvoord and Zuck, eds., *The Bible Knowledge Commentary*, Vol. 2, 20-21.

[232] "Then it goes and takes with it seven other spirits more wicked than itself, and they go in and live there. And the final condition of that person is worse than the first. That is how it will be with this wicked generation" (Mt. 12:45).

[233] Walvoord and Zuck, eds., *The Bible Knowledge Commentary*, Vol. 2, 145. Gilbrant, ed., *The Complete Biblical Library Commentary, Mark*, 251.

[234] "Matthew 17:14-21", In Henry, *Matthew Henry's Commentary on the Whole Bible*.

helped her up. The fever left her and she began to wait on them" (Mk. 1:31; cf. 5:41). Jesus not only delivers this boy from the "deaf and mute spirit", but He also completely restores the boy to full health and strength. Jesus then gives the boy to his father (Lk. 9:42) and the people "were all amazed at the greatness of God" (Lk. 9:43). The enemy had controlled this boy since childhood, but Jesus in a matter of moments, looses "the chains of injustice" and imparts life into the boy. [235]

When we study these gospels accounts, it becomes evident of what is lacking in the lives of the disciples. They lacked faith—having become part of an unbelieving generation and lacked confidence to carry out the ministry that Jesus had called them to fulfill. Likewise, they lacked prayer and fasting—which demonstrates that their devotional disciplines had eroded during Jesus' short absence. This context speaks loudly of the necessity of maintaining our spiritual lives in communion with the Lord. The principle that we learn here is that when prayer and fasting are combined as part of our spiritual disciplines, there are no limits to the works that we can accomplish, following His will.[236]

Please refer to *Fasting: Unlocking Spiritual Power and Breakthrough, Personal Reflections* under the heading "The Disciple's Fast" to complete the Personal Reflections section of this study.

The Ezra Fast

The Book of Ezra emphasizes two primary fasts: the first takes place while they were still in Babylon as they prayed and fasted for divine deliverance and guidance. The purpose of the Ezra Fast is to "untie the cords of the yoke" (Isa. 58:6). It assists in problem-solving and allowing the Holy Spirit to help us to lift burdens and overcome those obstacles that hinder personal and spiritual development in our lives and in the Church.

> There, by the Ahava Canal, I proclaimed a fast, so that we might humble ourselves before our God and ask him for a safe journey for us and our children, with all our possessions. I was ashamed to ask the king for soldiers and horsemen to protect us from enemies on the road, because we had told the king, "The gracious hand of our God is on everyone who looks to him, but his great anger is against all who forsake him". So we fasted and petitioned our God about this, and he answered our prayer (Ezra 8:21-23).

Ezra the priest was commissioned with restoring the Law of Moses among the Jewish remnant and rebuilding the temple in Jerusalem (Ezra 3:7-13). Even though Ezra had received permission by Artaxerxes, King of Persia to rebuild the temple, their enemies continued to oppose the work. Ezra and the leaders had proclaimed to the King that "The gracious hand of our God is on everyone who looks to him" and therefore Ezra "was ashamed to ask the king for soldiers and horsemen to protect us from enemies". They were forced to completely trust the Lord and not "soldiers and horsemen" for divine

---

[235] Gilbrant, ed., *The Complete Biblical Library Commentary, Mark*, 251.

[236] Warren W. Wiersbe, *The Bible Exposition Commentary*, Vol. 1 (Wheaton, IL: Victor Books, 1996), 208-09. Walvoord and Zuck, eds., *The Bible Knowledge Commentary*, Vol. 2, 60-61. Towns, *Fasting for Spiritual Breakthrough*, 20-21.

guidance and direction as they travelled some 900 miles without any military escort to their new home in Jerusalem.[237]

The reference to "a safe journey" יָשָׁר דֶּרֶךְ, *derekh yāshār*, literally means an unobstructed "straight way" free of obstacles and danger of any kind. The Jews before they would travel prayed the "prayer of the road" *tephillath hadderech*.[238] The principle of fasting that Ezra emphasizes is that fasting prepares us for a divine assignment and divine protection. Likewise, when we fast for a specific purpose, we may solve a debilitating problem (1 Sam. 1:1-20). As Ezra led a fast when seeking the favour of God in leading the Jews back to Jerusalem, Nehemiah also led the Jews in a fast before they departed for Jerusalem (Neh. 9). In the Book of Acts, Paul and Barnabas fasted before being sent out as missionaries (Acts 13:1-2). However, there is no greater example of this type of fast than when Jesus was led by the Holy Spirit into the wilderness to prepare for ministry (Lk. 4:1-13).

The second fast in Ezra shows how he set the example for the Jews to follow which subsequently led to their conviction and confession of their sins. Shekaniah, the son of Jehiel, recommended a renewal of the covenant and urged Ezra to lead the community in a reform and called for an assembly of all the tribes under threat of having all their property seized (cf. Ezra 7:26). In such passages as Ezra 10:6 and Esther 4:3, it is not clear whether fasting is used in its religious significance or simply as a natural expression of sorrow. This view explains the association of fasting with the mourning customs of antiquity.

> When the people of Jabesh Gilead heard what the Philistines had done to Saul, all their valiant men marched through the night to Beth Shan. They took down the bodies of Saul and his sons from the wall of Beth Shan and went to Jabesh, where they burned them. Then they took their bones and buried them under a tamarisk tree at Jabesh, and they fasted seven days (1 Sam. 31:11-13; cf. 2 Sam. 1:12).

As fasting was a perfectly natural human expression and evidence of the subject's grief, it readily claimed a place among those religious customs whose main object was the appeasement of the anger of God, or stirring up His compassion. Any and every act that would manifest the distressful state of the supplant would appeal to the Deity and move Him to pity.

> While Ezra was praying and confessing, weeping and throwing himself down before the house of God, a large crowd of Israelites—men, women and children—gathered around him. They too wept bitterly. Then Shekaniah son of Jehiel, one of the descendants of Elam, said to Ezra, "We have been unfaithful to our God by marrying foreign women from the peoples around us. But in spite of this, there is still hope for Israel. Now let us make a covenant before our God to send away all these women and their children, in accordance with the counsel of my lord and of those who fear the commands of our God. Let it be done according to the Law (Ezra 10:1-3).

---

[237] "Ezra 8:21-30", In Gilbrant, ed., *The Complete Biblical Library Commentary, Ezra-Job*. Towns, *Fasting for Spiritual Breakthrough*, 21. Peter Williams, *Opening Up Ezra*, Opening Up Commentary (Leominster: Day One Publications, 2006), 92-93.

[238] Gaebelein, *The Expositor's Bible Commentary, Volume 4*, 659.

In this passage in Ezra, we can see that Ezra was deeply moved over the desperate predicament of his people. The Hebrew verb for "weeping" בָּכָה *bākhāh*[239] refers to the oral and vocal aspects of weeping. It can denote a person's excitement or anxiety concerning the future or meeting someone for the first time or having not seen someone for a long time. It was not only Ezra's great ability in proclaiming the Law of Moses that moved the leaders and eventually all of the Israelites, including chief priests and leading Levites, to respond to Ezra's dilemma, but it was also Ezra's absolute devotion to the teachings of the Law in his own life as the Word of God that moved them. Ezra understood that his people were on the threshold of complete destruction, if they did not adhere to the Law. The phrase "now let us make a covenant before our God" or literally "cut a covenant" derives from the practice of cutting an animal in preparation for its sacrifice. Anyone disobeying the covenant should be cut up like the animals (Gen. 15:9-18).[240] The Book of Ezra shows him fasting over the idolatrous marriages of the Jews to foreign women.

> Then Ezra withdrew from before the house of God and went to the room of Jehohanan son of Eliashib. While he was there, he ate no food and drank no water, because he continued to mourn over the unfaithfulness of the exiles. A proclamation was then issued throughout Judah and Jerusalem for all the exiles to assemble in Jerusalem. Anyone who failed to appear within three days would forfeit all his property, in accordance with the decision of the officials and elders, and would himself be expelled from the assembly of the exiles (Ezra 10:6-8).

Ezra issues a decree for "all the exiles to assemble in Jerusalem" and even though calling an assembly for the entire community of Israel occurred regularly it was not as serious as this one—the threatened destruction of the remnant (Ezra 9:14). Ezra allowed three days for people to get to Jerusalem and had the authority of the Law of Moses and Artaxerxes I to enforce this oath, which included the leaders of Jerusalem. "Whoever does not obey the law of your God and the law of the king must surely be punished by death, banishment, confiscation of property, or imprisonment" (Ezra 7:26).

Ezra placed the priests, Levites, and the entire assembly of Israel under an oath and proclaimed, "Anyone who failed to appear within three days would forfeit all his property" (Ezra 10:8). This verse uses the verb יָחֳרַם *āyḥăram* from חָרַם *chāram* meaning to take things or people from their everyday lives and dedicate them exclusively to God. Moreover, "the verb is often used of completely destroying a conquered town's people and wealth in dedication to the Lord"[241] (e.g., Ex. 22:20; Deut. 13:13-17; cf. Lev. 27:28-29; Jos. 6:18-19; 7:1-26). This meant that anyone guilty of breaking this oath would lose their

---

[239] However, this root usually refers to emotional grief, such as mourning over the dead for the purpose of emotion rather than consolation. Weeping can also refer to lament over individual distress, or even a public lament. It can also be used in connection with acts of repentance, or even out of awe (although the latter is not common in the Old Testament). This root can also refer to cultic wailing over a deity. בָּכָה *bākhāh* "1098", In Gilbrant, ed., *The Complete Biblical Library Hebrew-English Dictionary, Aleph-Beth.*

[240] Gaebelein, *The Expositor's Bible Commentary*, Vol. 4, 669. "Ezra 10", In Gilbrant, ed., *The Complete Biblical Library Commentary, Ezra-Job.*

[241] חָרַם *chāram* "2868", In Gilbrant, ed., *The Complete Biblical Library Hebrew-English Dictionary, Heth-Yodh.* Gaebelein, *The Expositor's Bible Commentary, Volume 4*, 671.

legal rights and property as punishment for their disobedience. This was enforced in order to preserve the renewed exilic community as being separated unto God.[242] Ezra was justified in confiscating the property and the ban חֵרֶם *chāram* since most of the property had been the wealth given to the entire assembly (מִקְּהַל *miqqĕhal* from קָהָל *qāhāl*) of Israel (Ezra 1:6; 7:18-24; 8:24-29).[243]

In the Book of Ezra, we can see his priority in maintaining a distinct religious purity and it was through intermarrying with foreign women that this religious purity had been corrupted by idolatry. Ezra reprimanded and commanded them to separate from their foreign wives. Divorce was not God's will for His people (cf. Mal. 2:16; Mt. 19:4-6). However, God permitted divorce to preserve Jewish spiritual life (cf. Deut. 24:1-3). The separation of men from their foreign wives was so severe that the process took three months for a tribunal to hear every case. The Book of Ezra concludes by listing all those who were guilty of marrying foreign wives, beginning with the religious leaders: 17 priests, 10 Levites, and 86 men. No family and/or group escaped the sin or discipline. Each had to put away his foreign wife and offer a ram as a trespass offering. This somber conclusion is contrasted with the record of those who were honoured for their faith (Ezra 2). Moreover, Ezra's conclusion shows that the exiles still had further spiritual growth to accomplishment in doing God's work.[244]

Please refer to *Fasting: Unlocking Spiritual Power and Breakthrough, Personal Reflections* under the heading "The Ezra Fast" to complete the Personal Reflections section of this study.

The Samuel Fast

When they had assembled at Mizpah, they drew water and poured it out before the LORD. On that day they fasted and there they confessed, "We have sinned against the LORD". Now Samuel was serving as leader of Israel at Mizpah (1 Sam. 7:6).

Isaiah states that a true fast will "set the oppressed free", which included both physical and spiritual freedom and was especially directed towards revival and harvest (Isa. 58:6). The purpose of the Samuel Fast is to assist us in identifying bondage(s) to sin and suggest the spiritual direction necessary to be set free from enslavement to the darkness and shown the light. The Samuel Fast demonstrates how fasting defeats strongholds and dethrones idols.

The verb קָבַץ *qāvats* used here for "assembled" means "to gather" as in people or individuals, and is often used in reference to crops "to harvest".[245] Assembling "at Mizpah"[246] is significant since it is one of

---

[242] Walvoord and Zuck, eds., *The Bible Knowledge Commentary*, Vol. 1, 145. Gilbrant, ed., *The Complete Biblical Library Commentary, Mark*, 670-71.

[243] "Ezra 10:5-8", In Gilbrant, ed., *The Complete Biblical Library Commentary, Ezra-Job*. קָהָל *qāhāl* "7235", In Gilbrant, ed., *The Complete Biblical Library Hebrew-English Dictionary, Pe-Resh*.

[244] "Ezra 10:1-44", In Dockery, ed., In *Holman Concise Bible Commentary*, 181. Walvoord and Zuck, eds., *The Bible Knowledge Commentary*, Vol. 1, 670-71. Williams, *Opening Up Ezra*, 114. Knowles, *The Bible Guide*, 202. Paschall and Hobbs, eds., *The Teacher's Bible Commentary*, 257.

[245] קָבַץ *qāvats* "7192", In Gilbrant, ed., *The Complete Biblical Library Hebrew-English Dictionary, Pe-Resh*.

the three names Laban and Jacob gave to a heap of stones or "heap of witness" that they erected as a witness to their legally binding oral contract. This heap of stones was seen as a boundary marker, and God would watch over the keeping of the oath of peace between the two parties. It also served as the place where the Israelites gathered for religious events. This assembly has been seen as one of the greatest revivals in biblical history. For example, Samuel assembled the people at Mizpah for prayer after the Ark of the Covenant returned to Kirjath-Jearim (1 Sam. 7:5f.). Likewise, Saul was first announced as Israel's King (1 Sam. 10:9-27).

It is significant that the task of "they drew water" was customarily the function of the women, children and servants (Gen. 24:13, 20, 43, 45; Deut. 29:11; Jos. 9 21, 23, 27; 1 Sam. 9:11). Isaac met his wife Rebekah when she came to draw water from the well outside her town (Gen. 24 :13, 20, 43, 45), was a necessity for labourers (Ruth 2:9), military campaigns (1 Chr. 11:18; Nah. 3:14), and were located either inside the walls of a city or close by (1 Chr. 11:18). Underground tunnels allowed besieged cities access to water sources, while an important military strategy was to attempt to cut off an enemy's water supply. The salvation of the Lord is figuratively compared to the life-giving and life-sustaining qualities of drawn water in an arid and desolate wilderness (Isa. 12:3).[247]

The Hebrew verb שָׁפַךְ *shāphakh* used here for "poured out" is significant as it is used in the basic sense of "pouring a liquid", such as water (Ex. 4:9), broth (Jdg. 6:20), and many of its uses refer to the pouring of sacrificial blood (Ex. 29:12), and drink offerings (Isa. 57:6). It's symbolic meaning in that murder is the "pouring" out of a person's blood (Lev. 17:4), and the psalmist "pours" out his soul before the Lord (Ps. 42:4). The prophet Joel promised that one day the Holy Spirit would be "poured" out upon all people (Joel 2:28-29). Zechariah saw the "pouring" out of the grace of God and supplication when the messiah appears, (12:10). The most common metaphorical usage is God's anger being "poured" out upon rebellious people.

> Pour it out on the children in the street and on the young men gathered together; both husband and wife will be caught in it, and the old, those weighed down with years (Jer. 6:11).

The pouring out of the water perhaps symbolized their spirit being completely poured out before the Lord in devotion to him.[248] The context behind the Samuel Fast begins with the Ark of the Covenant being

---

[246] Modern Tell en-Nasbeh, is first mentioned in Genesis 31:49. Another location with this same name was a city of Benjamin in the area near Geba and Ramah (1 Kgs. 15:22). Mizpah was one of the cities that the prophet Samuel visited on his annual circuit to judge the people (cf. 1 Sam. 7:16f.). It was also one of the sites fortified against the kings of the northern tribes of Israel during the reign of King Asa (1 Kgs. 15:22). After Jerusalem was destroyed in 586 BC, Gedaliah was appointed governor of the people who were not taken into captivity. His residence was established at Mizpah (2 Kgs. 25:23, 25). It was resettled by the Jews who returned from Babylon (Neh. 3:7, 15, 19). The precise location of Mizpah is not mentioned in Scripture or in the writings of Josephus. מִצְפָּה *mitspāh* "4870", In Gilbrant, ed., *The Complete Biblical Library Hebrew-English Dictionary, Kaph-Mem.*

[247] שָׁאַב *shā'av* "8056", In Gilbrant, ed., *The Complete Biblical Library Hebrew-English Dictionary, Sin-Taw.*

[248] שָׁפַךְ "2444", In Harris, Archer, Jr., and Waltke, eds., *Theological Wordbook of the Old Testament*, 950.
שָׁפַךְ *shāphakh* "8581", In Gilbrant, ed., *The Complete Biblical Library Hebrew-English Dictionary, Sin-Taw.*

returned to Israel. The Philistines had discovered that the presence of God in the Ark had only brought them "disease and panic . . . and they resolve to return it to Israel". However, the Israelites were not worthy of the presence of God that accompanied it either. The Ark of the Covenant had been quarantined for twenty years in the house of Abinadab at Kiriath Jearim known as the "city of woods" situated between the tribes of Benjamin and Judah (1 Sam. 7:2-4). The Israelites mourn the loss of the presence of God, and begin to turn to Him again.

Sometime later, Samuel gives the Israelites an ultimatum that if they would return to the Lord wholeheartedly, forsaking all foreign gods, especially Astarte, the Baal-goddess of fertility and war, then God would set them free from the oppression of the Philistines. Samuel sends a message to all Israelites "assemble all Israel at Mizpah[249], and I will intercede with the Lord for you" (1 Sam. 7:5). At Mizpah, they pour out water in the presence of God, as a sign confessing that God alone can wash away they sin of disobedience. They fast, confess their guilt, and accept God's discipline through Samuel, their great leader, prophet, and priest.

When the Philistines learned that the Israelites were assembling at Mizpah and believe that they were about to be attacked they attempt to get one-step ahead of Israel, gathering their own army. The Israelites appeal to Samuel for God's help—a paradigm shift from their past—where they assumed that the presence of the Ark of the Covenant would automatically bring them victory. Samuel intercedes on behalf of the Israelites and sacrifices a burnt offering asking for divine help against the Philistines.

> While Samuel was sacrificing the burnt offering, the Philistines drew near to engage Israel in battle. But that day the Lord thundered with loud thunder against the Philistines and threw them into such a panic that they were routed before the Israelites. The men of Israel rushed out of Mizpah and pursued the Philistines, slaughtering them along the way to a point below Beth Car (1 Sam. 7:10-11).

It is interesting that Beth-Car denotes a place belonging to the Philistines, near Mizpah and its literal meaning is "place of a lamb".[250]

They had the advantage over the Philistines chasing them downhill. To commemorate their victory, Samuel erects a memorial stone and names it "Ebenezer" meaning "stone of God's help" and the site of their last defeat (1 Sam. 4:1) and now they were granted repentance and success. The stone was probably given the same name as the site of Israel's earlier defeat in order to encourage the people that this defeat

---

[249] Mizpah means "watchtower" and is a small settlement only a few miles north of Jerusalem, whose height above the valleys makes it a good rallying point. Samuel inaugurated the reformation that characterized his time by convening a great assembly of all Israel at Mizpeh, now the politico-religious centre of the nation. There, in deep humiliation on account of their sins, they renewed their vows and entered again into covenant with the God of their fathers. It was a period of great religious awakening and of revived national life. The Philistines heard of this assembly, and came up against Israel. The Hebrews charged the Philistine host with great fury, and they were totally routed. Samuel commemorated this signal victory by erecting a memorial-stone, which he called "Ebenezer" (q.v.), saying, "Hitherto hath the Lord helped us" (1 Sam. 7:7-12). "Mizpah", In Easton, *Easton's Bible Dictionary*.

[250] כַּר בֵּית *bêth kar* "1072", In Gilbrant, ed., *The Complete Biblical Library Hebrew-English Dictionary, Aleph-Beth*.

had now been reversed—the Philistines are vanquished, and the memorial stone is erected by Samuel.[251] Samuel was the leader who inaugurated the fast, which aroused within them a desire for change and to never again misuse the presence of God and allow the Ark to be captured again. The Israelites learned a valuable lesson that even though victory has been achieved that their relationship with God must remain solid, especially after victory which is often the precarious time to become complacent. Moreover, prayer and fasting must continue even after victory and revival.[252]

Samuel, as a man of prayer, was able to achieve much more than Samson who was gifted by God with extraordinary strength. Even though it may seem that this victory was insignificant, it was a turning point in weakening Philistine's dominance of Israelite territory following forty years of oppression (Jdg. 13:1). Samuel continued as judge over Israel all the days of his life. Each year he travelled on a judicial circuit of about 50 miles in circumference from Bethel to Gilgal to Mizpah, judging Israel in each place. But he always went back to Ramah, where his home was, and there he also judged Israel. And he built an altar there to the Lord, which became the national center for Israel worship (1 Sam. 7:15-17).[253]

The Samuel Fast communicates how the Israelites had wandered away from God, persecuted by the Philistines, and needed to separate themselves from the idolatrous practices of their surrounding neighbours. Besides ridding themselves "of the foreign gods and the Ashtoreths" Samuel instructed them to pray and fast.

Please refer to *Fasting: Unlocking Spiritual Power and Breakthrough, Personal Reflections* under the heading "The Samuel Fast" to complete the Personal Reflections section of this study.

The Elijah Fast

Isaiah continues his discussion on fasting by emphasizing another aspect of fasting seen in Elijah's forty day fast after he fled from Jezebel (1 Kgs. 19:7-18). The purpose of the Elijah Fast is to "break every yoke" (Isa. 58:6).

Now Ahab told Jezebel everything Elijah had done and how he had killed all the prophets with the sword. So Jezebel sent a messenger to Elijah to say, "May the gods deal with me, be it ever so severely, if by this time tomorrow I do not make your life like that of one of them". Elijah was afraid and ran for his life. When he came to Beersheba in Judah, he left his servant there, while he himself went a day's journey into the wilderness. He came to a broom bush, sat down under it and prayed that he might die. "I have had enough, LORD", he said. "Take my life; I am no better than my ancestors". Then he lay down under the bush and fell asleep. All at once an angel touched him and said, "Get up and eat". He looked around, and there by his head was some bread baked over hot coals, and a jar of water. He ate and drank and then lay down again. The angel of the LORD came back a second time and touched him and said, "Get up and eat, for the journey is too much for you". So he got up and ate and drank. Strengthened by that food, he traveled forty days and

---

[251] "Ebenezer", In Wood and Marshall, *New Bible Dictionary*, 287. "Ebenezer", In Easton, *Easton's Bible Dictionary*.

[252] Knowles, *The Bible Guide*, 134-35. Towns, *Fasting for Spiritual Breakthrough*, 21.

[253] Walvoord and Zuck, eds., *The Bible Knowledge Commentary*, Vol. 1, 438-39. "1 Samuel 7:3-17", In James E. Smith, *The Books of History*, Old Testament Survey Series (Joplin, MO: College Press, 1995).

forty nights until he reached Horeb, the mountain of God. There he went into a cave and spent the night (1 Kgs. 19:1-9).

The Elijah Fast is specifically directed towards breaking negative emotions—being victorious over the mental and emotional anxieties and stresses that can dominate our thinking, perception, our values and worldview. The context here refers to Elijah's victory over the prophets of Baal, which had resulted from being afraid of Jezebel, despair, and depression. It is interesting that Jezebel was not intimidated by Ahab's report and that the prophets of Baal had been miraculously annihilated through Elijah. This report infuriated her to the point that she promised to do to Elijah what he had done to her prophets. Jezebel sends a messenger to find and convey to Elijah that he would be dead within a day. If she meant this, why did she warn him? Perhaps she would not find anyone that evening who could carry out Elijah's execution that night of someone whose supernatural powers of God rested upon so mightily.

In a state of despair, "Elijah was afraid and ran for his life" into the wilderness and "prayed that he might die" (cf. Num. 11:11-15; Job 6:8-9; Jon. 4:8). An angel of the Lord appeared to him and gave him food to sustain him for "forty days and forty nights until he reached Horeb, the mountain of God" also known as Mt. Sinai where the Lord appeared to Moses (cf. Ex. 3; Ex. 19-20). Even though Scripture does not refer to this as a "fast", Elijah did fast under duress while he "ran for his life" from Jezebel and an angel of the Lord ministered to him in the wilderness.[254]

Even though Elijah complained that the Israelites had once again become the apostate people of God, but he was mistaken. God instructed Elijah to "Go out and stand on the mountain in the presence of the Lord, for the Lord is about to pass by" (v. 11) who brought a "great and powerful wind", "an earthquake", "a fire" "but the Lord was not in" these calamities. Finally, there "came a gentle whisper" which Elijah heard and responded to God. He learned that God works in wondrous ways—wind, earthquake, and fire—but He more often speaks through "a gentle whisper" or a still small voice. God later sends Elijah to anoint Hazael of Aram, Jehu of Israel, and the prophet Elisha who would ultimately bring an end to Ahab (1 Kgs. 22). The call of Elisha was the beginning of a large school of prophets.[255]

> The company of the prophets said to Elisha, "Look, the place where we meet with you is too small for us. Let us go to the Jordan, where each of us can get a pole; and let us build a place there for us to meet". And he said, "Go" (2 Kgs. 6:1-2).

Elijah's discouragement after the victory on Mount Carmel is quite similar to our moods today. No one is immune from despair. God is always there to strengthen and encourage us, and reveal Himself to us in a fresh way. We need to have our spiritual ears open to hear His still small voice, accept new challenges, and encourage others to look to Him and be strong. Through fasting we can receive a fresh vision ("still small voice"), clear direction, and break habits and emotional problems (1 Kgs. 19:2-18). If

---

[254] "1 Kings 19:1-4", In Smith, *The Books of History*.

[255] "1 Kings 19:1-21", In Dockery, ed., In *Holman Concise Bible Commentary*, 143. Walvoord and Zuck, eds., *The Bible Knowledge Commentary*, Vol. 1, 527-28. Paschall and Hobbs, eds., *The Teacher's Bible Commentary*, 204-05.

our fast focuses on our problem, God will show us how to overcome emotional defects and personal habits. It does not matter how many personal and/or spiritual victories we have overcome—there will always be a new enemy to overcome. We are often the most vulnerable to emotional attacks following a victory.[256]

The principle is usually felt to rest in the belief that if God's saints cause voluntary suffering on themselves to show their real sincerity with God, then God will more readily respond. He would look on their self-imposed afflictions in an anxious mood and rush to release them from their self-imposed hurt. But this cannot be correct. If it were, then the prophets of Baal in Elijah's time had the right idea. After crying to the Baals from morning to late afternoon without any response, they began to "cut themselves with knives and lancets, till the blood gushed out upon them" (1 Kgs. 18:28). It was like saying: "Look, Baal, we are suffering for you". Elijah mocked them to scorn. Such a thing was blatant heathenism. This type of "suffering" also applies to fasting. Simply being uncomfortable with gnawing pangs of hunger or thirst is not advocated in the Scriptures as a way of getting God's attention.

Please refer to *Fasting: Unlocking Spiritual Power and Breakthrough, Personal Reflections* under the heading "The Elijah Fast" to complete the Personal Reflections section of this study.

The Widow's Fast

> Elijah said to her, "Don't be afraid. Go home and do as you have said. But first make a small loaf of bread for me from what you have and bring it to me, and then make something for yourself and your son. For this is what the LORD, the God of Israel, says: 'The jar of flour will not be used up and the jug of oil will not run dry until the day the LORD sends rain on the land'". She went away and did as Elijah had told her. So there was food every day for Elijah and for the woman and her family. For the jar of flour was not used up and the jug of oil did not run dry, in keeping with the word of the LORD spoken by Elijah (1 Kgs. 17:13-16).

> There was also a prophetess, Anna, the daughter of Phanuel, of the tribe of Asher. She was very old; she had lived with her husband seven years after her marriage, and then was a widow until she was eighty-four. She never left the temple but worshiped night and day, fasting and praying (Lk. 2:36-37).

The Widow's Fast refers to the prophet Elijah and the Widow at Zarephath. In this context, the purpose is "to share your food with the hungry and to provide the poor wanderer with shelter"—to meet the humanitarian needs of others (Isa. 58:7). Warren Wiersbe states, "The worst sin toward our fellow creatures is not to hate them, but to be indifferent to them: that's the essence of inhumanity".[257] We are often so caught up in our own issues that we neglect, become apathetic or lack compassion towards those who struggle with the daily necessities of life. It's about denying ourselves of what we think we need so that we can use our resources to help them. Elijah announced that in Israel "there will be neither dew nor

---

[256] Paschall and Hobbs, eds., *The Teacher's Bible Commentary*, 204-05. Richards, *The Bible Reader's Companion*, electronic ed., 236.
[257] Wiersbe, *Be Determined*, 12.

rain in the next few years except at my word" (1 Kgs. 17:1) and he disappears into the desert where he is miraculously fed by ravens (vv. 2-6). When the Kerith Ravine dries up, God guides Elijah to the widow of Zarephath, a foreigner and a pagan who lived in Jezebel's own country and Elijah needs to depend upon her for refuge.

Elijah first meets the widow in the middle of the famine as she is about to prepare a last meal for herself and her son. Her faith is tested as he asks her to prepare some bread for him first, which she willingly does. The word that Elijah speaks over her and her son that "the jar of flour will not be used up and the jug of oil will not run dry until the day the LORD sends rain on the land" (1 Kgs. 17:14). Franklin states in reference to connecting fasting with poverty, health and healing: "fasting will break poverty from your life"; "when fasting is a lifestyle, poverty will not be" and "health and healing will follow fasting".[258]

Not only is the widow and her son blessed with food, but when her son suddenly dies and she assumes that God is punishing her for some secret sin, Elijah "stretched himself out on the boy three times" (1 Kgs. 17:21) and life returns to his body. As a result, the widow declares her faith in God and Elijah as a true messenger from God. A close parallel to this Elijah account is that of a widow of one of the sons of a prophet is sustained by "a small jar of olive oil" (2 Kgs. 4:2; cf. 4:42-44; Mt. 14:13-21; 15:32-38; Mk. 6:30-44; Lk. 9:10-17; Jn. 6:1-14). The Lord directing Elijah to the widow of Zarephath and her obedience to the Lord helped to relieve her hunger.[259]

The Widow's Fast can also be seen in the Gospel According to Luke,

> There was also a prophetess, Anna, the daughter of Phanuel, of the tribe of Asher. She was very old; she had lived with her husband seven years after her marriage, and then was a widow until she was eighty-four. She never left the temple but worshiped night and day, fasting and praying (Lk. 2:36-37).

Here we see the "prophetess, Anna, the daughter of Phanuel[260], of the tribe of Asher" whose name means "grace". Of the forty-three references to women in the Gospel According to Luke, and of the twelve widows in Scripture[261], Luke writes about three of them (Lk. 2:36-40; 7:11-15; 21:1-4). Therefore, there is an emphasis on the role of women in the Gospel of Luke. Widows in Scripture are presented as constantly struggling, often neglected, and exploited contrary to the law, "do not take advantage of a widow or an orphan" (Ex. 22:22); God "defends the cause of the fatherless and the widow" (Deut. 10:18); "plead the case of the widow" (Isa. 1:17). The prophetess Anna was a witness to the messianic identity of

---

[258] Franklin, *Fasting*, 71, 90.

[259] Knowles, *The Bible Guide*, 155-56. Richards, *The Bible Reader's Companion*, 234. "1 Kings 17:8", In Mays, ed., *Harper's Bible Commentary*. Towns, *Fasting for Spiritual Breakthrough*, 22.

[260] Anna's father's name Phanuel (*Phanuēl* in Greek) comes from *Penuel* in Hebrew, meaning "face of God". Thoralf Gilbrant, ed., *The Complete Biblical Library Commentary, Luke* (Springfield, IL: World Library Press, Inc., WORDsearch CROSS e-book, 1988), 79.

[261] Some of these prophetesses include: Miriam (Ex. 15:20), Deborah (Jdg. 4:4), Hulduh (2 Kgs. 22:14), Noadiah (Neh. 6:14), and the wife of Isaiah (Isa. 8:3). The evangelist Philip had four daughters who were prophetesses (Acts 21:8-9). Wiersbe, *The Bible Exposition Commentary*, Vol. 1, 177-79.

Jesus who "never left the temple but worshiped night and day, fasting and praying". She had the gift of declaring and interpreting God's message and spread the Gospel to those who were expecting the redemption of Israel (cf. Lk. 2:25).[262]

When we take a close look at the text, Anna was married seven years before she became a widow and then remained a widow and celibate until she was eighty-four years old. When we see that most Jewish women married in their mid-teens and if Anna married at this age then she would be over 100 years old. Women like Anna, who maintained a life of celibacy after they became a widow and were devoted to God were highly-esteemed among the Jewish population and early Christian church (1 Cor. 7:7-8; 1 Tim. 5:5). In the Book of Acts, Luke highlights fasting and prayer in relation to divine visitations and revelations and in his gospel account describes a persistent widow as an example of constant prayer (18:1-8).

> While they were worshiping the Lord and fasting, the Holy Spirit said, "Set apart for me Barnabas and Saul for the work to which I have called them". So after they had fasted and prayed, they placed their hands on them and sent them off (Acts 13:2-3; cf. 9:9, 11).

Luke states, "she never left the temple but worshiped night and day, fasting and praying" which probably should not be taken literally. However, it probably refers to the habitual frequency of being at the temple, daily worship, and devotion to the Lord (cf. "they earnestly serve God day and night", Acts 26:7).[263]

Please refer to *Fasting: Unlocking Spiritual Power and Breakthrough, Personal Reflections* under the heading "The Widow's Fast" to complete the Personal Reflections section of this study.

The Apostle Paul Fast

> Meanwhile, Saul was still breathing out murderous threats against the Lord's disciples. He went to the high priest and asked him for letters to the synagogues in Damascus, so that if he found any there who belonged to the Way, whether men or women, he might take them as prisoners to Jerusalem. As he neared Damascus on his journey, suddenly a light from heaven flashed around him. He fell to the ground and heard a voice say to him, "Saul, Saul, why do you persecute me?" "Who are you, Lord?" Saul asked. "I am Jesus, whom you are persecuting", he replied. "Now get up and go into the city, and you will be told what you must do". The men traveling with Saul stood there speechless; they heard the sound but did not see anyone. Saul got up from the ground, but when he opened his eyes he could see nothing. So they led him by the hand into Damascus. For three days he was blind, and did not eat or drink anything (Acts 9:1-9).

Isaiah's discourse on true fasting also describes the Apostle Paul Fast "Then your light will break forth like the dawn" (Isa. 58:8). The purpose here is to help us to make crucial decisions through bringing a clearer perspective to the situation. The emphasis here is that Paul "for three days he was blind, and did

---

[262] Wiersbe, *The Bible Exposition Commentary*, Vol. 1, 177-79. Ἄννα *Anna* "449", In Gilbrant, ed., *The Complete Biblical Library Greek-English Dictionary, Alpha-Gamma.* Φανουήλ *Phanouēl* "5161", In Gilbrant, ed., *The Complete Biblical Library Greek-English Dictionary, Sigma-Omega.*

[263] Gilbrant, ed., *The Complete Biblical Library Commentary, Luke*, 79.

not eat or drink anything" (v. 9). The conversion of Saul[264], Σαῦλος *Saulos*, is probably one of the most important events in the church since Pentecost—this is seen as Luke the Physician records this event three times in the Book of Acts (chs. 9, 22, 26). Paul's conversion prepares the readers for the gospel being preached to the Gentiles (ch. 10; Gal. 2:8; Eph. 3:8) was preceded by the Apostle Peter's evangelization of Cornelius' household (ch. 10).

It was after the stoning and death of Stephen that "Saul began to destroy the church. Going from house to house, he dragged off men and women and put them in prison" (Acts 8:3). Saul was a zealous and determined man to uphold what he believed to be true and would honour God, which led him to breathe "murderous threats against the Lord's disciples" (Acts 9:1). After he received healing for his blindness, he began to realize that his actions against Jesus and His church were blasphemous. It was during these three days that the light and love of Jesus was shone upon his heart, transforming his life.[265]

In classical Greek, the verb ἐμπνέω *empneō* (v. 1) means to "blow into or upon" or it can mean "to inspire", or "to create an atmosphere of violence" breathing out threatenings and slaughter against the disciples" in order to influence others to join Saul in his persecution of the Christians.[266] The Greek noun ἀπειλή *apeilē* (v. 1) used here is one of Satan's strongest weapons against the Church since he as "the prince of this world" (Jn. 12:31; 2 Cor. 4:4) can frighten and paralyze Christians and the propagation of the gospel. In a sense, Saul was used by Satan to attempt to bring Christianity to an end, but the Lord put an end to Saul's persecution.[267]

The Apostle Paul's Damascus Road encounter with Jesus Christ also relates to the martyrdom of Stephen since his testimony enraged Saul to completely annihilate Christianity (Acts 8:1-3). If what Stephen was saying was true then the Law was in jeopardy, which incited Saul to extinguish any witness of Jesus Christ (cf. Gal. 1:13; Phil. 3:6). After Saul's encounter with the Lord, Saul the persecutor became Paul the Apostle of Jesus Christ and his background and qualifications suited him eminently for the work that the Lord had called him to fulfill:

1. Paul was very well acquainted with Jewish culture and language (Acts 21:40; Phil. 3:5) and Greek culture and its philosophies (Acts 17:22-31; Tit. 1:12);
2. Paul was a Roman citizen (Acts 16:37; 22:23-29; 25:10-12);
3. He was educated and skilled in Jewish theology (Gal. 1:14);
4. Paul was skilled in trade and commerce and could support himself (Acts 18:3; 1 Cor. 9:4-18; 2 Cor. 11:7-11; 1 Th. 2:9; 2 Th. 3:8);

---

[264] Saul's conversion is related three times in Acts, Acts 9, and in two speeches of Paul; before a Jewish crowd in the temple yard (Acts 22:3-21), and in his address to King Agrippa (Acts 26:2-23). There are minor differences between the three accounts, mainly due to the different audiences to whom they were addressed. Dockery, Butler, Church et al., *Holman Bible Handbook*, 643.

[265] Thoralf Gilbrant, ed., *The Complete Biblical Library Commentary, Acts*, (Springfield, IL: wordseacrh, Inc., WORDsearch CROSS e-book, 1988), 213.

[266] ἐμπνέω *empneō* "1693", In Gilbrant, ed., *The Complete Biblical Library Greek-English Dictionary, Delta-Epsilon*.

[267] ἀπειλή *apeilē* "543", In Gilbrant, ed., *The Complete Biblical Library Greek-English Dictionary, Alpha-Gamma*.

5. God gave him zeal, leadership qualities, and theological insight.[268]

Paul, becoming blind, prayed and fasted—"did not eat or drink anything" (Acts 9:9)—for three days seeking God's will for his life (Acts 9:1-22). The possible reason why Paul did not eat or drink was because he was overwhelmed with his spiritual state of being. His past life of persecuting the Christians, his great sins, the dramatic change in worldview and vision, and possible grief over his loss of sight would have indisposed him to not "eat or drink anything". Overwhelming grief often produces this effect and produces involuntary fasting. This whole incident on the road to Damascus had left Paul in a state of no assurance of forgiveness, arrested, alarmed, and convinced that Jesus is the Messiah, that he still had no comfort. Being in a state of darkness was necessary to humble him, preparing him for the ministry to which the Lord would call him. The comfort and peace that Paul sought would only come when he submitted himself to the Lord. We can learn from Paul that rebelling and resisting the Lord only leaves us in a state of restlessness, perplexity, and a lack of peace.

Consequently, this allowed the Holy Spirit to reveal Jesus to his heart, soul, and mind in a powerful way. He probably realized that his perception of Jesus and those who followed Him was wrong, but even more so when he considered his interpretation of the Old Testament and its prophecies. Until his encounter, he had depended upon who he was and what he could do (cf. Phil. 3:5-6) and now his focus needed to be upon the Lord and not upon himself.

Please refer to *Fasting: Unlocking Spiritual Power and Breakthrough, Personal Reflections* under the heading "The Apostle Paul Fast" to complete the Personal Reflections section of this study.

The Daniel Fast

The chief official gave them new names: to Daniel, the name Belteshazzar; to Hananiah, Shadrach; to Mishael, Meshach; and to Azariah, Abednego. But Daniel resolved not to defile himself with the royal food and wine, and he asked the chief official for permission not to defile himself this way. Now God had caused the official to show favor and compassion to Daniel, but the official told Daniel, "I am afraid of my lord the king, who has assigned your food and drink. Why should he see you looking worse than the other young men your age? The king would then have my head because of you". Daniel then said to the guard whom the chief official had appointed over Daniel, Hananiah, Mishael and Azariah, "Please test your servants for ten days: Give us nothing but vegetables to eat and water to drink. Then compare our appearance with that of the young men who eat the royal food, and treat your servants in accordance with what you see". So he agreed to this and tested them for ten days. At the end of the ten days they looked healthier and better nourished than any of the young men who ate the royal food. So the guard took away their choice food and the wine they were to drink and gave them vegetables instead. To these four young men God gave knowledge and understanding of all kinds of literature and learning. And Daniel could understand visions and dreams of all kinds (Dan. 1:7-17).

---

[268] Walvoord and Zuck, eds., *The Bible Knowledge Commentary*, Vol. 2, 375. Knowles, *The Bible Guide*, 545. Towns, *Fasting for Spiritual Breakthrough*, 21. "Acts 9:9", In Albert Barnes, *Notes on the New Testament Explanatory and Practical*. Robert Frew, ed (WORD*search* CROSS e-book, 2012).

The Daniel Fast is the first recorded fast in the Book of Daniel and is different from the other fasts listed in Isaiah 58 since it involves abstinence from certain types of food, while consuming only "vegetables to eat and water to drink". The purpose of the Daniel Fast is for our "healing to quickly appear" (Isa. 58:8), to seek God's favor, and improve health and/or receive healing. The key verse is, "But Daniel resolved not to defile himself with the royal food and wine, and he asked the chief official for permission not to defile himself this way" (Dan. 1:8). The prophet Daniel, a young man and three of his Hebrew captives were taught Babylonian customs and prepared to serve in the court. However, they turned down the king's diet of wine and rich foods and he speaks with the chief official about an alternative diet, one that would not defile them by eating food offered to the Babylonian gods. This official becomes concerned with their health by only eating vegetables and drinking water for ten days. In following this fast, "they looked healthier and better nourished than any of the young men who ate the royal food" (1:15).[269]

The prophet Isaiah states that through fasting "your healing will quickly appear" (Isa. 58:8). Isaiah states that if the people demonstrated righteousness, which was revealed in an outward act of justice and mercy, the Lord promised that their "light will rise in the darkness" (Isa. 58:10) a picture of the light of God's blessing or "to break out" (cf. Deut. 28:1-14). The reference to healing speaks of spiritual restoration and righteousness speaks of high standards, protection from enemy attack, and answer to prayer. Moreover, if the people would literally remove from their midst "the yoke of oppression", sending out judgment "the pointing finger", the speaking of wickedness "malicious talk",

> if you spend yourselves in behalf of the hungry and satisfy the needs of the oppressed, then your light will rise break forth in the darkness, and your night will like the noonday (Isa. 58:9-10; cf. Ps. 112:4).

The Lord promises divine guidance, strengthening in their body and soul, provision for both natural and spiritual needs, and physical restoration "rebuild the ancient ruins".[270]

Scripture does not demand God's people to follow the Daniel Fast. This is a narrative that describes a young man's personal convictions regarding diet, even though it is a healthier way of eating. By choosing an alternative diet, he did not assimilate himself into the Babylonian culture, but separated himself unto God. Daniel proposed that they be given "vegetables" זֵרֹעִים *zfirō 'im* meaning "herbs" or "garden plants" grown from cultivated seeds to eat and "water to drink" (v. 12). This is Daniel's first recorded exercise of faith, which prepared him for the even greater testings that were to follow.[271]

---

[269] Towns, *Fasting for Spiritual Breakthrough*, 22-23.

[270] Walvoord and Zuck, eds., *The Bible Knowledge Commentary*, Vol. 1, 1113. זָרַח *zārach* "2311", In Gilbrant, ed., *The Complete Biblical Library Hebrew-English Dictionary, Gimel-Zayin*.

[271] זֵרֹעִים *zfirō 'im* "2322", In Gilbrant, ed., *The Complete Biblical Library Hebrew-English Dictionary, Gimel-Zayin*. Gaebelein, ed., *The Expositor's Bible Commentary, Volume 7*, 36.

Daniel's second recorded fast is when he read Jeremiah's prophecy and prayed for Judah's sins (cf. 2 Chr. 36:21; Jer. 29:10; Zech. 1:12; 7:5). He prayed and fasted to "encourage" the prophesied Israelite release from captivity[272] in Babylon.

> In the first year of Darius son of Xerxes (a Mede by descent), who was made ruler over the Babylonian kingdom—in the first year of his reign, I, Daniel, understood from the Scriptures, according to the word of the LORD given to Jeremiah the prophet, that the desolation of Jerusalem would last seventy years. So I turned to the Lord God and pleaded with him in prayer and petition, in fasting, and in sackcloth and ashes. I prayed to the LORD my God and confessed: "Lord, the great and awesome God, who keeps his covenant of love with those who love him and keep his commandments, we have sinned and done wrong (Dan. 9:1-5).

The following events occurred during the first year of the reign of Darius the Mede, approximately 539 BC and 66 years after Daniel had been exiled. The conquest of the Babylonian kingdom by the Medo-Persians had been revealed to Belshazzar through Daniel's interpretation of the writing on the wall (5:25-28, 30). The Babylonian conquest had set the stage for the deliverance of the Jews who had been in captivity from Nebuchadnezzar's first invasion of Jerusalem in 605 BC. The prophet Jeremiah not only prophesied the conquest but also that their captivity that would last 70 years,

> This whole country will become a desolate wasteland, and these nations will serve the king of Babylon seventy years. "But when the seventy years are fulfilled, I will punish the king of Babylon and his nation, the land of the Babylonians, for their guilt", declares the LORD, "and will make it desolate forever" (Jer. 25:11-12).

Daniel, encouraged by Darius' success, searched the Scriptures to comprehend the events that had taken place meant that the end of the 70-year captivity was soon approaching, leading to a significant event in the history of the Jews.[273]

This context shows how diligent Daniel was in studying Scripture and building his spiritual life of the known Scriptures of the time. Daniel presents the written and inspired prophetic word of Jeremiah as trustworthy and dependable—who had died a few decades earlier, probably as a Jewish martyr in the refugee colony of Tahpanhes, Egypt.[274] As Daniel read Jeremiah 25:11-13, it was clear that God had allowed His people Israel to remain in captivity for a period of seventy years (v. 2), and at the end of this time, Babylon would fall to the judgment of God. The words of Jeremiah 29:10-14 had grabbed the attention of Daniel,

> This is what the LORD says: "When seventy years are completed for Babylon, I will come to you and fulfill my good promise to bring you back to this place. For I know the plans I have for you", declares the LORD, "plans to prosper you and not to harm you, plans to give you hope and a

---

[272] Scripture sometimes speaks of "captivity" as referring to the restoration of the fortunes of the people of God (cf. Jer. 30:3; 31:23; 33:7)

[273] Walvoord and Zuck, eds., *The Bible Knowledge Commentary*, Vol. 1, 1359-60. Towns, *Fasting for Spiritual Breakthrough*, 22-23.

[274] "Jeremiah", In Wood and Marshall, *New Bible Dictionary*, 552.

future. Then you will call on me and come and pray to me, and I will listen to you. You will seek me and find me when you seek me with all your heart. I will be found by you", declares the LORD, "and will bring you back from captivity. I will gather you from all the nations and places where I have banished you", declares the LORD, "and will bring you back to the place from which I carried you into exile" (Jer. 29:10-14).

Daniel corporately identifies and confesses the sin of his people as their intercessory priest and accepts the punishment for their iniquity, which typifies Jesus the Messiah, the Sin-bearer and Great Intercessor. He pleads with God "in prayer and petition, in fasting, and in sackcloth and ashes". Daniel begins his prayer[275] with praise addressing God as "great and awesome", confessing the sin, wickedness, rebellion, and shame of the people, and the just punishment that God had brought upon them. [276]

Daniel's study of the Scriptures led him to turn to God and to pray a prayer of confession (vv. 3-14) and petition (vv. 15-19), with fasting. Wearing sackcloth and/or ashes was evidence of mourning in grief or repentance (cf. Gen. 37:34; Neh. 9:1; Est. 4:1, 3; Isa. 58:5; Jer. 49:3; Eze. 7:18; Joel 1:8; Mt. 11:21). Daniel begins by saying "So I turned to the Lord God" a formal beginning establishing the turning away from everything to focus on his prayer to the Lord—implying faith, devotion and worship. Daniel pleads with the Lord in prayer using the noun תְּפִלָּה *tephillāh* which is used seventy-seven times in the Old Testament meaning "to intervene", or "to interpose" and is used only in reference to petitions to the God of Israel. Daniel's prayer for God to end the Babylonian Exile was miraculously answered by the arrival of Gabriel the archangel with God's answer (Dan. 9:3, 17, 21).[277]

He also uses the plural form of the noun תַּחֲנוּן *tachănûn* from *chānan* meaning "to show favor", "to be gracious" resulting from "the outpourings of a troubled soul". It illustrates the level of Daniel's contrition for the corporate sins of his people, a parallel to "weeping" (Jer. 3:21; 31:9), and describes his extended period of fasting with sackcloth and ashes (Dan. 9:3, 17f., 23).[278] He next uses the noun for fasting צוֹם *tsôm* connected with the nouns for sackcloth שַׂק *saq* and ashes אֵפֶר *'fipher* to illustrate that[279]

---

[275] This prayer, with its elements of ascription, confession, and petition, closely resembles three other long prose prayers, Ezra 9:6-15; Nehemiah 1:5-11; and 9:6-37. "Daniel 9:1-27", In Mays, ed., *Harper's Bible Commentary*.

[276] "Daniel 9:1-27", In Jamieson, Fausset, and Brown, *Commentary Critical and Explanatory on the Whole Bible*. Walvoord and Zuck, eds., *The Bible Knowledge Commentary*, Vol. 1, 1359-60.

[277] תְּפִלָּה *tephillāh* "8940", In Gilbrant, ed., *The Complete Biblical Library Hebrew-English Dictionary, Sin-Taw*.

[278] It occurs eight times in the Psalms, almost always in the phrase "my supplications" (Ps. 28:2, 6; 31:22; 86:6; 116:1; 130:2; 140:6; 143:1).

[279] Walvoord and Zuck, eds., *The Bible Knowledge Commentary*, Vol. 1, 1359-60. תַּחֲנוּן *tachănûn* "8800", In Gilbrant, ed., *The Complete Biblical Library Hebrew-English Dictionary, Sin-Taw*. צוֹם *tsôm* "6948", In Gilbrant, ed., *The Complete Biblical Library Hebrew-English Dictionary, Pe-Resh*. שַׂק *saq* "8012", In Gilbrant, ed., *The Complete Biblical Library Hebrew-English Dictionary, Sin-Taw*. אֵפֶר *'fipher* "684", In Gilbrant, ed., *The Complete Biblical Library Hebrew-English Dictionary, Aleph-Beth*. John F. Walvoord, *Daniel: The Key to Prophetic Revelation* (Chicago, IL: Moody Press, 1989), 205-06.

it is only as we ourselves are truly humbled before God that we can humble ourselves for His people. Through grace, and the power of the Holy Spirit, we must put ourselves morally into the circumstances of those whose case we desire to present to God. The state of the people required prayer and supplications, with fasting, sackcloth, and ashes, and the prophet as one of them, understanding their condition, took this ground in the presence of God.[280]

The third recorded fast in Daniel is at the time of his vision of a man (Dan. 10:1-13) the climactic experience of the Book of Daniel. Daniel fasted as he prayed over a mysterious vision God had given him seeking solace for the great pressure he felt because of a dream he had experienced.

In the third year of Cyrus king of Persia, a revelation was given to Daniel (who was called Belteshazzar). Its message was true and it concerned a great war. The understanding of the message came to him in a vision. At that time I, Daniel, mourned for three weeks. I ate no choice food; no meat or wine touched my lips; and I used no lotions at all until the three weeks were over (Dan. 10:1-3).

In Daniel's final vision, approximately 536 BC, the exiles had already returned from Babylon, occupied Jerusalem, and as a nation seemed to live in peace, and had begun to rebuild the temple in Jerusalem. However, this vision crushed Israel's hope of lasting peace and freedom since "its message was true and it concerned a great war". Daniel uses the verb אָבַל *'āval* "mourned" which emphasizes an "outward behavior as contrasted with inner feelings (cf. Gen. 37:34; 1 Sam. 16:1; 2 Sam. 13:31-37; 14:2; Neh. 1:4; Dan. 10:2)". This "mourning for the dead" included weeping, wearing sackcloth with ashes, prostrating oneself, and shaving their head and beard.[281] Daniel ate "no choice food" לֶחֶם חֲמֻדֹות *leḥem ḥămudôt* meaning "the dainties of the king's table" or "bread of pleasures, of desires", "all desirable food" "personal grooming, such as fragrant oil on his hair or body". Daniel was consumed with interceding for his people and a guarantee that the Israelites would survive and fulfill God's mission as His witnesses to the surrounding nations with honour and faithfulness.[282]

Daniel did not even use lotions which was a Jewish sign of fasting, "I used no lotions at all until the three weeks were over" (Dan. 10:3). He uses the verb סוּךְ *sûkh* meaning "to anoint" or "to incite", which refers to Daniel not anointing himself during his twenty-one day fast. In most of occurrences in the Old Testament, it refers to anointing oneself with oil for cosmetic purposes, primarily after washing. When a person did not anoint themselves, it was a sign of mourning (2 Sam. 12:20; 14:2).

The pleasure of anointing the body with oil was highly esteemed among the ancients. It is impossible to fail to recognize, in this passage, the origin of the Essenian discipline. The Essenes abstained, from flesh, from wine, and from anointing themselves. Daniel thus abstained, as a sign

---

[280] "Daniel 9", In Edward Dennett, *Daniel the Prophet*, Rick Meyers, e-Sword, Version 10.2.1, 2000-2012, <http://www.e-sword.net>.

[281] אָבַל *'āval* "57", In Gilbrant, ed., *The Complete Biblical Library Hebrew-English Dictionary, Aleph-Beth.*

[282] Walvoord, *Daniel: The Key to Prophetic Revelation*, 240. Gaebelein, ed., *The Expositor's Bible Commentary, Volume 7*, 122. Walvoord and Zuck, eds., *The Bible Knowledge Commentary*, Vol. 1, 1365-66. Towns, *Fasting for Spiritual Breakthrough*, 22-23.

of sorrow for the *sin* of his people; they made this fast a perpetual discipline. They waited for the salvation of Israel, and endeavoured, by fasting, to hasten the coming of the Lord. The converse of this, that Daniel's fast is derived from the Essene discipline, is not to be thought of. It is a sign of a later development, when such practices of self-denial, from being the incidents of a life which occur on special occasions, become its rule.[283]

In the Book of Ruth, Naomi encouraged Ruth to bathe and anoint herself before she approached Boaz, her kinsmen redeemer (Ruth 3:3). The lack of oil also demonstrated divine judgment, which is seen as the prophets warned the people not to use oil or anoint themselves due to the deprivation associated with the Lord's coming judgment.[284]

> You will have olive trees throughout your country but you will not use the oil, because the olives will drop off (Deut. 28:40).

> You will plant but not harvest; you will press olives but not use the oil, you will crush grapes but not drink the wine (Mic. 6:15).

The result of the Daniel Fast is that his prayers and intercessions ascended quickly before the throne of God and the demonic principalities that ruled over the Babylonian nation were overcome by the forces of God. The passage speaks of spiritual warfare in the heavenlies between Satan's spirits and the angels of God. It was through Daniel's fasting that helped determine the ultimate outcome. Daniel was a man of great revelation, visions, signs and wonders. As a result of his extended fast, he received one of the most amazing chapters of revelation found in all of Scripture. Daniel's success was the result of understanding and operating in the principle of fasting.

Please refer to *Fasting: Unlocking Spiritual Power and Breakthrough, Personal Reflections* under the heading "The Daniel Fast" to complete the Personal Reflections section of this study.

The King Darius Fast

The purpose of the King Darius Fast is seen in his lack of wisdom, discernment, and subsequent emotional distress as he worries over Daniel's possible fate in the lion's den. In this Fast we can see "injustice", "cords of yoke" (government officials) setup against Daniel and in the end the oppressed are set free and every yoke is broken (Isa. 58:6).

> So the king gave the order, and they brought Daniel and threw him into the lions' den. The king said to Daniel, "May your God, whom you serve continually, rescue you!" A stone was brought and placed over the mouth of the den, and the king sealed it with his own signet ring and with the rings of his nobles, so that Daniel's situation might not be changed. Then the king returned to his palace and spent the night without eating and without any entertainment being brought to him. And he could not sleep. At the first light of dawn, the king got up and hurried to the lions' den. When he came near the den, he called to Daniel in an anguished voice, "Daniel, servant of the

---

[283] "Daniel 10:3", In Joseph S. Exell and Henry D. M. Spence-Jones, *The Complete Pulpit Commentary*, Rick Meyers, e-Sword, Version 10.2.1, 2000-2012, <http://www.e-sword.net>.

[284] סוּךְ *sûkh* "5665", In Gilbrant, ed., *The Complete Biblical Library Hebrew-English Dictionary, Nun-Ayin.*

living God, has your God, whom you serve continually, been able to rescue you from the lions?" Daniel answered, "May the king live forever! My God sent his angel, and he shut the mouths of the lions. They have not hurt me, because I was found innocent in his sight. Nor have I ever done any wrong before you, Your Majesty". The king was overjoyed and gave orders to lift Daniel out of the den. And when Daniel was lifted from the den, no wound was found on him, because he had trusted in his God (Dan. 6:16-23).

When King Darius assumed the throne (Dan. 5:30), one of his first duties was to restructure the conquered kingdom of Babylon. He appointed "120 satraps[285] to rule throughout the kingdom, with three administrators over them, one of whom was Daniel" (Dan. 6:1-2). Daniel was an exceptional administrator since he had 39 years' experience under the leadership of Nebuchadnezzar (2:48). This created friction between himself and the other two administrators and 120 satraps.[286] Even though Daniel knew that the decree that King Darius had signed,

> The royal administrators, prefects, satraps, advisers and governors have all agreed that the king should issue an edict and enforce the decree that anyone who prays to any god or man during the next thirty days, except to you, O king, shall be thrown into the lions' den. Now, Your Majesty, issue the decree and put it in writing so that it cannot be altered—in accordance with the law of the Medes and Persians, which cannot be repealed". So King Darius put the decree in writing. Now when Daniel learned that the decree had been published, he went home to his upstairs room where the windows opened toward Jerusalem. Three times a day he got down on his knees and prayed, giving thanks to his God, just as he had done before (Dan. 6:7-10).

Daniel was so successful that he provoked the other administrators and officials since he was faithful to God they conspired to have him executed for treason. They convinced King Darius to issue a decree ordering his subjects to worship him exclusively for one month and anyone violating this decree would be thrown into the lion's den. Daniel willingly defied the decree and openly prayed to the Lord as was his custom, and the conspirators reported him to the king. King Darius then realized that he had been deceived sought to pardon Daniel of guilt, but the administrator and officials reminded the king that

---

[285] Herodotus states that Darius I (521-486 BC) reorganized the empire into a total of twenty satrapies and placed a satrap "protector of the kingdom/kingship" in charge of each province, in order to bring more rigorous method to taxation and control throughout his vast empire. The satrap, often a close relative of the king, was generally appointed and removed by him. The satrap's court was modeled on that of the great king. Usually a wealthy man in his own right, he regularly spent of his own resources in the service of government while also having command over royal government resources within his satrapy. Generally the satrap's power of command extended over both civil and military affairs, but in some cases major fortresses and their garrisons were under commanders who reported directly to the Great King. Other means were available to the king for independently monitoring the satrap's activities. The "king's scribes" for example, regularly reported back to the court. There were also officials called "the eyes and ears of the king", who are assumed to have provided the central government with information on events in the provinces. Herodotus of Halicarnassus (484-425 BC), *The Histories*, <http://www. swartzentrover.com/cotor/E-Books/misc/Herodotus/THindex.htm>, 3.89ff. Accessed on November 28, 2013.

[286] Walvoord and Zuck, eds., *The Bible Knowledge Commentary*, Vol. 1, 1347-48.

"according to the law of the Medes and Persians no decree or edict that the king issues can be changed" (6:15).[287]

King Darius was distressed and tormented by his actions that "the king returned to his palace and spent the night without eating and without any entertainment being brought to him. And he could not sleep" (6:18). King Darius' last words to Daniel expressed hope that the God that Daniel served would rescue him from the lions. The king professed faith greater than his own personal faith.

> No one is more miserable than the person who presumptuously professes a faith that deep in his heart he does not believe in. The king's fasting and sleeplessness were not caused by diligent seeking of the true God, but by remorse and heart-sick grief over Daniel's being thrown into the lions' den. Despair is implied.[288]

Darius anxiously could not sleep the entire night and without eating breakfast he quickly went to the lion's den to see if Daniel was still alive, since he knew that Daniel had faith in God to deliver him. When he approached the lion's den he stated,

> A stone was brought and placed over the mouth of the den, and the king sealed it with his own signet ring and with the rings of his nobles, so that Daniel's situation might not be changed. Then the king returned to his palace and spent the night without eating and without any entertainment being brought to him. And he could not sleep. At the first light of dawn, the king got up and hurried to the lions' den. When he came near the den, he called to Daniel in an anguished voice, "Daniel, servant of the living God, has your God, whom you serve continually, been able to rescue you from the lions? (Dan. 6:17-20).

Darius probably thought that if Daniel had been killed that where could he find such a faithful and devoted administrator such as Daniel. It is interesting that Darius refers to Daniel, as the "servant of the living God", to see if his God was really alive or was he an unproved belief like the deities that the non-Jews worshipped. To Darius, if God really existed He would of course deliver His servant from the lions, who remained faithful to God even when it could have cost him his life.[289] This is clearly a fast due to emotional distress.[290]

Please refer to *Fasting: Unlocking Spiritual Power and Breakthrough, Personal Reflections* under the heading "The King Darius Fast" to complete the Personal Reflections section of this study.

---

[287] "Daniel 6:1-28", In Dockery, ed., In *Holman Concise Bible Commentary*, 335. Towns, *Fasting for Spiritual Breakthrough*, 22-23.

[288] "Daniel 6:18", In Thoralf Gilbrant, ed., *The Complete Biblical Library Commentary, Daniel-Malachi* (Springfield, IL: World Library Press, Inc., WORDsearch CROSS e-book), 1996.

[289] Gaebelein, ed., *The Expositor's Bible Commentary, Volume 7*, 81-82. "Daniel 6:18", In Gilbrant, ed., *The Complete Biblical Library Commentary, Daniel-Malachi*.

[290] Please refer to the section entitled "Fasting Due to Emotional Distress - (Dan. 6:18-24; Mt. 15:32; 2 Cor. 6:5; 11:27)".

The John the Baptist Fast

Isaiah's discourse on true fasting also describes the John the Baptist Fast (Mt. 3:4-6) "then your righteousness will go before you" (Isa. 58:8). The purpose of this fast is to bring power to the testimony of Jesus Christ in our lives and, therefore, empower us to become a true witness and influence for others to receive salvation through Jesus Christ.

> John's clothes were made of camel's hair, and he had a leather belt around his waist. His food was locusts and wild honey. People went out to him from Jerusalem and all Judea and the whole region of the Jordan. Confessing their sins, they were baptized by him in the Jordan River (Mt. 3:4-6).

> He will be a joy and delight to you, and many will rejoice because of his birth, for he will be great in the sight of the Lord. He is never to take wine or other fermented drink, and he will be filled with the Holy Spirit even before he is born. He will bring back many of the people of Israel to the Lord their God. And he will go on before the Lord, in the spirit and power of Elijah, to turn the hearts of the parents to their children and the disobedient to the wisdom of the righteous—to make ready a people prepared for the Lord" (Lk. 1:14-17).

John the Baptist was Jesus' cousin who was called to fulfill the prophecies that one like Elijah would "prepare the way for the Lord" (Mt. 11:7-19). John became known as "the Baptist" because he called Jews to repent of their sin and rededicate their lives to God through water baptism, a sacrament reserved for Gentile proselytes to Judaism.

> In those days John the Baptist came, preaching in the wilderness of Judea and saying, "Repent, for the kingdom of heaven has come near". This is he who was spoken of through the prophet Isaiah: "A voice of one calling in the wilderness, 'Prepare the way for the Lord, make straight paths for him'" (Mt. 3:1-3).

John the Baptist, seen as the forerunner of Jesus Christ, took the Nazirite Vow, and devoted himself to fasting from wine and strong drink—and was set apart for a special mission. This lifestyle, not a choice fast of today, symbolizes separation from worldly practices. John the Baptist taught that a person's faith in Jesus Christ involves personal commitment without dependence upon ancestral lineage. John met Jesus on the banks of the Jordan River where Jesus asks John to baptize Him in water even though Jesus did not need to repent of sin and subsequently be water baptized. John hesitates since he knew that Jesus is the one whom Isaiah called Immanuel, "God with us" (Isa. 1:23).[291]

The clothes that John the Baptist wore are significant since they were made of a course rough texture or woven camel's hair, symbolizing the prophetic office—humble, ascetic, and driven by his calling and sense of mission (Zech. 13:4). His appearance would remind those who came in contact with him of the prophet Elijah (2 Kgs. 1:8; cf. Mal. 4:5), in contrast with the elegant clothing used by those in King Herod's court (Lk. 7:25).

---

[291] "Matthew", In Dockery, ed., In *Holman Concise Bible Commentary*, 406. Towns, *Fasting for Spiritual Breakthrough*, 23.

After John's messengers left, Jesus began to speak to the crowd about John: "What did you go out into the wilderness to see? A reed swayed by the wind? If not, what did you go out to see? A man dressed in fine clothes? No, those who wear expensive clothes and indulge in luxury are in palaces. But what did you go out to see? A prophet? Yes, I tell you, and more than a prophet. This is the one about whom it is written: "'I will send my messenger ahead of you, who will prepare your way before you', I tell you, among those born of women there is no one greater than John; yet the one who is least in the kingdom of God is greater than he" (Lk. 7:24-28).

John the Baptist diet of locusts ἀκρίς *akris*, is a rare noun in the New Testament (cf. Mk. 1:6; Rev. 9:3-10) and was common diet among the poor people of Arabia, Africa, and Syria. The symbolic use in Revelation 9:3-10 refers to fiery locusts seen by the Apostle John in an apocalyptic vision which tormented men who did not have the seal of God on their foreheads. John describes them as horses prepared for battle, gold crowns on their head, faces like men, hair like women, teeth like lions, breastplates of iron, and tails like scorpions. The Law of Moses referred to locusts as clean food (Lev. 11:21-22) and the people would remove everything but the meaty thorax, dried them and would eat the thorax only when food was low. However, John ate them as part of his regular diet. Both "locusts and wild honey" suggests a poor man accustomed to living in the wilderness, and connected with the prophets (Mt. 3:1; 11:8-9). Moreover, in Zechariah's day, false prophets would cloth themselves like true prophets in order to deceive people. But Elijah and John wore ascetic clothes and followed a strict diet which confirmed their message and rejected the idolatrous physical and spiritual softness of the false prophets.[292]

Please refer to *Fasting: Unlocking Spiritual Power and Breakthrough, Personal Reflections* under the heading "The John the Baptist Fast" to complete the Personal Reflections section of this study.

The Esther Fast

The final fast spoken in Isaiah 58 is the Esther Fast, "the glory of the LORD will be your rear guard" (Isa. 58:8). The purpose of the Esther Fast is to protect us from the attack of the devil.

When Esther's words were reported to Mordecai, he sent back this answer: "Do not think that because you are in the king's house you alone of all the Jews will escape. For if you remain silent at this time, relief and deliverance for the Jews will arise from another place, but you and your father's family will perish. And who knows but that you have come to your royal position for such a time as this?" Then Esther sent this reply to Mordecai: "Go, gather together all the Jews who are in Susa, and fast for me. Do not eat or drink for three days, night or day. I and my attendants will fast as you do. When this is done, I will go to the king, even though it is against the law. And if I perish, I perish". So Mordecai went away and carried out all of Esther's instructions (Est. 4:12-17).

The Esther Fast (אֶסְתֵּר תַּעֲנִית) is called so since it was commanded by her to prevent imminent annihilation of the Jews.

---

[292] ἀκρίς *akris* "198", In Gilbrant, ed., *The Complete Biblical Library Greek-English Dictionary, Alpha-Gamma*. Gilbrant, ed., *The Complete Biblical Library Commentary, Matthew*, 51. Gaebelein, ed., *The Expositor's Bible Commentary, Volume 8*, 102. Brand, Draper, England, *Holman Illustrated Bible Dictionary*, 257.

The Jews to this day keep this fast on the 13th of Adar, the day which was appointed for their extirpation, and which precedes the feast of Purim, because it was ordained both by Esther and Mordecai, that it should continue a national fast, to be observed annually in commemoration of that eventful day (cf. Est. 9:31). . . . But this festival has long since ceased to be celebrated, and as early as the ninth century of the Christian era we find that the fast of Esther was again duly observed . . . and it has continued ever since to be one of the fasts in the Jewish calendar.[293]

On this day, the Jews devotedly abstained from eating and drinking, introduce into their daily service reciting penitential psalms, and offer prayers composed especially for this occasion. If this date occurs on a Sabbath Day, the fast is observed on the preceding Friday, since fasting was not allowed on the Sabbath. Some Jews extend this to three days, based upon the example of Esther (Est. 4:6).

The context here is a series of narratives between Esther and Mordecai. In the first narrative (4:4), no words are spoken as Esther sends clothes to Mordecai, which he rejects, who along with all the Jews, had been mourning and fasting in sackcloth and ashes. Mordecai's spontaneous act of grief evidenced the solidarity of the Jews. The custom of sackcloth and ashes included prayers of confession and worship (1 Kgs. 21:27-29; Neh. 9:1-3; Dan. 9:3). The second narrative (4:5-9) is both an oral and written message sent from Mordecai to Esther, but the words are not reported. The third narrative (4:10-17) is a dialogue between Esther and Mordecai. The key verses in the Book of Esther are verses 13-14 and the only time that Mordecai's words are recorded in direct speech. Elsewhere, Mordecai's words are only referred to indirectly.

This narrative moves from ignorance to understanding to decision and even though Esther initiates the dialogue between her and Mordecai, his words hold equal importance since he informs Esther of Haman's deception of King Ahasuerus (Xerxes) the King of Persia and his decision to annihilate the Jews because Mordecai refused to bow before him. He challenges her to risk her life to approach the king without notice, and convinces her to act courageously. In order to carry out her bold action to save her people, she must have the support of all the Jews, expressed in an exceptionally rigorous fasting—balanced against the task at hand. Mordecai warns Esther, "For if you remain silent at this time, relief and deliverance for the Jews will arise from another place" (v. 14). Esther had risen in royal status and even this could not protect her against the king's edict,

Hathach went back and reported to Esther what Mordecai had said. Then she instructed him to say to Mordecai, "All the king's officials and the people of the royal provinces know that for any man or woman who approaches the king in the inner court without being summoned the king has but one law: that he be put to death. The only exception to this is for the king to extend the gold scepter to him and spare his life. But thirty days have passed since I was called to go to the king". When Esther's words were reported to Mordecai, he sent back this answer: "Do not think that because you are in the king's house you alone of all the Jews will escape. For if you remain silent at this time, relief and deliverance for the Jews will arise from another place, but you and your father's family will perish. And who knows but that you have come to royal position for such a time as this?" Then Esther sent this reply to Mordecai: "Go, gather together all the Jews who are

[293] "Fast", In M'Clintock and Strong, eds., *Cyclopedia of Biblical and Ecclesiastical Literature*, <http://www.e-sword.net>.

in Susa, and fast for me. Do not eat or drink for three days, night or day. I and my maids will fast as you do. When this is done, I will go to the king, even though it is against the law. And if I perish, I perish". So Mordecai went away and carried out all of Esther's instructions (Est. 4:9-17).

Mordecai asks a question that has become the *locus classicus* of the doctrine of providence—the key to understanding the Book of Esther, "who knows but that you have come to your royal position for such a time as this?" Esther had two options, to either risk her own death or remain silent and risk the death of all Jews, including herself. If she failed, "relief and deliverance for the Jews will arise from another place". Esther's faith rose to the occasion and trusted in God, which became the turning point in the fate of her people, the Jews. This is seen as she requested an Absolute Fast of all Jews (Ezra 8:21-23; cf. Acts 13:3; 14:23). Her response to Mordecai was with courage and confidence in God's will for His people, "If I perish, I perish" (4:16; cf. Dan. 3:16-18). [294] Herodotus of Halicarnassus, in *The Histories*, mentions that anyone who approaches the king unannounced would be put to death, except if he raised his golden scepter to them. He also mentions that a person could send a letter asking for an audience. [295]

The final fast seen in Esther refers to the establishment of the Feast of Purim (Est. 9:20-32). [296]

> So Queen Esther, daughter of Abihail, along with Mordecai the Jew, wrote with full authority to confirm this second letter concerning Purim. And Mordecai sent letters to all the Jews in the 127 provinces of the kingdom of Xerxes—words of goodwill and assurance—to establish these days of Purim at their designated times, as Mordecai the Jew and Queen Esther had decreed for them, and as they had established for themselves and their descendants in regard to their times of fasting and lamentation. Esther's decree confirmed these regulations about Purim, and it was written down in the records (Est. 9:29-32).

The Feast of Purim was not part of the Mosaic Law, but was established by Mordecai (9:20-28) and by Esther (9:29-32) as a two-day feast to commemorate Yahweh protecting His people from annihilation through various circumstances. Purim was observed approximately thirty days before Passover. Mordecai writes a proclamation that the Jews were to commemorate the Feast of Purim annually,

> When Mordecai left the king's presence wearing royal garments of blue and white, a large crown of gold and a purple robe of fine linen. And the city of Susa held a joyous celebration. For the Jews it was a time of happiness and joy, gladness and honor. In every province and in every city, wherever the edict of the king went, there was joy and gladness among the Jews, with feasting and celebrating. And many people of other nationalities became Jews because fear of the Jews had seized them (Est. 8:15-17).

---

[294] "Esther 4:14", In Gilbrant, ed., *The Complete Biblical Library Commentary, Ezra-Job*. "Esther", In Dockery, ed., *Holman Concise Bible Commentary*, 195-96. "Esther 4:4-17", In Mays, ed., *Harper's Bible Commentary*. Gaebelein, *The Expositor's Bible Commentary, Volume 4*, 817. Towns, *Fasting for Spiritual Breakthrough*, 23.

[295] Herodotus of Halicarnassus (484-425 BC), *The Histories*, <http://www.swartzentrover.com/cotor/E-Books/misc/Herodotus/THindex.htm>, 3.118. Accessed on November 28, 2013. Gaebelein, *The Expositor's Bible Commentary*, Vol. 4, 817.

[296] "Antiquities of the Jews", In Josephus, *The Works of Josephus*, 11.292-296. "In the apocryphal book of 2 Maccabees (15:36), it is called the Day of Mordecai". "Festivals", In Brand, Draper, England, *Holman Illustrated Bible Dictionary*, 572.

Mordecai recorded these events, and he sent letters to all the Jews throughout the provinces of King Xerxes, near and far, to have them celebrate annually the fourteenth and fifteenth days of the month of Adar as the time when the Jews got relief from their enemies, and as the month when their sorrow was turned into joy and their mourning into a day of celebration. He wrote them to observe the days as days of feasting and joy and giving presents of food to one another and gifts to the poor. So the Jews agreed to continue the celebration they had begun, doing what Mordecai had written to them. For Haman son of Hammedatha, the Agagite, the enemy of all the Jews, had plotted against the Jews to destroy them and had cast the *pur* (that is, the lot) for their ruin and destruction. But when the plot came to the king's attention, he issued written orders that the evil scheme Haman had devised against the Jews should come back onto his own head, and that he and his sons should be hanged on the gallows. (Therefore these days were called Purim, from the word *pur*.) Because of everything written in this letter and because of what they had seen and what had happened to them, the Jews took it upon themselves to establish the custom that they and their descendants and all who join them should without fail observe these two days every year, in the way prescribed and at the time appointed. These days should be remembered and observed in every generation by every family, and in every province and in every city. And these days of Purim should never cease to be celebrated by the Jews, nor should the memory of them die out among their descendants (Est. 9:20-28).

The Feast of Purim was established to celebrate the deliverance of the Jews from Haman's conspiracy to annihilate the Jews. The holiday is preceded by the Esther Fast, which celebrates the gathering together and fasting before the deliverance of the Jews. It is ironic that this festival was established after Purim, פּוּר *pûr*, "lots" was cast to reveal the divine will and the date upon which the Jews would be annihilated. It was customary for princes and people of the East to not only invite their friends to a feast, but also to send a portion of the feast to those who could not attend whether due to distance, poverty, or in a state of sorrow, distress, or mourning. During the Feast of Purim, the Jews were known for their abundant almsgiving, in money and food, which the rich bestowed upon the poor so that they, both rich and poor, could participate with equal status in the celebration of the festival.[297]

> When Haman saw that Mordecai would not kneel down or pay him honor, he was enraged. Yet having learned who Mordecai's people were, he scorned the idea of killing only Mordecai. Instead Haman looked for a way to destroy all Mordecai's people, the Jews, throughout the whole kingdom of Xerxes. In the twelfth year of King Xerxes, in the first month, the month of Nisan, they cast the *pur* (that is, the lot) in the presence of Haman to select a day and month. And the lot fell on the twelfth month, the month of Adar (Est. 3:5-7).

The date of Haman's conspired Jewish holocaust was to take place "on the twelfth month, the month of Adar" (March / April) which was almost one year from the time of casting lots and subsequent public declaration. This two-day feast was observed on the 14th and 15th days of the "month of Adar". The Jews were well prepared for the Feast of Purim and some of their enemies who try to stand against them are destroyed. In Susa there is widespread bloodshed, and the ten sons of Haman are among those who are

---

[297] "Esther 9:19", In Jamieson, Fausset, and Brown, *Commentary Critical and Explanatory on the Whole Bible*. Achtemeier, ed., *Harper's Bible Dictionary*, 843. "Esther 9:20-32", In Thomas Coke, *A Commentary on the Holy Bible: Joshua to Job*, Vol. 2, 1901, Rick Meyers, e-Sword, Version 10.2.1, 2000-2012, <http://www.e-sword.net>.

killed (Est. 9:5-14).[298] The origin of Purim possibly referred to a Persian spring feast where lots were cast as a way of foretelling their destiny and prosperities for the following year. It seems as though modern Jews still read the *Megillah* or Book of Esther in their synagogues.[299]

> The copy read must not be printed, but written on vellum in the form of a roll; and the names of the ten sons of Haman are written on it a peculiar manner, being ranged, they say, like so many bodies on a gibbet. The reader must pronounce all these names in one breath. Whenever Haman's name is pronounced, they make a terrible noise in the synagogue. Some drum with their feet on the floor, and the boys have mallets with which they knock and make a noise. They prepare themselves for their carnival by a previous fast, which should continue three days, in imitation of Esther's; but they have mostly reduced it to one day.[300]

It is noteworthy that the Book of Esther uses the phrase "but they did not lay their hands on the plunder" three times (Est. 9:5-10, 15-16). The decree of King Xerxes

> granted the Jews in every city the right to assemble and protect themselves; to destroy, kill and annihilate any armed force of any nationality or province that might attack them and their women and children; and to plunder the property of their enemies (Est. 8:11).

However, the Jews refused to "lay their hands on the plunder", which speaks of obedience to God (Jos. 6:18f.; 1 Sam. 15:3). It was sometimes strictly forbidden for the Jews to plunder their enemies, yet other references point to Israel carrying off the plunder of their enemies with God's approval, "But the livestock and the plunder from the towns we had captured we carried off for ourselves" (Deut. 2:35; cf. 3:7). The point here is that the Jews did not want to do to the Persians what Haman conspired to do to the Jews. It was not about economic gain, but to condone excess and to plunder the spoils of their enemy was contrary to the purpose of the feast.

The Feast of Purim was about defending their honour, their lives, and avenging the crimes that were committed by Haman and his sons against the Jews. Through Esther, who had "come to royal position for such a time as this" (Est. 4:14), their enemy had been eliminated and her people protected.[301] In the Book of Esther, we can see the sovereign Hand of Yahweh protecting His people from extermination by the Persian Empire, even though they were presently in exile. Purim became the symbol of Yahweh using circumstances to deliver His people.[302]

Queen Esther's last contribution was to legitimize Mordecai's letters of "goodwill and assurance" using her royal authority (Est. 9:30). The NKJV with other Bible translation use "peace and truth". The

---

[298] Knowles, *The Bible Guide*, 216.

[299] Mays, ed., *Harper's Bible Commentary*. 393.

[300] "Esther 9:26", In Jamieson, Fausset, and Brown, *Commentary Critical and Explanatory on the Whole Bible*.

[301] "Esther 9:4-10", In Gilbrant, ed., *The Complete Biblical Library Commentary, Ezra-Job*. Dockery, ed., In *Holman Concise Bible Commentary*, 197.

[302] פּוּר *pûr* "1749", In Harris, Archer, Jr., and Waltke, eds., *Theological Wordbook of the Old Testament*, 720. פּוּר *pûr* "6575", In Gilbrant, ed., *The Complete Biblical Library Hebrew-English Dictionary, Pe-Resh*. Walvoord and Zuck, eds., *The Bible Knowledge Commentary*, Vol. 1, 712-13. Myers, *The Eerdmans Bible Dictionary*, 863.

Jews are instructed "to establish these days of Purim at their designated times, as Mordecai the Jew and Queen Esther had decreed for them, and as they had established for themselves and their descendants in regard to their times of fasting and lamentation" (Est. 9:31). In Zechariah 8:19—a prophecy at least forty to fifty years earlier also connects "peace and truth" with "fasting" like Esther does here. The context of Zechariah, discussed later, prophecies that, "This is what the LORD Almighty says: 'the fasts of the fourth, fifth, seventh and tenth months will become joyful and glad occasions and happy festivals for Judah. Therefore love truth and peace'" (Zech. 8:19). These words of "joyous celebration" "a time of happiness and joy, gladness and honor", and "feasting and celebrating" (Est. 8:15-17) describe the euphoria of the Jews when they heard the king's decree allowing them to defend themselves against their enemies. In both of these contexts of Zechariah and Esther, fasting becomes a time of joyful celebration and Esther 9:22 was a fulfillment of the prophecy of Zechariah 8:19. The Feast of Purim became a reversal of the fasts described in Zechariah:

1. The fast of the fourth month fell on the ninth of Tammuz, the day when the city walls were breached (2 Kgs. 25:3-4; Jer. 39:2).
2. The fast of the fifth month was on the ninth of Ab, when the house of God was destroyed by fire (2 Kgs. 25:8-10).
3. The fast of the seventh month was on the third of Tishri, the anniversary of the assassination of Gedaliah the son of Ahikam (ibid. 25; Jer. 41:2).
4. The fast of the tenth month fell on the tenth of Tebeth, which was the day when the King of Babylon laid siege to Jerusalem (2 Kgs. 25:1; Eze. 24:2).[303]

The Feast of Purim was not only a time of feasting and celebration, happiness and joy, gladness and honour of their deliverance, but also of the distress and suffering that had preceded this time of celebration (cf. Est. 4:3). In later times, the thirteenth day of Adar, which had been the time allotted for the annihilation at the hands of Haman, was a time observed by Jews as a day of humiliation (Est. 3).[304]

Please refer to *Fasting: Unlocking Spiritual Power and Breakthrough, Personal Reflections* under the heading "The Esther Fast" to complete the Personal Reflections section of this study.

Conclusion to the Fasts of Isaiah 58

Then you will call, and the LORD will answer; you will cry for help, and he will say: Here am I. "If you do away with the yoke of oppression, with the pointing finger and malicious talk, and if you spend yourselves in behalf of the hungry and satisfy the needs of the oppressed, then your light will rise in the darkness, and your night will become like the noonday. The LORD will guide you always; he will satisfy your needs in a sun-scorched land and will strengthen your

[303] "Fast", In M'Clintock and Strong, eds., *Cyclopedia of Biblical and Ecclesiastical Literature*, <http://www.e-sword.net>. "Esther 9:29-32", in Gilbrant, ed., *The Complete Biblical Library Commentary, Ezra-Job*. "Esther 9:31", In John Trapp, *A Commentary On the Old and New Testaments: Ezra to Psalms*, W. Webster and Hugh Martin, eds., Vol. 2. In Rick Meyers, e-Sword, Version 10.2.1, 2000-2012, <http://www.e-sword.net>. Gaebelein, *The Expositor's Bible Commentary, Volume 4*, 839.

[304] "Esther 9:1-32", In Dummelow, ed., *A Commentary on the Holy Bible*, <http://www.e-sword.net>.

frame. You will be like a well-watered garden, like a spring whose waters never fail. Your people will rebuild the ancient ruins and will raise up the age-old foundations; you will be called Repairer of Broken Walls, Restorer of Streets with Dwellings. "If you keep your feet from breaking the Sabbath and from doing as you please on my holy day, if you call the Sabbath a delight and the LORD's holy day honorable, and if you honor it by not going your own way and not doing as you please or speaking idle words, then you will find your joy in the LORD, and I will cause you to ride in triumph on the heights of the land and to feast on the inheritance of your father Jacob". For the mouth of the LORD has spoken (Isa. 58:9-14).

The true fast of Isaiah 58 means to serve others, releasing them from injustice and oppression, sharing our food, home, clothes, our possessions with those in need, including our relatives, "not to turn away from your own flesh and blood", then God promises to bless us and answer our prayers (Isa. 58:6-8).[305] If the Jews had demonstrated inner righteousness "do away with the yoke of oppression"—outward acts of justice and mercy (vs. 6-7) then the Lord would bless them, "then your light will rise in the darkness" (cf. Deut. 28:1-14). They would receive healing and spiritual restoration, guidance, satisfaction, strength, fertility, "you will be like a well-watered garden, like a spring whose waters never fail", physical restoration, and protection from trouble "your people will rebuild the ancient ruins", and answered prayer (vs. 8-9).

Isaiah next emphasizes the importance of keeping the Sabbath, which measured their faithfulness to the Mosaic Covenant (cf. 56:4-6). Through observing the Sabbath, the people acknowledged the importance of worshipping God and demonstrated their dependence upon Him. Their faithfulness to God and not remaining self-centered, "doing as you please" they would have the "joy in the Lord", spiritual salvation "ride in triumph on the heights of the land" and prosper "feast on the inheritance of your father Jacob".

True fasting was to encourage a person to respond positively to God's commands and a commitment to justice and to the poor. Isaiah describes man's responsibility and then God's response to man's obedience (Isa. 58:9-14). His purpose is to rebuke the Jews for their futile dependence on an outward form of worship, diligent in the external rites of their religion, and expecting God to prevent judgment without divine approval. He emphasizes that their religious spirit was not divinely accepted and the blessings that would result from righteous living and not meaningless ritual.

The text of Isaiah 58 highlights the don'ts and the do's while we are fasting:

We should not

1. seek other pleasures for food. We must deny ourselves these pleasures and focus ourselves on seeking after God.
2. boast about our fasting like the Pharisees (cf. Lk. 18:10-14).
3. allow sin to reign in our lives. Sins must be eradicated from our lives so that our fasting will accomplish its purpose in our lives and ascend as a pleasing aroma to God. Fasting can help you conquer these weaknesses in your life.

---

[305] Knowles, *The Bible Guide*, 292.

We should

1. disengage ourselves from anything that displeases God.
2. seek to lay aside physical and spiritual burdens as much as possible, since our focus should be upon God.
3. forgive and release those who have hurt, wronged, or offended us. "do to others what you would have them do to you" (Mt. 7:12).
4. lay aside every weight and sin that besets us, breaking yokes that bind us and hinder us from being spiritual. "Therefore, since we are surrounded by such a great cloud of witnesses, let us throw off everything that hinders and the sin that so easily entangles, and let us run with perseverance the race marked out for us" (Heb. 12:1).
5. give of ourselves to those who are in need. Feed those who are hungry, cloth the naked, and do not hide ourselves from our fellow man who is in need (Isa. 58:7).
6. anoint our head with oil, continue your practice of personal hygiene, and do not appear sullen or physically weak.
7. fast unto God in secret. Fast as discreetly as possible.

Therefore, the ten fasts of Isaiah 58 accomplish a particular purpose and objective:

1. The Disciple's Fast, to break addiction and addictive behaviours.
2. The Ezra Fast, to solve problems.
3. The Samuel Fast, for evangelism and revival.
4. The Elijah Fast, to break habits and emotional problems.
5. The Widow's Fast, to focus on the needs of others.
6. The Saint Paul Fast, for decision making.
7. The Daniel Fast, for health and healing.
8. The King Darius Fast, for wisdom, discernment, and emotional health.
9. The John the Baptist Fast, for testimony and influence.
10. The Esther Fast, for spiritual warfare.[306]

The following chart contrasts the Jewish fast or false fasting and God's fast or true fasting:

False Fasting, Jewish	True Fasting, Christian
1. The *motive* of their fasting was wrong—constituting a claim upon God.	1. Fasting should be accompanied with *repentance*.
2. The *method* of their fasting was wrong—self-serving.	2. Fasting should be associated with *almsgiving*.
3. The *accompaniment* of their fasting was wrong—promoting self.	3. Fasting must always be attended by *prayer*.

The type of fasting that God requires is a fast that encourages a person to respond positively to His commands.

---

[306] Knowles, *The Bible Guide*, 292. Walvoord and Zuck, eds., *The Bible Knowledge Commentary*, Vol. 1, 1113-14. "Isaiah 58", In Albert Barnes, *Albert Barnes' Notes on the Bible*, <http://www.e-sword.net>. "Isaiah 58:1-14", In Dockery, ed., In *Holman Concise Bible Commentary*, 288. "Isaiah 58", In Nicoll, Stoddart, and Moffatt, eds., *The Expositor's Dictionary of Texts*, <http://www.e-sword.net>.

Is it not to share your food with the hungry and to provide the poor wanderer with shelter—when you see the naked, to clothe them, and not to turn away from your own flesh and blood? (Isa. 58:7).

The Hebrew verb פָּרַס *pāras* means "to share", "to divide", or "to detach"; in Arabic "to kill", "to divide booty", and in Syriac "to separate".[307] The Jews were to divide their food among the poor, and the noun בַּיִת *bayith* meant sharing their home with "the poor wanderer" as if they were their extended family.[308] The verb רָאָה *rā'āh* "when you see" means "to visit someone in person" (2 Sam. 13:5f.; Ps. 41:6), "to observe" with the sense of providing for their needs (cf. Hos. 9:10; Deut. 33:9; Gen. 11:5; Jdg. 7:17).[309]

> In that day people will look to their Maker and turn their eyes to the Holy One of Israel. They will not look to the altars, the work of their hands, and they will have no regard for the Asherah poles and the incense altars their fingers have made (Isa. 17:7-8).

> That fading flower, his glorious beauty, set on the head of a fertile valley, will be like figs ripe before harvest—as soon as people see them and take them in hand, they swallow them (Isa. 28:4).

Isaiah states that instead of fasting in order to receive something for themselves, God desired that we would share and provide for the poor, the hungry, those without shelter, and cloth those who had insufficient clothing. Their primary concern was to be for their families and if everyone provided for their families no one would lack anything. The Israelites were to consider themselves members of one family who at one time had been slaves in Egypt. Therefore, they were not to neglect each other. When someone shared with one in need, it was a reminder that everything he owned belonged to the Lord.[310] Jesus stated it plainly in Matthew 25:31-46 and Galatians 6:10 exhorts us, "Therefore, as we have opportunity, let us do good to all people, especially to those who belong to the family of believers".[311]

Isaiah 58:8-12, describes the blessings God promises to the true worshipper.

> Then your light will break forth like the dawn, and your healing will quickly appear; then your righteousness will go before you, and the glory of the LORD will be your rear guard. Then you will call, and the LORD will answer; you will cry for help, and he will say: Here am I. "If you do away with the yoke of oppression, with the pointing finger and malicious talk, and if you spend yourselves in behalf of the hungry and satisfy the needs of the oppressed, then your light will rise in the darkness, and your night will become like the noonday. The LORD will guide you always;

---

[307] פָּרַס *pāras* "6788", In Gilbrant, ed., *The Complete Biblical Library Hebrew-English Dictionary, Pe-Resh.* פָּרַס "1821", In Harris, Archer, Jr., and Waltke, eds., *Theological Wordbook of the Old Testament*, 736.

[308] בַּיִת *bayith* "1041", In Gilbrant, ed., *The Complete Biblical Library Hebrew-English Dictionary, Aleph-Beth.* בַּיִת "241", In Harris, Archer, Jr., and Waltke, eds., *Theological Wordbook of the Old Testament*, 107-16.

[309] רָאָה *rā'āh* "7495", In Gilbrant, ed., *The Complete Biblical Library Hebrew-English Dictionary, Pe-Resh.* רָאָה "2095", In Harris, Archer, Jr., and Waltke, eds., *Theological Wordbook of the Old Testament*, 823-25.

[310] Walvoord and Zuck, eds., *The Bible Knowledge Commentary*, Vol. 1, 1113.

[311] "Isaiah 58:7", In Gilbrant, ed., *The Complete Biblical Library Commentary, Isaiah.*

he will satisfy your needs in a sun-scorched land and will strengthen your frame. You will be like a well-watered garden, like a spring whose waters never fail (Isa. 58:8-12).

He begins with "Then your light will break forth like the dawn" refers to light in the promises of Isaiah 9:2, "The people walking in darkness have seen a great light; on those living in the land of deep darkness a light has dawned" (cf. 60:1-3). Elsewhere Isaiah uses the verb בָּקַע *bāqaʿ* in reference to breaking forth of hatching eggs (59:5) and water breaking forth (35:6).[312] This Hebrew verb suggests suddenness, swiftness, and uniqueness. In the Near East the light of day follows almost immediately upon the darkness of night. God also pledges restoration of health, protection, and access to himself in prayer. Isaiah states that a new day will dawn, new flesh will appear where there was once a wound, and their defeats in the battle of life will be forgotten. They will march onward in victory with God-given righteousness leading the way and the glory of God as their rear guard talk (Isa. 58:9),[313]

> Then you will call, and the LORD will answer; you will cry for help, and he will say: Here am I. If you do away with the yoke of oppression, with the pointing finger and malicious talk.

Isaiah includes another amazing promise: "you will cry for help, and he will say: Here am I". "Here I am" is the typical and appropriate biblical response of a person called by a superior or by God. This was Isaiah's response when God commissioned him to be a prophet. However, here God takes those words of quintessential human response and speaks them to Isaiah. Now, God says, "Here am I", or in other words, "I am here for you". This occurs three times in the latter part of Isaiah (58:9; 52:6; 65:1), which shows the remarkable inclination toward incarnation of God, as portrayed in this material.[314] Isaiah proceeds to amplify what should be expected, not only on a fast day, but also in the fast from sin and greed that should be kept by every individual every day. Negatively, it means getting rid of the yoke of oppression, the extended finger in judging others and speaking falsely to cause harm or trouble. Positively, in verse 10, it means granting your soul or your desire what you want for yourself to the hungry. It means satisfying the humbled soul. Then the darkness and obscurity of life's problems will be replaced by light. When we do these things, God's blessing is upon us and he answers our prayers.[315]

> Then your light will break forth like the dawn, and your healing will quickly appear; then your righteousness will go before you, and the glory of the LORD will be your rear guard. Then you will call, and the LORD will answer; you will cry for help, and he will say: Here am I. "If you do away with the yoke of oppression, with the pointing finger and malicious talk, and if you spend yourselves in behalf of the hungry and satisfy the needs of the oppressed, then your light will rise in the darkness, and your night will become like the noonday (58:8-10).

---

[312] בָּקַע *bāqaʿ* "1260", In Gilbrant, ed., *The Complete Biblical Library Hebrew-English Dictionary, Aleph-Beth*. בָּקַע "271", In Harris, Archer, Jr., and Waltke, eds., *Theological Wordbook of the Old Testament*, 123.

[313] Gaebelein, ed., *The Expositor's Bible Commentary*, Vol. 6, 322. "Isaiah 58:8", In Gilbrant, ed., *The Complete Biblical Library Commentary, Isaiah*.

[314] <http://www.enterthebible.org/resourcelink.aspx?rid=477>, Accessed on September 3, 2013.

[315] Knowles, *The Bible Guide*, 292.

The Hebrew text of verses 10-11 clarifies how this works in its repeated use of the word for "soul" or "self" (נֶפֶשׁ *nephesh*): "If you offer your *nephesh* [your self, your soul] to the hungry and satisfy the *nephesh* of the afflicted....The Lord will...satisfy your *nephesh* in parched places". In other words, as you pour yourself out for others, you will find yourself—or, as Jesus said, "Those who find their life will lose it, and those who lose their life for my sake will find it" (Mt. 10:39). Moreover, verse 10 suggests that social concern is not just to be seen in an isolated episode, but it is to be a way of life for God's people.[316]

The LORD will guide you always; he will satisfy your needs in a sun-scorched land and will strengthen your frame. You will be like a well-watered garden, like a spring whose waters never fail (Isa. 58:11).

Isaiah uses the verb נָחָה *nāchāh* meaning that the Lord promises to "guide you always" or as the verb means "to look", or "to walk to one side". In this light, life that is fully provided for and strong is always refreshed (cf. Jer. 31:12) and ever refreshing others—can flourish under God's blessing (v. 11). Isaiah uses the verb וְהִשְׂבִּיעַ *wěhiśbîa* from שָׂבַע *sāvfi* meaning "to be satisfied" or "to be satiated". This verb refers to a state of being which implies sufficiency, though it generally does not imply excess. The verb often expresses a propriety, the correct amount, as opposed to abundance (cf. Ruth 2:14). *Sāvfi* is a verb frequently used to describe the condition of satiety or lack thereof in regard to food (Ex. 16:12) and drink (Isa. 66:11). Yahweh is the ultimate Source of physical satiety (Ps. 104:28). God's guidance will be continual—He will satisfy our soul, our desires, even in scorched land. Strong bones refer to inner strength, stability, and stamina. A pleasant, watered garden and an unfailing spring indicate provision for every need, both natural and spiritual.[317]

Your people will rebuild the ancient ruins and will raise up the age-old foundations; you will be called Repairer of Broken Walls, Restorer of Streets with Dwellings (Isa. 58:12).

In verse 12, Isaiah uses the verb בָּנָה *bānāh* meaning "to build" or "to construct", used about 200 times in the Old Testament in both a literal and figurative sense. For example, in a literal sense, the tower of Babel (Gen. 11:5); altars (Gen. 8:20; Jdg. 6:26; Jos. 22:16; 1 Sam. 14:35); cities (Num. 32:24); shrines (Eze. 16:24); the temple (2 Kgs. 12:11) and houses (Neh. 7:14). It is interesting that in reference to God taking a rib from Adam He "built" Eve (Gen. 2:22).[318]

---

[316] נֶפֶשׁ *nephesh* "5497", In Gilbrant, ed., *The Complete Biblical Library Hebrew-English Dictionary, Nun-Ayin*. "Isaiah 58", In Gilbrant, ed., *The Complete Biblical Library Commentary, Isaiah*, <http://www.enterthebible.org/resourcelink.aspx?rid=477>, Accessed on September 3, 2013.

[317] "Isaiah 58", In Gilbrant, ed., *The Complete Biblical Library Commentary, Isaiah*. נָחָה *nāchāh* "5328", In Gilbrant, ed., *The Complete Biblical Library Hebrew-English Dictionary, Nun-Ayin*. Gaebelein, ed., *The Expositor's Bible Commentary*, Vol. 6, 322. שָׂבַע *sāvfi* "7881", In Gilbrant, ed., *The Complete Biblical Library Hebrew-English Dictionary, Sin-Taw*.

[318] בָּנָה *bānāh* "1161", In Gilbrant, ed., *The Complete Biblical Library Hebrew-English Dictionary, Aleph-Beth*.

Figuratively, this verb means "to establish" as Rachel and Leah "together built up the house of Israel", referring to establishing the Israelites as a people (Ruth 4:11). The barren Sarai encouraged Abram to use her slave Hagar as a surrogate, so that "perhaps I can build a family through her" (Gen. 16:2; cf. 30:3). The Lord, in reference to Samuel, stated "I will firmly establish his house" who served as a loyal priest and prophet of the Lord throughout his life (1 Sam. 2:35). Concerning the coming Davidic King, Zechariah states, "It is he who will build the temple of the LORD" (6:13). The prophet Malachi refers to the prosperity of the wicked by saying, "the evildoers prosper" (3:15).

Isaiah refers to future generations who will "rebuild the ancient ruins" and those ("your people") alluded to in verse 9f. will "establish" the foundations of earlier generations (58:12). The phrase "Repairer of Broken Walls" refers to Ezekiel "I looked for a man among them who would build up the wall and stand before me in the gap on behalf of the land so I would not have to destroy it, but I found none" (22:30).

Ezekiel's point here is rhetorical. As God had spoken with Abraham regarding the number of righteous men needed to save the city of Sodom, He enquires as to there being sufficient righteousness to abort his judgment. Although there were such righteous men as Jeremiah, Habakkuk and Zephaniah, contemporary prophets living in Judah at the time of the fall of Jerusalem, there were not enough.[319]

Likewise, it refers to Nehemiah and the rebuilding of the "wall of Jerusalem", "You see the trouble we are in: Jerusalem lies in ruins, and its gates have been burned with fire. Come, let us rebuild the wall of Jerusalem, and we will no longer be in disgrace" (Neh. 2:17). Nehemiah raises up God's people to become "Repairer of Broken Walls" and the "Restorer of Streets with Dwellings". The Jews would not only be able to walk on quiet paths, but also dwell within Jerusalem.[320]

> If you keep your feet from breaking the Sabbath and from doing as you please on my holy day, if you call the Sabbath a delight and the LORD's holy day honorable, and if you honor it by not going your own way and not doing as you please or speaking idle words (Isa. 58:13).

In verse 13, Isaiah now brings us back to a feast day and not the fast day, which the Sabbath was an important covenant sign under the Law. Moses had referred to the Sabbath day as "a Sabbath of rest, a day of sacred assembly . . . a Sabbath to the LORD" (Lev. 23:3). The prophet addresses the abuse of the Sabbath by doing as they pleased. God had sanctified the Sabbath as a Holy day to worship Him—giving themselves wholeheartedly to Him "Love the LORD your God with all your heart and with all your soul and with all your strength" (Deut. 6:5).[321]

Isaiah uses the verb שׁוּב *shûv* which in essence means "to turn". Depending on context, the verb also connotes "to repent", "to return", "to turn back" or "to be restored".[322] Isaiah had earlier rebuked them for

---

[319] "Ezekiel 22:30", In Gilbrant, ed., *The Complete Biblical Library Commentary, Ezekiel*.

[320] "Isaiah 58", In Gilbrant, ed., *The Complete Biblical Library Commentary, Isaiah*. Wiersbe, *Be Comforted*, 150-51. "Isaiah 58:8-12", In Henry, *Matthew Henry's Commentary on the Whole Bible*.

[321] "Isaiah 58", In Gilbrant, ed., *The Complete Biblical Library Commentary, Isaiah*.

[322] שׁוּב *shûv* "8178", In Gilbrant, ed., *The Complete Biblical Library Hebrew-English Dictionary, Sin-Taw*.

their hypocritical claims of loyalty and their empty expressions of repentance "These people come near to me with their mouth and honor me with their lips, but their hearts are far from me. Their worship of me is made up only of rules taught by men" (Isa. 29:13; cf. 1:10-15; Mt. 15:8-9).[323] Their unjust and cruel behaviour made their fasts unacceptable. The Lord had called them to be holy and live righteously, and not perform detestable, empty, and meaningless rituals. If they had followed the commands of the Lord, it would have resulted in loosing "the chains of injustice", "untying the cords of the yoke", "setting the oppressed free", "breaking every yoke", "sharing your food with the hungry", "providing the poor wanderer with shelter", "to clothe" the naked, "and not to turn away from your own flesh and blood" (Isa. 58:6-7).

If they obeyed the Lord's commands, then they would experience the Lord's protective presence, enjoy His blessings, and witness the rebuilding of the land.[324] The Lord had commanded His people to observe one fast on the annual Day of Atonement,

> This is to be a lasting ordinance for you: On the tenth day of the seventh month you must deny yourselves and not do any work—whether native-born or an alien living among you—because on this day atonement will be made for you, to cleanse you. Then, before the LORD, you will be clean from all your sins. It is a Sabbath of rest, and you must deny yourselves; it is a lasting ordinance (Lev. 16:29-31).

However, instead of complying with the Lord's command they complained and were possibly trying to buy the Lord's blessings through fasting. The Lord was trying to teach them that worship involves more than an external form; it involves an inward obedience and submission to the Lord (cf. Mt. 6:16-18).

The lesson here speaks against "doing as you please on my holy day" and worshipping the Lord from a heart and life that is wholly surrendered to Him. Sabbath observance was a barometer of one's faithfulness to the Mosaic Covenant. True fasting will lead to humility before God and ministry to others. We deprive ourselves so that we might share with others and do so for the glory of God. If we fast in order to get something for ourselves from God, instead of becoming a better person for the sake of others, then we have missed the meaning of worship. It delights the Lord when we delight in the Lord.[325]

> then you will find your joy in the LORD, and I will cause you to ride in triumph on the heights of the land and to feast on the inheritance of your father Jacob". For the mouth of the LORD has spoken (Isa. 58:14).

Isaiah concludes this chapter by stating that if the people would walk in obedience and submission to the Lord, "then" they would find their joy in the Lord and not in doing things their own way. Isaiah uses the verb עָנֹג '*ānōgh* meaning "to pamper" or "to take pleasure in", which describes a person who has been raised to live a refined, sheltered life where luxury is the norm. When God's judgment strikes, even the

---

[323] שׁוּב *shûv* "8178", In Gilbrant, ed., *The Complete Biblical Library Hebrew-English Dictionary, Sin-Taw.*

[324] "The Major Prophets" In Dockery, ed., In *Holman Concise Bible Commentary*, 288.

[325] Wiersbe, *Be Comforted*, 150-51. Walvoord and Zuck, eds., *The Bible Knowledge Commentary*, Vol. 1, 1113-14.

person accustomed to a soft life will feel the full force of His anger (cf. Jer. 6:2; Deut. 28:56f.). The verb עָנֹג *ānōgh* frequently appears in a positive sense of the exquisite delight a person can take in someone or something.

Job's friend Eliphaz exhorted him, "Surely then you will find delight in the Almighty and will lift up your face to God" (Job 22:26), while Job declared that his enemy would not delight in the Almighty.

Will they find delight in the Almighty? Will they call on God at all times? (Job 27:10).

The prophet Isaiah called on the people to stop spending their wages on that which does not satisfy; if they would listen to God's Word, they would delight themselves in abundance (Isa. 55:2). David, in Psalms 37 uses the verb עָנֹג *ānōgh* two times: the instruction here is that those who take exquisite pleasure in the Lord (37:4) will inherit the land and delight in abundant prosperity (37:11).[326] Moreover, Jesus in His Sermon on the Mount stated, "But seek first his kingdom and his righteousness, and all these things will be given to you as well" (Mt. 6:33).

Not only would they experience bountiful joy, they would also "ride in triumph on the heights of the land". This phrase also occurs in numerous Old Testament references: "He made him ride on the heights of the land and fed him with the fruit of the fields" (Deut. 32:13); "The Sovereign Lord is my strength; he makes my feet like the feet of a deer, he enables me to go on the heights" (Hab. 3:19; cf. Ps. 18:33); Amos applies this phrase to God, "He who forms the mountains, creates the wind, and reveals his thoughts to man, he who turns dawn to darkness, and treads the high places of the earth—the Lord God Almighty is his name" (Am. 4:13).

Albert Barnes gives further significance to this phrase. Some of these include:

1. God would restore the exiled Jews to their own land—a land of mountains and elevated places, more lofty than the surrounding regions.
2. It refers to a conqueror, who on his horse or in his chariot, occupies mountains, hills, towers, and monuments, and subjects them to himself.
3. "I will place you in lofty and inaccessible places, where you will be safe from all your enemies".
4. The word "high places" here means fortress or stronghold, and that to walk over those strongholds, or to ride over them, is equivalent to possessing them, and that he who has possession of the fortress has possession of the whole country. The above expositions seems to be entirely free from difficulty, the general idea of prosperity and security is undoubtedly the main thing intended; but what is the specific sense couched under the phrase "to ride on the high places of the earth", does not seem to be sufficiently explained.[327]

---

[326] עָנֹג *ānōgh* "6253", In Gilbrant, ed., *The Complete Biblical Library Hebrew-English Dictionary, Nun-Ayin.*
[327] "Isaiah 58:14", In Albert Barnes, *Albert Barnes' Notes on the Bible*, <http://www.e-sword.net>.

Chapter 8: The Fasts of the Prophetical Books

The purpose of this chapter is to describe the fasts found within the prophetical books of the Word of God. Each fast presents the context and purpose in which the fasting occurs and then concludes by completing the relevant "Personal Reflections" section.

The Jeremiah Fast

In the fourth year of Jehoiakim son of Josiah king of Judah, this word came to Jeremiah from the LORD: "Take a scroll and write on it all the words I have spoken to you concerning Israel, Judah and all the other nations from the time I began speaking to you in the reign of Josiah till now. Perhaps when the people of Judah hear about every disaster I plan to inflict on them, each of them will turn from his wicked way; then I will forgive their wickedness and their sin". So Jeremiah called Baruch son of Neriah, and while Jeremiah dictated all the words the LORD had spoken to him, Baruch wrote them on the scroll. Then Jeremiah told Baruch, "I am restricted; I cannot go to the LORD's temple. So you go to the house of the LORD on a day of fasting and read to the people from the scroll the words of the LORD that you wrote as I dictated. Read them to all the people of Judah who come in from their towns. Perhaps they will bring their petition before the LORD, and each will turn from his wicked ways, for the anger and wrath pronounced against this people by the LORD are great". Baruch son of Neriah did everything Jeremiah the prophet told him to do; at the LORD's temple he read the words of the LORD from the scroll. In the ninth month of the fifth year of Jehoiakim son of Josiah king of Judah, a time of fasting before the LORD was proclaimed for all the people in Jerusalem and those who had come from the towns of Judah (Jer. 36:1-9).

The emphasis of Jeremiah 1-44 is primarily on Israel and Judah, while Jeremiah 45-51 deals with the surrounding nations of the Near East. Jeremiah 36 records the events that began "in the fourth year of Jehoiakim son of Josiah king of Judah" (605-604 BC, cf. Jer. 25:1) when God had commanded Jeremiah to "Take a scroll and write on it all the words I have spoken to you concerning Israel, Judah and all the other nations from the time I began speaking to you in the reign of Josiah till now" (627 BC; Jer. 1:2; 25:3). Documents in Jeremiah's time were recorded on papyrus or parchment, secured to a wooden roller at one or both ends, and then rolled up. This chapter presents three readings of Jeremiah's prophecies:

1. The scroll was read "from the room of Gemariah son of Shaphan the secretary, which was in the upper courtyard at the entrance of the New Gate of the temple, Baruch read to all the people at the Lord's temple the words of Jeremiah from the scroll" (Jer. 36:9-10; cf. 26:7ff.). This gave Baruch maximum exposure to the greatest number of people.
2. The scroll was read in the presence of "the princes". The ministers of state were in session in the statehouse, close to the Temple. After hearing a report of the first reading of the scroll, they became troubled and summoned Jeremiah and Baruch. Upon hearing the contents of "the book", they became concerned with the safety of Jeremiah and his scribe Baruch (Jer. 36:11-19).
3. The book/scroll was read in the presence of the king. It was the duty of "the princes" to report this to the king. However, before reporting the contents of the scroll to the king, they warned Jeremiah and Baruch to go into hiding. As the scroll was read, Jehoiakim showed his contempt by cutting up columns and throwing them into the fire to be completely burned. The king then ordered their arrest. He hoped to destroy any written record and cancel out their effectiveness. The Lord then instructed

Jeremiah to dictate another scroll to his scribe Baruch, which announced that Jehoiakim would be punished severely for his disrespect (Jer. 36:20-26).

The reader is not told why Jeremiah could not go to the Temple himself. However, Jeremiah was restricted from entering the temple, possibly because of earlier unpopular addresses there (cf. Jer. 7:1-15; 26:1-19). Perhaps he had been threatened with arrest if he appeared there again after his temple sermon from the first year of Jehoiakim's reign (26:1). Perhaps, in the intervening years, Jehoiakim had become so angry with Jeremiah that the prophet did not dare show up where the king could have him arrested.

The public persecution to which Jeremiah had been subjected had clearly demonstrated that it was no longer safe for him to speak in public. Therefore, like Amos and many prophets before him, when silenced, he resorted to writing. Jeremiah was one of the great prophetic souls who walked so close to God that he recognized in every conviction which came to him the promptings of the divine voice. Accordingly, as a God-given task, he wrote down all the words that God had spoken to him over the twenty-three years of ministry,

> Take a scroll and write on it all the words I have spoken to you concerning Israel, Judah and all the other nations from the time I began speaking to you in the reign of Josiah till now. Perhaps when the people of Judah hear about every disaster I plan to inflict on them, each of them will turn from his wicked way; then I will forgive their wickedness and their sin (Jer. 36:2-3).

In antiquity, the written word had a lot more credibility than the spoken word, and Jeremiah hoped that Judah would finally obey God's call to repentance through the reading of the scroll. The reading of the scroll was a petition aimed directly at the consciences of the rulers and people. Moreover, it solidified his authority as a true prophet confirming that his earlier messages had been fulfilled in the life of the nation. Jeremiah hoped that the reading of the scroll would result in national repentance and that God would withhold His judgment (Jer. 36:5-7).[328]

Jeremiah, to guarantee a good hearing of his written messages, chose a fast day and instructs Baruch to go to the house of the Lord when all the people would be assembled in the temple (v. 6). Baruch read the scroll in the fifth year of Jehoiakim, the ninth month, which describes a gap between Jeremiah's writing of the scroll and it being read to all the people. Prior to the fall of Jerusalem in 586 BC, fast days were not specified but were called in times of emergency (cf. 36:9; 2 Chr. 20:3; Joel 1:14; 2:15). Only after the fall of Jerusalem were regular fast days instituted (Zech. 7:3, 5; 8:19).

Fast days were not scheduled in the Pentateuchal legislation, as were feast days; fast days were specifically called events. After the Exile, fast days were specified (cf. Zech. 7:3, 5; 8:19), however, in earlier times, fast days were proclaimed in a time of crisis (cf. Joel 2:12, 15). Jeremiah had probably called this fast because of a public disaster, or possibly a drought.

The reference to צוֹם בְּיוֹם *beyom som*, "a fast day" and then added mention in v. 9 cannot apply to the Day of Atonement because (a) the former is too indefinite and (b) the latter falls on the

---

[328] "Chapter 19: The Defiant King (36:1-32)", In Smith, *The Major Prophets*.

tenth day of the seventh month (Lev. 16:29; 23:27), not the ninth month. Both cases come under the category of days of fasting announced during times of special national distress, here because of the terror of Nebuchadnezzar's victories. Since fasts, other than Atonement, were apparently not on fixed dates, a fast was chosen for the reading in order to take advantage of the crowds then assembled.[329]

On a larger scale, it was the perfect time to proclaim a fast since Jeremiah saw the importance of the Babylonians defeating the Egyptians at Carchemish in 605 BC. There was a feeling that turning to the Lord in a public fast might avert the judgment that had been conditionally predicted (Jer. 36:7-8). This seemed to be a time of imminent crisis, which could include the conquest of Nebuchadnezzar and destruction of Ashkelon, on the Philistine coast. Jeremiah's response was to proclaim a fast in Jerusalem, which was observed in the month of December 604 BC. This caused so much concern that people "came from the cities of Judah" to Jerusalem and the Temple (Jer. 36:9), which would have created a large audience for Baruch's reading of Jeremiah's scroll.[330]

This chapter highlights the fact that even though King Jehoiakim burned the scroll, he cannot destroy the Word of God. God told Jeremiah to write on another scroll all the words of the first scroll. However, he was to include an additional word for King Jehoiakim, which would bring judgment upon him and his descendants. By burning the first scroll, Jehoiakim showed contempt for the Word of the Lord and refused to believe God's warning about the King of Babylon. This judgment was threefold:

1. No descendant of his would permanently sit on the throne of David. His son Jehoiachin was not his successor (cf. 2 Kgs. 24:8-17), and was deposed by Nebuchadnezzar after a reign of only three months. No other descendant of Jehoiakim ascended the throne.
2. Jehoiakim would not receive a proper burial (cf. 22:18-19). Instead his body would be thrown out of the city and exposed to the elements.
3. Jehoiakim's children and his attendants would be judged for their wickedness. God would bring on them every disaster that He had pronounced because they had not listened.[331]

The end of this chapter (36:27-32) is quite significant since God instructs Jeremiah to write a second scroll, which was also dictated to Baruch since the first scroll was burned.

After the king burned the scroll containing the words that Baruch had written at Jeremiah's dictation, the word of the LORD came to Jeremiah: "Take another scroll and write on it all the words that were on the first scroll, which Jehoiakim king of Judah burned up. Also tell Jehoiakim king of Judah, 'This is what the LORD says: You burned that scroll and said, "Why did you write on it that the king of Babylon would certainly come and destroy this land and cut off both men and animals from it?" Therefore, this is what the LORD says about Jehoiakim king of Judah: He will have no one to sit on the throne of David; his body will be thrown out and exposed to the

[329] Gaebelein, ed., *The Expositor's Bible Commentary*, Vol. 6, 605.

[330] "Jeremiah 36", In Gilbrant, ed., *The Complete Biblical Library Commentary, Jeremiah-Lamentations*. Gaebelein, ed., *The Expositor's Bible Commentary, Volume 6*, 604-605. Charles Foster Kent, *The Kings and Prophets of Israel and Judah: From the Division of the Kingdom to the Babylonian Exile*, The Historical Bible (New York: Charles Scribner's Sons, 1909), 250.

[331] Walvoord and Zuck, eds., *The Bible Knowledge Commentary*, Vol. 1, 1181.

heat by day and the frost by night. I will punish him and his children and his attendants for their wickedness; I will bring on them and those living in Jerusalem and the people of Judah every disaster I pronounced against them, because they have not listened". So Jeremiah took another scroll and gave it to the scribe Baruch son of Neriah, and as Jeremiah dictated, Baruch wrote on it all the words of the scroll that Jehoiakim king of Judah had burned in the fire. And many similar words were added to them (Jer. 36:27-32).

The difference between the first and second scroll was that the second included an oracle condemning Jehoiakim for not fearing God, not tearing their clothes, cutting and burning the first scroll, and not listening to the wise counsel of his attendants (Jer. 36:29-31).

Whenever Jehudi had read three or four columns of the scroll, the king cut them off with a scribe's knife and threw them into the firepot, until the entire scroll was burned in the fire. The king and all his attendants who heard all these words showed no fear, nor did they tear their clothes. Even though Elnathan, Delaiah and Gemariah urged the king not to burn the scroll, he would not listen to them. Instead, the king commanded Jerahmeel, a son of the king, Seraiah son of Azriel and Shelemiah son of Abdeel to arrest Baruch the scribe and Jeremiah the prophet. But the LORD had hidden them (Jer. 36:23-26).

This second scroll also included "many similar words" of prophecy (Jer. 36:32). The harsh judgment that would follow was seen by God as "an appalling act of blasphemy and contempt for God's revelation in His written Word, Jehoiakim took a scribe's knife and cut off consecutive strips of the scroll as Jehudi read them and tossed them into the fire".[332] Moreover, "It may be that by burning the scroll Jehoiakim was not being merely disrespectful of Yahweh and of Yahweh's messenger; he may have intended to negate the effective power of the scroll's words by an action of the kind known as sympathetic magic. More than merely dismissing Yahweh's word, Jehoiakim may have been actively opposing it".[333]

The reference to Jehoiakim's death (Jer. 36:30-31) seems to agree somewhat with Jeremiah 22:18-19, but not with 2 Kings 24:1-7,

There is a noticeable relationship between the account in 2 Kings of Josiah's response to the "scroll of the law" found in the Temple (2 Kgs. 22:3-23:24) and Jehoiakim's to the scroll containing Jeremiah's prophecies: Josiah tore his clothes, sought prophetic guidance (2 Kgs. 22:11-14), and burned the offending ritual objects; whereas Jehoiakim, showing no fear, tore and burned only the scroll (Jer. 36:22-26). And this was despite the fact that the menacing content of the two scrolls was essentially the same (2 Kgs. 22:14, 16; Jer. 36:3, 29). From the standpoint of Jeremiah and those in exile who agreed with him, this comparison is highly unfavorable to Jehoiakim. It is possible that the narrative of Jeremiah 36 is consciously patterned after the Deuteronomistic account of Josiah's reaction to the scroll.[334]

The purpose in writing these scrolls was to announce the impending destruction promised by God if they did not repent from their wicked ways. However, if they did repent, God promised to forgive them

---

[332] Gaebelein, ed., *The Expositor's Bible Commentary, Volume 6*, 607.

[333] "Jeremiah 36:20-26", In Gilbrant, ed., *The Complete Biblical Library Commentary, Jeremiah-Lamentations*.

[334] Mays, ed., *Harper's Bible Commentary*. 639.

for their wickedness. The fast was likely to be an occasion on which Jeremiah would find a large crowd of Jews who were open and humble.[335]

Please refer to *Fasting: Unlocking Spiritual Power and Breakthrough, Personal Reflections* under the heading "The Jeremiah Fast" to complete the Personal Reflections section of this study.

The Joel Fast

> Put on sackcloth, O priests, and mourn; wail, you who minister before the altar. Come, spend the night in sackcloth, you who minister before my God; for the grain offerings and drink offerings are withheld from the house of your God. Declare a holy fast; call a sacred assembly. Summon the elders and all who live in the land to the house of the LORD your God, and cry out to the LORD (Joel 1:13-14).

The book does not mention when Joel lived, but many believe that he prophesied during the reign of King Joash (835-796 BC). Even though the date is important, the message of Joel far outweighs the dating. The Book of Joel has three main messages from different periods of the prophet's ministry. The first, 1:2-2:2, is a manual for rectifying what we refer to as natural disasters. Joel used language with a high emotional impact to speak to people in desperate situations. The second message, 2:28-32, says that God's Spirit would be poured out broadly on God's people, regardless of their societal status or gender, so that they would engage in prophetic activities and experiences. The third message, 3:1-21, describes a time of wrath against the nations who had exploited God's people.

Joel instructed the people to implore Yahweh to change their situation. The first section (1:2-2:2) describes a locust plague and drought which caused extensive agricultural damage. Joel made it clear that this destruction was ultimately the doing of Yahweh. The people were called to mourn and turn to God. On the basis of a central theological confession concerning Yahweh's faithfulness and mercy, Joel argued that it was possible to get Yahweh to change his mind and bring restoration. God would bring restoration to the land, along with gladness and joy. We must always remember that God is immutable in reference to His character. However, He can relent in His dealings with His people, as seen in various contexts.

In Joel 1:13-14, we have the first "Day of Yahweh" passage, which refers to the calamity which the people faced, not Christ's return. The physical destruction of the land resulted in an emotional devastation for the people. Even though God had allowed this destruction, He would not expect His people in a disastrous predicament to rejoice. Their natural inclination would be one of sorrow and to express their sorrow before God (cf. vv. 14ff.). Joel connects rejoicing with the prosperity of the land (2:21-24, 26) and sorrow with its destruction. In the Old Testament, God frequently applies physical pressure to the people,

---

[335] Paschall and Hobbs, eds., *The Teacher's Bible Commentary*, 472. Walvoord and Zuck, eds., *The Bible Knowledge Commentary*, Vol. 1, 1180. Richards, *The Bible Reader's Companion*, 470. "The Major Prophets", In Dockery, ed., In *Holman Concise Bible Commentary*, 305. "Jeremiah 36", In Robert Jamieson, A. R. Fausset, David Brown, *A Commentary: Critical, Experimental, and Practical on the Old and New Testaments* (Toledo, OH: Jerome B. Names & Co., 1884), WORD*search* CROSS e-book.

especially to motivate them (cf. Am. 4:6-12). The blessings and curses of Deuteronomy 28 are based on the assumption that people are not expected to ignore their physical circumstances.[336]

Joel instructs the people to "put on sackcloth" which was common in mourning a death (e.g., Gen. 37:34; cf. 2 Sam. 3:31), it also expressed hopelessness (Est. 4:1ff.), demonstrated repentance (Jon. 3:5-8), and humility before God

> When the king heard the woman's words, he tore his robes. As he went along the wall, the people looked, and they saw that, under his robes, he had sackcloth on his body (2 Kgs. 6:30; cf. Ps. 35:13).

To "put on sackcloth" symbolized a person's passionate desire for mercy from God (Dan. 9:3). The shape of the שַׂק saq was comparable to a loincloth or a beanbag, while its dark color signified lamentation, grief and sorrow. In reference to the colour of the sackcloth, Isaiah states "I clothe the sky with darkness and make sackcloth its covering" (Isa. 50:3). He symbolically compares the dark colour of sackcloth with the darkness of Israel's sky on account of their sin. The darkness of the sackcloth contrasted the colourful garments worn at festive times and celebrations. Therefore, an absence of colour indicated sadness, while the presence of colour indicated joy. Another use of the שַׂק saq could be a holder of items such as food (Gen. 42:25, 27, 35; Lev. 11:32; Jos. 9:4) or as a blanket for covering (2 Sam. 21:10; Joel 1:13).[337]

Joel connects wearing sackcloth and mourning. In Old Testament times, lamenting or mourning was a central part of their daily life. People would lament or mourn because of death, natural disaster, war, sickness, or awareness of sin. Joel calls a collective lamentation and petition by the spiritual leaders and the congregation of all people. He calls for the priests as the spiritual leaders to set the example for the people to follow. Lamentation is encouraged in the Psalms, both directly and simply by the fact that many Psalms provide the opportunity for God's people to address Him concerning negative circumstances. God does not expect us to hide our sorrow, pain, horror or fear. For example, Joseph wailed bitterly and mourned for seven days at the threshing floor at Atad following the death of his father, Jacob (Gen. 50:10). He also instructs the priests to יָלַל yālal or "wail" which refers to "howling" from a person being in distress, especially that which comes with judgment and ensuing lament (Jer. 47:2; Hos. 7:14; Am. 8:3). Even though "to wail" or "to howl" specifically referred to the Israelites, יָלַל yālal frequently designates judgment against foreign nations (Isa. 23:1, 14; Jer. 48:20; 51:8). It can also denote "howling" used to mock the God of Israel (Isa. 52:5). Joel states "mourn like a virgin in sackcloth grieving for the husband of her youth" (Joel 1:8). To wail or to howl like a virgin or young bride described the extreme intensity of the situation.[338]

---

[336] "Joel: Summary", In Gilbrant, ed., *The Complete Biblical Library Commentary, Daniel-Malachi*.

[337] שַׂק saq "8012", In Gilbrant, ed., *The Complete Biblical Library Hebrew-English Dictionary, Sin-Taw*.

[338] סָפַד sāphadh "5792", In Gilbrant, ed., *The Complete Biblical Library Hebrew-English Dictionary, Nun-Ayin*. יָלַל yālal "3321", In Gilbrant, ed., *The Complete Biblical Library Hebrew-English Dictionary, Heth-Yodh*. "Joel 1", In Gilbrant, ed., *The Complete Biblical Library Commentary, Daniel-Malachi*.

The priests, in verse 13, were required to be in mourning since because of the invasion of the locusts and the devastation of the land they could not perform their priestly duties without an offering. Joel begins by addressing the spiritual leaders who were adversely affected by this infestation of locusts. This was similar to the Book of Haggai as the people were not fulfilling their duty to support the rebuilding of the temple. Likewise, in the Book of Malachi, the people were not tithing and the priesthood had developed a cynical attitude.

The Prophet Joel states

> declare a holy fast; call a sacred assembly. Summon the elders and all who live in the land to the house of the LORD your God, and cry out to the LORD (Joel 1:14).

The prophet Joel uses the phrase קַדְּשׁוּ־צוֹם *qaddĕšû-ṣôm* "sanctify a fast", "declare a holy fast" or literally or "make holy a fast" referring to making someone or something holy accomplished by the grace and power of God, and therefore qualifying them to be used by God for His purposes (Ex. 29:44). This begins with the priests and leaders and ceremonial acts of obedience including the altar and tabernacle. Joel summons the priests, elders, "and all who live in the land to the house of the LORD your God, and cry out to the LORD" and sanctify—atoning and purifying themselves from sin. He calls the people to set aside or sanctify a time of worship to the Lord.[339] He addresses the priests and the spiritual leaders who were called to assemble all people at the temple for a time of solemn prayer and fasting.

Joel calls the congregation of all people to a national or corporate time of fasting, which was an extraordinary event (Neh. 9:1-3; Jer. 36:9). Times of devastation called for drastic measures. It was to be a time of mourning and lamenting led by the elders (Eze. 30:1-3; cf. 1 Kgs. 21:8-12). The prophet Hosea lamented that the people of the Northern Kingdom did not cry to the Lord from the heart in their assemblies but gathered themselves together only for the sake of their grain and new wine (7:14). Joel's observation was the same. The prophet was concerned that the people give a fervent cry of repentance and call on God for forgiveness, lest a greater judgment descend on them soon.

Joel then proceeded to explain the reasons for the repentant cry. He strongly warned his hearers that all the available evidence pointed to the fact that the Day of the Lord stood near at hand. The locust plague was a dire warning that the day of the Lord's judgment for Judah was imminent. Likewise, the prophet Amos, Joel's contemporary, reported that certain "prophets" had misunderstood the Day of the Lord. It was not to be one of vindication for Israel but was to signal its demise (Am. 5:16-20). Like Joel, Amos warned of judgment due to sin and moral decay (3:1-5:13), a condition that required repentance (5:17).

Likewise, Hosea's constant message was one of rebuke for Israel's spiritual and moral corruption and warning of judgment for her spiritual infidelity and sins. Joel's message was in accord with this same picture of life found in the early eighth century BC.—a scene of spiritual bankruptcy, despite great political and economic assets. Joel message of the Day of Yahweh was certain, "Alas for that day! For the

---

[339] קָדַשׁ *qādhash* "7227", In Gilbrant, ed., *The Complete Biblical Library Hebrew-English Dictionary, Pe-Resh*.

day of the LORD is near; it will come like destruction from the Almighty" (Joel 1:15). Joel uses a play on words as the Hebrew words for "destruction" שֹׁד *shōdh* and "Almighty" שַׁדָּי *shadday* come from the same root word.[340]

The second context of fasting is seen in Joel 2:12-17,

"Even now", declares the LORD, "return to me with all your heart, with fasting and weeping and mourning". Rend your heart and not your garments. Return to the LORD your God, for he is gracious and compassionate, slow to anger and abounding in love, and he relents from sending calamity. Who knows? He may turn and have pity and leave behind a blessing—grain offerings and drink offerings for the LORD your God. Blow the trumpet in Zion, declare a holy fast, call a sacred assembly. Gather the people, consecrate the assembly; bring together the elders, gather the children, those nursing at the breast. Let the bridegroom leave his room and the bride her chamber. Let the priests, who minister before the LORD, weep between the temple porch and the altar. Let them say, "Spare your people, O LORD. Do not make your inheritance an object of scorn, a byword among the nations. Why should they say among the peoples, 'Where is their God?'".

This is one of Israel's central confessions regarding the nature of God—relational, gracious, and compassionate (cf. Ex. 34:6f.; Neh. 9:17; Ps. 103:8; Jon. 4:2). The people of God while enduring trials and suffering are to remember His chief attributes. Joel, like his contemporaries, emphasized the need of true repentance and total reliance upon the God of all mercies, turning from their past inequities, recognizing that the repentant heart is the only soil in which the regenerated soul can grow. Joel pleaded with the people for broken and contrite hearts (cf. Ps. 51:17). Even though outward conformity to worship is important, the primary importance to God is always the heart condition (cf. Isa. 1:11-17; 58:3b-12; Am. 5:21-24; Mic. 6:6-8).

Joel uses the verb שׁוּב *shûv* meaning "to repent", "to return", "to turn back", "to be restored", and "to hold back". The usage "to hold back" (Mal. 2:6) literally means "to hold back from sin" (Eze. 18:8) "to be brought back" or "to be led back" (Gen. 42:28; 43:12; Ex. 10:8). Once Joel had stated and then reiterated his petition, he laid the foundational attitude for acceptance—"he is gracious and compassionate" for all who are in need (Jon. 4:2), but He is a God of abounding love who has revealed himself to man in redemptive grace, "slow to anger and abounding in love" (Ex. 34:6) revealing Himself to his people in redemptive grace. The height of His compassion is that it ascends to Himself. The length of His compassion is that He is "slow to anger"; the breadth of His compassion is that He is "abounding in love"—abundant in His righteous concern for man's spiritual welfare. The depth of His compassion is seen in His willingness to reach down in forgiveness to man in his evil condition, "he relents from sending calamity".

---

[340] "Joel 1", In Gilbrant, ed., *The Complete Biblical Library Commentary, Daniel-Malachi*. Gaebelein, ed., *The Expositor's Bible Commentary, Volume 7*, 242-243. שֹׁד *shōdh* "8160", In Gilbrant, ed., *The Complete Biblical Library Hebrew-English Dictionary, Sin-Taw*. שַׁדָּי *shadday* "8163", In Gilbrant, ed., *The Complete Biblical Library Hebrew-English Dictionary, Sin-Taw*.

The phrase "return to me with all your heart, with fasting and weeping and mourning" indicates the depth of their wickedness and the need for extraordinary humiliation. The outward marks of repentance are to signify the depth of their sorrow for sin. Joel then calls them to "rend your heart and not your garments". He uses the verb קָרַע qāra which occurs 63 times in the Old Testament and means to "to tear in pieces", "to tear away", "to cut in pieces", "to tear out or off", "to tear open", or "to tear at". To "rend your heart" literally means "to cause pain or distress to the heart or emotions", "to pull something apart violently", "to tear (the hair or clothing) as a sign of anger, grief, or despair", or "to lacerate mentally or emotionally".[341] God calls for the three signs of "fasting and weeping and mourning",

> True heart-felt repentance would display itself in various outward acts. In ancient Israelite culture heart-deep repentance surfaced in demonstrations of humility and distress. Here Yahweh called for three signs: fasting, weeping, and lamentation. Joel had already called for fasting as part of a national service of lamentation (cf. 1:14). In ancient Israel fasting served the purpose of indicating (a) self-renunciation; (b) submission to God and circumstances; and (c) earnestness in the petition which grew out of the fasting. Weeping and lamentation were evidence of sorrow over a life of sin.[342]

Frequently it refers to an act of heartfelt and grievous affliction—tearing one's upper and under garment in front of the breast baring the sorrow of the heart (cf. Lev. 10:6). "Rending" of one's clothes could be accompanied by putting on sackcloth (שַׂק saq, Gen. 37:34), putting dirt or ashes on the head (1 Sam. 4:12), removing the shoes (2 Sam. 15:30), and putting the hands on the head (2 Sam. 13:19).[343] Joel follows prophetic tradition and appeals for more than just an external or cultic return to Yahweh; their whole conduct must change, which must begin in the inner depths of their being (cf. Hos. 6:1-6; Jer. 4:4; Deut. 10:16).[344]

The promise of judgment is conditional upon man's failure to follow God's standards and for people to repent and meet God in His gracious provision is to avert His just judgment. It would seem as though God has relented or "changed His mind" concerning His judgment or the punishment for man's guilt

> When the angel stretched out his hand to destroy Jerusalem, the LORD relented concerning the disaster and said to the angel who was afflicting the people, "Enough! Withdraw your hand." The angel of the LORD was then at the threshing floor of Araunah the Jebusite (2 Sam. 24:16).

However, to assert that God changes His mind in specific circumstances does not imply that God's character changes from one situation to another. God might even restore the forfeited blessings and the fertility of the land so that the discontinued sacrifices might again be offered, this time out of a pure

---

[341] "rend", In *Merriam-Webster's Collegiate Dictionary*.

[342] "Joel 2:12-13", In James E. Smith, *The Minor Prophets*, Old Testament Survey Series (Joplin, MO: College Press, 1994).

[343] קָרַע qāra ', "2074", In Harris, Archer, Jr., and Waltke, eds., *Theological Wordbook of the Old Testament*, 816.

[344] Brown, Fitzmyer, and Murphy, *The Jerome Biblical Commentary*, Vol. 1, 441.

heart.[345] Joel, for the second time, states "declare a holy fast" (cf. 1:14), which reiterates what he had stated earlier (2:15a parallels 2:1a; 2:15b parallels 1:14a). This emphasizes involvement of the entire community—no one was exempt.[346]

Please refer to *Fasting: Unlocking Spiritual Power and Breakthrough, Personal Reflections* under the heading "The Joel Fast" to complete the Personal Reflections section of this study.

The Nineveh Fast

Then the word of the LORD came to Jonah a second time: "Go to the great city of Nineveh and proclaim to it the message I give you". Jonah obeyed the word of the LORD and went to Nineveh. Now Nineveh was a very important city—a visit required three days. On the first day, Jonah started into the city. He proclaimed: "Forty more days and Nineveh will be overturned". The Ninevites believed God. They declared a fast, and all of them, from the greatest to the least, put on sackcloth. When the news reached the king of Nineveh, he rose from his throne, took off his royal robes, covered himself with sackcloth and sat down in the dust. Then he issued a proclamation in Nineveh: "By the decree of the king and his nobles: Do not let any man or beast, herd or flock, taste anything; do not let them eat or drink. But let man and beast be covered with sackcloth. Let everyone call urgently on God. Let them give up their evil ways and their violence. Who knows? God may yet relent and with compassion turn from his fierce anger so that we will not perish". When God saw what they did and how they turned from their evil ways, he had compassion and did not bring upon them the destruction he had threatened (Jon. 3:1-10).

There are many references to the city of Nineveh נִינְוֵה *nînĕwēh*, "a very important city"[347], but first and most important reference, is found in Genesis,

Cush was the father of Nimrod, who grew to be a mighty warrior on the earth. He was a mighty hunter before the LORD; that is why it is said, "Like Nimrod, a mighty hunter before the LORD". The first centers of his kingdom were Babylon, Erech, Akkad and Calneh, in Shinar. From that land he went to Assyria, where he built Nineveh, Rehoboth Ir, Calah and Resen, which is between Nineveh and Calah; that is the great city (Gen. 10:8-12).

As seen here, Nimrod began his kingdom in Babylonia and then travelled to Assyria where he built the cities of Nineveh, Rehoboth Ir, Calah, and Resen. Scripture speaks of Nineveh as a wicked city and the greatest enemy of the Northern Kingdom of Israel and the Southern Kingdom of Judah. The majority of references to Nineveh concern its wickedness and its subsequent fall. The entire Book of Nahum "An oracle concerning Nineveh" rejoices over the Lord's anger against Nineveh and its fall. Nahum calls

---

[345] "Joel 2", In Gilbrant, ed., *The Complete Biblical Library Commentary, Daniel-Malachi*. Gaebelein, ed., *The Expositor's Bible Commentary*, Vol. 7, 250-251. שׁוּב *shûv* "8178", In Gilbrant, ed., *The Complete Biblical Library Hebrew-English Dictionary, Sin-Taw*. "Joel 2", In Jamieson, Fausset, Brown, *A Commentary: Critical, Experimental, and Practical on the Old and New Testaments*. קָרָע *qāra'* "7458", In Gilbrant, ed., *The Complete Biblical Library Hebrew-English Dictionary, Pe-Resh*.

[346] Mays, ed., *Harper's Bible Commentary*. 718.

[347] "A very important city" עִיר גְּדוֹלָה לֵאלֹהִים *ir-gedolah lelohim* translates "a city great for God". Gaebelein, ed., *The Expositor's Bible Commentary, Volume 7*, 381.

Nineveh, the Assyrian capital, "the city of blood, full of lies, full of plunder, never without victims! (Nah. 3:1). The prophet Zephaniah gives a brief description of the destruction of Assyria and the fall of Nineveh (Zeph. 2:13-15). The New Testament refers to Jonah and Nineveh in Matthew 12:39-42 and Luke 11:29-32.[348]

Jonah sets the example by repenting and in turn the Ninevites (Gentiles) repent. It seems as though the king of Nineveh understands that there is no reason for God giving them a forty-day warning period if there is not some chance, however slight, that God would relent in bringing the coming destruction of Nineveh. Therefore, he decrees an immediate response from all citizens and all animals to fast and wear sackcloth. Verse 5 is a key to the Book of Jonah. As Jonah "from inside the fish Jonah prayed to the LORD his God" (Jon. 2:1), likewise, "the Ninevites believed God" and declared a fast.

As outward symbols of inward contrition and humiliation they fasted (cf. 1 Sam. 7:6; 2 Sam. 1:12; Neh. 1:4; Zech. 7:5) and "put on sackcloth" (cf. Gen. 37:34; 1 Kgs. 21:27; Neh. 9:1; Est. 4:1-4; Lam. 2:10; Dan. 9:3; Joel 1:8). All people from the poor class to the upper class hoped that God might turn from His anger and spare them. They had heard the word of the Lord and believed *in* God. The Ninevites did not only observe the word of the Lord, they repented and turned *to* Him. This was demonstrated by fasting and wearing sackcloth.[349] It represented self-abasement as an outward expression and reflected an authentic and sincere turning from their former way of living and turning to God for hope and mercy. The wearing of sackcloth was the standard obligatory accompaniment of fasting at the time. In most cases, sackcloth and fasting go hand-in-hand.[350]

> Then David said to Joab and all the people with him, "Tear your clothes and put on sackcloth and walk in mourning in front of Abner." King David himself walked behind the bier. . . . Then they all came and urged David to eat something while it was still day; but David took an oath, saying, "May God deal with me, be it ever so severely, if I taste bread or anything else before the sun sets!" (2 Sam. 3:31, 35; cf. Isa. 58:5; Dan. 9:3).

It is interesting that in verse 6, that "the king of Nineveh" also humbled himself, fasted and wore sackcloth signifying that Jonah's message included everyone, no exceptions. Likewise, the focus must be upon his message to Nineveh and not to Assyria in general. Moreover, the name, titles, and achievements of the king of Nineveh are irrelevant since both him and the city are connected and will share the same fate. The existential crisis presented here is that the king and his people need to act urgently and their fate will be determined by their response.

---

[348] "Nineveh (Place)", In Freedman, ed., *The Anchor Yale Bible Dictionary*, Vol. 4, 1118.

[349] Sackcloth, a coarse cloth, often made of goat's hair, was the primary clothes worn by the poor, prisoners, and slaves, and those who mourned (Eze. 7:18). When the prophet wore sackcloth (2 Kgs. 1:8; Zech. 13:4; Mk. 1:6), it was partly to associate themselves with the poor, and also as a sign of mourning for the sins of the people. When used in mourning, it covered no more of the body than was demanded by decency. When used by the Ninevites, it expressed their complete inability to contend with the divine decree and that they were the slaves of the supreme God. Gaebelein, ed., *The Expositor's Bible Commentary, Volume 7*, 382

[350] Walvoord and Zuck, eds., *The Bible Knowledge Commentary*, Vol. 1, 1469. Paul Mackrell, *Opening Up Jonah*, Opening Up Commentary (Leominster: Day One Publications, 2007), 73-74.

Verse 7 depicts the scope of the repentance that not only included the king, and the people, but also the "beast, herd or flock"; "Do not let any man or beast, herd or flock, taste anything; do not let them eat or drink" (Jon. 3:7). Even though there are no Mesopotamian records of animal involvement in mourning rites, fasting, and wearing of sackcloth, there is nothing alien to the Oriental mind in it. Herodotus of Halicarnassus, in *"The Histories"* states that at the death of Masistius, the Persian Army lamented for him.

> When the horse reached the camp, Mardonius and all the Persian army made great lamentation for Masistius. They shaved off all the hair from their own heads, and cut the manes from their war-horses and their sumpter-beasts, while they vented their grief in such loud cries that all Boeotia resounded with the clamour, because they had lost the man who, next to Mardonius, was held in the greatest esteem, both by the king and by the Persians generally. So the barbarians, after their own fashion, paid honours to the dead Masistius (9.24).[351]

It is interesting that the king of Nineveh decreed that "beast, herd or flock" were also to be deprived of food and water. Even though they were not responsible for bringing God's judgment, man and "beast, herd or flock" were connected within the life of the community. They shared with man when there was abundance or a lack of food and water. It was therefore appropriate that the bellowing and moaning of distressed animals should mingle with the cries of the people as they sought God—one united voice ascending to the Lord, just as their wickedness had done (1:2). In the Book of Joel, the cattle, herds, and sheep also feel the effects of the devastation of locusts, "How the cattle moan! The herds mill about because they have no pasture; even the flocks of sheep are suffering" (1:18).[352]

In addition to the scope of Jonah's message, only a small percentage of the Ninevite population could be included. Of greater importance would be the Assyrian attitude toward others. The prophet Amos states that even though there was no written law, there was an accepted code of conduct. According to the Assyrians, they were above the lesser breeds and could ignore the dictates of conscience and compassion in their conduct towards their neighbors (Am. 1:3-2:3). It is interesting that Habakkuk applies this same word "violence" (חָמָס *chāmās*) to the Chaldeans (Hab. 1:9; 2:8, 17). It is very easy to slip into the concept that our position gives us the right to dominate others. Much racial prejudice and discrimination is the result of this.

In verse 8, the phrase, "Let them give up their evil ways and their violence" (3:8) is a Hebrew expression that connects the general with the specific. In Hebrew thinking, "evil ways" was all inclusive in relation to law and conscience. The noun used for "violence" *chāmās* refers to defying the law by someone who thinks that they are above the law or not responsible for their actions. It refers to the wickedness of people and the product of calloused hearts, "From their callous hearts comes iniquity; the evil conceits of their minds know no limits" (Ps. 73:7). The judgment that is administered by God is

---

[351] Herodotus of Halicarnassus (484-425 BC), *The Histories*, <http://www.swartzentrover.com/cotor/E-Books/misc/Herodotus/THindex.htm>, 9.24. Accessed on November 28, 2013.
[352] Mackrell, *Opening Up Jonah*, 80.

because He hates violence "I hate a man's covering himself with violence as well as with his garment" (Mal. 2:16).[353]

The operative phrase in verses 9-10 is that "God may yet relent and with compassion turn from his fierce anger" (Jon. 3:9-10; cf. Ps. 106:11-45). The focus in these verses is that God "relented", "had compassion" and did not carry out His judgment upon Nineveh. The verb נחם *nācham* used here means "to relent", "to repent", or "to comfort". "He who is the Glory of Israel does not lie or change his mind; for he is not a man, that he should change his mind" (1 Sam. 15:29). However, Exodus 32:14 states "Then the LORD relented and did not bring on his people the disaster he had threatened" and also Jeremiah 18:8, "if that nation I warned repents of its evil, then I will relent and not inflict on it the disaster I had planned". God cannot sin and never needs to turn away from evil deeds, thoughts, or behaviour or repent since it is not in His nature. God rejected King Saul, which led to his kingdom being taken from him because of the sins of impatience (ch. 13), pride (ch. 14), and disobedience (ch. 15). The context here refers to God's irrevocable decision to give the kingdom to David rather than His irreversible decision to reject Saul. God is truthful, "does not lie" and compassionate and man is deceitful and merciless. More often than not, it is the removal of threatened evil, punishment, and death that we experience. The opposite, however, is also true (cf. Jer. 18:9-10)—we realize that the change of mind, "repentance", is due to divine compassion for frail and mortal man.

In the end, "compassion" is not the best picture since it lacks the concept of change, but "relent" is a better representation of the idea in focus. God relenting was the result of the repentance of Ninevites who seemed to realize that true faith must be connected with true repentance. Jesus in referring to the men of Nineveh and their act of repentance argues for the historicity of this event. "The men of Nineveh will stand up at the judgment with this generation and condemn it; for they repented at the preaching of Jonah, and now one greater than Jonah is here" (Mt. 12:41).[354]

Please refer to *Fasting: Unlocking Spiritual Power and Breakthrough, Personal Reflections* under the heading "The Nineveh Fast" to complete the Personal Reflections section of this study.

The Fasts of Jewish Captivity

In the fourth year of King Darius, the word of the LORD came to Zechariah on the fourth day of the ninth month, the month of Kislev. The people of Bethel had sent Sharezer and Regem-Melek, together with their men, to entreat the LORD by asking the priests of the house of the LORD Almighty and the prophets, "Should I mourn and fast in the fifth month, as I have done for so many years?" Then the word of the LORD Almighty came to me: "Ask all the people of the land and the priests, 'When you fasted and mourned in the fifth and seventh months for the past seventy years, was it really for me that you fasted? And when you were eating and drinking, were

---

[353] חָמָס *chāmās* "2660", In Gilbrant, ed., *The Complete Biblical Library Hebrew-English Dictionary, Heth-Yodh.*

[354] Gaebelein, ed., *The Expositor's Bible Commentary, Volume 7*, 382-384. נחם *nācham* "5341", In Gilbrant, ed., *The Complete Biblical Library Hebrew-English Dictionary, Nun-Ayin.* "Jonah 3", In Gilbrant, ed., *The Complete Biblical Library Commentary, Daniel-Malachi.*

you not just feasting for yourselves? Are these not the words the LORD proclaimed through the earlier prophets when Jerusalem and its surrounding towns were at rest and prosperous, and the Negev and the western foothills were settled?'". "This is what the LORD Almighty says: 'Administer true justice; show mercy and compassion to one another. Do not oppress the widow or the fatherless, the alien or the poor. In your hearts do not think evil of each other'" (Zech. 7:1-10).

This is what the LORD Almighty says: "The fasts of the fourth, fifth, seventh and tenth months will become joyful and glad occasions and happy festivals for Judah. Therefore love truth and peace" (Zech. 8:19).

The fasts described above allude to the Lord's message to true fasting found in Isaiah 58 since both prophets speak of the people fasting for selfish reasons, which lacked religious significance and spiritual purpose. Therefore, like Isaiah, these fasts were rejected since they left God out of the picture and they tried to manipulate God for their own purposes.

The only required fast stipulated in the Law of Moses was to be observed on the Day of Atonement (Lev. 23:26-32) and is referred to in the Book of Acts as "the fast" (27:9). Besides the Day of Atonement, another Old Testament reference to fasting is during the Jewish captivity (Zech. 7:1-7; 8:19). "The purpose of chapters 7 and 8 is to impress on the people their need to live righteously in response to their past judgment and future glory".[355]

As can be seen early in the prophetic ministry of Zechariah (1:3-6) his interest was in the spiritual renewal of the postexilic community. In chapters seven and eight, he further confronts this issue as he speaks of the problem of fasting and the eschatological promise of restoration and rejoicing. It had been sixty-eight years after the destruction, when the rebuilding of the Temple was almost complete; the question naturally arose whether the time had not come to annul these fasts, since Jeremiah's prophecy about the duration of the exile might well be thought to have been fulfilled.

Moreover, it had been two years since Zechariah had exhorted the inhabitants of Jerusalem with his visions and sustained Haggai and encouraging a collaborative effort to build the temple in Jerusalem. These two chapters provide a limited perspective into Zechariah's prophetic ministry of conveying the Word of the Lord. Zechariah responds to an inquiry concerning fasting (7:1-3) in four messages (7:4, 8-9; 8:1-2, 18-19). These messages can be summed up as: (a) the message of rebuke (7:4-7); (b) the message of repentance (7:8-14); (c) the message of restoration (8:1-17); and (d) the message of rejoicing (8:18-23).[356]

Zechariah writes about a delegation from Bethel who raise a question about fasting, "Should I mourn and fast in the fifth month, as I have done for so many years?" (Zech. 7:3; cf. Ezra 2:28; Neh. 7:32; 11:31). This delegation included "Sharezer" שַׁר־אֶצֶר *śar-'eṣer* meaning "protect the king" and "Regem-Melech" וְרֶגֶם *wĕregem* meaning "heap of stones" and מֶלֶךְ *melek* meaning "king". This delegation was probably, based upon their foreign names, from Babylonia and addressed their question to the temple

---

[355] Gaebelein, ed., *The Expositor's Bible Commentary, Volume 7*, 643.

[356] "Zechariah 7:1", In Gilbrant, ed., *The Complete Biblical Library Commentary, Daniel-Malachi*. Walvoord and Zuck, eds., *The Bible Knowledge Commentary*, Vol. 1, 1559-61.

priests and divinely appointed prophets, which included Zechariah. The question raised is that should these exilic fasts continue to be observed since the fast was instituted in commemoration of the destruction of Jerusalem which was almost rebuilt? The Old Testament itself required only one fast day—on *Yom Kippur*, the Day of Atonement. According to 8:19, the question included all the fasts commemorating major events related to the fall and destruction of Jerusalem and the temple, namely, the "fasts of the fourth, fifth, seventh and tenth months". The four annual fasts, established in memory of national calamities and referred to by Zechariah (Zech. 8:19), had fallen into desuetude and not revived until after the destruction of Jerusalem by the Romans.[357]

The four Fasts of Jewish Captivity are referred to as "normal fasts" since they lasted for one 24 hour period.

1. The fast of the fourth month fell on the ninth of Tammuz, the day when the city walls were breached (2 Kgs. 25:3-4; Jer. 39:2).
2. The fast of the fifth month was on the ninth of Ab, when the house of God was destroyed by fire (2 Kgs. 25:8-10).
3. The fast of the seventh month was on the third of Tishri, the anniversary of the assassination of Gedaliah the son of Ahikam (2 Kgs. 25; Jer. 41:2).
4. The fast of the tenth month fell on the tenth of Tebeth, which was the day when the king of Babylon laid siege to Jerusalem (2 Kgs. 25:1; Eze. 24:2).[358]

The first fast was in the fourth month and the seventeenth day of Tammuz, known as the anniversary of the capture of Jerusalem by the Chaldeans. The Jews also commemorated the tablets of the covenant being broken into pieces because of the idolatry of the Israelites in creating the golden calf (Ex. 32:19). In the first of the four messages, Zechariah asks "all the people of the land and the priests"

> When you fasted and mourned in the fifth and seventh months for the past seventy years, was it really for me that you fasted? And when you were eating and drinking, were you not just feasting for yourselves? Are these not the words the LORD proclaimed through the earlier prophets when Jerusalem and its surrounding towns were at rest and prosperous, and the Negev and the western foothills were settled? (Zech. 7:5-7).

Their fasting and feasting for the past seventy years had been for selfish reasons and lacked religious motive and spiritual purpose. Therefore, it was rejected by God, which was in agreement with the Word of the Lord spoken through earlier prophets in times of abundance in Jerusalem (7:4-7).

The second fast was in the fifth month on the ninth of Ab (Num. 14:27), where the Jews commemorated the burning of the city and temple,

---

[357] "Fasting", In James Hastings, ed., *A Dictionary of Christ and the Gospels*, 12 Vols (New York: Charles Scribner's Sons, 1906), Rick Meyers, e-Sword, Version 10.2.1, 2000-2012, <http://www.e-sword.net>.

[358] "Fast", In M'Clintock and Strong, eds., *Cyclopedia of Biblical and Ecclesiastical Literature*, <http://www.e-sword.net>.

On the tenth day of the fifth month, in the nineteenth year of Nebuchadnezzar king of Babylon, Nebuzaradan commander of the imperial guard, who served the King of Babylon, came to Jerusalem. He set fire to the temple of the Lord, the royal palace and all the houses of Jerusalem. Every important building he burned down (Jer. 52:12-13).

Jeremiah 52 is parallel to 2 Kings 24:18-25:30, except for Jeremiah 52:28-30 which is missing in 2 Kings 25 and Gedaliah's death is missing in Jeremiah 52. The last chapter of Jeremiah is a detailed account of Jerusalem's fall to the Babylonians which is probably included to validate Jeremiah's prophetic message of judgment were fulfilled.[359]

In the second message, the Lord states "Administer true justice; show mercy and compassion to one another. Do not oppress the widow or the fatherless, the alien or the poor. In your hearts do not think evil of each other" (Zech. 7:9-10). The basis of this teaching insisted on an internal moral reformation and not external observances, which was founded upon the Israelites rejection of God and the subsequent calamities of their captivity and dispersion (7:8-14).

The third fast of the seventh month on the third day of Tisri (2 Kgs. 25) the anniversary and remembrance of the murder of Gedaliah,

In the seventh month Ishmael son of Nethaniah, the son of Elishama, who was of royal blood and had been one of the king's officers, came with ten men to Gedaliah son of Ahikam at Mizpah. While they were eating together there, Ishmael son of Nethaniah and the ten men who were with him got up and struck down Gedaliah son of Ahikam, the son of Shaphan, with the sword, killing the one whom the king of Babylon had appointed as governor over the land (Jer. 41:1-2).

The Jews still keep the fast of Gedaliah in the seventh month on the third day of the month—the first and second days are the New Year. Ishmael came from a collateral line of the Davidic family through Elishama, son of David (cf. 2 Sam. 5:16). Moreover, he was prominent in affairs of state with Zedekiah. The third message speaks of hope and promise and that holiness and abundance will be their near future. Zechariah's message of hope and abundance contrasts a past of suffering and division and exhorting the Jews to obedient living (8:1-17).[360]

The fourth fast was in the tenth month (Jer. 52:4; Eze. 33:21; 2 Kgs. 25:1) where the Jews celebrated the beginning of the siege of the holy city by Nebuchadnezzar.[361]

This is what the LORD Almighty says: "The fasts of the fourth, fifth, seventh and tenth months will become joyful and glad occasions and happy festivals for Judah. Therefore love truth and peace" (Zech. 8:19).

---

[359] "Jeremiah 52:1-34", In Dockery, ed., In *Holman Concise Bible Commentary*, 309. Gaebelein, ed., *The Expositor's Bible Commentary*, Vol. 6, 687. "Jeremiah 52:4-14", In Gilbrant, ed., *The Complete Biblical Library Commentary, Jeremiah-Lamentations*.

[360] Gaebelein, ed., *The Expositor's Bible Commentary, Volume 6*, 629.

[361] James M. Freeman and Harold J. Chadwick, *Manners & Customs of the Bible*, Revised edition (North Brunswick, NJ: Bridge-Logos Publishers, 1998), 416.

The final message foresees the response to Bethel's question, "Should I mourn and fast in the fifth month, as I have done for so many years?" (Zech. 7:3). It will be through reforming the fasts of the captivity into "joyful and glad occasions and happy festivals for Judah" (Zech. 8:19) and "many peoples and powerful nations" will join them in Jerusalem and together "seek the LORD Almighty and to entreat him" (Zech. 8:20-22). It will be an honour and a sense of protection to be associated with a Jew (Zech. 8:18-23).[362]

The "joyful and glad occasions" refers to the celebration of the dedication of the wall of Jerusalem subsequent to Israel's return from the Babylonian captivity. Zechariah uses the noun שִׂמְחָה simchāh to describe this celebration that was so loud that "The sound of rejoicing in Jerusalem could be heard far away" (Neh. 12:43).[363] In these two short messages, Zechariah instead of observing fasts which reminded them of their past, he calls them to look to the future when their times of mourning and fasting "will become joyful and glad occasions and happy festivals for Judah" (cf. Isa. 65:18f.; Jer. 31:10-14). He exhorts them to "love truth and peace" and that they will become the basis of blessing to Gentiles, for all the peoples of the earth will join them on pilgrimages to worship the Lord together in Jerusalem.

Apart from the two great commandments (Lev. 19:18, 34; Deut. 6:4-9), only Amos 5:15 describes the command to love in the Old Testament, though Psalms 31:23 is an exhortation to love the Lord. This love for the Lord inspires the whole covenant relationship and likewise the ethics set out under the covenant as the condition of blessing.[364]

> Do not seek revenge or bear a grudge against anyone among your people, but love your neighbor as yourself. I am the LORD. . . The foreigner residing among you must be treated as your native-born. Love them as yourself, for you were foreigners in Egypt. I am the LORD your God (Lev. 19:18, 34).

> Hear, O Israel: The LORD our God, the LORD is one. Love the LORD your God with all your heart and with all your soul and with all your strength. These commandments that I give you today are to be on your hearts. Impress them on your children. Talk about them when you sit at home and when you walk along the road, when you lie down and when you get up. Tie them as symbols on your hands and bind them on your foreheads. Write them on the doorframes of your houses and on your gates (Deut. 6:4-9).

Zechariah points out that their fasts were based upon selfish motives. These fasts, Zechariah charges, are self-centered: "when you were eating and drinking, were you not just feasting for yourselves?" (7:6). As with so much religious activity, one's relationship with God is abandoned. The people need to return to the teaching of the former prophets from which they could learn the things that please God (7:7). The Jews of Babylon, where the practice of fasting on these dates had originated, were expressing grief at

---

[362] Gaebelein, ed., *The Expositor's Bible Commentary*, Vol. 7, 642-643.

[363] שִׂמְחָה simchāh "7977", In Gilbrant, ed., *The Complete Biblical Library Hebrew-English Dictionary*, Sin-Taw.

[364] Gaebelein, ed., *The Expositor's Bible Commentary*, Volume 7, 654. M. F. Unger, *Commentary on Zechariah* (Grand Rapids, MI: Zondervan Publishing House, 1962), 148. Joyce C. Baldwin, *Haggai, Zechariah, Malachi: An Introduction and Commentary* (Downers Grove, IL: InterVarsity Press, 1972), 155, note 1. "Zechariah 8 18-23", In Gilbrant, ed., *The Complete Biblical Library Commentary, Daniel-Malachi*.

their situation, not sorrow that they had sinned so terribly against God. Zechariah's word from the Lord was that the Jews' fasting had been nothing but a hypocritical ritual motivated by self-interest rather than genuine sorrow and repentance for sin and the desire to renew their faithfulness to God.

Please refer to *Fasting: Unlocking Spiritual Power and Breakthrough, Personal Reflections* under the heading "The Fasts of Jewish Captivity" to complete the Personal Reflections section of this study.

Chapter 9: Fasting in the New Testament

The purpose of this chapter is to describe fasting in Greek antiquity, its function within Intertestamental Judaism, the foundational principles to fasting in the New Testament, the life and ministry of Jesus, and the Apostle Paul's use of fasting in relation to his good standing as a minister of the Lord.

Fasting in Greek Antiquity

When we think of fasting in Greek Antiquity, we need to consider the historical basis for fasting, which the earliest records date back to ancient Greece and the Near East. The philosophers Plato and Socrates were known to fast for mental efficiency and Pythagoras, an Ionian Greek philosopher and mathematician required his students to fast before entering his classes. This ancient type of fasting was referred to as therapeutic fasting, which the ancient Egyptians resolved syphilis with therapeutic fasting. Moreover, the Greek physician Hippocrates recognized therapeutic fasting as of primary importance in disease. Therapeutic fasting not only means zero calorie intake, but also abstaining from all food consumption, except for pure water.

In the fifth and fourth centuries BC, Hippocrates and Aristotle used *nēsteia* to refer to men who were starving because of a lack of food. Among the pagans, *nēsteia* referred to religious fasting, and the Greeks and Romans often fasted before approaching their gods or in expectation of blessing or the reception of some type of power. Moreover, Athenian women in the month of October celebrated the one day fast known as *Thesmophoria* in an attempt to receive favour from the goddess Demeter and become more fruitful in their womb. This day was called *Hē Nēsteia*, or "The Fast".[365]

It is interesting that five of the eight uses of *nēsteia* connect fasting with prayer, which builds upon the Old Testament emphasis of fasting. Moreover, many Greek manuscripts exclude any connection to fasting in three of these passages (Mt. 17:21; Mk. 9:29; 1 Cor. 7:5). The classical Greek adjective νῆστις *nēstis* suggests a specific period of time of abstaining from food, whether religious or non-religious and voluntarily or involuntarily. However, its usage in the New Testament does not refer to voluntary religious fasting, but to the same occasion (Mt. 15:32; Mk. 8:3). Jesus is moved with compassion, and hesitates to send the multitude away since they had been "fasting" for three days and did not want them to faint before they arrived at their homes.[366]

Some major ancient Greek manuscripts have "prayer and fasting" at the end of Mark 9:29. Perhaps the words were added at an earlier date by some scribes to the textual tradition to support asceticism. But

---

[365] νηστεία *nēsteia* "3383", In Gilbrant, ed., *The Complete Biblical Library Greek-English Dictionary, Lambda-Omicron*. Kittel, Bromiley and Friedrich, eds., *Theological Dictionary of the New Testament*, electronic ed., Vol. 4, 924-35.

[366] νηστεία *nēsteia* "3383", In Gilbrant, ed., *The Complete Biblical Library Greek-English Dictionary, Lambda-Omicron*. νῆστις *nēstis* "3385", In Gilbrant, ed., *The Complete Biblical Library Greek-English Dictionary, Lambda-Omicron*.

the words, if original, refer to a practical means of focusing one's attention more fully on God for a specific purpose, for a specific period of time.[367]

It is interesting that fasting in antiquity stands in no close connection with ethos and ethics. Conversely, the moral idea of ἐγκράτεια[368] which the philosophers proclaimed and sought to achieve in their schools never led to a demand for times of νηστεία *nēsteia*, though we do find the utopian desire for a life without any nourishment at all. The fasting practiced in the Graeco-Roman world is not asceticism. In the world of the Greeks, they were very familiar with spiritual asceticism in the sense of controlling their passions and performing righteous acts or consciously controlling their thoughts and desires. It is a rite which is observed for the sake of relations to the spirits and the gods.[369]

Fasting in Intertestamental Judaism

In Intertestamental Judaism, ascetic practices increased among religious groups, but also in prevalent piety. Fasting was seen an act of demonstrating faithfulness, commended like prayer and almsgiving (Tobit 12:8), was rewarded with divine favour (Judith 4:9), and cautions those who attempt to twist the divine will (Judith 8:16). Ben Sira emphasizes prophetic warnings against adherence to rituals (Sirach 36:26) and *The Testaments of the Twelve Patriarchs* frequently mention fasting as the symbol of piety (*Testament of Joseph* 3:4), "They that fast for God's sake receive beauty of face" (cf. Dan. 1:15; Mt. 6:16-18). In Matthew 6:16-18, voluntary fasting anticipates a religious exercise, but Jesus warns the disciples about making it an occasion for a parade of piety.

Flavius Josephus, in *The Wars of the Jews* (*Bellum Judaicum*), states that the ascetic practices of the Essenes included fasting. The Dead Sea Scrolls contain no specific reference to community observances except for the Day of Atonement, with possible alluding to individual practices and Philo of Alexandria describes the Egyptian Therapeuts as fasting during the day.[370] According to Luke, the devout Pharisee fasted two times per week and in the Mishnah reference to fasting concerned adherence to special devotions during times of famine, and not a regular pious devotion (Babylonian Talmud, *Ta'anit*, 12a; *Didache* 8:1). Nevertheless, the ascetic tendency of Pharisaism is indisputable, and the rabbinic warnings against the danger of excessive mourning fasts for the destruction of the Temple (Babylonian Talmud, *Ta'anit*, 57) only serve to underscore the point that asceticism was a customary reaction to such disasters.

---

[367] Walvoord and Zuck, eds., *The Bible Knowledge Commentary*, Vol. 2, 139.

[368] It may be derived from ἐν κράτος (ἔχων) with its implication of having power in oneself, or from ἐν κράτει (ὤν) implying a status of power. ἐγκρατής means one who has a status of power or rule, who has power over something, whether this power be factual or spiritual. It thus means "to have power or dominion over all things and over oneself", i.e., "to be inwardly strong", cf. Plato *Phaedrus*, 256b; Plato *Epistulae*, VII, 331d. . . ἐγκράτεια thus means the "dominion which one has over oneself or something" in the sense that one may or may not have it, that one can bear it, that one thus controls it. Kittel, Bromiley and Friedrich, eds., *Theological Dictionary of the New Testament*, electronic ed., Vol. 2, 340.

[369] Kittel, Bromiley and Friedrich, eds., *Theological Dictionary of the New Testament*, electronic ed., Vol. 1, 927. Kittel, Bromiley and Friedrich, eds., *Theological Dictionary of the New Testament*, electronic ed., Vol. 4, 494. Porphyrius of Tyre, *De Abstinentia*, I, 27: λεπτὸν δὲ τὸ σιτίον καὶ ἐγγὺς τεῖνον ἀποσιτίας cf. 37f.

[370] "The Wars of the Jews", In Flavius Josephus, *The Works of Josephus: Complete and Unabridged* (Peabody, MA: Hendrickson Publishers, 1987), 2.8.5. Philo of Alexandria and Yonge. *The Works of Philo, De vita contemplative*, 34.

In addition to the sects, there were individual ascetics during this period, such as Haninah ben Dosa (Babylonian Talmud, *Ta'anit*, 24b) and John the Baptist (Mt. 11:18). Haninah ben Dosa fasted to increase the effectiveness of his charismatic prayer and John the Baptist sought to evoke through his abstinence simplicity and dependence upon God. Therefore, in the historicity of the New Testament, there is extensive acceptance of voluntary fasting as a form of religious piety, and likewise, a spontaneous rise of individual and corporate asceticism. In the Roman world of the first century, "Fasting like a Jew" had become a proverbial ideology.[371]

Fasting in Early Christianity

When we think of fasting in the New Testament, we need to consider the historical basis for fasting. The practice of fasting in early Christianity was similar to the Jewish practice. When Christian leaders were appointed to a specific ministry or task, the church leaders fasted (Acts 13:2-3; 14:23). In the Gospel According to Luke, the prophetess Anna is a model of traditional piety of widows, expressed in prayer and fasting (Lk. 2:36-37; cf. Acts 6:1; 1 Tim. 5:5) and likewise, Cornelius, a God-fearer and a man of prayer and almsgiving (Acts 10:30-31).[372]

There are two synonyms that are used in reference to fasting. The first is the noun ἀσιτίας *asitias* (Acts 27:21) in the sense of "hunger" and the noun ταπεινοφροσύνη, *tapeinophrosunē* (Acts 20:19; Eph. 4:2; Phil 2:3; Col. 2:18, 23; 3:12; 1 Pet. 5:5) meaning "humiliation of mind" or "affliction of one's soul". This noun portrays a humility that innately develops out of a heart full of love for the Lord. This exemplifies the attitude of the Christian servant, which Jesus modeled. Jesus also lived and taught that only this "humiliation of mind"—a penitent heart is the foundation on which spiritual life can grow and prosper.[373]

In relation to Jewish practice, *Yom Kippur* כִּפֻּרִיוֹם , is the only New Testament fast recorded in Acts 27:9, but some devout Pharisees would fast twice a week (Lk. 18:12), while other Jews such as Anna might fast regularly (Lk. 2:37). The only occurrence of Jesus fasting is seen in His temptation in the wilderness (Mt. 4:1-11; Lk. 4:1-13). He emphasized that those who fast should be joyful during times of fasting and taught His followers to fast towards God and not towards man (Mt. 6:16-18). When the disciples of John came to Jesus and asked Him why His disciples do not fast, Jesus did not discourage them from fasting, but stated that as long as the bridegroom was with them that is would not be appropriate for them to fast (Mt. 9:14-17; Mk. 2:18-22; Lk. 5:33-39).

In the Book of Acts, church leaders fasted when choosing missionaries (13:2-3) and elders (14:23).

---

[371] "Fast, Fasting", In Freedman, ed., *The Anchor Yale Bible Dictionary*, Vol. 2, 774.

[372] Kittel, Bromiley and Friedrich, eds., *Theological Dictionary of the New Testament*, electronic ed., Vol. 4, 931.

[373] "Fast, Fasting", In Freedman, ed., *The Anchor Yale Bible Dictionary*, Vol. 2, 773. ἀσιτία *asitia* "770", In Gilbrant, ed., *The Complete Biblical Library Greek-English Dictionary, Alpha-Gamma*. ταπεινοφροσύνη *tapeinophrosunē* "4863", In Gilbrant, ed., *The Complete Biblical Library Greek-English Dictionary, Sigma-Omega*.

They preached the gospel in that city and won a large number of disciples. Then they returned to Lystra, Iconium and Antioch, strengthening the disciples and encouraging them to remain true to the faith. "We must go through many hardships to enter the kingdom of God," they said. Paul and Barnabas appointed elders for them in each church and, with prayer and fasting, committed them to the Lord, in whom they had put their trust (Acts 14:21-23).

Notice that this was done "in each church" not just in what might be considered Jewish churches where fasting might be considered a Jewish custom. The Apostle Paul referred to personal fasting twice (2 Cor. 6:5; 11:27). In 2 Corinthians 6:5, Paul uses the Greek noun νηστεία *nēsteia* for voluntary fasting—self-discipline. In 2 Corinthians 11:27, Paul mentions both involuntary "hunger and thirst" (λιμός καί δίψος *limos kai dipsos*) and voluntary going "without food" (νηστεία *nēsteia*), which was already discussed in the Apostle Paul Fast.[374]

In conclusion, the following has been discussed: (a) our Lord Jesus fasted in a time of temptation; (b) Jesus taught His disciples concerning fasting on several occasions; (c) He also foretold of a time when His disciples would fast; (d) He instructed His disciples that there are times when the combination of fasting and prayer might be more efficacious than prayer alone; (e) the early church fasted in their service to the Lord; (f) the Apostle Paul regarded fasting as a mark of his ministry; and (g) prayer and fasting are often connected and utilized whenever there was a strong desire for God's blessing and guidance. In view of these above stated times of fasting, one can conclude that fasting does indeed have a place in the lives of Christians today.[375]

Fasting in the Life of Jesus

The majority of the references in the Synoptic Gospels follow the established pattern of piety suggested in 1st century Judaism and early Christianity with the exception of Mark 2:18-22. The Matthean narrative is the longest of three gospel narratives and states that "after fasting forty days and forty nights, he was hungry" (Mt. 4:2; cf. Ex. 34:28). The Lukan narrative parallels the Matthean account in stating, "where for forty days he was tempted by the devil. He ate nothing during those days, and at the end of them he was hungry" (Lk. 4:2). He ate no food and appears to have had only water. The reason scholars conclude that Jesus drank water while on this fast was because Scripture says He was hungry, but does not say He was thirsty. The devil tempted Jesus with bread, but not with water. So could we assume this was a water only fast? We must always remember that we can never argue from silence since there is no evidence to prove this argument.[376]

In the temptation of Jesus, the first act of the Holy Spirit was to lead Jesus into the wilderness to expose Him to the temptation of Satan. It is of the utmost importance to understand that Jesus triumphed over the wiles of Satan and secured our salvation through fasting. We see Jesus standing on the threshold of the most important act in the history of the world and on His obedience and righteousness hangs the salvation of the world. No one can escape damnation without Jesus as the Servant who is obedient to

---

[374] Wood and Marshall, *New Bible Dictionary*, 364. Achtemeier, ed. *Harper's Bible Dictionary*, 304.

[375] Copeland, *Fasting: A Special Study*, <http://www.e-sword.net>. Accessed on June 12, 2014.

[376] "Fast, Fasting", In Freedman, ed., *The Anchor Yale Bible Dictionary*, Vol. 2, 773.

suffering, death, and resurrection. Of the countless things that Jesus could have done to overcome the threat to salvation, He is led by the Holy Spirit into the wilderness where He fasts for forty days.

If Satan had been successful in his attempt to persuade Jesus from a humble sacrificial obedience, we would be eternally lost, without any hope of salvation. Therefore, the salvation of mankind and living victorious over temptation and defeating Satan can be attributed to Jesus setting the example of fasting before entering ministry. This is something that we should not take lightly. Jesus began His ministry with fasting. He triumphed over the enemy through fasting and our salvation was accomplished through perseverance by fasting.[377]

The Markan narrative omits any reference to fasting, "he was in the desert forty days, being tempted by Satan. He was with the wild animals, and angels attended him" (Mk. 1:13; Mt. 4:1-11; Lk. 4:1-13). Mark uses the verb διηκόνουν *diēkonoun* meaning, "to serve, minister, help" or "to render a service". Matthew states "Then the devil left him, and angels came and attended him" which occurred after the temptation (Mt. 4:11) as in Mark, while Luke does not make any such statement.[378] Jesus demonstrates that fasting reconnects us with God. When we "deny ourselves" through fasting we demonstrate our depth of love for Him. Satan doesn't want you to know anything about the discipline of fasting, since it breaks the enemy's power over us. In Luke 4, we see how the devil suffers a humiliating defeat at the hand of Jesus after His forty days fasting in the wilderness. Therefore, the enemy will try everything he can to discourage or stop us from understanding the spiritual benefits of fasting and using this vital and offensive spiritual weapon to defeat him.

There are four primary examples when Jesus fasted or discussed fasting. The first is immediately after Jesus was baptized by John is the Jordan River, the Holy Spirit came upon Him in the form of a dove and led Him into the wilderness to be tempted by the devil (Mt. 4:1-9; Lk. 4:1-2). "Then Jesus was led by the Spirit into the wilderness to be tempted by the devil. After fasting forty days and forty nights, he was hungry" (Mt. 4:1-2). This is the only time recorded in Scripture where Jesus fasted (cf. Ex. 34:28; 1 Kgs. 19:8). Like the Old Testament prophets, Jesus opposed the flamboyant fasting of the Pharisees (Mt. 6:16-18; cf. Isa. 58:3-7; Jer. 14:12; Zech. 7:5). He viewed voluntary fasting as a valid means of attaining humility and reflecting God's Word (Mt. 9:14-15). Since fasting was a custom of the early church, Jesus assumed that His followers would fast and taught them to fast Godward and not like the Pharisees who fasted to be seen by others (Mt. 6:16-18). When Jesus was asked why His disciples did not fast like John's disciples, He replied,

> How can the guests of the bridegroom mourn while he is with them? The time will come when the bridegroom will be taken from them; then they will fast (Mt. 9:15; Mk. 2:18-22; Lk. 5:33-39).

The second example is Jesus' discussion on fasting in the Sermon on the Mount,

---

[377] Piper, *A Hunger for God*, 53f.
[378] "Fast, Fasting", In Freedman, ed., *The Anchor Yale Bible Dictionary*, Vol. 2, 775. διακονέω *diakoneō* "1241", In Gilbrant, ed., *The Complete Biblical Library Greek-English Dictionary, Delta-Epsilon.*

When you fast, do not look somber as the hypocrites do, for they disfigure their faces to show men they are fasting. I tell you the truth, they have received their reward in full. But when you fast, put oil on your head and wash your face, so that it will not be obvious to men that you are fasting, but only to your Father, who is unseen; and your Father, who sees what is done in secret, will reward you (Mt. 6:16-18).

Jesus begins by saying "when you fast", not "if" which assumes that the practice of fasting was a part of the disciples everyday life. Jesus' statement "do not look somber as the hypocrites do" literally means "stop" your practice of demonstrating spirituality through "being actors" or "pretenders". The point that Jesus makes here is that the Pharisees showed no internal contrition and were drawing attention to themselves—desiring the praises of men, which was all that they would receive. Moreover, fasting loses its spiritual value when it becomes mandatory and draws attention to itself.[379]

Since Jesus comments on fasting immediately after His discussion on the Lord's Prayer suggests the possible connection between prayer and fasting (e.g., Ps. 35:13; Dan. 9:3; cf. Lk. 2:37). Jesus distinguishes between fasting—expressing sorrow for sin—and its consequences in the Old Testament and now in the new covenant, fasting was an expression of joy because of forgiveness. Jesus' requirement in fasting was that the participants wash their face and be anointed with oil, which was a sign of great joy.

You have exalted my horn like that of a wild ox; fine oils have been poured on me (Ps. 92:10).

You drink wine by the bowlful and use the finest lotions, but you do not grieve over the ruin of Joseph (Am. 6:6; Mk. 14:3)

Fasting, according to Jesus, did not involve separating oneself externally from others in appearance and behaviour, but being set apart internally for service unto God in secret who will reward in secret.[380]

The third example is when Jesus is questioned by John's disciples concerning why His disciples did not need to fast—an act of mourning—but calls them to celebrate since He was still among them (Mt. 9:14-17; Mk. 2:18-20; Lk. 5:33-39).

Then John's disciples came and asked him, "How is it that we and the Pharisees fast often, but your disciples do not fast?" Jesus answered, "How can the guests of the bridegroom mourn while he is with them? The time will come when the bridegroom will be taken from them; then they will fast. "No one sews a patch of unshrunk cloth on an old garment, for the patch will pull away from the garment, making the tear worse. Neither do people pour new wine into old wineskins. If they do, the skins will burst; the wine will run out and the wineskins will be ruined. No, they pour new wine into new wineskins, and both are preserved" (Mt. 9:14-17).

The Pharisees questioned Jesus reasons for His involvement, "Why does your teacher eat with tax collectors and sinners?" (Mt. 9:11). Likewise, the disciples of John the Baptist questioned Jesus, "How is

---

[379] "Luke 5:33", In Robert James Utley, *The Gospel According to Luke*, Study Guide Commentary Series, Vol. 3a (Marshall, TX: Bible Lessons International, 2004).

[380] ὑποκριτής *hupokritēs* "5111", In Gilbrant, ed., *The Complete Biblical Library Greek-English Dictionary, Sigma-Omega*. Gaebelein, ed., *The Expositor's Bible Commentary, Volume 8*, 175. Gilbrant, ed., *The Complete Biblical Library Commentary, Matthew*, 113.

it that we and the Pharisees fast often, but your disciples do not fast?" John called people to repentance and to the coming kingdom, which seemed right for his disciples to fast, but why did Jesus' disciples not fast. His response was that the kingdom was like a great feast or a wedding banquet (cf. Mt. 22:2; Isa. 25:6), but since the King was among them it was not appropriate for Him or His disciples to fast. The wedding that Jesus is talking about would be a feast with people being happy, joyous, and celebrating not a time of mourning or fasting.

Jesus illustrates the relationship between the ministry of John the Baptist and His ministry. John, as a reformer, brought repentance to those immersed in Judaic tradition. Jesus did not come to place a "patch" or a temporarily fix on an old system by sewing "a patch of unshrunk cloth on an old garment, for the patch will pull away from the garment, making the tear worse" or "pour new wine into old wineskins" since they would burst and ruin the wineskins. Jesus wanted to teach them that true righteousness is not founded upon the Law or Judaic or Pharisaic traditions. Jesus' purpose was to institute something new— to lead Judaism into His Kingdom based upon Himself and His righteousness. In this passage, Jesus wanted to teach the disciples that fasting must have a place in their lives, but only at the appropriate time, not as a ceremonial rite.[381]

The final example is when Jesus connects the power of prayer with fasting. The disciples' failures are a recurring theme throughout this section (14:16-21, 26-27, 28-31; 15:16, 23, 33; 16:5, 22; 17:4, 10-11) and He becomes frustrated that His disciples lack the faith necessary to heal a boy who is possessed by a demon or perhaps epilepsy (Mt. 17:14-21).

> When they came to the crowd, a man approached Jesus and knelt before him. "Lord, have mercy on my son", he said. "He has seizures and is suffering greatly. He often falls into the fire or into the water. I brought him to your disciples, but they could not heal him". "You unbelieving and perverse generation", Jesus replied, "how long shall I stay with you? How long shall I put up with you? Bring the boy here to me". Jesus rebuked the demon, and it came out of the boy, and he was healed at that moment. Then the disciples came to Jesus in private and asked, "Why couldn't we drive it out?" He replied, "Because you have so little faith. Truly I tell you, if you have faith as small as a mustard seed, you can say to this mountain, 'Move from here to there', and it will move. Nothing will be impossible for you" (Mt. 17:14-21).

Mark's account and some manuscripts include, "He replied, 'this kind can come out only by prayer (and fasting)'" (Mk. 9:29). In the New Testament, the verb σεληνιάζεται *selēniazetai* is used two times, both in the Gospel According to Matthew meaning "to be moonstruck", "to be epileptic, or a lunatic" and makes the distinction between epilepsy and demonic possession. The first is in Matthew 4:24 where *selēniazomai* describes four unique types of sick people healed or delivered by Jesus during His ministry in Galilee.

These four types include:

---

[381] "Matthew 9:14-17", In Walvoord and Zuck, eds., *The Bible Knowledge Commentary*, Vol. 2. Copeland, *Fasting: A Special Study*, <http://www.e-sword.net>. Accessed on June 12, 2014.

(a) those who suffered from "divers diseases and torments"; (b) those who were "possessed with devils"; (c) those who were "lunatic" (*selēniazomai*); and (d) those "that had the palsy". Here the word *selēniazomai* is especially distinguished from *daimonizomai*, "demon possessed". By this distinction Matthew clearly showed that epilepsy and demonic possession are not one and the same. Although similar convulsions may be manifested in each, the cause is definitely different. *Selēniazomai* is a purely physical disorder, while *daimonizomai* finds its source in demons.[382]

Jesus asks the disciples to bring the boy to him, He rebukes His disciples, next the crowd for their lack of faith, and then "rebuked the demon" and the boy was healed (cf. Mt. 15:28). In private, the disciples asked Jesus, "Why couldn't we drive it out? He replied, Because you have so little faith", which contrasts the "great faith" of the Roman centurion (8:10) and the Canaanite woman (15:28). Jesus instructs the disciples that even with a small amount of faith "Nothing will be impossible" with God (cf. 19:26; Lk. 1:37). Jesus takes this moment with His disciples to teach them about their future ministries, to be careful about a lack of faith, and not seeking the Lord's direction. The Word of God is sufficient to produce the desired healing; however, their actions would require great faith and living a life of prayer. When faith, prayer and fasting are combined there is no limit to what the disciples can accomplish as they follow His will. Fasting joined with prayer can accomplish great things which normal faith may not.[383]

Fasting in the Ministry of the Apostle Paul

Fasting played a significant part in the ministry of the Apostle Paul who fasted with several churches. However, in the following passages, Paul mentions fasting as part of his good standing as a minister of Jesus Christ. The Apostle Paul refers to "fastings" as part of the suffering that he endured as an apostle of Jesus Christ.

> We put no stumbling block in anyone's path, so that our ministry will not be discredited. Rather, as servants of God we commend ourselves in every way: in great endurance; in troubles, hardships and distresses; in beatings, imprisonments and riots; in hard work, sleepless nights and hunger; in purity, understanding, patience and kindness; in the Holy Spirit and in sincere love; in truthful speech and in the power of God; with weapons of righteousness in the right hand and in the left; through glory and dishonor, bad report and good report; genuine, yet regarded as impostors; known, yet regarded as unknown; dying, and yet we live on; beaten, and yet not killed; sorrowful, yet always rejoicing; poor, yet making many rich; having nothing, and yet possessing everything (2 Cor. 6:3-10).

The Greek word used above for "hunger" is the noun νηστείαις *nēsteiais* from the noun νηστεία *nēsteia*, which is mentioned separately from normal hunger and thirst.[384] In the above verses, it is uncertain

---

[382] σεληνιάζομαι *selēniazomai* "4438", In Gilbrant, ed., *The Complete Biblical Library Greek-English Dictionary, Sigma-Omega*.

[383] Walvoord and Zuck, eds., *The Bible Knowledge Commentary*, Vol. 2, 60-61. Copeland, *Fasting: A Special Study*, <http://www.e-sword.net>. Accessed on June 12, 2014.

[384] νηστεία *nēsteia* "3383", In Gilbrant, ed., *The Complete Biblical Library Greek-English Dictionary, Lambda-Omicron*.

whether voluntary fasting or involuntary fasting is referred to here and this clarity depends upon whether it is read being connected with the preceding or with the following items.

Paul, in 2 Corinthians 11:27-28, later states "I have known hunger and thirst and have often gone without food" and so voluntary fasting is probably indicated.

> I have labored and toiled and have often gone without sleep; I have known hunger and thirst and have often gone without food; I have been cold and naked. Besides everything else, I face daily the pressure of my concern for all the churches (2 Cor. 11:27-28).

The phrase "have often gone without food" comes from the root noun νηστεία *nēsteia*, the common Greek word used for fasting. Paul may have undertaken some of his voluntary fasts ("I... have often gone without food"; cf. 6:5) because of his determination not to accept support from the Corinthians (1 Cor. 9:12, 15, 18; 2 Cor. 11:7-12). Fasting used above "gone without food" should not be understood as a self-imposed religious discipline, but rather voluntary abstinence from eating so that his work as a minister of Christ might not be hindered. His life with Jesus was far more important than eating or drinking since his impulse for ministry was realizing that "man shall not live on bread alone, but on every word that comes from the mouth of God" (Mt. 4:4) also "Then his disciples said to each other, 'Could someone have brought him food?' 'My food', said Jesus, 'is to do the will of him who sent me and to finish his work'" (Jn. 4:33-34).[385]

It is interesting that when Paul faces hardships in reference to food regulations among culturally mixed Christian communities (1 Cor. 8; Rom. 14) he willingly adopts their asceticism. It is interesting that extreme asceticism caused some problems in the first century church. In the church at Colossae, Paul confronted the "false humility and the worship of angels" (Col. 2:18), which is possibly Semitic for fasting since it was accompanied by "angel worship", i.e., intended to persuade angels to give visions and dreams. A few verses later (v. 23), Paul defines this term as "harsh treatment of the body" ἀφειδία σώματος *apheidia sōmatos*. He refrains from rejecting ascetic practice entirely, yet opposes this form, which is ineffective against fleshly desires and the unnecessary obedience to external regulations. Later, Paul regardless of radical perversions, states that "physical training is of some value" σωματικὴ γυμνασία *sōmatikē gumnasia*—beneficial up to a point (1 Tim. 4:8).

The Apostle Paul also exhorted the Corinthians to live a life of self-denial,

> Do you not know that in a race all the runners run, but only one gets the prize? Run in such a way as to get the prize. Everyone who competes in the games goes into strict training. They do it to get a crown that will not last; but we do it to get a crown that will last forever. Therefore I do not run like a man running aimlessly; I do not fight like a man beating the air. No, I beat my body and

---

[385] Gaebelein, *The Expositor's Bible Commentary, Volume 10: Romans through Galatians* (Grand Rapids, MI: Zondervan Publishing House, WORDsearch CROSS e-book, 1976), 392. Thoralf Gilbrant, ed., *The Complete Biblical Library Commentary, Romans-Corinthians* (Springfield, IL: World Library Press, Inc., WORDsearch CROSS e-book, 1988), 625. Copeland, *Fasting: A Special Study*, <http://www.e-sword.net>. Accessed on June 12, 2014.

make it my slave so that after I have preached to others, I myself will not be disqualified for the prize (1 Cor. 9:24-27).

Paul begins verse 27 by using the verb ὑπωπιάζω *hupōpiazō* which is a boxing term meaning "to strike under the eye" or "to give a black eye". These phrases were common among Eastern nations and meant to suffer public shame or damage a person's reputation. Luke used this verb figuratively to refer to the unjust judge who feared this consequence if he failed to listen to the widow's case, "yet because this widow keeps bothering me, I will see that she gets justice, so that she won't eventually come and attack me!'" (Lk. 18:5). The widow's continual pleading demonstrated that the judge is either incapable of fulfilling his duties as a judge or was guided by personal considerations. In both cases, his reputation is attacked and he is effectively disgraced or his face has been bruised as if he had been in a fight. Paul used this verb to describe how he would discipline his body for service as an athlete disciplines his body to compete.

Likewise, the Christian must discipline or "beat" their body to bring it into subjection.[386]

Paul says of himself that he does not contend like an undisciplined runner or boxer. He states that he aims his blows against his own body, beating it black and blue (*hypopiazo*; see the same word in Luke 18:5). The picture is graphic: the ancient boxers devastatingly punishing one another with knuckles bound with leather thongs. And so by pummeling his body, Paul enslaves it in order to gain the Christian prize. The ancient *keryx* was the herald in the Greek games who announced the rules of the contest, but the Christian herald—i.e., preacher—not only announces the rules but "plays" in the game as well. Paul had not only to preach the gospel but also to live the gospel.[387]

To bring his point home, Paul employs the image of an athlete common to the Greek Olympic Games as well as the Isthmian Games. He was quite fond of athletic images and used metaphors often in his epistles. These games, which included running and boxing, were quite familiar since they were hosted every other year by the citizens of Corinth. In Paul's time, a person needed to be a Greek citizen to participate in the games. Moreover, they must adhere to the rules in both their training and in their performing—anyone who broke these rules was automatically disqualified.[388]

Only the winner of the race would receive the olive-wreath crown, but *every* Christian can receive an incorruptible crown when they stand before the Judgment Seat of Christ. This crown is reserved for those who "beat their body", discipline themselves, keep their eyes on the goal, serve the Lord, and make disciples of Jesus Christ.[389] Christians do not run the race so that we can make it to heaven, but because we have been saved through faith in Jesus Christ,

---

[386] ὑπωπιάζω *hupōpiazō* "5137", In Gilbrant, ed., *The Complete Biblical Library Greek-English Dictionary, Sigma-Omega.* Gaebelein, ed., *The Expositor's Bible Commentary, Volume 8*, 1001.

[387] Gaebelein, *The Expositor's Bible Commentary, Volume 10*, 246.

[388] Wiersbe, *The Bible Exposition Commentary*, Vol. 1, 600-02. Gaebelein, *The Expositor's Bible Commentary*, Vol. 10, 246.

[389] Wiersbe, *The Bible Exposition Commentary*, Vol. 1, 600-02.

For it is by grace you have been saved, through faith—and this not from yourselves, it is the gift of God—not by works, so that no one can boast. For we are God's workmanship, created in Christ Jesus to do good works, which God prepared in advance for us to do (Eph. 2:8-10).

In Colossians, Paul warns against a type of fasting that is a "willpower religion" which stimulates spiritual pride of the flesh while at the same time conquering its physical appetites.

Since you died with Christ to the basic principles of this world, why, as though you still belonged to it, do you submit to its rules: "Do not handle! Do not taste! Do not touch!"? These are all destined to perish with use, because they are based on human commands and teachings. Such regulations indeed have an appearance of wisdom, with their self-imposed worship, their false humility and their harsh treatment of the body, but they lack any value in restraining sensual indulgence (Col. 2:20-23).

However, this type of fasting is contrary to Christian fasting,

Christian fasting moves from broken and contrite poverty of spirit to sweet satisfaction in the free mercy of Christ to ever greater desires and enjoyments of God's inexhaustible grace. Christian fasting does not bolster pride, because it rests with childlike contentment in the firmly accomplished justification of God in Christ, even while longing for all the fullness of God possible in this life. Christian fasting is the effect of what Christ has already done *for* us and *in* us. It is not our feat, but the Spirit's fruit. Recall that the last-mentioned fruit of the Spirit is "self-control" (Gal. 5:23).[390]

Paul throughout his epistles demonstrated that he was not influenced by physical comforts, because if he was, the suffering and hardships which he endured would have probably forced him to quit. Paul demonstrated that it was more important to finish the race strong and receive "the crown of righteousness", than to worry about the suffering and beatings that he endured for the sake of the gospel.

I have fought the good fight, I have finished the race, I have kept the faith. Now there is in store for me the crown of righteousness, which the Lord, the righteous Judge, will award to me on that day—and not only to me, but also to all who have longed for his appearing (2 Tim. 4:7-8).

Conversely, Paul also had a high regard for the body as the temple of the Holy Spirit, and he commanded believers to treat it as such, "Do you not know that your body is a temple of the Holy Spirit, who is in you, whom you have received from God? You are not your own; you were bought at a price. Therefore honor God with your body" (1 Cor. 6:19-20).[391]

Please refer to *Fasting: Unlocking Spiritual Power and Breakthrough, Personal Reflections* under the heading "Personal Reflections from the New Testament" to conclude this section of this study.

---

[390] Piper, *A Hunger for God*, 46.

[391] ὑπωπιάζω *hupōpiazō* "5137", In Gilbrant, ed., *The Complete Biblical Library Greek-English Dictionary, Sigma-Omega.*

Chapter 10: Fasting in the Early Church

The purpose of this chapter is to describe the practice of fasting and its observance throughout the Christian church era. It also includes fasting as a Jewish custom, its observance in the Church of Rome, and encouraged as a Christian duty in the Protestant Churches. Fasting in the Early Church and Early Church Fathers was a topic of great importance and was connected with reform and revival movements.

Fasting in the Christian Church

Throughout the era of the Christian church, fasting had been practiced as a method of self-discipline, mortification, and atonement. It appears either: (a) symbolically as repentance; or (b) to foster spiritual disciplines (e.g., prayer).

> But the ascetic tendency in the early Church led to reliance on fasting, etc., as not only helps to, but substitutes for, the inward and spiritual life. The theory which placed the origin and seat of sin in the body, also tended to give value to the practice of fasting. It came at last to be considered as an effectual means of securing forgiveness of sin. The earliest notices of fasting in the Christian writers are in a better vein. The days of holy consecration, of penitence and prayer, which individual Christians appointed for their own use, were oftentimes also a sort of fast days.[392]

On the topic of fasting and prayer, Philip Schaff states,

> After the Jewish custom, fasting was frequently joined with prayer, that the mind, unencumbered by earthly matter, might devote itself with less distraction to the contemplation of divine things. The apostles themselves sometimes employed this wholesome discipline, though without infringing the gospel freedom by legal prescriptions. As the Pharisees were accustomed to fast twice in the week, on Monday and Thursday, the Christians appointed Wednesday and especially Friday, as days of half-fasting or abstinence from flesh, in commemoration of the passion and crucifixion of Jesus. They did this with reference to the Lord's words: "When the bridegroom shall be taken away from them, then will they fast".[393]

The following fasts were observed in the Early Christian Church:

1. Lent, the annual fast of forty days before Easter. Initially it lasted forty hours and Gregory I extended it to thirty-six days and then in the 8th century, based upon the fasts of Moses and Jesus Christ was extended to forty days.
2. Quarterly fasts, no record beyond the 5th century.
3. A three day fast before the festival of the Ascension.
4. Monthly fasts, one day per month, excluding July and August.
5. Fasts before festivals, which were abolished in the 5th century.
6. Weekly fasts (*stations* or *statio*; Roman) on Wednesdays and Fridays, which honoured the practice of soldiers keeping guard.

---

[392] "Fasting in the Christian Church", In M'Clintock and Strong, eds., *Cyclopedia of Biblical and Ecclesiastical Literature*, <http://www.e-sword.net>.

[393] Philip Schaff and David Schley Schaff, *History of the Christian Church*, Vol. 2 (New York: Charles Scribner's Sons, 1910), 379.

7. Occasional fasts established in times of great danger, emergency, or distress.[394]

In the Church of Rome, observance to the institution of the holy Roman Church, which included fasting, and diligence to promote obedience to every command was advocated by the holy council. They stated that the Church commanded fasting and disobedience to these commands was seen as sin. In the Church in Greece, fasting was strictly observed. According to Greek tradition, there were four principle fasts: (a) Lent; (b) the Fast of the holy Apostles; (c) the Assumption of the Virgin (fourteen days before); and (d) forty days before Christmas.[395]

Moreover, in Protestant Churches, fasting was not imperative for membership, but recommended as a Christian responsibility, especially during national or individual affliction. The Church of England, under the reign of Queen Elizabeth, instituted a royal decree for fasting, recognizing it as an Ecclesiastical Law to retain prayers and fast days, without a specific diet. The type of fasting was the responsibility of the individual who could adapt fasting to their self-discipline. Likewise, Luther did not reject or disapprove of those who practiced fasting, but did not see fasting to be commendable. In this regard, he stated,

> We moreover teach that it is the duty of every man, by fasting and other exercises, to avoid giving any occasion to sin, but not to merit grace hey such works. But this watchfulness over our body is to be observed always, not on particular days only. On this subject Christ says, Take heed to yourselves lest at any time your hearts be overcharged with surfeiting (Lk. 21:34). Again, the devils are not cast out but by fasting and prayer (Mt. 17:21). And Paul says, I keep under my body, and bring it into subjection (1 Cor. 9:27). By which he wishes to intimate that this bodily discipline is not designed to merit grace, but to keep the body in a suitable condition for the several duties of our calling. We do not, therefore, object to fasting itself, but to the fact that it is represented as a necessary duty, and that specific days have, been fixed for its performance.[396]

John Calvin viewed fasting as a sign of humiliation, common to both public and private, was more frequently used in public and practiced in conjunction with prayer. For example, when the church in Antioch commissioned Paul and Barnabas, they fasted and prayed (Acts 13:1-3). Likewise, "Paul and Barnabas appointed elders for them in each church and, with prayer and fasting, committed them to the Lord" (Acts 14:23). Luke speaks of the prophetess Anna who "never left the temple but worshiped night and day, fasting and praying" (Lk. 2:37). Luke does not emphasize the worship of God in fasting, but suggests that the prophetess Anna focus was upon prayer. This constancy in prayer can also be seen in Nehemiah's fervent prayer for the deliverance of his people. Moreover, the Apostle Paul proclaims the benefits for those who practice abstinence from those things which we enjoy so that we can be free to devote ourselves to fasting and prayer. Jesus Himself has shown us by His own example that prayer and

---

[394] "Tertullian", In Alexander Roberts and James Donaldson, eds., *Ante-Nicene Fathers: The Writings of the Fathers Down To A.D. 325*, Vol. 3 (Edinburgh, UK: T. & T. Clark, 1867), WORDsearch CROSS e-book, "*De Jejuniis*", 13.

[395] "Fasting in the Christian Church", In M'Clintock and Strong, eds., *Cyclopedia of Biblical and Ecclesiastical Literature*, <http://www.e-sword.net>.

[396] "Fasting in the Christian Church", In M'Clintock and Strong, eds., *Cyclopedia of Biblical and Ecclesiastical Literature*, <http://www.e-sword.net>.

fasting are the first and most effective weapons against the forces of evil (cf. Mt. 4:1-11). Much more could be said of John Calvin's thoughts on fasting.[397]

When we correlate what Paul stated concerning the training and performing involved in running the race, finishing strong, receiving the prize, and fasting, we can see how fasting brings the flesh under subjection and disciplines the flesh so that it is not allowed to rule in your life. When we look at the life of Adam and how the lust of the flesh was the sin that resulted in the fall of humankind, the enemy will use the same temptation to cause us to sin. It is through fasting, which strengthens the spirit man that we can remain focused and serve the Lord instead of our fleshly desires. However, to the extent that we surrender to the indulgences of our flesh, to this same extent we lose spiritual sensitivity and power.

The phrase "will not be disqualified for the prize" is quite significant. The adjective ἀδόκιμος *adokimos* means "not passing the test", "incompetent", or "unqualified". It is difficult to adequately translate *adokimos* since the fundamental thought behind *adokimos* refers to something that has been proved false, worthless, or useless as a result of testing. This adjective is exclusively Pauline ("depraved", Rom. 1:28; 2 Tim. 3:8; "disqualified", 1 Cor. 9:27; "fail the test", 2 Cor. 13:5-7; "unfit", Tit. 1:16), except for Hebrews 6:8, "But land that produces thorns and thistles is worthless and is in danger of being cursed. In the end it will be burned", which speaks of harsh judgment that awaits those who willfully reject God

> Furthermore, just as they did not think it worthwhile to retain the knowledge of God, so God gave them over to a depraved mind, so that they do what ought not to be done (Rom. 1:28; cf. 2 Tim. 3:8; cf. 2 Cor. 13:5ff.).[398]

Fasting in the Early Church

The first century church did not reject the ascetic practice of fasting, yet at the same time it did not make it an official discipline, leaving it to the individual conscience. In regards to water baptism, there is no New Testament evidence that candidates should fast[399], and no New Testament evidence to a twice weekly Christian fast which either imitates or competes with rabbinic customs. The first appearance is in the *Didache* 8:1, and only during the second century that the statutory public fast on Good Friday was inaugurated. The Christian fast on Wednesdays and Fridays was contrasted with the Jewish practice, which probably resulted from the Quartodeciman controversy.[400] The Quartodecimans had adopted the

---

[397] "Fasting in the Christian Church", In M'Clintock and Strong, eds., *Cyclopedia of Biblical and Ecclesiastical Literature*, <http://www.e-sword.net>.

[398] ἀδόκιμος *adokimos* "95", In Gilbrant, ed., *The Complete Biblical Library Greek-English Dictionary, Alpha-Gamma*.

[399] Cf. *Didache* 7:4; Justin Martyr, *apologia*. 61.2, In Roberts and Donaldson, eds., *Ante-Nicene Fathers: The Writings of the Fathers Down To A.D. 325*, Vol. 1.

[400] The Quartodeciman controversy, which continued for over two centuries in Asia Minor (Canon no. 7 of the Synod of Laodicea, ca. 350), testifies with clarion voice to the perennial desire of many Anatolian Christians to maintain the Jewish heritage of the Christian observance of Easter/Passover. "Christianity: Christianity in Asia Minor", In Freedman, ed., *The Anchor Yale Bible Dictionary*, Vol. 2, 948.

anti-Jewish practice of fasting during the Feast of Passover and celebrated Easter the following day.[401] Upon the arrival of Easter, determined independently of the Jewish calendar and always on a Sunday, the conditions were instituted for Christian fasting to be held on the preceding Friday. Finally, as baptisms were customarily observed at Easter, partial abstinence during the preceding weeks of preparation began to be adhered to not only by the candidates, but also by all Church members as an annual Lenten fast of penitence.[402]

Fasting in the early church from the post-apostolic period onwards shows a different development, since fasting on specific days returns to being the normal practice. This demonstrates that the Christian who observes fasting on these days that they are watchful and expecting the coming of the Lord. There was no instruction in regards to fasting prior to the 3rd century. A person would fast *ex arbitrio, non ex imperio novae disciplinae pro temporibus et causis uniuscuiusque* (from the will, not at the command of the new discipline, and for the causes for the times of each). Wednesday was chosen since it was the day of the arrest of Jesus and Friday since it was the day of His crucifixion.

Eusebius of Caesarea in his *Historia Ecclesiastica* states that during the 2nd century, Christians were required to fast during the time the Lord was in the tomb, known as the Easter Fast (5.24. 12ff.). Fasting on Sundays was forbidden and the Apostle Paul broke his fast on Sunday so that he did not violate this command. It was common for the candidate to fast before baptism, which included those who were present with them and likewise before partaking in the Eucharist. The purpose for fasting was to strengthen prayer, prepare for divine revelation, express sorrow, to help the poor, and to reconcile penitents with God. Fasting that was established by the Early Church, from the 2nd century onwards, is a continuation of Old Testament and Jewish piety. Any criticism of fasting, was based upon the Old Testament prophets and the inclination to subordinate the custom to inwardness and to ethical concerns.[403]

Fasting in the Early Church Fathers

Fasting, according to the Early Church Fathers, was a prominent topic of discussion—including just over 800 references. Too often today, we think of fasting with little importance, however, it has been practiced by most nations from the beginning of civilization. Even though there are many examples among the Early Church Fathers, only a few of these will be highlighted. Some of these include, the Egyptians, Phoenicians, and Assyrians, which all practiced fasting, like the Jews and Christians. Porphyry asserts that the Egyptians, before their customary sacrifices, always fasted a number of days, up to and including six weeks.[404]

---

[401] cf. Eusebius of Caesarea, *Historia Ecclesiastica*, 5.23-25, <http://www.ccel.org/ccel/schaff/npnf201.html>, Accessed on September 3, 2013.

[402] "Fast, Fasting", In Freedman, ed., *The Anchor Yale Bible Dictionary*, Vol. 2, 774-75. Kittel, Bromiley and Friedrich, eds., *Theological Dictionary of the New Testament*, electronic ed., Vol. 4, 933.

[403] Kittel, Bromiley and Friedrich, eds., *Theological Dictionary of the New Testament*, electronic ed., Vol. 4, 934-35. Kittel, Friedrich and Bromiley, eds., *Theological Dictionary of the New Testament: Abridged in One Volume*, 633.

[404] "Fasting", In Charles Buck, *Buck's Theological Dictionary*, Rick Meyers, e-Sword, Version 10.2.1, 2000-2012, <http://www.e-sword.net>, 1802.

In the writings of the Early Church Fathers, there is a well-known theme on fasting which often includes almsgiving. The Shepherd of Hermas writes,

> Having fulfilled what is written, in the day on which you fast you will taste nothing but bread and water; and having reckoned up the price of the dishes of that day which you intended to have eaten, you will give it to a widow, or an orphan, or to some person in want, and thus you will exhibit humility of mind, so that he who has received benefit from your humility may fill his own soul, and pray for you to the Lord. If you observe fasting, as I have commanded you, your sacrifice will be acceptable to God, and this fasting will be written down; and the service thus performed is noble, and sacred, and acceptable to the Lord. These things, therefore, shall you thus observe with your children, and all your house, and in observing them you will be blessed; and as many as hear these words and observe them shall be blessed; and whatsoever they ask of the Lord they shall receive.[405]

The writings of the Early Church Fathers demonstrate that they clearly understood that whatever savings is realized through one's fasting belongs to the poor. Therefore, Gregory the Great preached, "The one who does not give to the poor what he has saved but keeps it for later to satisfy his own appetite, does not fast for God". Origen blessed those who fasted in order "to nourish the poor". For Augustine, in order to elevate the soul, fasting had to have two wings: prayer and works of mercy.[406]

Likewise, the Greeks observed fasting as did Roman kings and emperors, such as Numa Pompilius, Julius Caesar, Augustus, Vespasian, and others, observed customary fasts; and Julian the Apostate was so exact in this observation, that he surpassed the priests themselves. The Pythagoreans were known for their rigid, frequent, and prolonged fasts and their master Pythagoras, would fast for forty days. The Brachmans, and the Chinese, have their customary fasts and in the Church of Rome, fasting was considered as an important rite.[407]

Publius Cornelius Tacitus alludes to the "frequent fasts" of the Jews, "By their frequent fasts they still bear witness to the long hunger of former days, and the Jewish bread, made without leaven, is retained as a memorial of their hurried seizure of corn".[408] Likewise, Josephus mentions fasting in speaking of the dispersion of Jewish customs among the Gentile cities,

> Nay, farther, the multitude of mankind itself have had a great inclination of a long time to follow our religious observances; for there is not any city of the Grecians, nor any of the barbarians, nor any nation whatsoever, whither our custom of resting on the seventh day hath not come, and by

---

[405] "Pastor of Hermas", In *Ante-Nicene Fathers: The Writings of the Fathers Down To A.D. 325*, Vol. 2 (Edinburgh, UK: T. & T. Clark, 1867), WORDsearch CROSS e-book, Book 3, Similitude Fifth, Chapter 3.

[406] Thomas Ryan, *Fasting: A Fresh Look*, <http://americamagazine.org/issue/563/article/fasting-fresh-look>, Accessed on June 13, 2013.

[407] "Fasting", In Buck, *Buck's Theological Dictionary*, <http://www.e-sword.net>.

[408] Publius Cornelius Tacitus, *The Histories*, Trans. Church and Brodribb, <http://classics.mit.edu/Tacitus/histories.html>, 5.4.

which our fasts and lighting up lamps, and many of our prohibitions as to our food, are not observed.[409]

Polycarp, in his Epistle to the Philippians, refers to "persevering in fasting",

> Wherefore, forsaking the vanity of many, and their false doctrines, let us return to the word which has been handed down to us from the beginning; "watching unto prayer", and persevering in fasting; beseeching in our supplications the all-seeing God "not to lead us into temptation", as the Lord has said: "The spirit truly is willing, but the flesh is weak".[410]

The Pastor of Hermas speaks of the type of fasting that is acceptable to God,

> For fasting to God in this way you will do nothing for a righteous life; but offer to God a fasting of the following kind: Do no evil in your life, and serve the Lord with a pure heart: keep His commandments, walking in His precepts, and let no evil desire arise in your heart; and believe in God. If you do these things, and fear Him, and abstain from every evil thing, you will live unto God; and if you do these things, you will keep a great fast, and one acceptable before God.[411]

He continues on to state,

> "This fasting", he continued, "is very good, provided the commandments of the Lord be observed. Thus, then, shall you observe the fasting which you intend to keep. First of all, be on your guard against every evil word, and every evil desire, and purify your heart from all the vanities of this world. If you guard against these things, your fasting will be perfect. And you will do also as follows. Having fulfilled what is written, in the day on which you fast you will taste nothing but bread and water; and having reckoned up the price of the dishes of that day which you intended to have eaten, you will give it to a widow, or an orphan, or to some person in want, and thus you will exhibit humility of mind, so that he who has received benefit from your humility may fill his own soul, and pray for you to the Lord. If you observe fasting, as I have commanded you, your sacrifice will be acceptable to God, and this fasting will be written down; and the service thus performed is noble, and sacred, and acceptable to the Lord. These things, therefore, shall you thus observe with your children, and all your house, and in observing them you will be blessed; and as many as hear these words and observe them shall be blessed; and whatsoever they ask of the Lord they shall receive".[412]

---

[409] "Against Apion", In Josephus, *The Works of Josephus*, 2.40. "Fasting", In Hastings, ed., *A Dictionary of Christ and the Gospels*, <http://www.e-sword.net>.

[410] "Polycarp", In Alexander Roberts and James Donaldson, eds., *Ante-Nicene Fathers: The Writings of the Fathers Down To A.D. 325*, Vol. 1, "Epistle to the Philippians", Chapter 7. "Fasting in the Christian Church", In M'Clintock and Strong, eds., *Cyclopedia of Biblical and Ecclesiastical Literature*, <http://www.e-sword.net>.

[411] "Pastor of Hermas", In Alexander Roberts and James Donaldson, eds., *Ante-Nicene Fathers: The Writings of the Fathers Down To A.D. 325*, Vol. 2, Book Third, Similitude Fifth, Chapter 1. "Fasting in the Christian Church", In M'Clintock and Strong, eds., *Cyclopedia of Biblical and Ecclesiastical Literature* <http://www.e-sword.net>.

[412] "Pastor of Hermas", In Roberts and Donaldson, eds., *Ante-Nicene Fathers: The Writings of the Fathers Down To A.D. 325*, Vol. 2, Book Third, Similitude Fifth, Chapter 3. "Fasting in the Christian Church", In M'Clintock and Strong, eds., *Cyclopedia of Biblical and Ecclesiastical Literature*, <http://www.e-sword.net>. "Tertullian, Part Fourth", In Roberts and Donaldson, eds., *Ante-Nicene Fathers: The Writings of the Fathers Down To A.D. 325*, Vol. 4, "On Fasting", Chapter 6.

Clement of Alexandria writes concerning pagan worship and the priests who were required to abstain from meat and wine,

Paul declares that the kingdom of heaven consists not in meat and drink, neither therefore in abstaining from wine and flesh, but in righteousness and peace, and joy in the Holy Ghost. As humility is shown, not by the castigation of the body, but by gentleness of disposition, so also abstinence is a virtue of the soul, consisting not in that which is without, but is that which is within the man. Abstinence has reference not to some one thing alone, not merely to pleasure, but it is abstinence also to despise money, to tame the tongue, and to obtain by reason the dominion over sin (Strong lib. 3).[413]

Clement speaks of weekly fasts as a customary practice within the Church. It seems as though weekly fasts were the practice of the Church before the end of the 2nd century, but not prescribed as a means of grace. The Montanists were rigorous to excess in regard to fasting.

This rigidity appeared most in the Montanists. Besides the usual fasts, they observed special *Xerophagiae* as they were called; seasons of two weeks for eating only dry or properly uncooked food, bread, salt, and water. The Catholic church, with true feeling, refused to sanction these excesses as a general rule, but allowed ascetics to carry fasting even to extremes. A priest in Lyons, for example, lived on bread and water alone, but forsook that austerity when reminded that he gave offence to other Christians by so despising the gifts of God.[414]

Tertullian has an in-depth section entitled "On Fasting", which discusses various issues and topics in regards to fasting and also gives an excellent account of fasting in the Old Testament. Some of these include Moses, who fasted for forty days and forty nights on Mt. Sinai and "maintained a fast above the power of human nature". He also says that Moses heard God's voice with his ears, understood God's Law with his heart, and was taught that "man does not live on bread alone but on every word that comes from the mouth of the LORD" (Deut. 8:3; cf. Mt. 4:4; Lk. 4:4).

On the other hand, he whose "heart" was habitually found "lifted up" (cf. Ps. 86:4, in LXX. lxxxv. 4); Lam. 3:41 (in LXX. iii. 40). rather than fattened up, who in forty days and as many nights maintained a fast above the power of human nature, while spiritual faith subministered strength (to his body, twice over, cf. Ex. 24:18 and xxxiv. 28; Deut. 9:11, 25), both saw with his eyes God's glory, and heard with his ears God's voice, and understood with his heart God's law: while He taught him even then (by experience) that man liveth not upon bread alone, but upon every word of God; in that the People, though fatter than he, could not constantly contemplate even Moses himself, fed as he had been upon God, nor his leanness, sated as it had been with His glory! (cf. Ex. 33:18-19, with xxxiv. 4-9, 29-35).[415]

---

[413] "Fasting in the Christian Church", In M'Clintock and Strong, eds., *Cyclopedia of Biblical and Ecclesiastical Literature*, <http://www.e-sword.net>.

[414] Schaff and Schaff, *History of the Christian Church*, Vol. 2, 380.

[415] "Tertullian - Part Fourth", In Roberts and Donaldson, eds., *Ante-Nicene Fathers: The Writings of the Fathers Down To A.D. 325*, Vol. 4, "On Fasting", Chapter 6.

175

Likewise, Tertullian speaks of Elijah who devoted himself to fasting and after eating a single meal, fled from Jezebel and made his home in a cave.

> Then he lay down under the bush and fell asleep. All at once an angel touched him and said, "Get up and eat". He looked around, and there by his head was some bread baked over hot coals, and a jar of water. He ate and drank and then lay down again. The angel of the LORD came back a second time and touched him and said, "Get up and eat, for the journey is too much for you". So he got up and ate and drank. Strengthened by that food, he traveled forty days and forty nights until he reached Horeb, the mountain of God. There he went into a cave and spent the night (1 Kgs. 19:5-9).

> For Elijah withal had, by this fact primarily, that he had imprecated a famine (cf. Jas. 6:17), already sufficiently devoted himself to fasts: "The Lord liveth", he said, "before whom I am standing in His sight, if there shall be dew in these years, and rain-shower" (cf. 1 Kgs. 17:1 in LXX. 3 Kings ib.). Subsequently, fleeing from threatening Jezebel, after one single (meal of) food and drink, which he had found on being awakened by an angel, he too himself, in a space of forty days and nights, his belly empty, his mouth dry, arrived at Mount Horeb; where, when he had made a cave his inn, with how familiar a meeting with God was he received! (cf. 1 Kgs. 19:1-8. But he took two meals: see verses 6, 7, 8.) "What (doest) thou, Elijah, here?" (verses 9, 13). Much more friendly was this voice than, "Adam, where art thou?" (Gen. 3:9, in LXX). For the latter voice was uttering a threat to a fed man, the former soothing a fasting one. Such is the prerogative of circumscribed food, that it makes God tent-fellow (cf. Mt. 17:4; Mk. 9:5; Lk. 9:33) with man—peer, in truth, with peer![416]

Tertullian, also speaks of the king of the Assyrians, Sennacherib which "nothing else (but fasting) diverted him from his purpose",

> Similarly, when the king of the Assyrians, Sennacherib, after already taking several cities, was volleying blasphemies and menaces against Israel through Rabshakeh, nothing else (but fasting) diverted him from his purpose, and sent him into the Ethiopias. After that, what else swept away by the hand of the angel an hundred eighty and four thousand from his army than Hezekiah the king's humiliation? if it is true, (as it is), that on heating the announcement of the harshness of the foe, he rent his garment, put on sackcloth, and bade the elders of the priests, similarly habited, approach God through Isaiah—fasting being, of course, the escorting attendant of their prayers (cf. 2 Kgs. 18 xix; 2 Chr. 32; Isa. 36 xxxvii). For peril has no time for food, nor sackcloth any care for satiety's refinements. Hunger is ever the attendant of mourning, just as gladness is an accessory of fulness.[417]

Moreover, of great significance is the story of Daniel in the lion's den, which Tertullian states who after "six days fasting, he had breakfast provided him by an angel",

> About the dream of the King of Babylon all the sophists are troubled: they affirm that, without external aid, it cannot be discovered by human skill. Daniel alone, trusting to God, and knowing

---

[416] "Tertullian - Part Fourth", In Roberts and Donaldson, eds., *Ante-Nicene Fathers: The Writings of the Fathers Down To A.D. 325*, Vol. 4, "On Fasting", Chapter 6.

[417] "Tertullian - Part Fourth", In Roberts and Donaldson, eds., *Ante-Nicene Fathers: The Writings of the Fathers Down To A.D. 325*, Vol. 4, "On Fasting", Chapter 7.

what would tend to the deserving of God's favour, requires a space of three days, fasts with his fraternity, and—his prayers thus commended—is instructed throughout as to the order and signification of the dream; quarter is granted to the tyrant's sophists; God is glorified; Daniel is honoured; destined as he was to receive, even subsequently also, no less a favour of God in the first year, of King Darius, when, after careful and repeated meditation upon the times predicted by Jeremiah, he set his face to God in fasts, and sackcloth, and ashes. For the angel, withal, sent to him, immediately professed this to be the cause of the Divine approbation: "I am come", he said, "to demonstrate to thee, since thou art pitiable"—by fasting, to wit. If to God he was "pitiable", to the lions in the den he was formidable, where, six days fasting, he had breakfast provided him by an angel.[418]

Tertullian, in his *De Jejuniis*, criticizes the Catholic Church for not observing the practice of fasting and therefore devotes an entire section to the subject of fasting.[419] Origen, in Homily 10 on Leviticus, states that fast days in the Church at Alexandria were held on Wednesdays and Fridays, since he viewed that Jesus Christ was betrayed by Judas on Wednesday and was crucified on a Friday. The Second Council of Orleans, in the 6th century, declared that any person failing to observe the established fast days would be treated as a violator of the laws of the Church.[420] Fasting in the 8th century was regarded as meritorious and anyone violating this observance was subjected to being excommunicated (cf. Lev. 23:26-32; cf. 16:29-31).

> Those who do not deny themselves on that day must be cut off from their people. I will destroy from among their people anyone who does any work on that day (Lev. 23:29-30).

In The Letter of Saint Jerome "To Eustochium", in reference to fasting, he speaks of people who "invariably worship what they like best",

> There are, in the Scriptures, countless divine answers condemning gluttony and approving simple food. But as fasting is not my present theme and an adequate discussion of it would require a treatise to itself, these few observations must suffice of the many which the subject suggests. By them you will understand why the first man, obeying his belly and not God, was cast down from paradise into this vale of tears; and why Satan used hunger to tempt the Lord Himself in the wilderness; and why the apostle cries: "Meats for the belly and the belly for meats, but God shall destroy both it and them;" and why he speaks of the self-indulgent as men "whose God is their belly". For men invariably worship what they like best. Care must be taken, therefore, that abstinence may bring back to Paradise those whom satiety once drove out.[421]

He later speaks of the attitude of fasting with selfish motives,

---

[418] "Tertullian - Part Fourth", In Roberts and Donaldson, eds., *Ante-Nicene Fathers: The Writings of the Fathers Down To A.D. 325*, Vol. 4, "On Fasting", Chapter 7.

[419] "Tertullian, Part Fourth", In Roberts and Donaldson, eds., *Ante-Nicene Fathers: The Writings of the Fathers Down To A.D. 325*, Vol. 4, "On Fasting".

[420] "Fasting in the Christian Church", In M'Clintock and Strong, eds., *Cyclopedia of Biblical and Ecclesiastical Literature*, 12 Vols, <http://www.e-sword.net>.

[421] "The Letters of St. Jerome", In Philip Schaff, ed., *The Nicene & Post-Nicene Fathers of the Christian Church: Second Series* (Edinburgh, UK: T. & T. Clark, 1886), WORDsearch CROSS e-book, "Letter XXII - To Eustochium", 10.

If you have fasted two or three days, do not think yourself better than others who do not fast. You fast and are angry; another eats and wears a smiling face. You work off your irritation and hunger in quarrels. He uses food in moderation and gives God thanks. Daily Isaiah cries: "Is it such a fast that I have chosen, saith the Lord?" and again: "In the day of your fast ye find your own pleasure, and oppress all your laborers. Behold ye fast for strife and contention, and to smite with the fist of wickedness. How fast ye unto me?" What kind of fast can his be whose wrath is such that not only does the night go down upon it, but that even the moon's changes leave it unchanged?[422]

In St. Jerome's letter "To Paula", he speaks of fasts that are displeasing and an enemy to God, "you deny yourself food, not to fast but to gratify your grief; and such abstinence is displeasing to me. Such fasts are my enemies. I receive no soul which forsakes the body against my will". In his Letter to Nepotian, he cautions the length of the fasting and also divinely acceptable fasting "lay upon yourself only as much fasting as you can bear, and let your fasts be pure, chaste, simple, moderate, and not superstitious".[423]

In the Epistles of Cyprian, he speaks of prayer and fasting of little value unless it is supported by almsgiving,

> Raphael the angel also witnesses the like, and exhorts that alms should be freely and liberally bestowed, saying, "Prayer is good, with fasting and alms; because alms doth deliver from death, and it purgeth away sins". He shows that our prayers and fastings are of less avail, unless they are aided by almsgiving; that entreaties alone are of little force to obtain what they seek, unless they be made sufficient by the addition of deeds and good works. The angel reveals, and manifests, and certifies that our petitions become efficacious by almsgiving, that life is redeemed from dangers by almsgiving, that souls are delivered from death by almsgiving.[424]

In the Letters of Saint Augustin, Letter 36 - Casulanus, he refers to fasting as "symbolical of humiliation",

> "Now, on the first day of the feast of unleavened bread, the disciples came to Jesus, saying unto Him, Where wilt Thou that we prepare for Thee to eat the passover?" —the Lord suffered on the sixth day of the week, as is admitted by all: wherefore the sixth day also is rightly reckoned a day for fasting, as fasting is symbolical of humiliation; whence it is said, "I humbled my soul with fasting".[425]

Even though there are hundreds of other references to fasting in the Early Church Fathers, these select few highlight the fact that fasting was an integral part, written and probably practiced by most of the

---

[422] "The Letters of St. Jerome", In Schaff, ed., *The Nicene & Post-Nicene Fathers of the Christian Church: Second Series*, "Letter XXII - To Eustochium", 37.

[423] "The Letters of St. Jerome", In Schaff, ed., *The Nicene & Post-Nicene Fathers of the Christian Church: Second Series*, "Letter XXXIX - To Paula", 3 and "Letter LII - To Nepotian", 12.

[424] "The Epistles of Cyprian", In Roberts and Donaldson, eds., *Ante-Nicene Fathers: The Writings of the Fathers Down To A.D. 325*, Vol. 5, "Treatise 8, On Works and Alms", 5.

[425] "Letters of St. Augustin", In Philip Schaff, ed., *The Nicene & Post-Nicene Fathers of the Christian Church: First Series*, Vol. 1 (Edinburgh, UK: T. & T. Clark, 1886), WORD*search* CROSS e-book, Second Edition, "Letter 36 - To Casulanus".

Fathers. Therefore, since it was a highly important part of their lives, it should likewise become part of our lives today.

Fasting in History and Revival Movements

The spiritual discipline of fasting has throughout Christianity been connected with history, reform, and revival movements. The Monastics regularly fasted as a spiritual discipline and later practiced fasting as a means of attaining salvation. The possibility exists that early monks fasted for the purpose of the church to experience reform and revival. The reformers of the 16th century fasted like those of the revivals in the subsequent centuries.

In the 16th century, the famous Swiss physician *Philippus Paracelsus*, who is known as one of the three fathers of Western medicine stated, "Fasting is the greatest remedy—the physician within" and Dr. Hoffman, in the 17th century wrote a book entitled *"Description of the Magnificent Results Obtained Through Fasting In All Diseases"*. Jonathan Edwards (1703-1758), before preaching his famous sermon entitled "Sinners in the Hands of An Angry God" fasted for 22 hours. In the 18th century, Dr. Von Seeland, of Russia stated, "Fasting is a therapeutic of the highest degree possible" and also Dr. Adolph Mayer of Germany stated, "Fasting is the most efficient means of correcting any disease". Likewise, Dr. Moeller stated, "Fasting is the only natural evolutionary method whereby through a systemic cleansing you can restore yourself by degrees to physiological normality".[426]

During the Layman's Prayer Revival Movement of 1859 in Northeastern USA, believers fasted during the lunch hour. Prayer and fasting was also prominent during the awakening of 1906, and Billy Graham prayed and fasted during his voyage to England in preparation for his first British crusades in the early 1950s. These English revival movements have been described as some of the greatest revivals of all time since they increased the awareness of the role of fasting and the need to return to the practice of this spiritual discipline.[427]

The physician, Herbert Shelton (1895-1985), who researched the fasting of over 40,000 participants stated, "Fasting must be recognized as a fundamental and radical process that is older than any other mode of caring for the sick organism, for it is employed on the plane of instinct". Hippocrates, Plato, Socrates, Aristotle, and Galen understood, practiced, and praised fasting for its intrinsic benefits in both health and healing therapy. Early healing arts recognized the revitalizing and rejuvenating power fasting promoted. It was by the end of the 19th century that fasting attracted the attention of social anthropologists who researched and compared fasting in various religious cultures with the purpose of developing a theory of its origin and expansion. Some scholars embraced fasting from an individualistic viewpoint which created an enlightened state of awareness, resulting in visions and dreams, and were identified as the ground of all religious conceptuality.[428]

---

[426] <http://fasting.ms11.net/fasting.html>, Accessed on September 3, 2013.
[427] Towns, *Fasting for Spiritual Breakthrough*, 27.
[428] <http://www.allaboutfasting.com/history-of-fasting.html>, Accessed on September 3, 2013.

Fasting is limiting our intake of food in response to God's call and for the building of His kingdom. Almost all the great men and women of God throughout history have known and practiced the secret of fasting. They have understood the power and the privilege of fasting. We cannot fast unless we have God's permission. When we fast we have the opportunity to be in the forefront of His work. We are honoured to be chosen to have such an important part in the Spirit's movement. Fasting is a power, privilege, opportunity, and honour. But only those who have unlocked this spiritual power and breakthrough recognize this.

The following table describes the revivals and results of each revival seen in Scripture.[429]

Leader	Reference and Results
Jacob (Gen. 35:1-4)	Jacob returns to Bethel, where God had revealed Himself to him. Jacob settles there, and builds an altar (35:1-15), a memorial to the God who called him, who gave him a new name, and who confirmed transmission of the promises given Abraham to Jacob/Israel's children. Rachel dies in giving birth to Benjamin (35:16-20). Jacob finds his father, Isaac, in time to join Esau in burying him (35:21-29).
Samuel (1 Sam. 7:3-6)	In Israel the ark is received with joy, but when a number of Israelites fail to show respect and peer inside, 70 die (6:19-7:1). These events stimulated a true revival (7:2-7). When the Philistines launch an attack against a gathering of God's people for worship, God intervenes and the Philistine forces are slaughtered (7:8-13a). Throughout Samuel's years as judge, God aids Israel against the Philistines (7:13b-17).
Moses (Ex. 14:31-15:12)	But the pillar leads them into an apparent trap—and Moses is told that Pharaoh has sent a chariot army to recapture his slaves (14:1-9). The approach of the Egyptian army creates panic (14:10-20), until Moses parts the sea so his people can cross (14:21-22). The pursuing Egyptians rush in after them, and are destroyed when the waters rush back at Moses' command (14:23-31). The triumphant Israelites join Moses in a song of praise (15:1-21). But in just three days, when the water supply runs out, the Hebrews have forgotten all God's miracles and grumble (15:22-27).
David (1 Chr. 15:25-28; 16:1-43; 29:10-25; 1 Chr. 29)	**1 Chronicles 15-16**, David's first attempt to bring the ark of God to Jerusalem failed (13:1-14). Now he tries again. This time he observes the rules for its transportation (15:1-15). The grand procession proceeds, and the ark is accompanied by marching bands, choirs, the military, and the elders of Israel, with David himself at the head of the celebrating throng (15:16-28). Only Michal, the daughter of Saul, seems to find no joy in the occasion (15:29). The ark is placed inside a tent David has constructed for it (16:1-3). Levites are assigned to lead in perpetual worship (16:4-6) and David contributes an original psalm of thanksgiving in praise of God's greatness (16:7-36). At last daily offerings are made and daily worship is conducted in Jerusalem, Israel's capital city and the place God has chosen to be forever identified with His name (16:37-43).
	1 Chronicles 29, David also challenges the leading men to give generously to the temple project. He sets the example by not only committing the nation's resources, but also by giving all "my personal treasures" (29:1-5). David's officials respond to the challenge. Together they commit some 375 tons of gold to the project (29:6-9; cf. 1 Kgs. 5-6). David expresses his joy and confidence in the Lord in a brief prayer (29:10-20). He acknowledges Solomon as king (29:21-25) and then, his lifework well and truly done, David dies (29:26-30).

---

[429] The "Leader" section has been adapted from Towns, *Fasting for Spiritual Breakthrough*, 70-72. The "Reference and Results" section has been adapted from Richards, *The Bible Reader's Companion*, electronic ed.

Solomon (1 Kgs. 5-8)	**1 Kings 5-6**, Solomon strengthens relations with Tyre and contracts for materials with which to build the temple that David had dreamed of erecting (5:1-12). Solomon drafts thousands of Israelite workers (5:13-18), and in the fourth year of his reign (968 BC), begins construction (6:1-7). The structure is magnificent, of the best marble and cedar wood, richly adorned with gold overlay and furnished with gold furniture (6:8-36). The project takes seven years, but at last the building is complete (6:37-38). Illustration, Solomon's Temple. **1 Kings 7**, An enthusiastic builder, Solomon not only builds a magnificent temple for the Lord, but goes on to construct a grand personal palace and national administrative center (7:1-12). Yet vast wealth and skills are poured out in equipping the temple. A skilled Israelite craftsman is brought from Tyre (7:13-14) to make massive bronze fixtures for the temple court (7:15-47) and delicate gold within (7:48-51). **1 Kings 8**, When the temple is complete, Solomon calls all Israel together (8:1-2). As the ark of the covenant is placed in the temple's inner room, a cloud symbolizing God's presence fills the temple (8:3-13). Solomon blesses the people in God's name (8:14) and, after giving a word of personal testimony (8:15-21), offers one of the Old Testament's most notable prayers (8:22-53). He acknowledges that God is too great to be contained in any structure (8:22-28). Yet Solomon asks God to be aware of prayers directed to Him at the temple whether the worshiper comes for help or for forgiveness (8:29-53). Solomon again blesses the people, and reminds them that their hearts must be "fully committed to the LORD our God" (8:54-61). The temple is then dedicated (8:62-66).
Asa (1 Kgs. 15:11-15)	The division of Solomon's empire into two rival kingdoms is complete. The author of Kings now provides a quick survey of the rulers of both kingdoms between 913 BC. and 874 BC. In Judah, Rehoboam is succeeded by a wicked son, Abijah (15:1-8). In just three years he gives way to Asa, Judah's first godly king. Asa's 41-year reign is marked by strife, but also by one of those religious revivals stimulated by Judah's all-too-infrequent pious rulers (15:9-24). In Israel, Jeroboam's dynasty is brought to a bloody end as Baasha assassinates Nadab (15:25-32).
Jehoshaphat (2 Chr. 19)	Home after the disastrous campaign with Ahab (2 Chr. 18), Jehoshaphat accepts the rebuke of the prophet Jehu (19:1-3). He remains committed to the Lord and appoints judges to administer the Old Testament's law code throughout Judah (19:4-11).
Elijah (1 Kgs. 18:21-40)	Three years of drought have drained the land of Israel of its vitality, and the next battle in the invisible war for the hearts of God's people is about to take place. God sends Elijah to Ahab (18:1). On the way he meets Obadiah, a court official who has remained faithful to the Lord, and arranges a meeting with the king (18:2-15). Elijah challenges Ahab to call the prophets of Baal and Asherah to a now-famous contest at Mount Carmel. The prophets, trailed by crowds of people, come from all over the land (18:16-19). There Elijah cries out to the wavering people of Israel to follow the deity who is truly God. Baal does not respond to the cries of his prophets. But the Lord does answer Elijah, with fire from heaven that consumes his sacrifice. Now the people decide! "The LORD, He is God!" (18:20-39) At Elijah's command they enthusiastically slaughter the prophets of Baal (18:40). A tiny cloud appears on the horizon, and soon a heavy rain falls at last on the parched land. God's people, though not the king and queen, have acknowledged Him again. And He is quick to bless them.
Jehu (2 Kgs. 10:15-28)	Elijah's prediction is thus literally fulfilled (cf. 1 Kgs. 21:23). Jehu then proceeds to wipe out the rest of the family (2 Kgs. 10:1-11). He also assembles all officials of the Baal cult, supposedly to worship, but in fact to destroy them (10:12-35). The massacre is a political expedient intended to wipe out a religion closely linked with the royal house. Because Jehu fails to turn to the Lord, his rule is marked by a series of military defeats and by the gradual reduction in size of the Northern Kingdom.
Jehoiada (2 Kgs. 11:17-20)	In Judah, Athaliah, the daughter of Jezebel and mother of the dead King Ahaziah, decides to seize the throne herself. She murders the entire royal family, but overlooks the infant Joash

	(11:1-3). Some seven years later the high priest Jehoiada and the commanders of the royal guards resolve to make Joash king. He is crowned, and the evil Athaliah is killed (11:4-16). Jehoiada then leads the people in a ceremony of covenant renewal, recommitting themselves to the Lord. In a surge of religious enthusiasm, the temple of Baal is torn down and rampaging crowds smash Baal shrines and kill Mattan, Baal's high priest (11:17-19). The boy king, just seven years old, is escorted in triumph to the palace (11:20-21).
Hezekiah (2 Chr. 29-31)	Hezekiah became king at a critical time in Judah's history. During his years the Northern Kingdom was defeated and stripped of its Hebrew population by Assyria. Judah's fortified cities were also razed. Jerusalem itself was threatened, and only divine intervention prevented its fall. How can the survival of Judah be explained? The chronicler answers by focusing on the piety of Hezekiah. He devotes three full chapters to describing Hezekiah's religious reforms and the spiritual impact of Hezekiah's reign. First, Hezekiah ritually purifies the temple (29:1-19) and re-establishes regular worship there (29:20-36). Then the king calls all his people together to celebrate Passover (30:1-20). The joy of the people is so great that they extend the week-long celebration another seven days (30:21-27). Once again enthusiastic for Yahweh, the people spread out throughout Judah and smash shrines devoted to pagan gods (31:1). Freewill offerings pour into the temple from all over Judah (31:2-15). Genealogical records are consulted, and the descendants of Aaron, supported by the gifts of the people, once again serve the Lord in the temple that represents God's presence in the land (31:16-21). Thus it is because Hezekiah sought God, did what was "good and right and faithful", and was devoted to the service of God at His temple that Judah prospered in Hezekiah's day.
Manasseh (2 Chr. 33:10-20)	Despite the lessons of faith taught during Hezekiah's reign, his son Manasseh leads Judah into a depravity so deep that "they did more evil than the [Canaanite] nations the Lord had destroyed" at the time of the conquest (33:1-10). In time Manasseh is taken captive by the Assyrians. He turns to God, humbles himself, and is restored to his throne (33:11-14). Although in his remaining years Manasseh purges Jerusalem of idolatry, he is unable to reach the people his own evil ways have influenced (33:15-20). And Manasseh is unable to influence his own son Amon who, after a short idolatrous reign, is assassinated (33:21-25).
Josiah (2 Kgs. 22-23)	One final revival, led by zealous King Josiah, fails to reverse Judah's slide toward destruction. Josiah becomes king at 8 years of age (22:1-2). At 16 he makes a decisive commitment to the Lord, and at 20 begins a purge of idolatry in Jerusalem (cf. 2 Chr. 34:3). But the key event of his reign is discovery of a lost book of God's Law, probably Deuteronomy, in the Jerusalem temple (2 Kgs. 22:3-10). Josiah is stunned to discover the terrible punishments his peoples' sins merit. The Prophetess Huldah confirms Scripture's grim vision of Judah's future, but promises the humble Josiah peace in his lifetime (22:11-20).
	Josiah intensifies his efforts to bring about a reformation. He leads his people in a covenant renewal ceremony (23:1-3). He purges the temple of every vestige of pagan worship (23:4), executes pagan priests, and tears down shrines erected to Baal and Asherah (23:5-7). He shuts down local shrines and restores the temple to its central place in worship (23:8-9). He continues his purge by desecrating Judah's Topheth, a park where child sacrifices were conducted in his grandfather's time, and where their charred corpses were buried in urns dedicated to pagan deities (23:10). He smashes every reminder of Judah's preceding half century of enthusiastic idolatry (23:11-14). Josiah even leads an expedition into the lost territory of Israel, and fulfills a 300-year-old prophecy by demolishing Israel's worship center at Bethel. Having purged Judah (23:15-20), Josiah calls his people together to celebrate Passover (23:21-24). Yet Josiah's reforms come too late. The people of Judah, corrupted for generations by idolatry, must face the fierce anger of God (23:25-28). Josiah is killed by Pharaoh Neco of Egypt, and Judah is left to face the future without the sheltering faith of her most pious king (23:29-37).

Ezra (Ezra 9-10)	When Ezra has been in Judea for a little over four months he faces the problem of mixed marriages. Deuteronomy 7:1-5 and Exodus 34:11-16 prohibit intermarriage with pagan peoples because, as God's chosen people, the Jews are to be "holy to the LORD". Ezra is appalled to learn that even some of the priests have married Canaanites. He tears his clothes as a mark of public shame and guilt (9:1-5). He then utters one of the Old Testament's most powerful prayers of confession, in which he identifies himself with God's sinning people (9:6-15). Ezra's emotional prayer moves others to promise to support Ezra in enforcing the Law (10:1-6). A proclamation orders all the men of Judah to appear in Jerusalem, where Ezra boldly confronts them. The assembly agrees that pagan wives must be divorced and their children sent away (10:7-15). Each case is investigated, and the guilty are forced to divorce their foreign wives (10:16-17). A list follows (10:18-44).
Nehemiah (Neh. 13)	When Nehemiah returns for a second term as governor of Judea, he finds that the Jews' old enemy Tobiah has actually been provided guest quarters in the temple compound itself (13:1-9). He also learns that services at the temple have been abandoned. God's tithes have not been paid, and the Levites who served at the temple have been forced to go back to their farms in order to survive (13:10-14). The people work on the Sabbath, and at Jerusalem the holy day of rest has been transformed into a market day! (13:15-22) Once again some men of Judah, including one of the sons of the high priest, have married foreign wives (13:23-31). Nehemiah vigorously corrects each abuse, calling on God to "remember" his faithful service . . . and the priests who defiled their office (13:29-30). Thus the last of the Old Testament's historical books ends on a note of uncertainty. If the people of God so quickly abandoned His Law in the brief absence of Nehemiah, what will happen to them in the centuries that lie ahead? Will they be ready when God's Deliverer, from David's line, comes?
Jonah (Jon. 3)	Given a second chance, Jonah now travels to Nineveh. Trudging through its suburbs he begins to announce that the city is to be destroyed (3:1-4). Amazingly, the people of Nineveh believe the foreign prophet's message, and the king decrees both a ritual fast and moral repentance (3:5-9). God then relents, and withholds the predicted destruction (3:10).
Esther (Est. 9:17-22)	When the appointed day arrives, the Jews take vengeance on their enemies (9:1-10). In Susa they are even given permission to extend the massacre an extra day (9:11-17). The annual festival of the Feast of Purim is established to observe the Jews' survival and triumph (9:18-32).
John the Baptist (Lk. 3:2-18)	Luke now carefully identifies just when John the Baptist began to utter his prophetic call to repentance (3:1-3). His message is urgent for the Messiah is about to appear, and so the people must turn to God now, before it is too late (3:4-14). John's ministry excited the people and aroused speculation that he himself might be the Messiah—especially when he dared rebuke Herod Antipas, ruler of Galilee (3:15-20). But John spoke of Jesus, whom God identified as His own Son at Christ's baptism (3:21-22), even though His human ancestry could be traced back to Adam (3:23-38). John was the forerunner. Jesus, Son of God and Child of humanity, is the Messiah of whom the prophets speak.
Jesus (Jn. 4:28-42)	When Jesus is traveling through Samaria He engages a woman at a well in conversation (4:1-8). When Jesus speaks of the "water" He can provide that will quench her deepest thirst, and shows that He knows her sins, she turns the conversation to theological controversy (4:9-26). Convinced that Jesus is the Messiah, the woman hurries to call her fellow villagers out to see Him (4:27-30). The salvation of the woman at the well is deeply satisfying to Jesus (4:31-38). And when the Samaritans come to see Jesus for themselves, He stays two more days and many more believe (4:39-42). Arriving back in Galilee, Jesus is approached by a royal official desperate over the illness of his son. Jesus promises the boy will live, and the official takes Jesus at His word. His trust is vindicated when the child is found well, his recovery dating from the moment Jesus had made His promise (4:43-54).

Philip (Acts 8:5-12)	After Stephen's stoning intense persecution scattered the Jerusalem believers (8:1-3). But those who fled the holy city shared Christ wherever they went (v. 4). Philip, one of the seven deacons (cf. Acts 6:1-7), not only preached in Samaria but also healed there (8:5-8), astonishing not only ordinary people but even a charlatan named Simon who had made his living impressing others with his supposedly supernatural powers (8:9-13). This revival in Samaria brought Peter and John to check on what was happening (8:14); and the apostles, discerning the conversions were authentic, prayed that the Samaritans too might be given the Holy Spirit (8:15-25). Meanwhile Philip himself was directed away from the cities and towns to wait by a desert road. There he shared the Gospel with a single traveler, an Ethiopian official, who believed and immediately was baptized by Philip. Then Philip returned to his preaching to the crowds (8:26-40).
Peter (Acts 9)	Saul sets out for Damascus with authority to arrest any Christians found in the Jewish community there (9:1-2). On the way Jesus appears to him, and Saul falls, stunned and blinded, to the ground (9:3-9). A Damascus believer called Ananias is sent by God to restore Paul's sight and tell him that he has been selected by God to carry Christ to the Gentiles (9:10-19). Paul's conversion is real. He begins at once to preach Christ in Damascus. There he is so effective some Jews conspire to kill him. Saul escapes and returns to Jerusalem, where only Barnabas is willing to take a chance on this one-time persecutor of the church. But in Jerusalem too Paul's zeal stirs up persecution, and the brothers escort the fiery evangelist to Caesarea and "send him off" to his home in Tarsus (9:20-31). Meanwhile Peter continues to minister in the Jewish homeland, performing notable miracles, even raising one much loved female believer from the dead (9:32-43).
Paul (Acts 19:11-20)	Paul moves on to Ephesus, site of a spectacular temple and center of the cult of the goddess Artemis in Asia. There Paul meets others who know only John's baptism but who quickly believe (19:1-7). At first Paul teaches in the synagogue, but when the Jews refuse to believe he continues his mission in a public lecture hall (19:8-10). Paul's teaching is supported by miracles of healing and exorcism, and because of them many turn from occult practices to adopt Christianity (19:11-22). The revival is so great that it threatens the livelihood of silversmiths, who make and sell religious trinkets to tourists. Their leader, Demetrius, plays on both financial and religious motivations to stir up a riot against Paul (19:23-34). But the city officials, fearing they will have to answer to Rome for any rioting, succeed in quieting the crowd and disbursing it (19:35-41).

Chapter 11: The Fasts of the New Testament

The purpose of this chapter is to describe the fasts found within the New Testament. Each fast presents the context and purpose in which the fasting occurs and then concludes by completing the relevant "Personal Reflections" section.

The Bridegroom or Jesus Fast

Then John's disciples came and asked him, "How is it that we and the Pharisees fast, but your disciples do not fast?" Jesus answered, "How can the guests of the bridegroom mourn while he is with them? The time will come when the bridegroom will be taken from them; then they will fast. "No one sews a patch of unshrunk cloth on an old garment, for the patch will pull away from the garment, making the tear worse. Neither do men pour new wine into old wineskins. If they do, the skins will burst, the wine will run out and the wineskins will be ruined. No, they pour new wine into new wineskins, and both are preserved" (Mt. 9:14-17)

The verses preceding this context speak of Jesus calling Matthew to come and follow Him (Mt. 9:9-13). This is the first time in the Gospel According to Matthew that Jesus refers to His departure or impending death (cf. Isa. 53:8). Subsequent to Jesus crucifixion and death, there would be a time of fasting, mourning, weeping, yet this would only be temporary (Jn. 16:20). There was no fasting preceding the ascension of Jesus since He ate periodically with His disciples (Lk. 24:41-42; Jn. 21:12-13; Acts 1:4). This dinner probably included many tax collectors and sinners who were enemies of the Jews. The Jews hated tax collectors primarily since they supported the Romans and were dishonest in charging more than required, pocketing the extra amount that was collected. As the Book of Acts progresses, there were times of fasting—especially before ministry (Acts 13:2). The spiritual discipline of fasting in the first century church was not a required observance on particular days and times. However, as the church began to degenerate that some adopted the Pharisaic practice of fasting.[430]

The Pharisees and also the disciples of John the Baptist questioned Jesus participating in the feast with the tax collectors and sinners. John and his disciples fasted because they called people to repentance and to the coming kingdom. They also questioned why Jesus and His disciples did not fast. Jesus responds by stating that the kingdom is like a great feast (cf. Mt. 22:2; Isa. 25:6) and His disciples refrained from fasting since it was inappropriate to fast while He was still among them.

Jesus expresses His power over traditions by using four parables (Lk. 5:34-39) of His ministry. As the physician of all physicians, He brings spiritual health to those who are sick (sinners). As the bridegroom, literally "the sons of the brides chamber", Jesus brings spiritual joy to those who take up their cross and follow Him. Their life should demonstrate a life feasting and celebration and not a life that is spiritually dead like those who do not know Jesus. His parable of the cloth refers to Jesus who brings spiritual wholeness to His people. Finally, in the parable of the wineskins, Jesus teaches that spiritual fullness comes only from Him. He points out that Jewish religion was like a worn-out wineskin that would burst if filled with the new wine of the Gospel. Jesus did not come to renovate Mosaic Law or even mix law and

---

[430] Gilbrant, ed., *The Complete Biblical Library Commentary, Matthew*, 173.

grace. He came with new life! Jesus had come to lead a group out of Judaism into the kingdom based on Him and His righteousness. True righteousness is not built on the Law or Pharisaic traditions.[431]

Jesus told us that we would fast after he returned to the Father. Mourning for the return of the Bridegroom is not mourning out of despair but actually a fasting of hope. This type of fasting increases our spiritual capacity to be filled with the Holy Spirit, who is promised to us in the absence of Jesus. The bridegroom or Jesus Fast is a fast for preparation for ministry and the task ahead. Jesus called for a new perspective on sin, forgiveness, and transformation. Even though we are called and loved we still need to consecrate ourselves to the One who called us.

The question here is that Jesus was accused of failing to observe the ceremonial laws, especially those regarding fasting on certain days. He alludes to rabbinic ordinances pertaining to the rites of mourning and being postponed during the marriage week. The probable reason for this is that fasting, as a sign of mourning, would be contrary to the joy which is experienced during the marriage week. Jesus adds that days of mourning are coming and approves of fasting which emotion spontaneously seeks expression. This is clearly expressed in the parables that follow in the old garment and old wineskins, which speaks of the futility of grafting the freedom that comes through the Gospel into the body of old observances and practices.

His point was that to combine His teachings and Judaism was like trying to sew a piece of un-shrunken cloth on an old garment. To confine His teaching on the ultimate meaning of life to the narrow and rigid ideology adhered to by Judaism was like putting new and unfermented wine into old and weak wine-skins. The teachings of Jesus not only disclosed the independence and breadth of His own vision, it also disclosed the deep chasm that existed between legalistic Judaism and Christianity, which His disciples throughout the generations to come would appreciate the significance of what He was teaching here. Likewise, it is even more futile to attempt to graft an entire new system into an ancient mold. Jesus emphasizes that new piety needs a new relevant expression of its own and used these illustrations to show how ridiculous it would be to constrict His message of hope and joy by Jewish ceremonialism. The truth that Jesus proclaimed must be expressed in new ways.[432]

Please refer to *Fasting: Unlocking Spiritual Power and Breakthrough, Personal Reflections* under the heading "The Bridegroom or Jesus Fast" to complete the Personal Reflections section of this study.

The Cornelius Fast

Cornelius answered: "Four days ago I was in my house praying at this hour, at three in the afternoon. Suddenly a man in shining clothes stood before me and said, 'Cornelius, God has heard your prayer and remembered your gifts to the poor. Send to Joppa for Simon who is called

---

[431] Wiersbe, *The Bible Exposition Commentary*, Vol. 1, 35. Walvoord and Zuck, eds., *The Bible Knowledge Commentary*, Vol. 2, 39-40.

[432] Charles Foster Kent, *The Life and Teachings of Jesus: According to the Earliest Records*, The Historical Bible (New York: Charles Scribner's Sons, 1913), 90. "Fasting", In Hastings, ed., *A Dictionary of Christ and the Gospels*, 2 Vols, <http://www.e-sword.net>. "Fasting", in Joel B. Green and Scot McKnight, eds., *Dictionary of Jesus and the Gospels* (Downers Grove, IL: InterVarsity Press, 1992), WORDsearch CROSS e-book, 233-34.

Peter. He is a guest in the home of Simon the tanner, who lives by the sea'. So I sent for you immediately, and it was good of you to come. Now we are all here in the presence of God to listen to everything the Lord has commanded you to tell us". Then Peter began to speak: "I now realize how true it is that God does not show favoritism but accepts from every nation the one who fears him and does what is right (Acts 10:30-35).

Many Bible versions use the word "praying", while a few use "fasting" or "fasting and praying". "Three o'clock in the afternoon" or the ninth hour was known as the hour of afternoon prayer, which is possibly why many versions use "prayer" instead of "fasting". However, the Greek uses the verb νηστεύων *nēsteuōn* from νηστεύω *nēsteuō* meaning "to fast" or "abstain from food". The emphasis here is not upon the time of evening prayer in Judaism, but to express that Cornelius received the vision "at this very hour" while he was praying and fasting. "Fulness breeds forgetfulness; but fasting maketh a man capable of heavenly visions of divine glory".[433]

This event occurred approximately ten years after Pentecost and is so important that Luke repeats it three times (Acts 10; Acts 11; 15:6-9). It speaks of the geographical expansion of the gospel in the Book of Acts, "I say to you that many will come from the east and the west, and will take their places at the feast with Abraham, Isaac and Jacob in the kingdom of heaven" (Mt. 8:11). The question arises why it took so long for the gospel to reach the Gentiles, since the gospel was "first for the Jew, then for the Gentile" (Rom. 1:16). Jesus instructed His disciples to "go and make disciples of all nations". Acts 10 is pivotal as it records that salvation has now come to the Gentiles. Peter had previously opened the door of faith for the Jews (Acts 2), and subsequently for the Samaritans (Acts 8), and he now brings the gospel to the Gentiles who are welcomed into the Church (cf. Gal. 3:27-28; Eph. 2:11-22).[434]

This passage is very significant since the Jew believed that other nations were beyond the reach of the mercy of God and a devout Jew would have absolutely no contact with a Gentile, especially if they failed to observe the Law. However, when Cornelius' emissaries arrived and knowing the Jewish outlook, they did not enter until Peter invited them in and showed them hospitality (Acts 10:23, 27). The barriers between Jew and Gentile had started to be broken down.[435] Moreover, the significance of this passage lies in Cornelius, a centurion, and "and all his family were devout and God-fearing; he gave generously to those in need and prayed to God regularly" (Acts 10:2). An "angel of God" appears and Cornelius recognizes him "What is it, Lord?" (Acts 10:3-4). When the angel answers him it has to do with

[433] Gaebelein, ed., *The Expositor's Bible Commentary, Volume 9: John and Acts* (Grand Rapids, MI: Zondervan Publishing House, 1981, WORDsearch CROSS e-book), 391. νηστεύω *nēsteuō* "3384", In Gilbrant, ed., *The Complete Biblical Library Greek-English Dictionary, Lambda-Omicron*. "Acts 10:30", In Trapp, *A Commentary on the Old and New Testaments: Matthew to Revelation*, Vol. 5. W. Webster and Hugh Martin. eds. In Rick Meyers, e-Sword, Version 10.2.1, 2000-2012, <http://www.e-sword.net>.

[434] Wiersbe, *The Bible Exposition Commentary*, Vol. 1, 444-47.

[435] "Acts 10:17-33", In William Barclay, *Daily Study Bible*, Rick Meyers, e-Sword, Version 10.2.1, 2000-2012, <http://www.e-sword.net>.

Cornelius' "prayers and gifts to the poor", which reminds us of the kind of fast that reaches the heart of God like a fragrant offering.[436]

> Is not this the kind of fasting I have chosen: to loose the chains of injustice and untie the cords of the yoke, to set the oppressed free and break every yoke? Is it not to share your food with the hungry and to provide the poor wanderer with shelter—when you see the naked, to clothe him, and not to turn away from your own flesh and blood? (Isa. 58:6-7).

Please refer to *Fasting: Unlocking Spiritual Power and Breakthrough, Personal Reflections* under the heading "The Cornelius Fast" to complete the Personal Reflections section of this study.

The Elder's Fast

> In the church at Antioch there were prophets and teachers: Barnabas, Simeon called Niger, Lucius of Cyrene, Manaen (who had been brought up with Herod the tetrarch) and Saul. While they were worshiping the Lord and fasting, the Holy Spirit said, "Set apart for me Barnabas and Saul for the work to which I have called them". So after they had fasted and prayed, they placed their hands on them and sent them off (Acts 13:1-3).

The phrase "While they were worshiping the Lord and fasting" in Greek describes a typical public service which included the congregation. The church at Antioch, situated on the Orontes River had become the home church for Paul's ministry, yet Jerusalem remained the mother church. The church at Antioch seems to be a multicultural church, seen in the diversity of those listed in verse 1. Luke begins by describing some of the "prophets and teachers" who were ministering in the church. These included, Barnabas, who was a Jew from Cyprus (Acts 4:36-37; 9:27; 11:22-26) may have been mentioned first since he was a delegate from the Jerusalem church and a held leadership position. Simeon called Niger, who had dark complexion, was a Jew who travelled in Roman circles. Lucius of Cyrene could have been one of the founders of the church at Antioch who was from North Africa (Acts 11:20) and could be the Simon of Cyrene who carried Jesus' cross (Mt. 27:32; Mk. 15:21), though debatable. Manaen was a close friend of Herod Antipas, who beheaded John the Baptist and disrespected Jesus at His trial, and Saul a Jew educated in rabbinical schools. Even though these men were from diverse cultures they functioned as a united group in setting apart Saul and Barnabas for ministry.

Frequently in the Book of Acts the Holy Spirit directed leaders to make decisions (Acts 10:19-20; cf. 8:29; 13:4). In this context, the Holy Spirit, "While they were worshiping the Lord and fasting" directed the "prophets and teachers" to set apart "Barnabas and Saul" underscoring the principle of these two men working together. The verb Ἀφορίσατε *Aphorisate* from the verb ἀφορίζω *aphorizō* is used three times in reference to the life of Saul:

---

[436] Walvoord and Zuck, eds., *The Bible Knowledge Commentary*, Vol. 2, 379. Wiersbe, *The Bible Exposition Commentary*, Vol. 1, 444-47. Mays, ed., *Harper's Bible Commentary*. 1093. Frank K. Sanders and Charles Foster Kent, eds., *The Messages of the Apostles*, Vol. XII, The Messages of the Bible (New York: Charles Scribner's Sons, 1900), 53-54.

1. He was set apart at birth to God (Gal. 1:15);
2. He was set apart at his conversation on the road to Damascus to preach the Gospel (Rom. 1:1);
3. In the church at Antioch, he was set apart for the "for the work to which I have called them" (Acts 13:2).[437]

In verse 3, Luke states "after they had fasted and prayed, they placed their hands on them and sent them off". The laying on of hands in the Old Testament communicates blessing, but in this context it indicates ordination (Num. 27:18, 23; cf. Acts 11:25) and was similar to the Jewish practice of Semikah in ordaining rabbis (cf. 1 Tim. 4:14; 2 Tim. 1:6). Rabbis practiced the laying on of hands only when it involved sacrifices and ordaining scholars. If this is true, then the "prophets and teachers" viewed the ministry of Barnabas and Saul with great importance—identifying their ministry and acknowledging God's direction upon their lives.[438] In the time of Jesus, Jewish people fasted to mourn in times of crisis such as a famine, to repent of their sins, or to seek the Lord for revelation. In this context, they were seeking the Lord in prayer and the phrase "the Holy Spirit said" who was known as the Spirit of prophecy referred to a prophetic word spoken by the prophets.[439]

In the second reference we can see that as the elders fasted and set apart Paul and Barnabas for ministry, they now appoint elders in each church and "committed them to the Lord".

> They preached the good news in that city and won a large number of disciples. Then they returned to Lystra, Iconium and Antioch, strengthening the disciples and encouraging them to remain true to the faith. "We must go through many hardships to enter the kingdom of God", they said. Paul and Barnabas appointed elders for them in each church and, with prayer and fasting, committed them to the Lord, in whom they had put their trust. After going through Pisidia, they came into Pamphylia, and when they had preached the word in Perga, they went down to Attalia (Acts 14:21-25).

In this context, we can see that Paul and Barnabas faced various hardships on their missionary journeys in Asia Minor. In Iconium, they faced opposition as they preached the Gospel and fled for their lives (Acts 14:1-7). In Lystra and Derbe the people looked to them as if "The gods have come down to us in human form!" (Acts 14:11) and to "offer sacrifices to them" (Acts 14:13).

> When the crowd saw what Paul had done, they shouted in the Lycaonian language, The gods have come down to us in human form!" Barnabas they called Zeus, and Paul they called Hermes because he was the chief speaker. The priest of Zeus, whose temple was just outside the city, brought bulls and wreaths to the city gates because he and the crowd wanted to offer sacrifices to them (Acts 14:11-13).

---

[437] ἀφορίζω aphorizō "866", In Gilbrant, ed., *The Complete Biblical Library Greek-English Dictionary, Alpha-Gamma.*

[438] "Acts 6:1-7", In Keener, *The IVP Bible Background Commentary, New Testament.*

[439] "Acts 12:25-13:3", In Keener, *The IVP Bible Background Commentary, New Testament.* Gilbrant, ed., *The Complete Biblical Library Commentary, Acts*, 304. Walvoord and Zuck, eds., *The Bible Knowledge Commentary*, Vol. 2, 387. "Acts 13", In Wiersbe, *The Bible Exposition Commentary*, Vol. 1, 456-59.

Some of the Jews had joined them in Antioch and Iconium on their missionary journey to hinder their ministry and incited the crowd against them. They stoned Paul and left him for dead, but as the disciples gather around him, he gets up and goes back into the city and continues to preach the Gospel. This demonstrates that nothing—no persecution, hardship, trial or tribulation—could hinder Paul from preaching the Gospel. Despite facing various hardships, they return home and report that a "large number of disciples" who were Gentiles received the Gospel (Acts 14:21-28).[440] He lived what Jesus had said,

> If anyone would come after me, he must deny himself and take up his cross and follow me. For whoever wants to save his life will lose it, but whoever loses his life for me and for the gospel will save it. What good is it for a man to gain the whole world, yet forfeit his soul? Or what can a man give in exchange for his soul? If anyone is ashamed of me and my words in this adulterous and sinful generation, the Son of Man will be ashamed of him when he comes in his Father's glory with the holy angels (Mk. 8:34-38).

In this context, we can see that Paul and Barnabas on their return trip to Antioch in Syria were involved in several aspects of ministry. They, first of all, preached the Gospel and made many disciples. Second, "they returned to Lystra, Iconium and Antioch" and strengthened and encouraged the disciples. Luke uses the verb στηρίζω *stērizō* which means "to fix something so that it stands upright and immovable", "to support oneself on something", "to commit oneself to something".[441] Paul desired that those who respond to the Gospel would be able to stand upright and immovable in their faith in God and find support in other believers. Paul wanted them to know that the Christian life was not an easy life, but full of trials and sufferings and their reward would be waiting for them through Jesus Christ.

Third, Paul and Barnabas established leaders in the churches that they had planted (Acts 14:23-25). These churches were planted as an organism that was organized, not as an organized organism, which was Paul's focus for the body of Christ. The focus of our churches must, first of all, be upon being an organism, since if the focus is upon organization or being organized the tendency is for the church to function as a business. Jesus instituted His Body to be based upon servant leadership (bottom up) not a hierarchical system (top down).

The reference in Acts 14:23 is not to congregational election but that these elders are nominated by Paul and Barnabas and then with "prayer and fasting" they are appointed and committed to the Lord for ministry in the churches of Pisidia and Lycaonia. Luke uses the verb χειροτονήσαντες *cheirotonēsantes* from the verb χειροτονέω *cheirotoneō* meaning "choose, select, nominate, elect by raising the hand" and also meant "elect or appoint". "It was used, however, in the writings of later church fathers and described the ordination process of bishops and deacons".[442] Luke describes the method that Paul and Barnabas used in appointing elders to serve in the churches of Lystra, Iconium, and Antioch in Galatia.

---

[440] Richards, *The Bible Reader's Companion*, 721.

[441] Kittel, Bromiley and Friedrich, eds., *Theological Dictionary of the New Testament*, electronic ed., Vol. 7, 653-54.

[442] χειροτονέω *cheirotoneō* "5336", In Gilbrant, ed., *The Complete Biblical Library Greek-English Dictionary, Sigma-Omega*.

The following diagram shows the difference between an organized organism (left) and an organism that is organized (right). In an organized organism, the focus is upon the organization, but in the organism that is organized, the focus is upon being an organism, which is the biblical model seen throughout the Pauline Epistles.

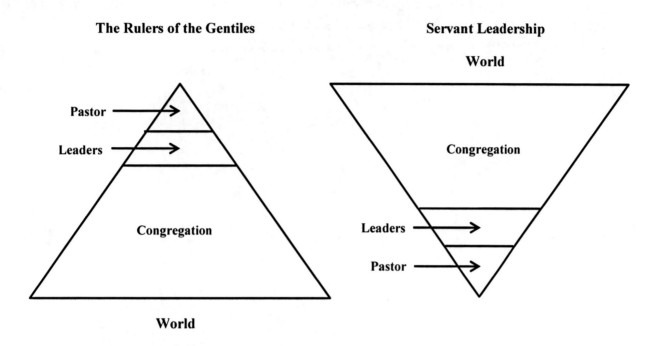

Luke then uses the verb παρέθεντο *parethento* from the verb παρατίθημι *paratithēmi* for "committed" and in ancient Greek, Jewish, and Roman thought an object was legally entrusted to someone to guard over the object for a specific period of time. This object was to be guarded, kept free, and undamaged at all costs until it was returned to the person who committed the object to the trustee. It was of the utmost importance that the trustee was trustworthy and dependable to be entrusted to protect someone or something that had been committed to him / her. Its New Testament usage literally means "to lay food before someone" (Mk. 6:41) and Jesus who quotes from Psalms 30:6—an evening prayer of pious Jews, entrusts His spirit into the hands of His Father (Ps. 30:6; Lk. 23:46; cf. Acts 7:59).[443] Moreover, "those who suffer according to God's will should commit themselves to their faithful Creator and continue to do good" (1 Pet. 4:19). Paul at his departure entrusts the churches and the appointed elders to the abiding faithfulness of God (Acts 14:23; 20:32).[444]

Paul and Barnabas knew that in order to strengthen the churches they had planted they needed to appoint elders or leaders in each church. Through the guidance and direction of the Holy Spirit they discerned which members had attained sufficient degree of spiritual maturity to become the servant

---

[443] παρατίθημι *paratithēmi* "3769", In Thoralf Gilbrant, ed., *The Complete Biblical Library Greek-English Dictionary, Pi-Rho* (Springfield, MO: Complete Biblical Library, WORDsearch CROSS e-book, 1991).

[444] Kittel, Bromiley and Friedrich, eds., *Theological Dictionary of the New Testament*, electronic ed., Vol. 8, 162-63.

leaders within these churches—serving their fellow believers. They also knew that these leaders could instruct and encourage these fellow believers to face hardship, persecution and maintain their Christian witness. Rather than inheriting leadership, the house church structure imparted, through the hosts, actual leadership which in turn determined the form of church life (cf. 1 Cor. 16:16). [445]

Please refer to *Fasting: Unlocking Spiritual Power and Breakthrough, Personal Reflections* under the heading "The Elder's Fast" to complete the Personal Reflections section of this study.

---

[445] Kittel, Bromiley and Friedrich, eds., *Theological Dictionary of the New Testament*, electronic ed., Vol. 9, 437. χειροτονέω *cheirotoneō* "5336", In Gilbrant, ed., *The Complete Biblical Library Greek-English Dictionary, Sigma-Omega*. Wiersbe, *The Bible Exposition Commentary*, Vol. 1, 456-59.

Chapter 12: Thematic Fasts

The purpose of this chapter is to describe the various fasts based upon themes along with a brief description of their context and concludes by completing the relevant "Personal Reflections" sections.

In Scripture, we can find various types of fasts based upon a particular theme. These thematic fasts can also be found in this study under other headings.

Fasting to Receive Healing

1. Hannah pours out herself to the Lord so that she can conceive a son (1 Sam. 1:5-11, 18-20).

   But to Hannah he gave a double portion because he loved her, and the LORD had closed her womb. And because the LORD had closed her womb, her rival kept provoking her in order to irritate her. This went on year after year. Whenever Hannah went up to the house of the LORD, her rival provoked her till she wept and would not eat. Elkanah her husband would say to her, "Hannah, why are you weeping? Why don't you eat? Why are you downhearted? Don't I mean more to you than ten sons?" Once when they had finished eating and drinking in Shiloh, Hannah stood up. Now Eli the priest was sitting on a chair by the doorpost of the LORD's temple. In bitterness of soul Hannah wept much and prayed to the LORD. And she made a vow, saying, "O LORD Almighty, if you will only look upon your servant's misery and remember me, and not forget your servant but give her a son, then I will give him to the LORD for all the days of his life, and no razor will ever be used on his head" . . . . She said, "May your servant find favor in your eyes". Then she went her way and ate something, and her face was no longer downcast. Early the next morning they arose and worshiped before the LORD and then went back to their home at Ramah. Elkanah lay with Hannah his wife, and the LORD remembered her. So in the course of time Hannah conceived and gave birth to a son. She named him Samuel, saying, "Because I asked the LORD for him" (1 Sam. 1:5-11, 18-20).

2. David fasted in an attempt to show his remorse for his sin of adultery with Bathsheba so that his son would live (receive healing), however, he died (2 Sam. 12:15-17, 21-23).

   After Nathan had gone home, the LORD struck the child that Uriah's wife had borne to David, and he became ill. David pleaded with God for the child. He fasted and went into his house and spent the nights lying on the ground. The elders of his household stood beside him to get him up from the ground, but he refused, and he would not eat any food with them. . . . His servants asked him, "Why are you acting this way? While the child was alive, you fasted and wept, but now that the child is dead, you get up and eat!" He answered, "While the child was still alive, I fasted and wept. I thought, 'Who knows? The LORD may be gracious to me and let the child live'. But now that he is dead, why should I fast? Can I bring him back again? I will go to him, but he will not return to me" (2 Sam. 12:15-17, 21-23).

3. The prophet Isaiah states that through fasting "your healing will quickly appear" (Isa. 58:8).

   Then your light will break forth like the dawn, and your healing will quickly appear; then your righteousness will go before you, and the glory of the LORD will be your rear guard (Isa. 58:8).

4. Saul was temporarily blinded in his encounter with Jesus on the road to Damascus and subsequently received healing (Acts 9:9, 17-19).

For three days he was blind, and did not eat or drink anything. . . . Then Ananias went to the house and entered it. Placing his hands on Saul, he said, "Brother Saul, the LORD—Jesus, who appeared to you on the road as you were coming here—has sent me so that you may see again and be filled with the Holy Spirit". Immediately, something like scales fell from Saul's eyes, and he could see again. He got up and was baptized, and after taking some food, he regained his strength (Acts 9:9, 17-19).

Please refer to *Fasting: Unlocking Spiritual Power and Breakthrough, Personal Reflections* under the heading "Fasting to Receive Healing" to complete the Personal Reflections section of this study.

Fasting to Receive A Solution to Individual / National Crisis

This type of fast was prevalent in the Old Testament and was called by the leaders of Israel whenever a national crisis loomed. It was also known as corporate fasting when a group of believers joined together in fasting and prayer. This group may be a family, such as when Esther told her uncle Mordecai to fast and pray, or may be a group from a church or churches. In fact, it can incorporate any group of believers even if they are separated by miles. This fasting is most often connected with specific prayer requests. If we fast and pray for revival, God will pour Himself on His people.

1. Samuel gathers the Israelites together at Mizpah and they fast and confessed their sin against the Lord (1 Sam. 7:2-17). Fasting frequently accompanied repentance as an outward and genuine indication of sorrow for apostasy.

    When they had assembled at Mizpah, they drew water and poured it out before the LORD. On that day they fasted and there they confessed, "We have sinned against the LORD". And Samuel was leader of Israel at Mizpah (1 Sam. 7:6).

2. King of Nineveh heeds the word of the prophet and averts the hand of the Lord (Jon. 3:5-10).

    The Ninevites believed God. They declared a fast, and all of them, from the greatest to the least, put on sackcloth. When the news reached the king of Nineveh, he rose from his throne, took off his royal robes, covered himself with sackcloth and sat down in the dust. Then he issued a proclamation in Nineveh: "By the decree of the king and his nobles: Do not let any man or beast, herd or flock, taste anything; do not let them eat or drink. But let man and beast be covered with sackcloth. Let everyone call urgently on God. Let them give up their evil ways and their violence. Who knows? God may yet relent and with compassion turn from his fierce anger so that we will not perish". When God saw what they did and how they turned from their evil ways, he had compassion and did not bring upon them the destruction he had threatened (Jon. 3:5-4:1).

3. A call to national repentance (Joel 1; Joel 2).

Please refer to *Fasting: Unlocking Spiritual Power and Breakthrough, Personal Reflections* under the heading "Fasting to Receive A Solution to Individual / National Crisis" to complete the Personal Reflections section of this study.

Fasting to Prevent Divine Judgment

This fast was used by Tertullian and Cyprian of the reparation made for sin by fasting, almsgiving, and other good works, which are regarded in Scripture as means of averting Divine punishment (cf. Dan. 4:27; Lk. 16:9).[446]

> Then once again I fell prostrate before the LORD for forty days and forty nights; I ate no bread and drank no water, because of all the sin you had committed, doing what was evil in the LORD's sight and so provoking him to anger. . . . I lay prostrate before the LORD those forty days and forty nights because the LORD had said he would destroy you (Deut. 9:18, 25).

> Then you will call, and the LORD will answer; you will cry for help, and he will say: Here am I. "If you do away with the yoke of oppression, with the pointing finger and malicious talk, and if you spend yourselves in behalf of the hungry and satisfy the needs of the oppressed, then your light will rise in the darkness, and your night will become like the noonday (Isa. 58:9-10).

Please refer to *Fasting: Unlocking Spiritual Power and Breakthrough, Personal Reflections* under the heading "Fasting to Prevent Divine Judgment" to complete the Personal Reflections section of this study.

Fasting to Experience God's Power

We all desire to experience the power of God in new and fresh ways on a continual basis. However, we often feel as though something is hindering us from growing deeper in our relationship with the Lord and struggle to break free from these obstacles. Fasting takes our focus off of ourselves and opens us to experience God's power. There are countless testimonies of people who have experienced God's power in miraculous ways as a result of fasting.

Please refer to *Fasting: Unlocking Spiritual Power and Breakthrough, Personal Reflections* under the heading "Fasting to Experience God's Power" to complete the Personal Reflections section of this study.

Fasting to Humble Oneself

David had fasted and prayed for his enemies when they were ill, putting on sackcloth (cf. Ps. 30:11; cf. Gen. 37:34), and when his prayers were not answered, he mourned and wept for them.[447]

> Yet when they were ill, I put on sackcloth and humbled myself with fasting. When my prayers returned to me unanswered, I went about mourning as though for my friend or brother. I bowed my head in grief as though weeping for my mother (Ps. 35:13-14).

> When I weep and fast, I must endure scorn; when I put on sackcloth, people make sport of me (Ps. 69:10-11).

Please refer to *Fasting: Unlocking Spiritual Power and Breakthrough, Personal Reflections* under the heading "Fasting to Humble Oneself" to complete the Personal Reflections section of this study.

---

[446] Cross and Livingstone, *The Oxford Dictionary of the Christian Church*, 1466.
[447] Walvoord and Zuck, eds., *The Bible Knowledge Commentary*, Vol. 1, 820-21.

Fasting in Sorrow and Mourning

Apparently before a person was stoned for blasphemy, the people mourned the sin and coming execution with fasting.[448]

So she wrote letters in Ahab's name, placed his seal on them, and sent them to the elders and nobles who lived in Naboth's city with him. In those letters she wrote: "Proclaim a day of fasting and seat Naboth in a prominent place among the people. But seat two scoundrels opposite him and have them testify that he has cursed both God and the king. Then take him out and stone him to death". So the elders and nobles who lived in Naboth's city did as Jezebel directed in the letters she had written to them. They proclaimed a fast and seated Naboth in a prominent place among the people. Then two scoundrels came and sat opposite him and brought charges against Naboth before the people, saying, "Naboth has cursed both God and the king". So they took him outside the city and stoned him to death. Then they sent word to Jezebel: "Naboth has been stoned and is dead" (1 Kgs. 21:8-14).

Please refer to *Fasting: Unlocking Spiritual Power and Breakthrough, Personal Reflections* under the heading "Fasting in Sorrow and Mourning" to complete the Personal Reflections section of this study.

Fasting for Divine Direction

Then the Israelites, all the people, went up to Bethel, and there they sat weeping before the LORD. They fasted that day until evening and presented burnt offerings and fellowship offerings to the LORD. And the Israelites inquired of the LORD. (In those days the ark of the covenant of God was there, with Phinehas son of Eleazar, the son of Aaron, ministering before it.) They asked, "Shall we go up again to battle with Benjamin our brother, or not?" The LORD responded, "Go, for tomorrow I will give them into your hands" (Jdg. 20:26-28).

After this, the Moabites and Ammonites with some of the Meunites b came to wage war against Jehoshaphat. Some people came and told Jehoshaphat, "A vast army is coming against you from Edom, from the other side of the Dead Sea. It is already in Hazezon Tamar" (that is, En Gedi). Alarmed, Jehoshaphat resolved to inquire of the LORD, and he proclaimed a fast for all Judah. The people of Judah came together to seek help from the LORD; indeed, they came from every town in Judah to seek him (2 Chr. 20:1-4).

There, by the Ahava Canal, I proclaimed a fast, so that we might humble ourselves before our God and ask him for a safe journey for us and our children, with all our possessions. I was ashamed to ask the king for soldiers and horsemen to protect us from enemies on the road, because we had told the king, "The gracious hand of our God is on everyone who looks to him, but his great anger is against all who forsake him". So we fasted and petitioned our God about this, and he answered our prayer (Ezra 8:21-23).

In the church at Antioch there were prophets and teachers: Barnabas, Simeon called Niger, Lucius of Cyrene, Manaen (who had been brought up with Herod the tetrarch) and Saul. While they were worshiping the Lord and fasting, the Holy Spirit said, "Set apart for me Barnabas and Saul for the

---

[448] צוּם "1890", In Harris, Archer, Jr., and Waltke, eds., *Theological Wordbook of the Old Testament*, 758.

work to which I have called them". So after they had fasted and prayed, they placed their hands on them and sent them off (Acts 13:1-3).

They preached the good news in that city and won a large number of disciples. Then they returned to Lystra, Iconium and Antioch, strengthening the disciples and encouraging them to remain true to the faith. "We must go through many hardships to enter the kingdom of God", they said. Paul and Barnabas appointed elders for them in each church and, with prayer and fasting, committed them to the Lord, in whom they had put their trust. After going through Pisidia, they came into Pamphylia, and when they had preached the word in Perga, they went down to Attalia (Acts 14:21-25).

Please refer to *Fasting: Unlocking Spiritual Power and Breakthrough, Personal Reflections* under the heading "Fasting for Divine Direction" to complete the Personal Reflections section of this study.

Fasting for Remorse Over Committed Sin

Wicked King Ahab fasted over his sin,

"Dogs will eat those belonging to Ahab who die in the city, and the birds of the air will feed on those who die in the country". (There was never a man like Ahab, who sold himself to do evil in the eyes of the LORD, urged on by Jezebel his wife. He behaved in the vilest manner by going after idols, like the Amorites the LORD drove out before Israel.) When Ahab heard these words, he tore his clothes, put on sackcloth and fasted. He lay in sackcloth and went around meekly (1 Kgs. 21:24-27).

Please refer to *Fasting: Unlocking Spiritual Power and Breakthrough, Personal Reflections* under the heading "Fasting for Remorse Over Committed Sin" to complete the Personal Reflections section of this study.

Fasting for Spiritual Deliverance

Alarmed, Jehoshaphat resolved to inquire of the LORD, and he proclaimed a fast for all Judah. The people of Judah came together to seek help from the LORD; indeed, they came from every town in Judah to seek him (2 Chr. 20:3-4).

Is not this the kind of fasting I have chosen: to loose the chains of injustice and untie the cords of the yoke, to set the oppressed free and break every yoke? (Isa. 58:6).

He replied, "Because you have so little faith. I tell you the truth, if you have faith as small as a mustard seed, you can say to this mountain, 'Move from here to there' and it will move. Nothing will be impossible for you". But this kind does not go out except by prayer and fasting (Mt. 17:20-21).
He replied, "This kind can come out only by prayer and fasting" (Mk. 9:29).

Please refer to *Fasting: Unlocking Spiritual Power and Breakthrough, Personal Reflections* under the heading "Fasting for Spiritual Deliverance" to complete the Personal Reflections section of this study.

Fasting for Revival, Renewal, and Righteousness

Anna and John the Baptist gave themselves to fasting (Lk. 2:26-37) praying for the Messiah to come. The fasts in the Book of Joel were to avert the national crisis, but also for the Holy Spirit to breakthrough over the nation. Jesus tells us that there is a blessing over those who hunger and thirst for righteousness.

There was also a prophetess, Anna, the daughter of Phanuel, of the tribe of Asher. She was very old; she had lived with her husband seven years after her marriage, and then was a widow until she was eighty-four. She never left the temple but worshiped night and day, fasting and praying. Coming up to them at that very moment, she gave thanks to God and spoke about the child to all who were looking forward to the redemption of Jerusalem. (Lk. 2:36-38).

Please refer to *Fasting: Unlocking Spiritual Power and Breakthrough, Personal Reflections* under the heading "Fasting for Revival, Renewal, and Righteousness" to complete the Personal Reflections section of this study.

Fasting for Material Provision

Are they servants of Christ? (I am out of my mind to talk like this.) I am more. I have worked much harder, been in prison more frequently, been flogged more severely, and been exposed to death again and again. Five times I received from the Jews the forty lashes minus one. Three times I was beaten with rods, once I was stoned, three times I was shipwrecked, I spent a night and a day in the open sea, I have been constantly on the move. I have been in danger from rivers, in danger from bandits, in danger from my own countrymen, in danger from Gentiles; in danger in the city, in danger in the country, in danger at sea; and in danger from false brothers. I have labored and toiled and have often gone without sleep; I have known hunger and thirst and have often gone without food; I have been cold and naked. Besides everything else, I face daily the pressure of my concern for all the churches (2 Cor. 11:23-28).

Please refer to *Fasting: Unlocking Spiritual Power and Breakthrough, Personal Reflections* under the heading "Fasting for Material Provision" to complete the Personal Reflections section of this study.

Fasting Rejected By God

The prophets protest against the view that purely external fasting gains a hearing with God (cf. Jer. 14:12; Isa. 58:1ff.). For them true fasting is a bowing down of the soul that leads to moral action. Fasting here is rejected because of strife, disobedience, and selfish motives.[449]

1. Described, (Isa. 58:4-5)

Your fasting ends in quarreling and strife, and in striking each other with wicked fists. You cannot fast as you do today and expect your voice to be heard on high. Is this the kind of fast I have chosen, only a day for a man to humble himself? Is it only for bowing one's head like a reed

---

[449] Kittel, Friedrich and Bromiley, eds., *Theological Dictionary of the New Testament: Abridged in One Volume*, 632-33.

and for lying on sackcloth and ashes? Is that what you call a fast, a day acceptable to the LORD? (Isa. 58:4-5)

2. Rejected, (Isa 58:1-3; Jer. 14:12; Zech. 7:5)

Shout it aloud, do not hold back. Raise your voice like a trumpet. Declare to my people their rebellion and to the descendants of Jacob their sins. For day after day they seek me out; they seem eager to know my ways, as if they were a nation that does what is right and has not forsaken the commands of its God. They ask me for just decisions and seem eager for God to come near them. "Why have we fasted", they say, "and you have not seen it? Why have we humbled ourselves, and you have not noticed?" (Isa. 58:1-3).

Then the LORD said to me, "Do not pray for the well-being of this people. Although they fast, I will not listen to their cry; though they offer burnt offerings and grain offerings, I will not accept them. Instead, I will destroy them with the sword, famine and plague" (Jer. 14:11-12).

Then the word of the LORD Almighty came to me: "Ask all the people of the land and the priests, 'When you fasted and mourned in the fifth and seventh months for the past seventy years, was it really for me that you fasted? And when you were eating and drinking, were you not just feasting for yourselves? Are these not the words the LORD proclaimed through the earlier prophets when Jerusalem and its surrounding towns were at rest and prosperous, and the Negev and the western foothills were settled?'" (Zech. 7:4-7).

3. Ostentatious,

When you fast, do not look somber as the hypocrites do, for they disfigure their faces to show men they are fasting. I tell you the truth, they have received their reward in full. But when you fast, put oil on your head and wash your face, so that it will not be obvious to men that you are fasting, but only to your Father, who is unseen; and your Father, who sees what is done in secret, will reward you (Mt. 6:16-18).

4. Boasted of, before God, (Lk. 18:9-12)

To some who were confident of their own righteousness and looked down on everybody else, Jesus told this parable: "Two men went up to the temple to pray, one a Pharisee and the other a tax collector. The Pharisee stood up and prayed about himself: 'God, I thank you that I am not like other men—robbers, evildoers, adulterers—or even like this tax collector. I fast twice a week and give a tenth of all I get'" (Lk. 18:9-12).

Please refer to *Fasting: Unlocking Spiritual Power and Breakthrough, Personal Reflections* under the heading "Fasting Rejected By God" to complete the Personal Reflections section of this study.

Fasting Due to Emotional Distress

This type of fasting was probably seen as an involuntary fast since when a person is emotionally distressed they usually do not feel like eating and often isolate themselves from other people.

1. Jacob after hearing of Joseph's possible death isolates himself, puts on sackcloth, throws dirt upon himself, and probably refuses to eat. However, Scripture does not say that he fasted, but can be assumed since sackcloth, mourning, and weeping are often connected with fasting.

   He recognized it and said, "It is my son's robe! Some ferocious animal has devoured him. Joseph has surely been torn to pieces". Then Jacob tore his clothes, put on sackcloth and mourned for his son many days. All his sons and daughters came to comfort him, but he refused to be comforted. "No", he said, "in mourning will I go down to the grave to my son". So his father wept for him (Gen. 37:33-35).

2. Saul becomes distressed and does not eat for one day over hearing his fate at the hands of the Amalekites and that of the Israelites from Samuel who has been brought back from the dead as a spirit (1 Sam. 28:20).

   The LORD will deliver both Israel and you into the hands of the Philistines, and tomorrow you and your sons will be with me. The LORD will also give the army of Israel into the hands of the Philistines". Immediately Saul fell full length on the ground, filled with fear because of Samuel's words. His strength was gone, for he had eaten nothing all that day and night (1 Sam. 28:19-20).

3. No desire for food because of anxiety, sorrow, or mental distress. Darius fasted as he worried over Daniel's fate.

   Then the king returned to his palace and spent the night without eating and without any entertainment being brought to him. And he could not sleep. At the first light of dawn, the king got up and hurried to the lions' den. When he came near the den, he called to Daniel in an anguished voice, "Daniel, servant of the living God, has your God, whom you serve continually, been able to rescue you from the lions?" Daniel answered, "O king, live forever! My God sent his angel, and he shut the mouths of the lions. They have not hurt me, because I was found innocent in his sight. Nor have I ever done any wrong before you, O king". The king was overjoyed and gave orders to lift Daniel out of the den. And when Daniel was lifted from the den, no wound was found on him, because he had trusted in his God. At the king's command, the men who had falsely accused Daniel were brought in and thrown into the lions' den, along with their wives and children. And before they reached the floor of the den, the lions overpowered them and crushed all their bones (Dan. 6:18-24).

4. A person finds themselves in a situation where no food is available (Mt. 15:32; 2 Cor. 6:3-10; 11:27-28).[450]

   Jesus called his disciples to him and said, "I have compassion for these people; they have already been with me three days and have nothing to eat. I do not want to send them away hungry, or they may collapse on the way" (Mt. 15:32).

   We put no stumbling block in anyone's path, so that our ministry will not be discredited. Rather, as servants of God we commend ourselves in every way: in great endurance; in troubles,

---

[450] <http://www.faithcycleministry.org/Fasting/Fasting4.html>, Accessed on September 3, 2013.

hardships and distresses; in beatings, imprisonments and riots; in hard work, sleepless nights and hunger; in purity, understanding, patience and kindness; in the Holy Spirit and in sincere love; in truthful speech and in the power of God; with weapons of righteousness in the right hand and in the left; through glory and dishonor, bad report and good report; genuine, yet regarded as impostors; known, yet regarded as unknown; dying, and yet we live on; beaten, and yet not killed; sorrowful, yet always rejoicing; poor, yet making many rich; having nothing, and yet possessing everything (2 Cor. 6:3-10).

I have labored and toiled and have often gone without sleep; I have known hunger and thirst and have often gone without food; I have been cold and naked. Besides everything else, I face daily the pressure of my concern for all the churches (2 Cor. 11:27-28).

Please refer to *Fasting: Unlocking Spiritual Power and Breakthrough, Personal Reflections* under the heading "Fasting Due to Emotional Distress" to complete the Personal Reflections section of this study.

Chapter 13: Topical Fasts

The purpose of this chapter is to describe the topical fasts that are found in Scripture. Each fast presents the context and purpose in which the fasting occurs and then concludes by completing the relevant "Personal Reflections" section.

The Circumstance Fast

Just before dawn Paul urged them all to eat. "For the last fourteen days", he said, "you have been in constant suspense and have gone without food—you haven't eaten anything. Now I urge you to take some food. You need it to survive. Not one of you will lose a single hair from his head". After he said this, he took some bread and gave thanks to God in front of them all. Then he broke it and began to eat. They were all encouraged and ate some food themselves. Altogether there were 276 of us on board. When they had eaten as much as they wanted, they lightened the ship by throwing the grain into the sea (Acts 27:33-38).

In Acts 27:9, Luke refers to this time as being after "the Fast" or observance of the Day of Atonement on the 10th day of the 7th month of the Jewish year. In the midst of the storm, Paul assures the 276 crew and passengers and prisoners of the Ship of Adramyttium (Acts 27:2) that everything is going to be alright and takes some bread, broke it, and gave thanks. Paul's confidence was in the Lord during this storm and could therefore remain calm and encouraged everyone to eat. Even though some believe that the breaking of bread here refers to observing the Lord's Supper, it was probably not, since the majority of the 276 crew and passengers were not Christians. Paul gave thanks for the bread, which was the usual custom among the Hebrews (Mt. 14:19). Even though Paul was among non-Christians, he was not ashamed of acknowledging God's sovereignty, publicly giving testimony of his faith in Jesus Christ, his dependence upon Him, and expressing his gratitude for His mercy. He recognized that everyone needed to eat and gain strength for the circumstances that are ahead of them.

The crew, passengers and prisoners had "gone without food" for fourteen days, and the Greek structure implies that they were expecting the worst—that the storm would destroy the ship and everything would be lost including their lives. Luke uses the adjective ἄσιτος *asitos* instead of the common word for fasting, νηστεύω *nēsteuō*—the only New Testament occurrence meaning literally "foodless", or "without eating, or "fasting". The adjective ἄσιτος *asitos* is from the negative *a* and *sitos* meaning "grain".[451] It can also refer to "a fast, hunger" "lack of appetite" or "a lack of hunger due to anxiety or seasickness".[452] It describes the condition of the shipwrecked companions of Paul who had gone "without eating" perhaps because of stress (Acts 27:33).

---

[451] ἄσιτος *asitos* "771", In Gilbrant, ed., *The Complete Biblical Library Greek-English Dictionary, Alpha-Gamma.*

[452] William Arndt, F. Wilbur Gingrich, Frederick W. Danker and Walter Bauer, *A Greek-English Lexicon of the New Testament and Other Early Christian Literature: A Translation and Adaption of the Fourth Revised and Augmented Edition of Walter Bauer's Griechisch-Deutsches Worterbuch Zu Den Schrift En Des Neuen Testaments Und Der Ubrigen Urchristlichen Literatur* (Chicago, IL: University of Chicago Press, 1979), 116.

These men had been fourteen successive anxious nights waiting for dawn, seeing land, and being saved. In Paul's time, ancient ships had no tables, and each person who wanted food or refreshment needed to get it for themselves. However, due to the storm, they had lost their appetite through fear and being afraid for their life they had no desire for food. Their physical condition had resulted from their spiritual despair, which Paul encourages them in their faith, "Not one of you will lose a single hair from his head" (Acts 27:34). He then takes "some bread and gave thanks to God in front of them all. Then he broke it and began to eat. They were all encouraged and ate some food themselves" (Acts 27:35-36).[453]

It must be noted that some scholars have supposed that they could not have possibly gone entirely without food, but that they had no time to make a regular meal. However, this cannot be true, since everyone had "gone without food—you haven't eaten anything" (Acts 27:33). Everyone had been in "constant suspense", danger, engaged with survival, and anxious for their safety that they did not eat. There is no mention of drinking water, so we cannot argue from silence that they must have or that they did not drink water.[454]

Please refer to *Fasting: Unlocking Spiritual Power and Breakthrough, Personal Reflections* under the heading "The Circumstance Fast" to complete the Personal Reflections section of this study.

The Intercessory Fast

The Scripture references and study for the Intercessory Fast have already been discussed under the following fasts: the Moses Fast (Deut. 9:9, 18, 25-29); The Ezra Fast (Ezra 8:21-23; 10:6); The Daniel Fast (Dan. 9:1-3); The Joel Fast (Joel 2:12-18); and The Nineveh Fast (Jon. 3:1-10). Please refer to these studies for further information.

When I went up on the mountain to receive the tablets of stone, the tablets of the covenant that the LORD had made with you, I stayed on the mountain forty days and forty nights; I ate no bread and drank no water. . . . Then once again I fell prostrate before the LORD for forty days and forty nights; I ate no bread and drank no water, because of all the sin you had committed, doing what was evil in the LORD's sight and so provoking him to anger. . . . I lay prostrate before the LORD those forty days and forty nights because the LORD had said he would destroy you. I prayed to the LORD and said, "O Sovereign LORD, do not destroy your people, your own inheritance that you redeemed by your great power and brought out of Egypt with a mighty hand. Remember your servants Abraham, Isaac and Jacob. Overlook the stubbornness of this people, their wickedness and their sin. Otherwise, the country from which you brought us will say, 'Because the LORD was not able to take them into the land he had promised them, and because he hated them, he brought them out to put them to death in the desert'. But they are your people,

---

[453] "Acts 27", In Ray C. Stedman, *Ray Stedman: Commentary on Selected Books of the Bible*, Copyright © 2010 by Ray Stedman Ministries, <http://www.raystedman.org>, Accessed on September 3, 2013, Rick Meyers, e-Sword, Version 10.2.1, 2000-2012, <http://www.e-sword.net>. 1971. Henry Alford, *The Greek Testament: An Exegetical and Critical Commentary*, 531-32, In Rick Meyers, e-Sword, Version 10.2.1, 2000-2012, <http://www.e-sword.net>.

[454] Gilbrant, ed., *The Complete Biblical Library Commentary, Acts*, 651. Walvoord and Zuck, eds., *The Bible Knowledge Commentary*, Vol. 2, 428. "Acts 27:33", In Albert Barnes, *Notes on the New Testament Explanatory and Practical*. Mays, ed., *Harper's Bible Commentary*. 1116. "The Life of Flavius Josephus", In Flavius Josephus, *The Works of Josephus: Complete and Unabridged* (Peabody, MA: Hendrickson Publishers, 1987), 15.

your inheritance that you brought out by your great power and your outstretched arm" (Deut. 9:9, 18, 25-29).

There, by the Ahava Canal, I proclaimed a fast, so that we might humble ourselves before our God and ask him for a safe journey for us and our children, with all our possessions. I was ashamed to ask the king for soldiers and horsemen to protect us from enemies on the road, because we had told the king, "The gracious hand of our God is on everyone who looks to him, but his great anger is against all who forsake him". So we fasted and petitioned our God about this, and he answered our prayer (Ezra 8:21-23).

Then Ezra withdrew from before the house of God and went to the room of Jehohanan son of Eliashib. While he was there, he ate no food and drank no water, because he continued to mourn over the unfaithfulness of the exiles (Ezra 10:6).

In the first year of Darius son of Xerxes (a Mede by descent), who was made ruler over the Babylonian kingdom—in the first year of his reign, I, Daniel, understood from the Scriptures, according to the word of the LORD given to Jeremiah the prophet, that the desolation of Jerusalem would last seventy years. So I turned to the LORD God and pleaded with him in prayer and petition, in fasting, and in sackcloth and ashes (Dan. 9:1-3).

"Even now", declares the LORD, "return to me with all your heart, with fasting and weeping and mourning". Rend your heart and not your garments. Return to the LORD your God, for he is gracious and compassionate, slow to anger and abounding in love, and he relents from sending calamity. Who knows? He may turn and have pity and leave behind a blessing—grain offerings and drink offerings for the LORD your God. Blow the trumpet in Zion, declare a holy fast, call a sacred assembly. Gather the people, consecrate the assembly; bring together the elders, gather the children, those nursing at the breast. Let the bridegroom leave his room and the bride her chamber. Let the priests, who minister before the LORD, weep between the temple porch and the altar. Let them say, "Spare your people, O LORD. Do not make your inheritance an object of scorn, a byword among the nations. Why should they say among the peoples, 'Where is their God?'" Then the LORD will be jealous for his land and take pity on his people (Joel 2:12-18).

The Ninevites believed God. They declared a fast, and all of them, from the greatest to the least, put on sackcloth. When the news reached the king of Nineveh, he rose from his throne, took off his royal robes, covered himself with sackcloth and sat down in the dust. Then he issued a proclamation in Nineveh: "By the decree of the king and his nobles: Do not let any man or beast, herd or flock, taste anything; do not let them eat or drink. But let man and beast be covered with sackcloth. Let everyone call urgently on God. Let them give up their evil ways and their violence. Who knows? God may yet relent and with compassion turn from his fierce anger so that we will not perish". When God saw what they did and how they turned from their evil ways, he had compassion and did not bring upon them the destruction he had threatened (Jon. 3:5-4:1).

Please refer to *Fasting: Unlocking Spiritual Power and Breakthrough, Personal Reflections* under the heading "The Intercessory Fast" to complete the Personal Reflections section of this study.

The Sexual Fast

Now for the matters you wrote about: "It is good for a man not to have sexual relations with a woman". But since sexual immorality is occurring, each man should have sexual relations with his own wife, and each woman with her own husband. The husband should fulfill his marital duty to his wife, and likewise the wife to her husband. The wife's body does not belong to her alone but also to her husband. In the same way, the husband's body does not belong to him alone but also to his wife. Do not deprive each other except by mutual consent and for a time, so that you may devote yourselves to prayer. Then come together again so that Satan will not tempt you because of your lack of self-control. I say this as a concession, not as a command (1 Cor. 7:1-6).

The purpose of the Sexual Fast is for a husband and wife to set aside time for mutual abstinence from sexual intimacy and devotion to fasting and prayer. The issue that the Apostle Paul addresses here is that some of the Corinthians were practicing celibacy within the marriage relationship—a unilateral decision and not a mutual agreement. A further issue was that this practice sometimes led the other spouse to commit acts of sexual immorality (v. 5b; cf. v. 2). Paul commands that those practicing the Sexual Fast must immediately stop unless three conditions were adhered to: (a) abstaining with mutual consent; (b) abstaining with an agreed upon time period; or (c) abstaining to devote themselves to fasting and prayer.[455]

The Apostle Paul had just written that in everything, the spiritual must govern the physical, since our bodies are the temple of the Holy Spirit,

Do you not know that your body is a temple of the Holy Spirit, who is in you, whom you have received from God? You are not your own; you were bought at a price. Therefore honor God with your body (1 Cor. 6:19-20).

Paul states that "each man should have his own wife, and each woman her own husband" (1 Cor. 7:2), arguing against both polygamous and homosexual "marriages". He begins by using the verb ἀποστερεῖτε *apostereite* for "deprive" in reference to the marital rights of a spouse, which was parallel to denying a spouse food and clothing (Ex. 21:10) and in 1 Timothy 5:8 is equivalent to denying them the Christian faith. Committing such an act was worse than that of an unbeliever. Paul refers to the Mosaic Covenant and that sexual obligations was a divine institution (Ex. 21:10).[456] He specifically addresses the issue of "do not deprive each other" μή ἀποστερεῖτε ἀλλήλους *mē apostereite allēlous* due to the prevalence of sexual immorality πορνεία *porneia* in the Corinthian culture. He understood the temptation that a husband or a wife could fall into during this type of fasting, which is the reason why he emphasizes this caution.[457]

Paul next uses the adjective συμφώνου *sumphōnou* meaning "harmonious, unison of sounds". Paul uses this unique appearance in the New Testament to instruct couples not to deprive their spouse of sexual

---

[455] Walvoord and Zuck, eds., *The Bible Knowledge Commentary*, Vol. 2, 517.

[456] σύμφωνος *sumphōnos* "4710", In Gilbrant, ed., *The Complete Biblical Library Greek-English Dictionary, Sigma-Omega*.

[457] Gaebelein, *The Expositor's Bible Commentary, Volume 10*, 228. Wiersbe, *The Bible Exposition Commentary*, Vol. 1, 590-94.

obligations unless there is harmonious agreement. Paul's focus is that the marital relationship must function like a symphony. He refers to Satan's tempting one's character and possible trapping of the Christian who lacks self-control to express themselves in an illicit manner such as fornication or adultery. He uses the Greek phrase τη νηστείᾳ καὶ τη προσευχη, *tē nēsteia kai tē proseuchē* for fasting and prayer even though some manuscripts exclude τη νηστείᾳ καὶ "for the fasting and". Some manuscripts include the noun for fasting νηστεία *nēsteia*, which along with prayer give spiritual power to breaking the enemies hold over a marriage.[458]

The central principle in the Sexual Fast is that fasting breaks the trappings of self-indulgence and enhances our sensitivity and awareness to the needs of others, especially our spouse. Many people tend to walk around with self-indulgent attitudes most of the time, like: "I want what I want when I want it". However, when a couple agrees to mutually fast and pray together in this way, they create an atmosphere where the woman tends to feel more cherished and the man learns self-control.

Please refer to *Fasting: Unlocking Spiritual Power and Breakthrough, Personal Reflections* under the heading "The Sexual Fast" to complete the Personal Reflections section of this study.

The Eucharistic Fast

> For I received from the Lord what I also passed on to you: The Lord Jesus, on the night he was betrayed, took bread, and when he had given thanks, he broke it and said, "This is my body, which is for you; do this in remembrance of me". In the same way, after supper he took the cup, saying, "This cup is the new covenant in my blood; do this, whenever you drink it, in remembrance of me". For whenever you eat this bread and drink this cup, you proclaim the Lord's death until he comes. Therefore, whoever eats the bread or drinks the cup of the Lord in an unworthy manner will be guilty of sinning against the body and blood of the Lord. A man ought to examine himself before he eats of the bread and drinks of the cup. For anyone who eats and drinks without recognizing the body of the Lord eats and drinks judgment on himself. That is why many among you are weak and sick, and a number of you have fallen asleep. But if we judged ourselves, we would not come under judgment. When we are judged by the Lord, we are being disciplined so that we will not be condemned with the world (1 Cor. 11:23-32).

By this is commonly understood complete abstinence from food and drink for a period preceding the reception of The Lord's Supper. Unlike other forms of fasting, it is designed less as a form of asceticism than to honour to the Eucharistic Gifts. This fast began from the previous midnight and its earliest discussion occurred in the Council of Hippo AD 393 allowing an exception on Maundy Thursday[459], which was re-enacted at Carthage in AD 397. St. Augustine promoted the Eucharistic Fast, since he believed in its universal observance, along with the Middle Ages and the Reformers, dating back to

---

[458] ἀποστερέω *apostereō* "644", In Gilbrant, ed., *The Complete Biblical Library Greek-English Dictionary, Alpha-Gamma*. σύμφωνος *sumphōnos* "4710", In Gilbrant, ed., *The Complete Biblical Library Greek-English Dictionary, Sigma-Omega*. Gilbrant, ed., *The Complete Biblical Library Commentary, Romans-Corinthians*, 331.

[459] The traditional English name for the Thursday preceding Easter, derived from the first antiphon of the ceremony of the washing of the feet, "*mandatum novum*" (Jn. 13:34). Its special celebration in commemoration of the Lord's Institution of the Eucharist on that day is attested already for the 4th century by the Council of Hippo (393). Cross and Livingstone, *The Oxford Dictionary of the Christian Church*, 1065.

Apostolic times. The Eucharistic Fast, within Protestantism, lost its focus and ceased to be practiced and in England seems to have disappeared in the 18th century. In the 19th century, the Tractarians[460] and their followers persistently encouraged the Eucharistic Fast.[461]

Please refer to *Fasting: Unlocking Spiritual Power and Breakthrough, Personal Reflections* under the heading "The Eucharistic Fast" to complete the Personal Reflections section of this study.

---

[460] A name for the earlier stages of the Oxford Movement, derived from the *Tracts for the Times* issued under its aegis. The purpose of the tracts was to disseminate Church principles "against Popery and Dissent". . . . They secured a wide circulation, and their influence, as the first public utterances of the Oxford Movement, was enormous. Their form gradually changed from brief leaflets to learned treatises and catenae assembled from the 17th-century. Cross and Livingstone, *The Oxford Dictionary of the Christian Church*, 1645.

[461] Cross and Livingstone, *The Oxford Dictionary of the Christian Church*, 572.

Chapter 14: Warnings and Abuses Concerning Fasting

The purpose of this chapter is to discuss how fasting can become an external show of godliness without the internal transformation of the heart. The Old Testament prophets strictly warned and harshly criticized any abuse of the Mosaic Law in relation to the Day of Atonement (*Yom Kippur*). Likewise, Jesus in the New Testament harshly criticized the Pharisees for their open display of religiosity without an inner transformation through repentance. Each fast presents the context and purpose in which the fasting occurs and then concludes by completing the relevant "Personal Reflections" section.

Warnings Concerning Fasting

It is important to become aware of some of the warnings associated with fasting. First of all, the discipline of fasting can easily become like the Pharisees who demonstrated an external show and ceremonial ritual. Not only did the prophets address this, but Jesus also spoke out harshly against this external practice with little or no internal transformation. Second, the strongest confrontation of this type of fasting can be seen in Isaiah 58 where the people complained that God did not pay attention to their fast, since their motives were not congruent with God's standard of fasting (Isa. 58:3-4). God requires more than just an external show. The kind of fasting that pleases God includes: (a) "to loose the chains of injustice"; (b) "untie the cords of the yoke"; (c) "to set the oppressed free"; (d) "break every yoke"; (e) "to share your food with the hungry"; (f) "to provide the poor wanderer with shelter"; and (g) "when you see the naked, to clothe him" (Isa. 58:6-7). The Lord's response to true fasting is that their prayers would be heard (Isa. 58:9). True fasting requires true repentance.[462] Other warnings include:

1. Fasting can never serve as a substitute for personal godliness. Isaiah delivers a blistering rebuke to those who would fast and then go about their own pleasure (Isa. 58:3-5).
2. Fasting must not be used as an occasion for putting on a religious front (Mt. 6:16-18).
3. Fasting must never cause one to develop a sense of complacency and self-righteousness (Lk. 18:9-14).
4. Today some religious groups have made a mockery of fasting by their "Mardi Gras" (fat Tuesday) a day of inhibited indulgence in foods in preparation for the fast of "Lent". There will always be those who "fast to be seen of men". But our avoidance of such extremes should not be used as an excuse to avoid fasting for the spiritual benefit it provides.
5. Fasting is not a way of showing off one's spirituality, but of drawing closer to God and seeking His guidance.

Abuses Concerning Fasting

The abuses concerning fasting are usually seen in the belief that if God's people voluntarily self-inflict suffering upon themselves in an attempt to demonstrate their sincerity with God, then God will quickly respond to their need. However, this cannot be true since if it was true then the prophets of Baal in Elijah's time were correct. They had cried from morning to late afternoon without any response, then they began to "slashed themselves with swords and spears, as was their custom, until their blood flowed"

---

[462] Copeland, *Fasting: A Special Study*, <http://www.e-sword.net>. Accessed on June 12, 2014.

(1 Kgs. 18:28). The prophets of Baal were literally telling God, look at us and our suffering, why do you not pay attention. Simply being uncomfortable with gnawing pangs of hunger or thirst is not advocated in Scripture as a way of getting God's attention.

The following fasts are some examples of the abuses of fasting.[463]

The Queen Jezebel Fast

> So Ahab went home, sullen and angry because Naboth the Jezreelite had said, "I will not give you the inheritance of my fathers". He lay on his bed sulking and refused to eat. His wife Jezebel came in and asked him, "Why are you so sullen? Why won't you eat?" He answered her, "Because I said to Naboth the Jezreelite, 'Sell me your vineyard; or if you prefer, I will give you another vineyard in its place'. But he said, 'I will not give you my vineyard'". Jezebel his wife said, "Is this how you act as king over Israel? Get up and eat! Cheer up. I'll get you the vineyard of Naboth the Jezreelite". So she wrote letters in Ahab's name, placed his seal on them, and sent them to the elders and nobles who lived in Naboth's city with him. In those letters she wrote: "Proclaim a day of fasting and seat Naboth in a prominent place among the people. But seat two scoundrels opposite him and have them testify that he has cursed both God and the king. Then take him out and stone him to death". So the elders and nobles who lived in Naboth's city did as Jezebel directed in the letters she had written to them. They proclaimed a fast and seated Naboth in a prominent place among the people. Then two scoundrels came and sat opposite him and brought charges against Naboth before the people, saying, "Naboth has cursed both God and the king". So they took him outside the city and stoned him to death. Then they sent word to Jezebel: "Naboth has been stoned and is dead". . . . When Ahab heard these words, he tore his clothes, put on sackcloth and fasted. He lay in sackcloth and went around meekly (1 Kgs. 21:4-14, 27).

When the Israelites settled in the Promised Land in the days of Joshua, each tribe and family were allotted land, which was to belong to them permanently and could not be transferred to any other owner. The Law of Moses taught that God was the owner of Canaan and that the people, as its tenants, could not dispose of their land (Lev. 25:23; Num. 27:1-11; 36:1-12). Even though Ahab knew the Law of Moses and this principle of justice, he still coveted Naboth's vineyard, which made him sick. Naboth's refusal to sell his family's vineyard was a courageous act of obedience in adhering to the Law of Moses. After Ahab realizes that the vineyard that he had coveted could not be attained, his wife Jezebel devises a scheme to get the vineyard at any cost (1 Kgs. 21:7-14). Although it was Ahab's wife Jezebel who carried out this evil deed, Ahab was held responsible as the king for failing to stop his wicked wife.

In Israelite society, land could not be transferred or taken away from the landowner since it was protected by law. Naboth's refusal to transfer or "exchange" to King Ahab is both a religious and economic statement and wanted to profit from the harvest of the land. Likewise, Naboth knew that to sell or exchange the land for profit was a sin according to Israelite Law. As the king, Ahab could have demanded the vineyard to be given to him, but he understood and respected the religious aspect of land distribution. However, Queen Jezebel had Canaanite religious roots and a princess from the Phoenician city of Tyre knew how to use Israelite Law to her advantage.

---

[463] Towns, *Fasting for Spiritual Breakthrough*, 238-39.

209

The context here refers to the Elijah era and the spiritual conflict which demanded a decision. At Mount Carmel and the war with Syria, God has revealed His power and now Ahab responds. He coveted Naboth's vineyard (1 Kgs. 21:1-6) and Jezebel promises him that she will acquire the vineyard at any cost. The author of Kings uses the verb סַר *sar* meaning "to be stubborn or rebellious" which indicates "smoldering anger which is about to be unleashed". This verb is used exclusively in reference to King Ahab and describes his emotional state after he was rebuked by a prophet, "Sullen and angry, the king of Israel went to his palace in Samaria" (1 Kgs. 20:43) and Naboth's refused to give him "the inheritance of my fathers" (1 Kgs. 21:4f.). Even though Ahab seems to have not showed his emotional state to anyone, his rage was apparent to his wife.[464] Jezebel had grown up in a culture where the rights of individuals were not honoured as they were in Israel and she criticizes Ahab for not taking what he wanted since he was the king, which is how, according to her, a king should act.

The author of Kings uses the verb וְלֹא־אָכַל *wĕlō' ākal* with the noun לֶחֶם *lāḥem* meaning "refused to eat" (1 Kgs. 21:4). It was not that Naboth had been rude or disrespected King Ahab that he had become "sullen and angry", but his resentful and irritable behaviour demonstrates selfish motives in not attaining what he coveted. This led him to return to his room where "He lay on his bed sulking and refused to eat" (1 Kgs. 21:4). The Hebrew noun used here מִטָּה *mittāh* means "couch" or "bed" and King Ahab reclined upon his couch during meals, which was common among the Jews and Orientals (Am. 6:4; Eze. 23:41). However, he turns his back, refuses to converse with his guests, and refuses to eat, typifying a child pouting because they did not get their own way.[465]

Jezebel sent letters to "the elders and nobles" who lived in the same town as Naboth to "Proclaim a day of fasting and seat Naboth in a prominent place among the people. But seat two scoundrels opposite him and have them testify that he has cursed both God and the king. Then take him out and stone him to death" (1 Kgs. 21:9-10). The elders and nobles, who were comprised of Judges and officials (Deut. 16:18) could, at their discretion, call an assembly to fast as though the city had committed a serious sin (cf. 1 Sam. 7:6) and the penalty needed to be averted (cf. Lev. 4:13-21; Deut. 21:1-9; 2 Chr. 20:2-4; Joel 1:14-15). Queen Jezebel demanded that "the elders and nobles . . . proclaim a day of fasting" and seat literally בְּלִיַּעַל *belîya'al* two sons of corruption beside Naboth. This refers to a person who "deliberately deprives others of justice or good, through false testimony, defamation, oppression". Likewise, it refers to someone who is "notoriously wicked or wretched in character" or a professional perjurer.[466]

It was a custom in the Old Testament during national disasters to "proclaim a day of fasting" (Joel 1:14), likewise following military defeats (Jdg. 20:26; 1 Sam. 31:13), corporate sin (1 Sam. 7:6; Joel 2:12), perceived adversity (2 Chr. 20:2-4), and was a sign of repentance. This conspiracy against Naboth

---

[464] סַר *sar* "5821", In Gilbrant, ed., *The Complete Biblical Library Hebrew-English Dictionary, Nun-Ayin.*

[465] "1 Kings 21:1-29", In Albert Barnes, *Albert Barnes' Notes on the Bible*, Rick Meyers, e-Sword, Version 10.2.1, 2000-2012, <http://www.e-sword.net>. מִטָּה *mittāh* "4433", In Gilbrant, ed., *The Complete Biblical Library Hebrew-English Dictionary, Kaph-Mem.*

[466] בְּלִיַּעַל *belîya'al* "1139", In Gilbrant, ed., *The Complete Biblical Library Hebrew-English Dictionary, Aleph-Beth.*

did not only concern him, but "to publish the fact that a grievous fault was resting upon the city, which must be expiated". Naboth was made an example of "so that the public indignation might be the more vividly expressed, if one who was worthy of such distinction, on account of his God-fearing sentiment, should be convicted of being such a grievous sinner".[467] This has been referred to as one of the most wicked deeds recorded in Bible history.[468]

Under Israelite Law, at least two witnesses were required to condemn a person and cursing God was a crime punishable by stoning. Naboth was accused of blaspheming both God and the king. The penalty for this crime was death by stoning (Deut. 13:10-11; 17:5), and the convicted along with his sons were dragged outside the city (cf. the stoning of Stephen, Acts 7:54-60) and stoned until dead (Lev. 24:14; Deut. 22:24). However, before the convicted was stoned the witnesses would lay their hands on them (Lev. 24:14) and cast the first stones (cf. Jn. 8:7). Since the entire community was responsible for carrying out the punishment, they would then join the witnesses in stoning the accused. Naboth is charged with blasphemy and treason (1 Kgs. 21:7-14) and after he is stoned to death, King Ahab, on his way to take possession of the vineyard is met by Elijah who announces God's judgment upon him and his family (1 Kgs. 21:15-26). However, King Ahab humbles himself, "he tore his clothes, put on sackcloth and fasted. He lay in sackcloth and went around meekly", and God promises that "because he has humbled himself, I will not bring this disaster in his day, but I will bring it on his house in the days of his son" (1 Kgs. 21:27-29).

The principle that is emphasized here is that King Ahab fasted to be forgiven for his wicked act against Naboth and his family. Fasting here is seen as the natural expression of grief and the customary mode of proving to others the inner emotion of sorrow. Ahab's example demonstrates that each person must choose good or evil and face the consequences. Even though Ahab was the most wicked king in Israel, God showed him mercy and prolonged his life. God postponing his punishment did not mean that He had changed His opinion of the character of Ahab's reign (cf. 1 Kgs. 22:37-38).[469] In the end, King Ahab coveting Naboth's vineyard is an appropriate illustration of contempt for the worship of Yahweh in the Northern Kingdom of Israel. Naboth's death by perjured testimony led to the collapse of the lineage of Omri, the longest-lived and most successful dynastic house of the Northern Kingdom.[470]

---

[467] Richards, *The Bible Reader's Companion*, 293. "1 Kings 21:1-29", In John Peter Lange, *Commentary on the Holy Scriptures: Critical, Doctrinal, and Homiletical* (25 volumes), Philip Schaff, ed., Rick Meyers, e-Sword, Version 10.2.1, 2000-2012, <http://www.e-sword.net>.

[468] "1 Kings 21:1-29", In Arno Clement Gaebelein, *Annotated Bible*, Rick Meyers, e-Sword, Version 10.2.1, 2000-2012, http://www.e-sword.net, 1919. "1 Kgs. 21:1-4", In Jamieson, Fausset, and Brown, *Commentary Critical and Explanatory on the Whole Bible*.

[469] "1 Kings 21:1-29", In Dockery, ed., In *Holman Concise Bible Commentary*, 143-44. Paschall and Hobbs, eds., *The Teacher's Bible Commentary*, 205-06. Larry Richards and Lawrence O. Richards, *The Teacher's Commentary* (Wheaton, IL: Victor Books, 1987), 264. Richards, *The Bible Reader's Companion*, 238.

[470] Richards, *The Bible Reader's Companion*, 238. "1 Kings 21:5-10", In Walvoord and Zuck, eds., *The Bible Knowledge Commentary*, Vol. 1, 532. Gaebelein, *The Expositor's Bible Commentary, Volume 4*, 159-160. "1 Kings 21:8-10", In Gilbrant, ed., *The Complete Biblical Library Commentary, Kings*. נָבוֹת *nāvôth* "5197", In Gilbrant, ed., *The Complete Biblical Library Hebrew-English Dictionary, Nun-Ayin*.

Please refer to *Fasting: Unlocking Spiritual Power and Breakthrough, Personal Reflections* under the heading "The Queen Jezebel Fast" to complete the Personal Reflections section of this study.

The Hypocrites' Fast

> Shout it aloud, do not hold back. Raise your voice like a trumpet. Declare to my people their rebellion and to the descendants of Jacob their sins. For day after day they seek me out; they seem eager to know my ways, as if they were a nation that does what is right and has not forsaken the commands of its God. They ask me for just decisions and seem eager for God to come near them. "Why have we fasted", they say, "and you have not seen it? Why have we humbled ourselves, and you have not noticed?" Yet on the day of your fasting, you do as you please and exploit all your workers. Your fasting ends in quarreling and strife, and in striking each other with wicked fists. You cannot fast as you do today and expect your voice to be heard on high (Isa. 58:1-4).

The Hebrew prophet Isaiah in this context does not condemn all fasting, but he does expose their hypocritical behaviour of displaying a form of fasting—denial of food, covering themselves in sackcloth and ashes, postures of mourning and humiliation, being recognized by God for their alleged suffering— while living a lifestyle of unrighteousness, injustice, selfishness, and neglect of the needs of others. While Isaiah is rebuking his countrymen for their hypocritical lifestyle, he asks the question, "Is this the kind of fast I have chosen" (Isa. 58:5) and "Is not this the kind of fasting I have chosen" (Isa. 58:6). Isaiah's response is, "of course not" and he continues on to explain true fasting (cf. "The Fasts of Isaiah 58"). Isaiah's countrymen were fasting as an external display with no internal transformation, which was vain and worthless and wonderfully explained,

> The one true repentance is to turn from the ways of sin into the ways of righteousness. The fear of the Lord is to depart from evil, and if a man be departing from evil he need not trouble about any further confession or repentance, except in so far as his own heart should compel him. In departing from evil he is fasting the fast which God chooses, which is not to afflict his soul with abstinence for a day, and to bow down his head as a bulrush, but to "loosen the bands of wickedness", and to "deal his bread to the hungry".[471]

The people wondered why God did not bless them, which was because they did not demonstrate the attitudes and activities that fasting represented (cf. Isa. 58:6-7). They did not deny themselves of anything and neglected the physical, emotional, spiritual needs of others. Instead, they pursued their personal interests, worked while they fasted, and forced their employees to work. They practiced religious rituals and attempted to manipulate God so that He would bless them. They demonstrated external repentance without the internal transformation of the heart. "But repentance is not for the purpose of getting God to

---

[471] "Isaiah 58:1-14", In William Robertson Nicoll, ed., *The Sermon Bible: Isaiah to Malachi*, Vol. 4, Rick Meyers, e-Sword, Version 10.2.1, 2000-2012, <http://www.e-sword.net>.

do anything; it is an expression of the conviction that my ways are wrong and God's ways are right, whether he does anything for me or not".[472]

Please refer to *Fasting: Unlocking Spiritual Power and Breakthrough, Personal Reflections* under the heading "The Hypocrites' Fast" to complete the Personal Reflections section of this study.

The Pharisee Fast

> To some who were confident of their own righteousness and looked down on everyone else, Jesus told this parable: "Two men went up to the temple to pray, one a Pharisee and the other a tax collector. The Pharisee stood up and prayed about himself: "God, I thank you that I am not like other men—robbers, evildoers, adulterers—or even like this tax collector. I fast twice a week and give a tenth of all I get" (Lk. 18:9-12).

Luke 18 brings together some important incidents that relate to parables and people. The parable of the persistent widow teaches we should persevere and be patient in prayer (Lk. 18:1-8). The parable of the Pharisee and the tax collector teaches that only those who recognize their sinful state will trust God and His mercy and truly experience forgiveness (Lk. 18:9-14). Jesus' short discussion concerning children demonstrates complete dependence upon God (Lk. 18:15-17), which is also the truth that He teaches concerning the rich young ruler (Lk. 18:18-30). Jesus, once again, predicts His coming death (Lk. 18:31-34) heals a blind beggar who cries out "Jesus, Son of David, have mercy on me!" (Lk. 18:35-43). When our true dependence is upon God, we are freed from our own circumstances and can without reservation care for those who are poor and in need.[473]

Jesus describes "Two men went up to the temple to pray" who represent two extremes, yet relevant situations. He, first of all, describes the Pharisee, who stands while praying (Mt. 6:5; Mk. 11:25), which alone was not unethical since its origin was to maintain a piety in contrast to pagan Hellenism. Pharisees were known for their piety in Palestinian Jewish society, while tax collectors were known as the most contemptuous and traitors to others. The issue with the Pharisee was that he "stood up and prayed about himself" and probably in a place to be seen by everyone, which contrasted the tax collector who "stood at a distance" (Lk. 18:13). The prayer of the Pharisee was self-centered and self-righteous, while the tax collector humbly cried out "God, have mercy on me, a sinner".

The Pharisee describes how thankful that he is "not like other men—robbers, evildoers, adulterers—or even like this tax collector". Luke uses the adjective ἅρπαξ *harpax* which in classical Greek means "preying, ravenous, extortion" and also as a substantive "robber, thief". Matthew states "watch out for false prophets. They come to you in sheep's clothing, but inwardly they are ferocious wolves" (Mt. 7:15). "It is so easy for men to consider the real values of life—the salvation of the soul and eternal things—as insignificant. From this follows an attitude that sins directed toward the inner life are less serious than

[472] "Isaiah 58:1-5", In Thomas L. Constable, *The Expository Notes of Dr. Constable*, 2012, Rick Meyers, e-Sword, Version 10.2.1, 2000-2012, <http://www.e-sword.net>.
[473] Richards, *The Bible Reader's Companion*, 669.

those that rob us of earthly values".[474] The Greek adjective conveys the idea that such people steal the goods of others by force and violence and take advantage of the necessities of others, the poor and the oppressed, and extort their property. However, Jesus viewed life quite differently since someone who preyed on others or robbed others spiritually—who destroys the souls of men—is equally guilty and deserves to be punished like a person who physically robs another. In the early church era, the tax collector was seen as a greedy politician—a person who was a social outcast—who was viewed as a recipient of the grace of God contrasted with the Pharisee who was self-absorbed in his justification.[475]

> While Jesus was in one of the towns, a man came along who was covered with leprosy. When he saw Jesus, he fell with his face to the ground and begged him, "Lord, if you are willing, you can make me clean". . . . After this, Jesus went out and saw a tax collector by the name of Levi sitting at his tax booth. "Follow me", Jesus said to him, and Levi got up, left everything and followed him (e.g., Lk. 5:12, 27-28; cf. 7:34, 37; 15:1-2; 16:20),

Next, Luke uses the adjective ἄδικος *adikos* from two dominant Hebrew nouns שֶׁקֶר *sheqer* meaning "falsehood, deception" and עַוְלָה *'awlāh* meaning "wickedness". The Greek adjective may also describe a "wrong, perverse, or unfair act", including sexual immorality (e.g., Gen. 19:8), bearing false witness (Ex. 23:1; Lev. 19:12); the latter being a reflection of its frequent legal context (e.g., Lev. 19:15, 35; Deut. 19:16, 18). Likewise, it refers to a person who is incongruent with what is right.[476] These types of people are unjust in their business deals with others and attain the property of others through fraud. The difference between ἅρπαξ *harpax* and ἄδικος *adikos* is that those who are unjust may have the appearance of honesty; in the other case there is not. The Pharisee finally says that he was not an adulterer μοιχός *moichos*, meaning "the violator of the marriage bond".[477] It also means "to seduce or violate a woman" or "to be, or to allow oneself to be seduced", of the woman "to commit adultery".[478]

The Pharisee arrives at the pinnacle of arrogance and self-evaluation in comparing himself to the tax collector, "or even like this tax collector". In Judaism, thanking God for their own righteousness is seen as a pious act, but don't want to receive credit. In this context, those who heard this parable would not see the Pharisee as being boastful, but as being grateful to God for his piety.[479] He sought to paint a picture of the tax collector as the lowest, most despicable person so that he could be elevated in the eyes of others.

---

[474] ἅρπαξ *harpax* "721", In Gilbrant, ed., *The Complete Biblical Library Greek-English Dictionary, Alpha-Gamma.*

[475] ἅρπαξ *harpax* "721", In Gilbrant, ed., *The Complete Biblical Library Greek-English Dictionary, Alpha-Gamma.*

[476] ἄδικος *adikos* "93", In Gilbrant, ed., *The Complete Biblical Library Greek-English Dictionary, Alpha-Gamma.* עַוְלָה *'awlāh* "5983", In Gilbrant, ed., *The Complete Biblical Library Hebrew-English Dictionary, Nun-Ayin.* שֶׁקֶר *sheqer* "8632", In Gilbrant, ed., *The Complete Biblical Library Hebrew-English Dictionary, Sin-Taw.*

[477] μοιχός *moichos* "3295", In Gilbrant, ed., *The Complete Biblical Library Greek-English Dictionary, Lambda-Omicron.*

[478] "μοιχεύω", In Kittel, Bromiley and Friedrich, eds., *Theological Dictionary of the New Testament*, electronic ed., Vol. 4, 729.

[479] "Luke 18:9-14", In Keener, *The IVP Bible Background Commentary, New Testament.*

The purpose of this parable was to illustrate that to trust in one's own righteousness was futile and we should not show contempt or think of ourselves as better than others, "Do not think of yourself more highly than you ought, but rather think of yourself with sober judgment, in accordance with the measure of faith God has given you" (Rom. 12:3).

In essence, he was using others as his criterion for determining righteousness. The tax collector used God's criterion for determining righteousness and he needed to rely upon God's mercy for attaining forgiveness, which pointed back to Jesus stating, "Indeed there are those who are last who will be first, and first who will be last" (Lk. 13:30). The tax collector's prayer in verse 13, "God, have mercy on me, a sinner" in Greek is literally translated "God be propitiated towards me, the sinner".[480]

Finally, Jesus states, that the Pharisees "fast twice a week". Pharisees were known to fast two times per week (Monday and Thursdays), even though they were commanded to fast one day per year on the Day of Atonement (Lev. 16:29-31). This fast commemorated Moses ascending and descending Mount Sinai to receive the Law. In Isaiah's time, God had rebuked the Israelites for just going through the motions of fasting without a changed life (Isa. 38:1-7). Likewise, Jesus cautioned against practicing a fast to impress others (Mt. 6:16-18). Like fasting, the most pious exaggerated their tithing to the fullest extent of the law, which included several different tithes equaling about twenty percent of their income. The issue that Jesus points to here is that the Pharisees depended upon works, while neglecting the mercy and grace of God.[481] The Pharisee boasted, "I . . . give a tenth of all I get". The Greek word used here for "all I get" is κτάομαι *ktaomai* and refers to something that is "acquired" or "obtained" in the sense that it becomes the possession of the one acquiring it.[482] They tithed "a tenth of your mint, rue and all other kinds of garden herbs, but you neglect justice and the love of God" (Lk. 11:42).

The point here is that the Pharisee revealed righteousness as being outside of oneself—it cannot be attained through personal pursuit. Likewise, we should never perceive what others do or not do with contempt. We cannot judge the motives of another person; only God can do this, which Jesus condemned them for trying to judge someone's motives. The Pharisees in judging the motives of another were in essence trying to be God and Jesus knowing their thoughts and heart exposed these cancerous emotional behaviours. The Pharisee, in comparing himself with the Tax Collector, concluded that his righteousness was far superior and should therefore receive more in return for his external behaviour. The Tax Collector compared his righteousness with God's standard and realized that he fell quite short and humbled himself before God and asked for mercy and forgiveness. Jesus finished this parable by saying, "For everyone who exalts himself will be humbled, and he who humbles himself will be exalted" (Lk. 18:14).[483]

---

[480] Gilbrant, ed., *The Complete Biblical Library Commentary, Luke*, 529. "Luke 18:9-14", In Arno Clement Gaebelein, *Annotated Bible*, http://www.e-sword.net, 1919.

[481] Gilbrant, ed., *The Complete Biblical Library Commentary, Luke*, 529-531. Gaebelein, ed., *The Expositor's Bible Commentary, Volume 8*, 1002-1003. "Luke 18:9-14", In Keener, *The IVP Bible Background Commentary, New Testament*. "Luke 18:11", In Barnes, *Notes on the New Testament*. Walvoord and Zuck, eds. *The Bible Knowledge Commentary*, Vol. 2, 250.

[482] κτάομαι *ktaomai* "2904", In Gilbrant, ed., *The Complete Biblical Library Greek-English Dictionary, Zeta-Kappa*.

[483] Walvoord and Zuck, eds., *The Bible Knowledge Commentary*, Vol. 2, 250.

Please refer to *Fasting: Unlocking Spiritual Power and Breakthrough, Personal Reflections* under the heading "The Pharisee Fast" to complete the Personal Reflections section of this study.

The Conspiracy Fast

> The next morning the Jews formed a conspiracy and bound themselves with an oath not to eat or drink until they had killed Paul. More than forty men were involved in this plot. They went to the chief priests and the elders and said, "We have taken a solemn oath not to eat anything until we have killed Paul" (Acts 23:12-14).

The Conspiracy Fast is an example of using the spiritual discipline of fasting for selfish or personal gain. There are a number of passages in the Book of Acts, where "the Jews formed a conspiracy" to kill the Apostle Paul. From the time of Paul's encounter with the Messiah on the road to Damascus (Acts 9:1-19), his life had been in danger by a Jewish conspiracy to kill him. After his conversion, Paul went to Jerusalem where the Hellenistic (Grecian) Jews tried to kill him; "He talked and debated with the Grecian Jews, but they tried to kill him" (Acts 9:29). After Paul and Barnabas had been consecrated and then sent out (Acts 13:1-3), they went to Antioch in Pisidia where the Jews "expelled them from their region" (Acts 13:50-51).

In Lystra, "There was a plot afoot among the Gentiles and Jews, together with their leaders, to mistreat them and stone them" (Acts 14:5), however, "they found out about it and fled to the Lycaonian cities of Lystra and Derbe and to the surrounding country, where they continued to preach the good news" (Acts 14:6-7). In Lystra, "They stoned Paul and dragged him outside the city, thinking he was dead" (Acts 14:19) and in Corinth, "the Jews made a united attack on Paul and brought him into court" (Acts 18:12). In Ephesus, Paul "served the Lord with great humility and with tears, although I was severely tested by the plots of the Jews" (Acts 20:19) and had earlier plotted to kill him at sea (Acts 20:1-3). Paul's first epistle to the Thessalonians becomes more significant when we reflect upon his suffering at the hands of his own countrymen,

> For you, brothers, became imitators of God's churches in Judea, which are in Christ Jesus: You suffered from your own countrymen the same things those churches suffered from the Jews, who killed the Lord Jesus and the prophets and also drove us out. They displease God and are hostile to all men in their effort to keep us from speaking to the Gentiles so that they may be saved. In this way they always heap up their sins to the limit. The wrath of God has come upon them at last (1 Th. 2:14-16).

In Acts 21, there is another conspiracy from Asian Jews to kill Paul,

> When the seven days were nearly over, some Jews from the province of Asia saw Paul at the temple. They stirred up the whole crowd and seized him, shouting, Men of Israel, help us! This is the man who teaches all men everywhere against our people and our law and this place. And besides, he has brought Greeks into the temple area and defiled this holy place. The whole city was aroused, and the people came running from all directions. Seizing Paul, they dragged him from the temple, and immediately the gates were shut. While they were trying to kill him, news

216

reached the commander of the Roman troops that the whole city of Jerusalem was in an uproar. He at once took some officers and soldiers and ran down to the crowd. When the rioters saw the commander and his soldiers, they stopped beating Paul (Acts 21:27-28, 30-32).

These false charges against Paul were similar to the false charges brought against Stephen (Acts 6:8-15; cf. Acts 7). The Jews accused Paul of bringing "Greeks into the temple area" which "defiled this holy place" (Acts 21:28). Gentiles were permitted in the court of the Gentiles, but not the temple area. Two inscriptions have been found on a balustrade separating the court of the Gentiles from the rest of the temple area as a warning to the Gentiles. Failing to adhere to this warning would bring death to any Gentile who trespassed (cf. Eph. 2:14). This was not the first time that the Romans and the Jews had cooperated in this type of plot (Mt. 28:11-15).[484]

The hatred against Paul (cf. 9:23; 20:3; also 9:29; 20:19) had grown so much that over forty fanatical Jews (23:13, 21) "formed a conspiracy and bound themselves with an oath not to eat or drink until they had killed Paul". This Jewish conspiracy against Paul was meticulously planned and elaborately described included a radical fast (Acts 23:12, 14, 21), the "chief priests and elders" (v. 14; 25:15; also 4:23; 22:30; 25:2), and repeated references to their determination to kill Paul (23:12, 14, 15, 21, 27).[485] Luke, the Physician uses the verb ἀναθεματίζω anathematizō from ἀνάθεμα anathema meaning "accursed", or "dedicated to destruction". It is used three times in this passage (cf. Acts 23:12, 14, 21) and the only other reference is used of Peter when he denied Jesus (Mk. 14:71).[486]

This verb for taking an oath also means to "bind with an oath, bind by a curse" and literally meant that the person placed himself under a curse if he does not fulfill his oath. It is possible that these forty men were later released from this oath by lawyers since Paul's circumstances changed through specific events.[487] However, these forty "chief priests and elders" (Acts 23:14) who were fasting and plotting against Paul failed to realize that Jesus had called Paul on the road to Damascus to be an apostle. Paul had been chosen as the Lord's instrument "to carry my name before the Gentiles and their kings and before the people of Israel. I will show him how much he must suffer for my name" (Acts 9:15-16). The Lord promised to deliver Paul from his enemies (Acts 9:15-16; 26:16-17)—a promise that Paul held on to for his entire life, and God was faithful.[488]

Please refer to *Fasting: Unlocking Spiritual Power and Breakthrough, Personal Reflections* under the heading "The Conspiracy Fast" to complete the Personal Reflections section of this study.

---

[484] Walvoord and Zuck, eds., *The Bible Knowledge Commentary*, Vol. 2, 417.

[485] Mays, ed., *Harper's Bible Commentary*. 1111.

[486] ἀναθεματίζω anathematizō "330", In Gilbrant, ed., *The Complete Biblical Library Greek-English Dictionary, Alpha-Gamma.*

[487] Walvoord and Zuck, eds., *The Bible Knowledge Commentary*, Vol. 2, 410. ἀναθεματίζω anathematizō "330", In Gilbrant, ed., *The Complete Biblical Library Greek-English Dictionary, Alpha-Gamma.*

[488] Wiersbe, *The Bible Exposition Commentary*, Vol. 1, 488-91.

The False Teacher's Fast

The Spirit clearly says that in later times some will abandon the faith and follow deceiving spirits and things taught by demons. Such teachings come through hypocritical liars, whose consciences have been seared as with a hot iron. They forbid people to marry and order them to abstain from certain foods, which God created to be received with thanksgiving by those who believe and who know the truth (1 Tim. 4:1-3).

The Apostle Paul, in chapter 2, had given brief directions concerning worship and in chapter 3 on leadership. In this context, he gives instruction concerning false teachers and their morally corrupt teachings that had weakened the vitality of the church—depriving her of divine blessings. The first five verses predict an imminent apostasy and give a solemn warning regarding false teaching. Paul instructs Timothy.

Have nothing to do with godless myths and old wives' tales; rather, train yourself to be godly. For physical training is of some value, but godliness has value for all things, holding promise for both the present life and the life to come (1 Tim. 4:7-8).

Even though Timothy is young, his effectiveness in ministry was the result of setting "an example for the believers in speech, in life, in love, in faith and in purity" (1 Tim. 4:12), devotion "to the public reading of Scripture, to preaching and to teaching" (1 Tim. 4:13), and finally "Watch your life and doctrine closely. Persevere in them, because if you do, you will save both yourself and your hearers" (1 Tim. 4:16).[489]

Paul begins by using the verb ἀποστήσονται *apostēsontai* which conveys "the idea of removal from a place, thing, or especially, persons", "causing to revolt", or "leading astray".[490] This refers to apostates who instead of being led by the Holy Spirit, willfully "abandon the faith" willfully "follow deceiving spirits and things taught by demons". This statement literally means that they have cognitively cast aside belief in the true God and have adopted and are promoting the "doctrines" of supernatural evil beings (cf. Eph. 6:11ff.). The Greek verb προσέχοντες *prosechontes* for "follow" comes for the mouth of the prophets (Isa. 28:23; 49:1; 55:3; Hos. 5:1), which God's people refused to obey (Jer. 6:19; 7:24, 26; 25:4). This was probably rooted in the Law of God to obey His commandments

Pay attention to him and listen to what he says. Do not rebel against him; he will not forgive your rebellion, since my Name is in him (Ex. 23:21; cf. 34:11-12; cf. Deut. 6:12; 8:11; 11:16; 12:13).

---

[489] Richards, *The Bible Reader's Companion*, 836.

[490] ἀποστήσονται *apostēsontai* "861", In Gilbrant, ed., *The Complete Biblical Library Greek-English Dictionary, Alpha-Gamma*. Gilbrant, ed., *The Complete Biblical Library Commentary, Galatians-Philemon*, 400. Herodotus of Halicarnassus (484-425 BC), *The Histories*, <http://www.swartzentrover.com/cotor/E-Books/misc/Herodotus/THindex.htm>, 1.76. Accessed on November 28, 2013. "Antiquities of the Jews", In Josephus, *The Works of Josephus*, 8.7.5.

This Greek verb also means to "guard against" or "watch out for" in reference to anything that is detrimental to one's relationship with God (cf. Ex. 10:28 of Pharaoh's warning Moses; cf. Ex. 19:12).[491]

Paul next speaks of "hypocritical liars" ὑπόκρισις ψευδολόγος *hupokrisis pseudologos* who were probably false teachers and had plagued the Ephesian church and the forerunners of the Gnostic movement in the second century. They had merged Jewish legalism with Eastern asceticism and taught that the spirit was good and matter was evil. The essence of this word is that they speak falsehood rather than truth by saying things about the gospel that are not true, which is how Satan operates by choosing those who are weak in the faith.[492]

> For such men are false apostles, deceitful workmen, masquerading as apostles of Christ. And no wonder, for Satan himself masquerades as an angel of light. It is not surprising, then, if his servants masquerade as servants of righteousness. Their end will be what their actions deserve (2 Cor. 11:13-15).

Next, Paul states that the consciences of the "hypocritical liars" have been cauterized. Paul uses the noun συνείδησις *suneidēsis*, a compound noun from *sun*, "with, together" and *eidēsis*, "knowledge", *suneidēsis* which conveys moral implications—a "knowledge" of right from wrong. Paul's concern for believers was that their conscience be protected so that it would not be exploited by "hypocritical liars" who sought to steal their freedom in Christ. This is why he asked the rhetorical question: "why should my freedom be judged by another's conscience?" (1 Cor. 10:29).[493]

In the 4th to 5th century BC, Hippocrates used the verb καυτηριάζω *kautēriazō* in the medical sense of cauterizing—"to make insensible: deaden".[494] This is the fourth time in First Timothy that Paul uses this verb, "The goal of this command is love, which comes from a pure heart and a good conscience and a sincere faith" (1 Tim. 1:5, 19; 3:9; 4:2). The perfect participle conveys an initial act with continuous consequences, which these "hypocritical liars" had become anesthetized to moral distinctions. In New Testament times, habitual criminals were often cauterized with a distinguishing mark so that they could be easily identified. Once our consciences had been cauterized, it would be easy for Satan to use these people as his instruments to carry out his plan. This verb also indicates ownership by Satan.[495]

In this context, the Apostle Paul mentions two of their false teachings, "They forbid people to marry and order them to abstain from certain foods". This ascetic practice which had infiltrated the church in the

---

[491] Gaebelein, ed., *The Expositor's Bible Commentary, Volume 11: Ephesians through Philemon* (Grand Rapids, MI: Zondervan Publishing House. Database © 2010 WORDsearch CROSS e-book, 1981), 371. προσέχω *prosechō* "4196", In Gilbrant, ed., *The Complete Biblical Library Greek-English Dictionary, Pi-Rho*. Gilbrant, ed., *The Complete Biblical Library Commentary, Galatians-Philemon*, 400.

[492] ψευδολόγος *pseudologos* "5408", In Gilbrant, ed., *The Complete Biblical Library Greek-English Dictionary, Sigma-Omega*. Wiersbe, *The Bible Exposition Commentary*, Vol. 2, 224-25.

[493] συνείδησις *suneidēsis* "4743", In Gilbrant, ed., *The Complete Biblical Library Greek-English Dictionary, Sigma-Omega*.

[494] "Cauterize", In *Merriam-Webster's Collegiate Dictionary*. καυτηριάζω *kautēriazō* "2713B", In Gilbrant, ed., *The Complete Biblical Library Greek-English Dictionary, Zeta-Kappa*.

[495] Walvoord and Zuck, eds., *The Bible Knowledge Commentary*, Vol. 2, 739-40. Gilbrant, ed., *The Complete Biblical Library Commentary, Galatians-Philemon*, 400.

first century became more prominent under Gnosticism. The Gnostics also believed that all bodily desires or cravings such as, sexual desires "forbid people to marry" and food appetites "abstain from certain foods" were evil and should be denied (cf. Col. 2:21). They believed that physical pleasure was sin and holiness was equated with asceticism, which is the same error of the Essenes. Paul now uses the verb ἀπέχεσθαι apechesthai meaning "to abstain" or "to have in full".

One of the best illustrations occurs in the writings of Plutarch, which is quite similar to the parable of the Pharisee and the Tax Collector (Lk. 18:9-14). God promises to bless those who give to the poor and answer those who pray and fast, but not those who give, pray or fast openly for selfish gain and "to be honored by men" (Mt. 6:1-18). Jesus declared that "they have received their reward in full" (Mt. 6:2). The root ἀπέχω apechō also means "to abstain" from something or "to give up" something (e.g., Acts 15:20), "abstain from pollutions of idols" (1 Th. 4:3), "abstain from fornication" (1 Th. 5:22), "abstain from all appearance of evil" (1 Tim. 4:3), "abstain from meats" (1 Pet. 2:11), "abstain from fleshly lusts".[496]

Scripture clearly states that everything that God has created is good, "God saw all that he had made, and it was very good" (Gen. 1:31) and Paul reiterates this, "For everything God created is good, and nothing is to be rejected if it is received with thanksgiving, because it is consecrated by the word of God and prayer" (1 Tim. 4:4-5). These false teachers were legalistic with their "forbidding" and "abstaining", but Paul states that "nothing is to be rejected" since God has created and called it good. Satan is the master counterfeiter and deceiver, taking what God has created to be good and using it "to steal and kill and destroy" (Jn. 10:10). For example, adultery is an abuse of the marital sexual relationship, and gluttony is an abuse of a normal appetite for food and these abuses must certainly be rejected and all of God's creation is good and should be "received with thanksgiving".[497] Wiersbe states,

> A true church seeks to win converts to Jesus Christ and to build them spiritually; conversely, a cult proselytizes, steals converts from others, and makes them servants (even slaves!) of the leaders of the cult. However, not all apostates are in cults; some of them are in churches *and pulpits*, teaching false doctrine and leading people astray.[498]

Please refer to *Fasting: Unlocking Spiritual Power and Breakthrough, Personal Reflections* under the heading "The False Teacher's Fast" to complete the Personal Reflections section of this study.

---

[496] It also provides an excellent analogy to Jesus' use of *apechō* in the Sermon on the Mount (cf. Mt. 6:2, 5, 16; Lk. 6:24). "The Lacedaemonians carried him with them to Sparta, where, giving the rewards of valour to Eurybiades, and of wisdom and conduct to Themistocles, they crowned him with olive, presented him with the best chariot in the city, and sent three hundred young men to accompany him to the confines of their country. And at the next Olympic games, when Themistocles entered the course, the spectators took no farther notice of those who were contesting the prizes, but spent the whole day in looking upon him, showing him to the strangers, admiring him, and applauding him by clapping their hands, and other expressions of joy, so that he himself, much gratified, confessed to his friends that he then reaped the fruit of all his labours for the Greeks". Plutarch, *Themistocles*, trans. by John Dryden, 75 ACE, <http://classics.mit.edu/Plutarch/themisto.html>, Accessed on September 3, 2013. ἀπέχω *apechō* "563", In Gilbrant, ed., *The Complete Biblical Library Greek-English Dictionary, Alpha-Gamma*. Gaebelein, ed., *The Expositor's Bible Commentary, Volume 11*, 371-372.

[497] Walvoord and Zuck, eds., *The Bible Knowledge Commentary*, Vol. 2, 739-40.

[498] Wiersbe, *The Bible Exposition Commentary*, Vol. 2, 224.

Appendix 1: Principles of Biblical Fasts

1. Fasting brings divine direction.
2. Fasting brings about a fresh vision ("still small voice") and clear direction.
3. The Israelites sought God's guidance with increasing earnestness—tears of penitence, fasting for grief, and sacrifices for forgiveness and peace.
4. Fasting brings healing.
5. Fasting defeats strongholds and dethrones idols in our life.
6. Fasting can prevent individual and/or national crisis.
7. Fasting can prevent divine judgment.
8. Fasting over the loss of a friend.
9. Fasting helps break negative emotions.
10. Fasting calls on God for protection.
11. Fasting opens the door to God's favor.
12. Fasting for remorse over committed sin.
13. Fasting to humble oneself.
14. Fasting encourages a person to respond positively to God's commands.
15. Fasting brings spiritual deliverance.
16. Fasting brings knowledge and understanding.
17. Fasting can be involuntary and voluntary.
18. Fasting to break selfish motives.
19. Fasting sets us apart from the world.
20. Fasting increases our spiritual capacity.
21. Fasting for revival, renewal, and righteousness.
22. Fasting brings strength to experience God's deliverance.
23. Fasted brings material provision.
24. Fasting brings personal transformation.
25. Fasting for mutual abstinence from sexual intimacy and devotion to prayer.
26. Fasting to honour the Eucharistic Gifts.[499]

---

[499] <http://users.stic.net/fortress/pr-fast-8fasts.htm>, Accessed on September 3, 2013.

Appendix 2: Occasions for Fasting[500]

Abstinence from Sexual Relationships	Do not deprive each other except by mutual consent and for a time, so that you may devote yourselves to prayer. Then come together again so that Satan will not tempt you because of your lack of self-control (1 Cor. 7:5).
Confession of Sin	When they had assembled at Mizpah, they drew water and poured it out before the LORD. On that day they fasted and there they confessed, "We have sinned against the LORD". And Samuel was leader of Israel at Mizpah (1 Sam. 7:6). On the twenty-fourth day of the same month, the Israelites gathered together, fasting and wearing sackcloth and having dust on their heads. Those of Israelite descent had separated themselves from all foreigners. They stood in their places and confessed their sins and the wickedness of their fathers. They stood where they were and read from the Book of the Law of the LORD their God for a quarter of the day, and spent another quarter in confession and in worshiping the LORD their God (Neh. 9:1-3).
During Periods of National Mourning	When the people of Jabesh Gilead heard of what the Philistines had done to Saul, all their valiant men journeyed through the night to Beth Shan. They took down the bodies of Saul and his sons from the wall of Beth Shan and went to Jabesh, where they burned them. Then they took their bones and buried them under a tamarisk tree at Jabesh, and they fasted seven days (1 Sam. 31:11-13). They mourned and wept and fasted till evening for Saul and his son Jonathan, and for the army of the LORD and the house of Israel, because they had fallen by the sword (2 Sam. 1:12). Then they all came and urged David to eat something while it was still day; but David took an oath, saying, "May God deal with me, be it ever so severely, if I taste bread or anything else before the sun sets!" (2 Sam. 3:35). When all the inhabitants of Jabesh Gilead heard of everything the Philistines had done to Saul, all their valiant men went and took the bodies of Saul and his sons and brought them to Jabesh. Then they buried their bones under the great tree in Jabesh, and they fasted seven days (1 Chr. 10:11-12).
Humiliation	Then once again I fell prostrate before the LORD for forty days and forty nights; I ate no bread and drank no water, because of all the sin you had committed, doing what was evil in the LORD's sight and so provoking him to anger (Deut. 9:18). Yet when they were ill, I put on sackcloth and humbled myself with fasting (Ps. 35:13). When I weep and fast, I must endure scorn; when I put on sackcloth, people make sport of me (Ps. 69:10-11). When Ahab heard these words, he tore his clothes, put on sackcloth and fasted. He lay in sackcloth and went around meekly (1 Kgs. 21:27). On the twenty-fourth day of the same month, the Israelites gathered together, fasting and wearing sackcloth and having dust on their heads (Neh. 9:1).
Lamenting	And Mordecai sent letters to all the Jews in the 127 provinces of the kingdom of Xerxes—words of goodwill and assurance—to establish these days of Purim at their designated times, as Mordecai the Jew and Queen Esther had decreed for them, and as they had established for themselves and their descendants in regard to their times of fasting and lamentation (Est. 9:30-31).

---

[500] See Towns, *Fasting for Spiritual Breakthrough*, 224-31.

Mourning	They mourned and wept and fasted till evening for Saul and his son Jonathan, and for the army of the LORD and the house of Israel, because they had fallen by the sword (2 Sam. 1:12).
	When Ahab heard these words, he tore his clothes, put on sackcloth and fasted. He lay in sackcloth and went around meekly (1 Kgs. 21:27).
	In every province to which the edict and order of the king came, there was great mourning among the Jews, with fasting, weeping and wailing. Many lay in sackcloth and ashes (Est. 4:3).
	When I heard these things, I sat down and wept. For some days I mourned and fasted and prayed before the God of heaven (Neh. 1:4).
	"Even now", declares the LORD, "return to me with all your heart, with fasting and weeping and mourning" (Joel 2:12).
	Then Ezra withdrew from before the house of God and went to the room of Jehohanan son of Eliashib. While he was there, he ate no food and drank no water, because he continued to mourn over the unfaithfulness of the exiles (Ezra 10:6).
Personal Demeanor	"But when you fast, put oil on your head and wash your face" (Mt. 6:17).
Prayer	So we fasted and petitioned our God about this, and he answered our prayer (Ezra 8:23).
	When I heard these things, I sat down and wept. For some days I mourned and fasted and prayed before the God of heaven (Neh. 1:4).
	Yet when they were ill, I put on sackcloth and humbled myself with fasting (Ps. 35:13).
	So I turned to the Lord God and pleaded with him in prayer and petition, in fasting, and in sackcloth and ashes (Dan. 9:3).
	They said to him, "John's disciples often fast and pray, and so do the disciples of the Pharisees, but yours go on eating and drinking" (Lk. 5:33).
Reading the Scriptures	On the twenty-fourth day of the same month, the Israelites gathered together, fasting and wearing sackcloth and having dust on their heads. Those of Israelite descent had separated themselves from all foreigners. They stood in their places and confessed their sins and the wickedness of their fathers. They stood where they were and read from the Book of the Law of the LORD their God for a quarter of the day, and spent another quarter in confession and in worshiping the LORD their God (Neh. 9:1-3).
	So you go to the house of the LORD on a day of fasting and read to the people from the scroll the words of the LORD that you wrote as I dictated. Read them to all the people of Judah who come in from their towns (Jer. 36:6).
	In the ninth month of the fifth year of Jehoiakim son of Josiah king of Judah, a time of fasting before the LORD was proclaimed for all the people in Jerusalem and those who had come from the towns of Judah. From the room of Gemariah son of Shaphan the secretary, which was in the upper courtyard at the entrance of the New Gate of the temple, Baruch read to all the people at the LORD's temple the words of Jeremiah from the scroll (Jer. 36:9-10).
When Challenged By Personal Concerns	After Nathan had gone home, the LORD struck the child that Uriah's wife had borne to David, and he became ill. David pleaded with God for the child. He fasted and went into his house and spent the nights lying on the ground. The elders of his household stood beside him to get him up from the ground, but he refused, and he would not eat any food with them. . . . His servants asked him, "Why are you acting this way? While the child was alive, you fasted and wept, but now that the child is dead, you get up and eat!" He answered, "While the

	child was still alive, I fasted and wept. I thought, 'Who knows? The LORD may be gracious to me and let the child live'. But now that he is dead, why should I fast? Can I bring him back again? I will go to him, but he will not return to me" (2 Sam. 12:15-17, 21-23).
When Communion with God Is Broken	Jesus answered, "How can the guests of the bridegroom mourn while he is with them? The time will come when the bridegroom will be taken from them; then they will fast (Mt. 9:15).
	Jesus answered, "How can the guests of the bridegroom fast while he is with them? They cannot, so long as they have him with them. But the time will come when the bridegroom will be taken from them, and on that day they will fast (Mk. 2:19-20).
	Jesus answered, "Can you make the guests of the bridegroom fast while he is with them? But the time will come when the bridegroom will be taken from them; in those days they will fast" (Lk. 5:34-35).
When Concerned for the Welfare of Others	Yet when they were ill, I put on sackcloth and humbled myself with fasting (Ps. 35:13).
When Engaged In Spiritual Warfare	"But this kind does not go out except by prayer and fasting" (Mt. 17:21).
	He replied, "This kind can come out only by prayer [and fasting]" (Mk. 9:29).
When Facing Danger	Some men came and told Jehoshaphat, "A vast army is coming against you from Edom, from the other side of the Sea. It is already in Hazazon Tamar" (that is, En Gedi). Alarmed, Jehoshaphat resolved to inquire of the LORD, and he proclaimed a fast for all Judah. The people of Judah came together to seek help from the LORD; indeed, they came from every town in Judah to seek him (2 Chr. 20:2-4).
	There, by the Ahava Canal, I proclaimed a fast, so that we might humble ourselves before our God and ask him for a safe journey for us and our children, with all our possessions. I was ashamed to ask the king for soldiers and horsemen to protect us from enemies on the road, because we had told the king, "The gracious hand of our God is on everyone who looks to him, but his great anger is against all who forsake him". So we fasted and petitioned our God about this, and he answered our prayer (Ezra 8:21-23).
	Then Esther sent this reply to Mordecai: "Go, gather together all the Jews who are in Susa, and fast for me. Do not eat or drink for three days, night or day. I and my maids will fast as you do. When this is done, I will go to the king, even though it is against the law. And if I perish, I perish" (Est. 4:15-16).
When Facing the Judgment of God	When Ahab heard these words, he tore his clothes, put on sackcloth and fasted. He lay in sackcloth and went around meekly (1 Kgs. 21:27).
	Put on sackcloth, O priests, and mourn; wail, you who minister before the altar. Come, spend the night in sackcloth, you who minister before my God; for the grain offerings and drink offerings are withheld from the house of your God. Declare a holy fast; call a sacred assembly. Summon the elders and all who live in the land to the house of the LORD your God, and cry out to the LORD (Joel 1:13-14).
	"Even now", declares the LORD, "return to me with all your heart, with fasting and weeping and mourning" (Joel 2:12).
	On the first day, Jonah started into the city. He proclaimed: "Forty more days and Nineveh will be overturned". The Ninevites believed God. They declared a fast, and all of them, from the greatest to the least, put on sackcloth (Jon. 3:4-5)

When Ordaining Ministers of the Gospel	While they were worshiping the Lord and fasting, the Holy Spirit said, "Set apart for me Barnabas and Saul for the work to which I have called them". So after they had fasted and prayed, they placed their hands on them and sent them off (Acts 13:2-3).
	Paul and Barnabas appointed elders for them in each church and, with prayer and fasting, committed them to the Lord, in whom they had put their trust (Acts 14:23).
Weeping	They mourned and wept and fasted till evening for Saul and his son Jonathan, and for the army of the LORD and the house of Israel, because they had fallen by the sword (2 Sam. 1:12).
	When I heard these things, I sat down and wept. For some days I mourned and fasted and prayed before the God of heaven (Neh. 1:4).
	In every province to which the edict and order of the king came, there was great mourning among the Jews, with fasting, weeping and wailing. Many lay in sackcloth and ashes (Est. 4:3).
	When I weep and fast, I must endure scorn; when I put on sackcloth, people make sport of me (Ps. 69:10-11).
	"Even now", declares the LORD, "return to me with all your heart, with fasting and weeping and mourning" (Joel 2:12).
Worship	On the twenty-fourth day of the same month, the Israelites gathered together, fasting and wearing sackcloth and having dust on their heads. Those of Israelite descent had separated themselves from all foreigners. They stood in their places and confessed their sins and the wickedness of their fathers. They stood where they were and read from the Book of the Law of the LORD their God for a quarter of the day, and spent another quarter in confession and in worshiping the LORD their God (Neh. 9:1-3).

Abstinence from Sexual Relationships	Do not deprive each other except by mutual consent and for a time, so that you may devote yourselves to prayer. Then come together again so that Satan will not tempt you because of your lack of self-control (1 Cor. 7:5).
Confession of Sin	When they had assembled at Mizpah, they drew water and poured it out before the LORD. On that day they fasted and there they confessed, "We have sinned against the LORD". And Samuel was leader of Israel at Mizpah (1 Sam. 7:6).
	On the twenty-fourth day of the same month, the Israelites gathered together, fasting and wearing sackcloth and having dust on their heads. Those of Israelite descent had separated themselves from all foreigners. They stood in their places and confessed their sins and the wickedness of their fathers. They stood where they were and read from the Book of the Law of the LORD their God for a quarter of the day, and spent another quarter in confession and in worshiping the LORD their God (Neh. 9:1-3).
Humiliation	Then once again I fell prostrate before the LORD for forty days and forty nights; I ate no bread and drank no water, because of all the sin you had committed, doing what was evil in the LORD's sight and so provoking him to anger (Deut. 9:18).
	Yet when they were ill, I put on sackcloth and humbled myself with fasting (Ps. 35:13).
	When I weep and fast, I must endure scorn; when I put on sackcloth, people make sport of me (Ps. 69:10-11).
	When Ahab heard these words, he tore his clothes, put on sackcloth and fasted. He lay in sackcloth and went around meekly (1 Kgs. 21:27).
	On the twenty-fourth day of the same month, the Israelites gathered together, fasting and wearing sackcloth and having dust on their heads (Neh. 9:1).
Lamenting	And Mordecai sent letters to all the Jews in the 127 provinces of the kingdom of Xerxes—words of goodwill and assurance—to establish these days of Purim at their designated times, as Mordecai the Jew and Queen Esther had decreed for them, and as they had established for themselves and their descendants in regard to their times of fasting and lamentation (Est. 9:30-31).
Mourning	They mourned and wept and fasted till evening for Saul and his son Jonathan, and for the army of the LORD and the house of Israel, because they had fallen by the sword (2 Sam. 1:12).
	When Ahab heard these words, he tore his clothes, put on sackcloth and fasted. He lay in sackcloth and went around meekly (1 Kgs. 21:27).
	When I heard these things, I sat down and wept. For some days I mourned and fasted and prayed before the God of heaven (Neh. 1:4).
	In every province to which the edict and order of the king came, there was great mourning among the Jews, with fasting, weeping and wailing. Many lay in sackcloth and ashes (Est. 4:3).
	"Even now", declares the LORD, "return to me with all your heart, with fasting and weeping and mourning" (Joel 2:12).
	Then Ezra withdrew from before the house of God and went to the room of Jehohanan son of Eliashib. While he was there, he ate no food and drank no water, because he continued to mourn over the unfaithfulness of the exiles (Ezra 10:6).

---

[501] See Towns, *Fasting for Spiritual Breakthrough*, 228-30.

Personal Demeanor	"But when you fast, put oil on your head and wash your face" (Mt. 6:17).
Prayer	So we fasted and petitioned our God about this, and he answered our prayer (Ezra 8:23). When I heard these things, I sat down and wept. For some days I mourned and fasted and prayed before the God of heaven (Neh. 1:4). Yet when they were ill, I put on sackcloth and humbled myself with fasting (Ps. 35:13). So I turned to the LORD God and pleaded with him in prayer and petition, in fasting, and in sackcloth and ashes (Dan. 9:3). They said to him, "John's disciples often fast and pray, and so do the disciples of the Pharisees, but yours go on eating and drinking" (Lk. 5:33).
Reading the Scriptures	On the twenty-fourth day of the same month, the Israelites gathered together, fasting and wearing sackcloth and having dust on their heads. Those of Israelite descent had separated themselves from all foreigners. They stood in their places and confessed their sins and the wickedness of their fathers. They stood where they were and read from the Book of the Law of the LORD their God for a quarter of the day, and spent another quarter in confession and in worshiping the LORD their God (Neh. 9:1-3). So you go to the house of the LORD on a day of fasting and read to the people from the scroll the words of the LORD that you wrote as I dictated. Read them to all the people of Judah who come in from their towns (Jer. 36:6). From the room of Gemariah son of Shaphan the secretary, which was in the upper courtyard at the entrance of the New Gate of the temple, Baruch read to all the people at the LORD's temple the words of Jeremiah from the scroll (Jer. 36:10).
Weeping	They mourned and wept and fasted till evening for Saul and his son Jonathan, and for the army of the LORD and the house of Israel, because they had fallen by the sword (2 Sam. 1:12). When I heard these things, I sat down and wept. For some days I mourned and fasted and prayed before the God of heaven (Neh. 1:4). In every province to which the edict and order of the king came, there was great mourning among the Jews, with fasting, weeping and wailing. Many lay in sackcloth and ashes (Est. 4:3). When I weep and fast, I must endure scorn; when I put on sackcloth, people make sport of me (Ps. 69:10-11). "Even now", declares the LORD, "return to me with all your heart, with fasting and weeping and mourning" (Joel 2:12).
Worship	On the twenty-fourth day of the same month, the Israelites gathered together, fasting and wearing sackcloth and having dust on their heads. Those of Israelite descent had separated themselves from all foreigners. They stood in their places and confessed their sins and the wickedness of their fathers. They stood where they were and read from the Book of the Law of the LORD their God for a quarter of the day, and spent another quarter in confession and in worshiping the LORD their God (Neh. 9:1-3).

Appendix 4: Promised Blessings Associated with Fasting[502]

Answered Prayer, Insight, and Restoration	Then you will call, and the LORD will answer; you will cry for help, and he will say: Here am I. "If you do away with the yoke of oppression, with the pointing finger and malicious talk, and if you spend yourselves in behalf of the hungry and satisfy the needs of the oppressed, then your light will rise in the darkness, and your night will become like the noonday. The LORD will guide you always; he will satisfy your needs in a sun-scorched land and will strengthen your frame. You will be like a well-watered garden, like a spring whose waters never fail. Your people will rebuild the ancient ruins and will raise up the age-old foundations; you will be called Repairer of Broken Walls, Restorer of Streets with Dwellings (Isa. 58:9-12).
Effects of Fasting	Then the word of the LORD came to Elijah the Tishbite: "Have you noticed how Ahab has humbled himself before me? Because he has humbled himself, I will not bring this disaster in his day, but I will bring it on his house in the days of his son" (1 Kgs. 21:28-29). "My knees give way from fasting; my body is thin and gaunt" (Ps. 109:24). Jesus called his disciples to him and said, "I have compassion for these people; they have already been with me three days and have nothing to eat. I do not want to send them away hungry, or they may collapse on the way" (Mt. 15:32). "I have compassion for these people; they have already been with me three days and have nothing to eat. If I send them home hungry, they will collapse on the way, because some of them have come a long distance" (Mk. 8:2-3).
Joy, Gladness and Cheerfulness	This is what the LORD Almighty says: "The fasts of the fourth, fifth, seventh and tenth months will become joyful and glad occasions and happy festivals for Judah. Therefore love truth and peace" (Zech. 8:19).
Rewarded by God the Father	But when you fast, put oil on your head and wash your face, so that it will not be obvious to men that you are fasting, but only to your Father, who is unseen; and your Father, who sees what is done in secret, will reward you (Mt. 6:17-18).
Spiritual Power Over Demons	"But this kind does not go out except by prayer and fasting" (Mt. 17:21). He replied, "This kind can come out only by prayer [and fasting]" (Mk. 9:29).

---

[502] See Towns, *Fasting for Spiritual Breakthrough*, 231-33.

Appendix 5: Proclamations of Fasts[503]

Esther	Then Esther sent this reply to Mordecai: "Go, gather together all the Jews who are in Susa, and fast for me. Do not eat or drink for three days, night or day. I and my maids will fast as you do. When this is done, I will go to the king, even though it is against the law. And if I perish, I perish" (Est. 4:15-16).
Ezra	There, by the Ahava Canal, I proclaimed a fast, so that we might humble ourselves before our God and ask him for a safe journey for us and our children, with all our possessions. I was ashamed to ask the king for soldiers and horsemen to protect us from enemies on the road, because we had told the king, "The gracious hand of our God is on everyone who looks to him, but his great anger is against all who forsake him". So we fasted and petitioned our God about this, and he answered our prayer (Ezra 8:21-23).
Jehoiakim	In the ninth month of the fifth year of Jehoiakim son of Josiah king of Judah, a time of fasting before the LORD was proclaimed for all the people in Jerusalem and those who had come from the towns of Judah (Jer. 36:9).
Jehoshaphat	Alarmed, Jehoshaphat resolved to inquire of the LORD, and he proclaimed a fast for all Judah (2 Chr. 20:3).
Joel	Blow the trumpet in Zion, declare a holy fast, call a sacred assembly (Joel 2:15).
The King of Nineveh	The Ninevites believed God. They declared a fast, and all of them, from the greatest to the least, put on sackcloth. When the news reached the king of Nineveh, he rose from his throne, took off his royal robes, covered himself with sackcloth and sat down in the dust. Then he issued a proclamation in Nineveh: "By the decree of the king and his nobles: Do not let any man or beast, herd or flock, taste anything; do not let them eat or drink. But let man and beast be covered with sackcloth. Let everyone call urgently on God. Let them give up their evil ways and their violence. Who knows? God may yet relent and with compassion turn from his fierce anger so that we will not perish" (Jon. 3:5-9).
Saul	Now the men of Israel were in distress that day, because Saul had bound the people under an oath, saying, "Cursed be any man who eats food before evening comes, before I have avenged myself on my enemies!" So none of the troops tasted food (1 Sam. 14:24).
Purim	And Mordecai sent letters to all the Jews in the 127 provinces of the kingdom of Xerxes—words of goodwill and assurance—to establish these days of Purim at their designated times, as Mordecai the Jew and Queen Esther had decreed for them, and as they had established for themselves and their descendants in regard to their times of fasting and lamentation (Est. 9:30-31).
***Yom Kippur* (Day of Atonement)**	"The tenth day of this seventh month is the Day of Atonement. Hold a sacred assembly and deny yourselves, and present an offering made to the LORD by fire (Lev. 23:27).

---

[503] See Towns, *Fasting for Spiritual Breakthrough*, 233-35.

Appendix 6: Examples of Individuals Fasting[504]

Ahab	So Ahab went home, sullen and angry because Naboth the Jezreelite had said, "I will not give you the inheritance of my fathers". He lay on his bed sulking and refused to eat. His wife Jezebel came in and asked him, "Why are you so sullen? Why won't you eat?" (1 Kgs. 21:4-5).
	So she wrote letters in Ahab's name, placed his seal on them, and sent them to the elders and nobles who lived in Naboth's city with him. In those letters she wrote: "Proclaim a day of fasting and seat Naboth in a prominent place among the people. But seat two scoundrels opposite him and have them testify that he has cursed both God and the king. Then take him out and stone him to death". So the elders and nobles who lived in Naboth's city did as Jezebel directed in the letters she had written to them. They proclaimed a fast and seated Naboth in a prominent place among the people. Then two scoundrels came and sat opposite him and brought charges against Naboth before the people, saying, "Naboth has cursed both God and the king". So they took him outside the city and stoned him to death. Then they sent word to Jezebel: "Naboth has been stoned and is dead" (1 Kgs. 21:8-14).
	When Ahab heard these words, he tore his clothes, put on sackcloth and fasted. He lay in sackcloth and went around meekly (1 Kgs. 21:27).
Anna	There was also a prophetess, Anna, the daughter of Phanuel, of the tribe of Asher. She was very old; she had lived with her husband seven years after her marriage, and then was a widow until she was eighty-four. She never left the temple but worshiped night and day, fasting and praying (Lk. 2:36-37).
Cornelius	Cornelius answered: "Four days ago I was in my house praying at this hour, at three in the afternoon. Suddenly a man in shining clothes stood before me and said, 'Cornelius, God has heard your prayer and remembered your gifts to the poor (Acts 10:30-31).
Daniel	So I turned to the LORD God and pleaded with him in prayer and petition, in fasting, and in sackcloth and ashes (Dan. 9:3).
	At that time I, Daniel, mourned for three weeks. I ate no choice food; no meat or wine touched my lips; and I used no lotions at all until the three weeks were over (Dan. 10:2-3).
Darius	Then the king returned to his palace and spent the night without eating and without any entertainment being brought to him. And he could not sleep (Dan. 6:18).
David	Then they all came and urged David to eat something while it was still day; but David took an oath, saying, "May God deal with me, be it ever so severely, if I taste bread or anything else before the sun sets!" (2 Sam. 3:35).
	After Nathan had gone home, the LORD struck the child that Uriah's wife had borne to David, and he became ill. David pleaded with God for the child. He fasted and went into his house and spent the nights lying on the ground. The elders of his household stood beside him to get him up from the ground, but he refused, and he would not eat any food with them (2 Sam. 12:15-17).
	Yet when they were ill, I put on sackcloth and humbled myself with fasting (Ps. 35:13).
	When I weep and fast, I must endure scorn; when I put on sackcloth, people make sport of me (Ps. 69:10-11).
	My knees give way from fasting; my body is thin and gaunt (Ps. 109:24).

---

[504] See Towns, *Fasting for Spiritual Breakthrough*, 243-47.

An Egyptian Servant	They found an Egyptian in a field and brought him to David. They gave him water to drink and food to eat—part of a cake of pressed figs and two cakes of raisins. He ate and was revived, for he had not eaten any food or drunk any water for three days and three nights (1 Sam. 30:11-12).
Elijah	So he got up and ate and drank. Strengthened by that food, he traveled forty days and forty nights until he reached Horeb, the mountain of God (1 Kgs. 19:8).
Esther	In every province to which the edict and order of the king came, there was great mourning among the Jews, with fasting, weeping and wailing. Many lay in sackcloth and ashes (Est. 4:3). When Esther's words were reported to Mordecai, he sent back this answer: "Do not think that because you are in the king's house you alone of all the Jews will escape. For if you remain silent at this time, relief and deliverance for the Jews will arise from another place, but you and your father's family will perish. And who knows but that you have come to your royal position for such a time as this?" Then Esther sent this reply to Mordecai: "Go, gather together all the Jews who are in Susa, and fast for me. Do not eat or drink for three days, night or day. I and my attendants will fast as you do. When this is done, I will go to the king, even though it is against the law. And if I perish, I perish". So Mordecai went away and carried out all of Esther's instructions (Est. 4:12-17). So Queen Esther, daughter of Abihail, along with Mordecai the Jew, wrote with full authority to confirm this second letter concerning Purim. And Mordecai sent letters to all the Jews in the 127 provinces of the kingdom of Xerxes—words of goodwill and assurance—to establish these days of Purim at their designated times, as Mordecai the Jew and Queen Esther had decreed for them, and as they had established for themselves and their descendants in regard to their times of fasting and lamentation. Esther's decree confirmed these regulations about Purim, and it was written down in the records (Est. 9:29-32).
Ezra	Then Ezra withdrew from before the house of God and went to the room of Jehohanan son of Eliashib. While he was there, he ate no food and drank no water, because he continued to mourn over the unfaithfulness of the exiles (Ezra 10:6).
Hannah	This went on year after year. Whenever Hannah went up to the house of the LORD, her rival provoked her till she wept and would not eat (1 Sam. 1:7).
Jesus	Then Jesus was led by the Spirit into the desert to be tempted by the devil. After fasting forty days and forty nights, he was hungry (Mt. 4:1-2). Jesus, full of the Holy Spirit, returned from the Jordan and was led by the Spirit in the desert, where for forty days he was tempted by the devil. He ate nothing during those days, and at the end of them he was hungry (Lk. 4:1-2).
John the Baptist	For John came neither eating nor drinking, and they say, 'He has a demon' (Mt. 11:18). For John the Baptist came neither eating bread nor drinking wine, and you say, 'He has a demon' (Lk. 7:33).
Jonathan	Jonathan got up from the table in fierce anger; on that second day of the month he did not eat, because he was grieved at his father's shameful treatment of David (1 Sam. 20:34).
Joseph[505]	When his master heard the story his wife told him, saying, "This is how your slave treated me", he burned with anger. Joseph's master took him and put him in prison, the place where the king's prisoners were confined. But while Joseph was there in the prison, the LORD was with him; he showed him kindness and granted him favor in the

---

[505] According to history, only the prisoner's family members were allowed to bring them food, and Joseph's entire family was in another country. Franklin, *Fasting*, 91.

231

	eyes of the prison warden. So the warden put Joseph in charge of all those held in the prison, and he was made responsible for all that was done there. The warden paid no attention to anything under Joseph's care, because the LORD was with Joseph and gave him success in whatever he did (Gen. 39:19-23).
Moses	Then the LORD said to Moses, "Write down these words, for in accordance with these words I have made a covenant with you and with Israel". Moses was there with the LORD forty days and forty nights without eating bread or drinking water. And he wrote on the tablets the words of the covenant—the Ten Commandments (Ex. 34:27-28).
	When I went up on the mountain to receive the tablets of stone, the tablets of the covenant that the LORD had made with you, I stayed on the mountain forty days and forty nights; I ate no bread and drank no water. . . . Then once again I fell prostrate before the LORD for forty days and forty nights; I ate no bread and drank no water, because of all the sin you had committed, doing what was evil in the LORD's sight and so provoking him to anger (Deut. 9:9, 18).
Nehemiah	When I heard these things, I sat down and wept. For some days I mourned and fasted and prayed before the God of heaven. Then I said: "O LORD, God of heaven, the great and awesome God, who keeps his covenant of love with those who love him and obey his commands, let your ear be attentive and your eyes open to hear the prayer your servant is praying before you day and night for your servants, the people of Israel. I confess the sins we Israelites, including myself and my father's house, have committed against you. We have acted very wickedly toward you. We have not obeyed the commands, decrees and laws you gave your servant Moses (Neh. 1:4-7).
	On the twenty-fourth day of the same month, the Israelites gathered together, fasting and wearing sackcloth and having dust on their heads. Those of Israelite descent had separated themselves from all foreigners. They stood in their places and confessed their sins and the wickedness of their fathers. They stood where they were and read from the Book of the Law of the LORD their God for a quarter of the day, and spent another quarter in confession and in worshiping the LORD their God (Neh. 9:1-3).
Paul	For three days he was blind, and did not eat or drink anything (Acts 9:9).
	Rather, as servants of God we commend ourselves in every way: in great endurance; in troubles, hardships and distresses; in beatings, imprisonments and riots; in hard work, sleepless nights and hunger (2 Cor. 6:4-5).
	I have labored and toiled and have often gone without sleep; I have known hunger and thirst and have often gone without food; I have been cold and naked (2 Cor. 11:27).
Saul	Immediately Saul fell full length on the ground, filled with fear because of Samuel's words. His strength was gone, for he had eaten nothing all that day and night (1 Sam. 28:20).
Uriah	Uriah said to David, "The ark and Israel and Judah are staying in tents, and my master Joab and my lord's men are camped in the open fields. How could I go to my house to eat and drink and lie with my wife? As surely as you live, I will not do such a thing!" (2 Sam. 11:11).

Appendix 7: Examples of Corporate Fasting[506]

Crew and Passengers on the Ship of Adramyttium	Just before dawn Paul urged them all to eat. "For the last fourteen days", he said, "you have been in constant suspense and have gone without food—you haven't eaten anything (Acts 27:33).
Israel at Mizpah	When they had assembled at Mizpah, they drew water and poured it out before the LORD. On that day they fasted and there they confessed, "We have sinned against the LORD". And Samuel was leader of Israel at Mizpah (1 Sam. 7:6).
Israel before the Battle against Benjamin	Then the Israelites, all the people, went up to Bethel, and there they sat weeping before the LORD. They fasted that day until evening and presented burnt offerings and fellowship offerings to the LORD (Jdg. 20:26).
Jews Committed to Killing Paul	The next morning the Jews formed a conspiracy and bound themselves with an oath not to eat or drink until they had killed Paul. More than forty men were involved in this plot (Acts 23:12-13).
Jews During the Reign of Ahasuerus	In every province to which the edict and order of the king came, there was great mourning among the Jews, with fasting, weeping and wailing. Many lay in sackcloth and ashes. . . . Then Esther sent this reply to Mordecai: "Go, gather together all the Jews who are in Susa, and fast for me. Do not eat or drink for three days, night or day. I and my maids will fast as you do. When this is done, I will go to the king, even though it is against the law. And if I perish, I perish" (Est. 4:3, 15-16).
Judah	Alarmed, Jehoshaphat resolved to inquire of the LORD, and he proclaimed a fast for all Judah. The people of Judah came together to seek help from the LORD; indeed, they came from every town in Judah to seek him (2 Chr. 20:3-4).
Leaders of the Church at Antioch	In the church at Antioch there were prophets and teachers: Barnabas, Simeon called Niger, Lucius of Cyrene, Manaen (who had been brought up with Herod the tetrarch) and Saul. While they were worshiping the Lord and fasting, the Holy Spirit said, "Set apart for me Barnabas and Saul for the work to which I have called them". So after they had fasted and prayed, they placed their hands on them and sent them off (Acts 13:1-3).
Men of Jabesh Gilead	When the people of Jabesh Gilead heard of what the Philistines had done to Saul, all their valiant men journeyed through the night to Beth Shan. They took down the bodies of Saul and his sons from the wall of Beth Shan and went to Jabesh, where they burned them. Then they took their bones and buried them under a tamarisk tree at Jabesh, and they fasted seven days (1 Sam. 31:11-13). When all the inhabitants of Jabesh Gilead heard of everything the Philistines had done to Saul, all their valiant men went and took the bodies of Saul and his sons and brought them to Jabesh. Then they buried their bones under the great tree in Jabesh, and they fasted seven days (1 Chr. 10:11-12).
Mighty Men of David	They mourned and wept and fasted till evening for Saul and his son Jonathan, and for the army of the LORD and the house of Israel, because they had fallen by the sword (2 Sam. 1:12).
Multitudes Following Jesus	Jesus called his disciples to him and said, "I have compassion for these people; they have already been with me three days and have nothing to eat. I do not want to send them away hungry, or they may collapse on the way" (Mt. 15:32; Mk. 8:2-3).

---

[506] See Towns, *Fasting for Spiritual Breakthrough*, 239-43.

People of Judah (During the Reign of Jehoiakim)	In the ninth month of the fifth year of Jehoiakim son of Josiah king of Judah, a time of fasting before the LORD was proclaimed for all the people in Jerusalem and those who had come from the towns of Judah. From the room of Gemariah son of Shaphan the secretary, which was in the upper courtyard at the entrance of the New Gate of the temple, Baruch read to all the people at the LORD's temple the words of Jeremiah from the scroll (Jer. 36:9-10).
People of Nineveh	The Ninevites believed God. They declared a fast, and all of them, from the greatest to the least, put on sackcloth. When the news reached the king of Nineveh, he rose from his throne, took off his royal robes, covered himself with sackcloth and sat down in the dust. Then he issued a proclamation in Nineveh: "By the decree of the king and his nobles: Do not let any man or beast, herd or flock, taste anything; do not let them eat or drink. But let man and beast be covered with sackcloth. Let everyone call urgently on God. Let them give up their evil ways and their violence. Who knows? God may yet relent and with compassion turn from his fierce anger so that we will not perish" (Jon. 3:5-9).
Pharisees and the Disciples of John the Baptist	Then John's disciples came and asked him, "How is it that we and the Pharisees fast, but your disciples do not fast?" (Mt. 9:14). Now John's disciples and the Pharisees were fasting. Some people came and asked Jesus, "How is it that John's disciples and the disciples of the Pharisees are fasting, but yours are not?" (Mk. 2:18). They said to him, "John's disciples often fast and pray, and so do the disciples of the Pharisees, but yours go on eating and drinking" (Lk. 5:33).
Remnant in Jerusalem After the Captivity	On the twenty-fourth day of the same month, the Israelites gathered together, fasting and wearing sackcloth and having dust on their heads. Those of Israelite descent had separated themselves from all foreigners. They stood in their places and confessed their sins and the wickedness of their fathers. They stood where they were and read from the Book of the Law of the LORD their God for a quarter of the day, and spent another quarter in confession and in worshiping the LORD their God (Neh. 9:1-3).
Remnant Returning After the Captivity	There, by the Ahava Canal, I proclaimed a fast, so that we might humble ourselves before our God and ask him for a safe journey for us and our children, with all our possessions. I was ashamed to ask the king for soldiers and horsemen to protect us from enemies on the road, because we had told the king, "The gracious hand of our God is on everyone who looks to him, but his great anger is against all who forsake him". So we fasted and petitioned our God about this, and he answered our prayer (Ezra 8:21-23).
Saul's Army	Now the men of Israel were in distress that day, because Saul had bound the people under an oath, saying, "Cursed be any man who eats food before evening comes, before I have avenged myself on my enemies!" So none of the troops tasted food (1 Sam. 14:24).

Appendix 8: Specialized Fasts[507]

Abstaining from Questionable Foods	Do not destroy the work of God for the sake of food. All food is clean, but it is wrong for a man to eat anything that causes someone else to stumble. It is better not to eat meat or drink wine or to do anything else that will cause your brother to fall (Rom. 14:20-21). Therefore, if what I eat causes my brother to fall into sin, I will never eat meat again, so that I will not cause him to fall (1 Cor. 8:13).
No Cereals or Grains (Feast of Firstfruits)	You must not eat any bread, or roasted or new grain, until the very day you bring this offering to your God. This is to be a lasting ordinance for the generations to come, wherever you live (Lev. 23:14).
No Grapes or Grape Products (Nazirite Vow)	The LORD said to Moses, "Speak to the Israelites and say to them: 'If a man or woman wants to make a special vow, a vow of separation to the LORD as a Nazirite, he must abstain from wine and other fermented drink and must not drink vinegar made from wine or from other fermented drink. He must not drink grape juice or eat grapes or raisins. As long as he is a Nazirite, he must not eat anything that comes from the grapevine, not even the seeds or skins (Num. 6:1-4).
Vegetarian Fast (Daniel in Babylon)	"Please test your servants for ten days: Give us nothing but vegetables to eat and water to drink. Then compare our appearance with that of the young men who eat the royal food, and treat your servants in accordance with what you see". So he agreed to this and tested them for ten days. At the end of the ten days they looked healthier and better nourished than any of the young men who ate the royal food. So the guard took away their choice food and the wine they were to drink and gave them vegetables instead (Dan. 1:12-16).

---

[507] See Towns, *Fasting for Spiritual Breakthrough*, 247-48.

Appendix 9: Fasting Quotations[508]

Spiritual Benefits

"Fasting cleanses the soul, raises the mind, subjects one's flesh to the spirit, renders the heart contrite and humble, scatters the clouds of concupiscence, quenches the fire of lust, and kindles the true light of chastity. Enter again into yourself".--Saint Augustine (354-430 A.D.; *"On Prayer and Fasting"*, Sermon lxxii; Doctor of the Catholic Church).

"Fasting with a pure heart and motives, I have discovered, brings personal revival and adds power to our prayers. Personal revival occurs because fasting is an act of humility. Fasting gives opportunity for deeper humility as we recognize our sins, repent, receive God's forgiveness, and experience His cleansing of our soul and spirit. Fasting also demonstrates our love for God and our full confidence in His faithfulness".--Bill Bright (1921-2003; "The Coming Revival"; American founder of "Campus Crusade for Christ").

"Renew yourselves and fast, for I tell you truly that Satan and his plagues may only be cast out by fasting and by prayer. Go by yourself and fast alone, and show your fasting to no man. The living God shall see it, and great shall be your reward. And fast till Beelzebub and all his evils depart from you, and all the angels of our Earthly Mother come and serve you. For I tell you truly, except you fast, you shall never be freed from the power of Satan and from all diseases that come from Satan. Fast and pray fervently, seeking the power of the living God for your healing. While you fast, eschew the Sons of Men and seek our Earthly Mother's angels, for he that seeks shall find" ("Essene Gospel of Peace")--Jesus Christ (c. 8-4 B.C.-29? AD).

"Fasting is the soul of prayer; mercy is the lifeblood of fasting. So, if you pray, fast; if you fast, show mercy. If you want your petition to be heard, hear the petition of others. If you do not close your ear to other, you open God's ear to yourself".--Saint Peter Chrysologus (c.380-c. 450; Doctor of the Catholic Church).

"Fasting of the body is food for the soul". - "As bodily food fattens the body, so fasting strengthens the soul. Imparting it an easy flight, it makes it able to ascend on high, to contemplate lofty things, and to put the heavenly higher than the pleasant and pleasurable things of life". - "It is necessary, most of all, for one who is fasting to curb anger, to accustom her- or himself to meekness and condescension, to have a contrite heart, to repulse impure thoughts and desires, to examine one's conscience, to put one's mind to the test, and to verify what good has been done by us in this or any other week, and which deficiency we have corrected in ourself in the present week. This is true fasting". - "Do you fast? Then feed the hungry, give drink to the thirsty, visit the sick, do not forget the imprisoned, have pity on the tortured, comfort those who grieve and who weep, be merciful, humble, kind, calm, patient, sympathetic, forgiving, reverent, truthful and pious, so that God might accept your fasting and might plentifully grant you the fruits of repentance".--Saint John Chrysostom (347-407 A.D.; Doctor of the Catholic Church).

"Fasting is an institution as old as Adam. It has been resorted to for self-purification or for some ends, noble as well as ignoble". - "True happiness is impossible without true health. True health is impossible without the rigid control of the palate". - "A complete fast is a complete and literal denial of self. It is the truest prayer". - "A genuine fast cleanses the body, mind and soul. It crucifies the flesh and, to that extent, sets the soul free". - "What the eyes are for the outer world, fasts are for the inner". - "My religion teaches me that whenever there is distress which one cannot remove, one must fast and pray". - Fasting will bring spiritual rebirth to those of you who cleanse and purify your bodies. The light of the world will illuminate within you when you fast and purify yourself". - "More caution and perhaps more restraint are necessary in breaking a fast than in keeping it". - "Experience has taught me that it was wrong to have dwelt upon the relish of food. One should eat not in order to please the palate, but just to keep the body going. When each organ of sense subserves the body and, through the body, the soul, its special relish disappears, and then alone does it begin to function in the way Nature intended it to do".--Mahatma Gandhi (1869-1948; Indian Independence Movement leader).

"Every request needs humility of spirit. Fast then, and you will receive from the Lord what you ask". - "When you are going to fast, observe it in this way: first, avoid any evil and desire, and purify your heart of all the vain things in the world. Your fast will be perfect if you do this".--Hermas (A.D. 55-150; "The Shepherd"; Roman Christian).

"Fasting and prayer are religious exercises; the enjoining them, an act of discipline".--Thomas Jefferson (1743-1826; "The Writings of Thomas Jefferson"; 3rd U.S. President).

"Be on your guard when you begin to mortify your body by abstinence and fasting--lest you imagine yourself to be perfect and a saint--for perfection does not consist in this virtue. It is only a help, a disposition, a means, though a fitting one, for the attainment of true perfection".--Saint Jerome (340-420 A.D., Doctor of the Catholic Church).

"The goal of fasting is inner unity. This means hearing, but not with the ear; hearing, but not with the understanding; it is hearing with the spirit, with your whole being. The hearing that is only in the ears is one thing. The hearing of the understanding is another, but the hearing of the spirit is not limited to any one faculty, to the ear, or to the mind. Hence, it demands the emptiness of the faculties, and when the faculties are empty, then your whole being listens. There is then a direct grasp of what is right before you that can never be heard with the ear or understood with the mind. Fasting of the heart empties the faculties, frees you from limitations and from preoccupations".--Father Thomas Merton (1915-1968; "The Living Bread"; American Trappist monk, writer and poet).

"Prayer carries us half way to God, fasting brings us to the door of His palace, and alms-giving procures us admission".--Muslim proverb.

"Dear Brothers and Sisters! In our own day, fasting seems to have lost something of its spiritual meaning, and has taken on, in a culture characterized by the search for material well-being, a therapeutic value for the care of one's body. Fasting certainly bring benefits to physical well-being, but for believers, it is, in the first place, a 'therapy' to heal all that prevents them from conformity to the will of God. The faithful practice of fasting contributes, moreover, to conferring unity to the whole person, body and soul, helping to avoid sin and grow in intimacy with the Lord". - "Denying material food, which nourishes our body, nurtures an interior disposition to listen to Christ and be fed by His saving word. Through fasting and praying, we allow Him to come and satisfy the deepest hunger that we experience in the depths of our being: the hunger and thirst for God. At the same time, fasting is an aid to open our eyes to the situation in which so many of our brothers and sisters live. Voluntary fasting enables us to grow in the spirit of the Good Samaritan, who bends low and goes to the help of his suffering sister and brother. This practice needs to be rediscovered and encouraged again in our day". - "It seems abundantly clear that fasting represents an important ascetical practice, a spiritual arm to do battle against every possible disordered attachment to ourselves. Freely chosen detachment from the pleasure of food and other material goods helps the disciple of Christ to control the appetites of nature, weakened by original sin, whose negative effects impact the entire human person. Quite opportunely, an ancient hymn of the Lenten Liturgy exhorts: 'Let us use sparingly words, food and drink, sleep and amusements. May we be more alert in the custody of our senses'. Since all of us are weighed down by sin and its consequences, fasting is proposed to us as an instrument to restore friendship with God".--Pope Benedict XVI ("The Great Joy of Fasting" 12.11.08).

"The penitential practices suggested by the Church include fasting. This traditional form of penance has not lost its meaning; indeed, perhaps it ought to be rediscovered, especially in those parts of the world and in those circumstances where not only is there food in plenty, but where one even comes across illnesses from overeating". - "Penitential fasting can be considered therapy for the soul. In fact, practiced as a sign of conversion, it helps one in the interior effort of listening to God. Fasting is to reaffirm to oneself what Jesus answered Satan when he tempted him at the end of his forty days of fasting in the wilderness: 'Man shall not live by bread alone, but by every word that proceeds from the mouth of God'" (Matthew 4:4) - "Today, especially in affluent societies, St. Augustine's warning is more timely than ever: 'Enter again into yourself'. Yes, we must enter again into ourselves, if we want to find ourselves. Not only our spiritual life is at stake, but indeed, our personal, family and social equilibrium, itself. One of the meanings of penitential fasting is to help us recover an interior life. Moderation, recollection and prayer go hand in hand". - "Sisters and Brothers, let us learn from the Blessed Virgin. The Gospel tells that she pondered in her heart the events of her life (Luke 2:19), seeking in them the unfolding of God's plan. Mary is the model to whom we can all look. Let us ask her to give us the secret of that 'spiritual fast' which sets us free from the slavery of things, strengthens our soul, and makes it ever ready to meet the Lord" ("Penitential Fasting Is Therapy for the Soul", 3.10.96) - "With physical fasting and, even more so, with interior fasting, the Christian prepares her-/himself to follow Christ and to be His faithful witness in every circumstance. Moreover, fasting helps us to understand better the difficulties and sufferings of so many of our brothers and sisters who are oppressed by hunger, severe poverty and war. In addition, it prompts us to a concrete solidarity and sharing with those who are in need" ("Angelus", 3.2.03)--Pope John Paul II.

"If thou wouldst preserve a sound body, use fasting and walking; if a healthful soul, fasting and praying. Walking exercises the body; praying exercises the soul. Fasting cleanses both".--Francis Quarles (1592-1644, English poet).

"Fasting as a religious act increases our sensitivity to that mystery always and everywhere present to us. It is an invitation to awareness, a call to compassion for the needy, a cry of distress, and a song of joy. It is a discipline of self-restraint, a ritual of purification, and a sanctuary for offerings of atonement. It is a wellspring for the spiritually dry, a compass for the spiritually lost, and inner nourishment for the spiritually hungry".--Father Thomas Ryan (Dir., Catholic Paulist Society's North American Office for Ecumenical and Interfaith Relations, Washington, DC).

"Fasting possesses great power. If practiced with the right intention, it makes one a friend of God. The demons are aware of that".--Quintus Tertullian (160-220 A.D.; Christian Ecclesiastical author, perhaps most famous for coining the term ''Trinity').

"I desired as many as could to join together in fasting and prayer, that God would restore the spirit of love and of a sound mind to the poor deluded rebels in America". - "Is not the neglect of this plain duty--I mean, fasting, ranked by our Lord with almsgiving and prayer--one general occasion of deadness among Christians? Can any one willingly neglect it, and be guiltless?"--John Wesley (1703-1791; "Collected Works of John Wesley", 1771; founder of the Methodist Church).

Fastings and vigils without a special object in view are time run to waste.--David Livingstone.

If you say "I will fast when God lays it on my heart", you never will. You are too cold and indifferent to take the yoke upon you.--D. L. Moody.

Fasting in the biblical sense is choosing not to partake of food because your spiritual hunger is so deep, you determination in intercession so intense, or your spiritual warfare so demanding that you have temporarily set aside even fleshly needs to give yourself to prayer and meditation.--Wesley L. Duewel, Touch the World Through Prayer.

The purpose of fasting is to loosen to some degree the ties which bind us to the world of material things and our surroundings as a whole, in order that we may concentrate all our spiritual powers upon the unseen and eternal things.--Ole Hallesby.

Physical Benefits

"Fasting is an effective and safe method of detoxifying the body. . .a technique that wise men have used for centuries to heal the sick. Fast regularly and help the body heal itself and stay well. Give all of your organs a rest. Fasting can help reverse the aging process, and if we use it correctly, we will live longer, happier lives".--James Balch, M. D ("Prescription For Natural Healing").

"If a person makes fasting part of her or his life, s/he'll experience a heightened spiritual awareness. By taking a long fast or two, and then fasting one day a week, s/he'll gradually find a growing peace and personal integration. America badly needs to go on a diet. It should do something drastic about excessive, unattractive, life-threatening fat. It should get rid of it in the quickest possible way, and this is by fasting".--Allan Cott, M. D ("Fasting: The Ultimate Diet").

"I often observe in fasting participants that. . .concentration seems to improve, creative thinking expands, depression lifts, insomnia stops, anxieties fade, the mind becomes more tranquil, and a natural joy begins to appear. It is my hypothesis that when the physical toxins are cleared from the brain cells, mind-brain function automatically and significantly improves, and spiritual capacities expand".--Gabriel Cousens, M. D (Founder, Tree of Life Rejuvenation Center, Patagonia, AZ).

"Fasting is the master key to mental and spiritual unfoldment and evolution".--Dr. Arnold Ehret (1866-1922; German Father of Naturopathy, a.k.a. Naturopathic Medicine).

"Life is slow suicide. Nine humans in ten are suicides". - "To lengthen thy life, lessen thy meals". - "The best of all medicines are rest and fasting".--Benjamin Franklin, LL.D. (1706-1790; American founding father, statesman and inventor--bifocal glasses, iron furnace stove and lightning rod).

"Fasting is the greatest remedy, the physician within".--*Philippus Paracelsus*, M.D. (1493-1541; Swiss physician and alchemist. . .considered one of the three Fathers of Western Medicine).

"I fast for greater physical and mental efficiency".--Plato (428-348 B.C., Greek philosopher and mathematician--student of Socrates; teacher of Aristotle; laid foundations of Western Philosophy).

"A little starvation can really do more for the average sick man than can the best medicines and the best doctors. I do not mean a restricted diet; I mean total abstinence from food. I speak from experience;

239

starvation has been my cold and fever doctor for 15 years, and has accomplished a cure in all instances".--Mark Twain (1835-1910; American author and humorist).

Spiritual and Physical Benefits

"There is both a physical and a spiritual fast. In the physical fast, the body abstains from food and drink. In the spiritual fast, the faster abstains from evil intentions, words and deeds. One who truly fasts abstains from anger, rage, malice, and vengeance. One who truly fasts abstains from idle and foul talk, empty rhetoric, slander, condemnation, flattery, lying and all manner of spiteful talk. In a word, a real faster is one who withdraws from all evil". - "As much as you subtract from the body, so much will you add to the strength of the soul". - "By fasting, it is possible both to be delivered from future evils, and to enjoy the good things to come. We fell into disease through sin; let us receive healing through repentance, which is not fruitful without fasting".--Saint Basil (329-379 A.D.; Doctor of the Catholic Church).

Subject Index

and wore sackcloth – 56, 150
church leaders – 160
Daniel – 44, 49, 118, 121,
  122, 133, 203
Darius – 122, 124, 133, 200
David – 60, 71, 95, 96, 193
early church – 161
Israelites – 69, 94
Ninevites – 69
Paul and Barnabas – 60, 106
prayed and – 20, 105, 117,
  119, 179
sackcloth and – 40, 62, 197,
  209, 211, 222, 223, 224,
  226, 230
seven days – 106, 222, 233
wept and – 45, 76, 95, 222,
  223, 225, 226, 227, 233
fasting
  a time of – 140, 185, 223, 229,
    234
  absence of – 20, 29
  abuses of – 209
  an expression of joy – 163
  ancient Israel – 148
  ancient type of – 158
  and prayer – 3, 5, 25, 35, 39,
    43, 55, 57, 104, 115, 161,
    169, 170, 194, 205, 206,
    237, 238
  and praying – 2, 42, 43, 64,
    113, 114, 115, 170, 187,
    198, 230, 237, 238
  and wearing sackcloth – 92,
    150, 222, 223, 225, 226,
    227, 232, 234
  and weeping –, 147, 148, 204,
    223, 224, 225, 226, 227
  an expression of piety – 102
  ate no bread – 51, 67, 71, 74,
    195, 203, 222, 226, 232
  ate no food – 74, 107, 161,
    204, 223, 227, 231
  attitude of – 63, 171
  before appointing elders – 23
  benefits of – 4, 39, 40, 162
  biblical – 4, 19, 35, 43, 44, 54
  biblical perspective on – 20
  blessings through – 138
  Christian – 18, 19, 25, 35, 36,
    168, 172
  Church of Rome – 169, 170,
    173
  concept of – 61, 63
  conception of – 2

corporate – 1, 194, 233
corporate time of – 146
criticism(s) of – 57, 172
criticized – 103
day(s) of – 9, 40, 71, 140, 142,
  196, 209, 210, 223, 227,
  230, 238
did not eat – 79, 115, 117,
  194, 203, 231, 232
discipline of – 1, 5, 7, 20, 21,
  22, 50, 162, 179, 185, 208,
  216
divinely acceptable – 178
do not eat – 11, 41, 74. 126,
  128, 224, 229, 231, 233
does not eat – 81, 200
drank no water – 51, 67, 71,
  74, 107, 195, 203, 204, 222,
  223, 226, 227, 231, 232
due to emotional distress –
  124, 199, 201
example of – 162
expresses repentance – 60
expressing sorrow – 163
extended period of – 120
external – 198
false – 133
fear of – 8
feasting and – 70
for divine direction – 196, 197
for grief – 76, 221
for material provision – 198
for remorse over committed
  sin – 197, 221
for revival, renewal, and
  righteousness – 198, 221
for spiritual deliverance – 197
forty days – 9, 35, 42, 44, 47,
  50, 51, 52, 53, 60, 69, 71,
  74, 75, 111, 112, 161, 162,
  169, 170, 173, 175, 176,
  195, 203, 222, 226, 231,
  232, 238
goal of true – 100, 101
Graeco-Roman – 54, 159
Greeks observed – 173
had eaten nothing – 79, 81,
  200, 232
heart of – 25, 27
historical basis for – 158, 160
humbled myself with – 58, 94,
  195, 222, 223, 224, 226,
  227, 230
in every church – 64
in sorrow and mourning – 196

individual(s) – 37, 47, 50, 57,
  69, 74
infrequent – 69, 70
involuntary – 117, 166, 199,
  221
Jesus – 52, 160
Jewish sign of – 121
joy of – 238
key component to – 39
length of the – 178
method – 22, 44, 71, 133
moderate – 39
month dedicated to – 92
Moses – 74
mourning and – 54, 70, 127,
  156
must not eat bread – 85, 87
national – 62
not drink water – 203
observe – 65, 173, 174
of antiquity – 106
of the Pharisees – 162
outward act of – 4
penitential – 238
perception of – 4
persevering in – 174
practice of – 4, 8, 54, 95, 156,
  160, 163, 169, 171, 172,
  177, 185, 237
prayer and – 2, 21, 25, 42, 43,
  58, 59, 98, 103, 104, 105,
  111, 146, 158, 160, 161,
  163, 165, 170, 178, 179,
  189, 190, 197, 224, 225,
  228, 236
preparation for – 8
principle of – 106, 122
private – 57, 63
problem of – 153
proclaim a day of – 40, 196,
  209, 210, 230
proper – 19, 98
psychological benefits to – 54
public – 57
purpose for – 39, 53, 54, 91,
  172
purpose of – 43, 54, 55, 57,
  58, 239
rejected – 198, 199
relevance of – 1
religious – 7, 60, 158
religious activity of – 98
rigorous – 127
Roman kings and emperors –
  173

244

strike – 55

idleness – 28, 29
idol(s) – 11, 15, 40, 74, 75, 85,
    98, 108, 197, 220, 221
    pollutions of – 220
idolatrous – 93, 94, 97, 107,
    111, 126, 182
    marriages – 107
idolatrous nations – 93
idolatry – 87, 108, 154, 182
indulgence – 31, 171, 208
indulgences
    perverted life of – 15
    sensual – 11, 168
insomnia – 239

Jerusalem
    City of – 55, 90, 91, 217
    destruction of – 19, 50, 62,
        154
    wall of – 90, 93, 137, 156
Jewish
    calendar – 37, 92, 127, 172
    captivity – 67, 152, 153, 154,
        157
    conspiracy – 216, 217
    custom – 55, 92, 161, 169,
        173
    legalism – 219
    remnant – 90, 105
    superficial view of
        purification – 14
    theology – 116
Jews
    and Gentiles – 9
    deliverance of the – 119, 129
Jezreel Valley – 80
Judah's sins – 119
Judaism – 56, 63, 125, 158, 159,
    161, 164, 186, 187, 214
judgment
    divine – 122, 195, 221
    eternal – 13
justice – 38, 41, 97, 98, 99, 102,
    103, 104, 105, 118, 122,
    132, 138, 153, 155, 167,
    188, 197, 208, 209, 210,
    212, 215

Kibroth Hattaavah – 14, 33, 34

lamentation – 45, 61, 65, 67,
    128, 131, 145, 148, 151,
    223, 226, 229, 231

Law of the Lord – 92, 222, 223,
    225, 226, 227, 232, 234
Lent – 36, 49, 53, 169, 170, 172,
    208
Levites – 79, 84, 92, 107, 108,
    180, 183
lifestyle
    unrestrained – 15
locusts – 125, 126, 146, 151
lusts
    unbridled – 14

martyrs – 16
message
    of rebuke – 153
    of rejoicing – 153
    of repentance – 153
    of restoration – 153
Mizpah – 40, 41, 44, 75, 108,
    109, 110, 111, 155, 194,
    222, 226, 233
Mosaic Covenant – 97, 132,
    138, 205
Mosaic Law – 19, 65, 128, 185,
    208
Moses
    Law of – 12, 34, 49, 79, 89,
        93, 105, 107, 126, 153, 209
    Mount Carmel – 112, 181, 210
    Mount Ebal – 76, 84
    Mount Gilboa – 95
    Mount Horeb – 51, 176
    Mount Seir – 89
    Mount Sinai – 9, 50, 51, 52, 55,
        71, 74, 75, 112, 175, 215

Naboth's vineyard – 209, 210,
    211
national crisis – 194, 198, 221
national emergency – 19
national trauma – 19
Nazareth – 21
Nazirite Vow – 78, 125, 235
necromantic ritual – 81
New Covenant – 9, 52, 62, 163,
    206
Nineveh – 40, 47, 48, 49, 62, 72,
    73, 149, 150, 151, 152, 183,
    194, 203, 204, 224, 229,
    234
    fall of – 150
    wicked city – 149
oath(s) – 8, 9, 30, 44, 45, 46, 55,
    83, 95, 107, 109, 150, 216,

217, 222, 229, 230, 233,
    234
offering(s)
    burnt – 40, 44, 54, 68, 75, 76,
        93, 97, 110, 196, 199, 233
    fellowship – 40, 44, 75, 76,
        196, 233
    sin – 76
oppression
    yoke of – 118, 131, 132, 134,
        135, 195, 228
orgy – 14

Parable of the Good Samaritan –
    90
peace – 4, 29, 36, 50, 67, 68, 76,
    97, 98, 102, 109, 117,
    121,130, 131, 153, 155,
    156, 175, 182, 221, 228,
    236, 239
penitence – 53, 57, 65, 69, 76,
    89, 98, 169, 172, 221
personal habits – 113
perverted actions – 14
Pharisaism – 159
piety
    Jewish – 172
    parade of – 159
    religious – 160
plague(d) – 14, 27, 33, 54, 62,
    144, 146, 199, 219, 236
poor and needy – 27, 28, 29, 30,
    63, 69
prayed – 1, 20, 21, 23, 35, 56,
    62, 64, 68, 76, 77, 79, 90,
    91, 105, 106, 111, 112, 115,
    117, 119, 121, 123, 150,
    170, 179, 184, 187, 188,
    189, 193, 195, 197, 199,
    203, 213, 223, 224, 225,
    226, 227, 232, 233
    Hannah – 79
prayer
    charismatic – 160
    Hannah's – 78
    Moses' – 75
    of the road – 106
    persevering – 104
    practice of – 4, 65, 98, 104
    Samuel's – 75
    solemn – 59, 146
praying – 1, 2, 25, 28, 42, 43,
    44, 64, 66, 90, 106, 113,
    114, 115, 170, 186, 187,

Scripture Index

248

254

256

257

Hebrew, Greek, and Latin Indexes

Hebrew Index

chānan – 120

'innah nepēš – 67

Megillah – 130

tephillath hadderech – 106

אָבֵל 'āval – 47, 91, 121

אֶגְרֹף 'eghrōph – 101, 102

אֶגְרֹף 'egrōp – 102

אָחוֹת 'āchôth – 28

אֵלֶּה – 45

אֲסַפְסֻף 'ăsaphsuph – 33

אַףחָרִיב – 79

אֵפֶר 'fipher – 72, 73, 120

אִישׁ וְעַד אִשָּׁה – 93

צוֹם בְּיוֹם beyom som – 141

בַּיִת bayith – 134

כַּר בֵּית bêth kar – 110

בָּכֹה – 91

בָּכֹה bākhāh – 91, 107

בְּכֹרָה bekhōrāh – 31

בְּלִיַעַל beliya'al – 210

בָּנָה bānāh – 136

בַּסָּתֶר bassāter – 84

בָּקַע bāqa' – 135

גֵּאָה gā'â – 28

גָּאוֹן gā'ôn – 28

גָּבַהּ gāvahh – 28

יָשָׁר דֶּרֶךְ derekh yāshār – 106

קִבְרוֹת הַתַּאֲוָה qivrôth hatta'ăwāh – 14, 34

וְהִשְׂבִּיעַ wĕhiśbîa' – 136

מֵירֹאשׁ וְהִשְׁקִתִים wĕhišqitîm mê-rō'š – 29

הֶחֱזִיקָה לֹא וְאֶבְיוֹן וְיַדעָנִי wĕyad-'ānî wĕ'ebyôn lō' heḥĕzîqâ – 29

וְלֹא'אָכַל wĕlō'-'ākal – 210

וְנִקָּה wĕnikkâ – 84

וְרֶגֶם wĕregem – 153

הַשְׁקֵט וְשַׁלְוַת wĕšalwat hašqēṭ – 29

זָרַח zārach – 118

זֵרֹעִים zfirō'îm – 118

חָמָס chāmās – 151, 152

חֲצֵרוֹת chătsfirôth – 14

חָרַם chāram – 107, 108

יְהוֹשֻׁעַ yehôshua' – 9

יוֹם yôm – 65

יַחֲרֵם 'āyhăram – 107

יָלַל yālal – 145

יַעֲקֹב ya'ăqōv – 30

יָשַׁב yāshav – 91

כִּפֻּרִים kippurîm – 65

כָּרַת kārath – 65

לָחֶם lāḥem – 210

חֲמֻדוֹת לֶחֶם lehem ḥămudôt – 121

לְעֵנָה la'ănāh – 29

לִשְׁמֹעַ מֵבִין כֹּל – 93

מִטָּה mittāh – 210

מְלֹאקוֹמָתוֹ mĕlō'-qômātô – 80

מֶלֶךְ melek – 153

מִןהָעָם min-hā'ām – 85

מַצָּה matstsāh – 101

מִצְפָּה mitspāh – 109

מִקְּהַל miqqĕhal – 108

מִתְאַבֵּל mit'abbēl – 47

נָבוֹת nāvôth – 211

נָחָה nāchāh – 136

נָחַם nācham – 152

נִינְוֵה nînĕwēh – 149

נָכָה – 101

נָכָה – 84

נָכָה nākhāh – 84, 101

נֶפֶשׁ nephesh – 66, 136

נָצָה nātsāh – 101

נָצַח – 101

סוּךְ sûkh – 121, 122

סָפַד sāphadh – 145

סַר sar – 210

עוֹלָה 'awlāh – 214

עָיֵף 'āyfiph – 32, 33

לֵאלֹהִים גְּדוֹלָה עִיר ir-gedolah lelohim – 149

עֹל 'ōl – 85

עָלַל 'ālal – 85

עַם 'am – 85

עָנֹג 'ānōgh – 138, 139

ענה 'nh – 66, 67

עָנָה 'ānāh – 66, 100

עָנִי 'ānî – 30

עֵשָׂו 'ēśāw – 30

פּוּר pûr – 129, 130

פָּלַל pālal – 91

פָּרַס pāras – 134

צוֹם – 56, 61, 63, 69, 90, 91, 96, 196

צוֹם tsôm – 120

צוּם tsûm – 62

צַרלִי ṣar-lî – 80

קָבַץ qāvats – 108

קָדַשׁ qādhash – 146

קַדְּשׁוּצוֹם qaddĕšû-ṣôm – 146

קָהָל qāhāl – 108

קוֹמָה qômāh – 80

קָרָא qārā' – 99, 100

קֶרָא qŏrā' – 99

קָרַע qāra – 148, 149

רָאָה rā'āh – 134

רִיב rîv – 101

רָשַׁע rāshā' – 102

שָׁאַב shā'av – 109

שָׂבֵעַ sāvfi' – 136

שִׁבְעָה siv'āh – 29

שִׁבְעַתלֶחֶם śib'at-lehem – 29

שֹׁד shōdh – 147

שַׁדַּי shadday – 147

שׁוּב shûv – 137, 138, 147, 149

שָׁלֹשׁ šālōš – 26

שְׁמוּאֵל shemû'fil – 79

שִׂמְחָה simchāh – 156

שָׁפַךְ – 78, 109

שָׁפַךְ shāphakh – 78, 109

259

Author and Person Index

References Cited

Achtemeier, Paul J., ed. *Harper's Bible* Dictionary. 1st ed. San Francisco, CA: Harper & Row, 1985.

Alford, Henry, *The Greek Testament: An Exegetical and Critical Commentary*, In Rick Meyers, e-Sword, Version 10.2.1, 2000-2012, <http://www.e-sword.net>.

Arndt, William, F. Wilbur Gingrich, Frederick W. Danker and Walter Bauer. *A Greek-English Lexicon of the New Testament and Other Early Christian Literature: A Translation and Adaption of the Fourth Revised and Augmented Edition of Walter Bauer's Griechisch*. Chicago, IL: University of Chicago Press, 1979.

Baldwin, Joyce C. *Haggai, Zechariah, Malachi: An Introduction and Commentary*. Downers Grove, IL: InterVarsity Press, 1972.

Barclay, William. *Daily Study Bible*. In Rick Meyers, e-Sword, Version 10.2.1, 2000-2012. <http://www.e-sword.net>, n.d.

Barnes, Albert. *Albert Barnes' Notes on the Bible*. In Rick Meyers, e-Sword, Version 10.2.1, 2000-2012. <http://www.e-sword.net>, n.d.

_____. *Notes on the New Testament Explanatory and Practical*. Robert Frew. ed. WORDsearch CROSS e-book, n.d.

Barry, John D. and Lazarus Wentz, eds. *The Lexham Bible Dictionary*. Bellingham, WA: Logos Bible Software, 2012.

Brand, Chad, Charles Draper, Archie England et al. *Holman Illustrated Bible Dictionary*. Nashville, TN: Holman Bible Publishers, 2003.

Bray, Tamara L., ed. *The Archaeology and Politics of Food and Feasting in Early States and Empires*. New York: Kluwer Academic Publishers, 2002.

Broadbent III, Gordon P. *A Call to Biblical Fasting: A Written Sermon. Doctoral unpublished manuscript*. Sun Valley, CA: The Master's Seminary, October 30, 2006.

Brooks, Keith. *Summarized Bible: Complete Summary of the Old Testament*. Bellingham, WA: Logos Bible Software, 2009.

Brown, Raymond Edward, Joseph A. Fitzmyer, and Roland Edmund Murphy. *The Jerome Biblical Commentary*. Vol. 1. Englewood Cliffs, NJ: Prentice-Hall, 1996.

Brueggemann, Walter. *First and Second Samuel. Interpretation: A Bible Commentary for Teaching and Preaching*. Louisville, KY: John Knox, 1990.

Buck, Charles. *Buck's Theological Dictionary*. In Rick Meyers, e-Sword, Version 10.2.1, 2000-2012. <http://www.e-sword.net>, 1802.

Calvin, John. *Institutes of the Christian Religion*. Bellingham, WA: Logos Bible Software, 1997.

Carlson, R. A. *David the Chosen King: A Traditio-Historical Approach to the Second Book of Samuel*. Stockholm, Sweden: Almqvist and Wiksell, 1964.

Carroll, B. H. *An interpretation of the English Bible*. In Rick Meyers, e-Sword, Version 10.2.1, 2000-2012. <http://www.e-sword.net>, n.d.

Coke, Thomas. *A Commentary on the Holy Bible: Joshua to Job*. Vol. 2. In Rick Meyers, e-Sword, Version 10.2.1, 2000-2012. <http://www.e-sword.net>, 1901.

Complete Pulpit Commentary, The. In Rick Meyers, e-Sword, Version 10.2.1, 2000-2012. <http://www.e-sword.net>, n.d.

Constable, Thomas L. *The Expository Notes of Dr. Constable*. In Rick Meyers, e-Sword, Version 10.2.1, 2000-2012. <http://www.e-sword.net>, 2012.

Copeland, Mark A. *Fasting: A Special Study*. In Rick Meyers, e-Sword, Version 10.2.1, 2000-2012. <http://www.e-sword.net>, 1992-2007.

Cross, F. L. and Elizabeth A. Livingstone. *The Oxford Dictionary of the Christian Church*. 3rd revised edition. New York: Oxford University Press, 2005.

Dennett, Edward. *Daniel the Prophet*. In Rick Meyers, e-Sword, Version 10.2.1, 2000-2012, <http://www.e-sword.net>, 1909.

Dockery, David S., ed. *Holman Concise Bible Commentary: Simple, Straightforward Commentary on Every Book of the Bible*. Nashville, TN: Broadman & Holman Publishers, 1998.

Dockery, David S., Trent C. Butler, Christopher L. Church et al. *Holman Bible Handbook*. Nashville, TN: Holman Bible Publishers, 1992.

Dods, Marcus and G. Reith, trans. *Epistle of Barnabas 3.1ff*. In Rick Meyers, e-Sword, Version 10.2.1, 2000-2012. <http://www.e-sword.net>, n.d.

Dummelow, J. R., ed. *A Commentary on the Holy Bible*. In Rick Meyers, e-Sword, Version 10.2.1, 2000-2012. <http://www.e-sword.net>, n.d.

Easton, M. G. *Easton's Bible Dictionary*. New York: Harper & Brothers, 1893.

Ellsworth, Roger. *Opening Up Philippians, Opening Up Commentary*. Leominster: Day One Publications, 2004.

Exell, Joseph S. and Henry D. M. Spence-Jones. *The Complete Pulpit Commentary*. In Rick Meyers, e-Sword, Version 10.2.1, 2000-2012. <http://www.e-sword.net>, 1880-1919.

Exell, Joseph S., ed. *The Biblical Illustrator*. In Rick Meyers, e-Sword, Version 10.2.1, 2000-2012. <http://www.e-sword.net>, 1849.

Eyre, Stephen D. *Drawing Close to God: The Essentials of a Dynamic Quiet Time: A Lifeguide Resource*. Downers Grove, IL: InterVarsity Press, 1995.

Foster, Richard. *The Celebration of Discipline*. New York: Harper & Row, 1978.

Franklin, Jentezen. *Fasting*. Lake Mary, FL: Charisma House, 2008.

Freedman, David Noel, ed. *The Anchor Yale Bible Dictionary*. 6 Vols. New York: Doubleday, 1992.

Freeman, James M., and Harold J. Chadwick. *Manners & Customs of the Bible*. Revised edition. North Brunswick, NJ: Bridge-Logos Publishers, 1998.

Gaebelein, Arno Clement. *Annotated Bible: Old and New Testaments*. In Rick Meyers, e-Sword, Version 10.2.1, 2000-2012. <http://www.e-sword.net>, 1919.

Gaebelein, Frank E., ed. *The Expositor's Bible Commentary, Volume 2: Genesis, Exodus, Leviticus, Numbers*. Grand Rapids, MI: Zondervan Publishing House. Database © 2010 WORDsearch CROSS e-book, 1990.

_____. *The Expositor's Bible Commentary, Volume 3: Deuteronomy, Joshua, Judges, Ruth, 1 & 2 Samuel*. Grand Rapids, MI: Zondervan Publishing House. Database © 2010 WORDsearch CROSS e-book, 1992.

_____. *The Expositor's Bible Commentary, Volume 4: 1 & 2 Kings, 1 & 2 Chronicles, Ezra, Nehemiah, Esther, Job*. Grand Rapids, MI: Zondervan Publishing House. Database © 2010 WORDsearch CROSS e-book, 1988.

_____. *The Expositor's Bible Commentary, Volume 5: Psalms, Proverbs, Ecclesiastes, Song of Songs*. Grand Rapids, MI: Zondervan Publishing House. Database © 2010 WORDsearch CROSS e-book, 1991.

_____. *The Expositor's Bible Commentary, Volume 6: Isaiah, Jeremiah, Lamentations, Ezekiel*. Grand Rapids, MI: Zondervan Publishing House. Database © 2010 WORDsearch CROSS e-book, 1986.

_____. *The Expositor's Bible Commentary, Volume 7: Daniel and the Minor Prophets*. Grand Rapids, MI: Zondervan Publishing House. Database © 2010 WORDsearch CROSS e-book, 1985.

_____. *The Expositor's Bible Commentary, Volume 8: Matthew, Mark, Luke*. Grand Rapids, MI: Zondervan Publishing House. Database © 2010 WORDsearch CROSS e-book, 1984.

_____. *The Expositor's Bible Commentary, Volume 9: John and Acts*. Grand Rapids, MI: Zondervan Publishing House. Database © 2010 WORDsearch CROSS e-book, 1981.

_____. *The Expositor's Bible Commentary, Volume 10: Romans through Galatians*. Grand Rapids, MI: Zondervan Publishing House, WORDsearch CROSS e-book, 1976.

_____. *The Expositor's Bible Commentary, Volume 11: Ephesians through Philemon*. Grand Rapids, MI: Zondervan Publishing House. Database © 2010 WORDsearch CROSS e-book, 1981.

Gilbrant, Thoralf, ed. *The Complete Biblical Library Commentary, Acts.* Springfield, IL: wordseacrh, Inc., WORDsearch CROSS e-book, 1988.

_____. *The Complete Biblical Library Commentary, Daniel-Malachi.* Springfield, IL: World Library Press, Inc., WORDsearch CROSS e-book, 1996.

_____. *The Complete Biblical Library Commentary, Deuteronomy.* Springfield, IL: World Library Press, Inc., WORDsearch CROSS e-book, 1996.

_____. *The Complete Biblical Library Commentary, Ezekiel.* Springfield, IL: World Library Press, Inc., WORDsearch CROSS e-book, 1996.

_____. *The Complete Biblical Library Commentary, Ezra-Job.* Springfield, IL: World Library Press, Inc., WORDsearch CROSS e-book, 1996.

_____. *The Complete Biblical Library Commentary, Galatians-Philemon.* Springfield, IL: World Library Press, Inc., WORDsearch CROSS e-book, 1995.

_____. *The Complete Biblical Library Commentary, Isaiah.* Springfield, IL: World Library Press, Inc., WORDsearch CROSS e-book, 1996.

_____. *The Complete Biblical Library Commentary, Jeremiah-Lamentations.* Springfield, IL: World Library Press, Inc., WORDsearch CROSS e-book, 1996.

_____. *The Complete Biblical Library Commentary, Kings.* Springfield, IL: World Library Press, Inc., WORDsearch CROSS e-book, 1996.

_____. *The Complete Biblical Library Commentary, Luke.* Springfield, IL: World Library Press, Inc., WORDsearch CROSS e-book, 1988.

_____. *The Complete Biblical Library Commentary, Mark.* Springfield, IL: World Library Press, Inc., WORDsearch CROSS e-book, 1988.

_____. *The Complete Biblical Library Commentary, Matthew.* Springfield, IL: World Library Press, Inc., WORDsearch CROSS e-book, 1988.

_____. *The Complete Biblical Library Commentary, Romans-Corinthians.* Springfield, IL: World Library Press, Inc., WORDsearch CROSS e-book, 1988.

_____. *The Complete Biblical Library Commentary, Samuel.* Springfield, IL: World Library Press, Inc., WORDsearch CROSS e-book, 1996.

_____. *The Complete Biblical Library Commentary, Chronicles.* Springfield, IL: World Library Press, Inc., WORDsearch CROSS e-book, 1996.

_____. *The Complete Biblical Library Commentary, Psalms.* Springfield, IL: World Library Press, Inc., WORDsearch CROSS e-book, 1996.

_____. *The Complete Biblical Library Greek-English Dictionary, Alpha-Gamma.* Springfield, MO: Complete Biblical Library, WORDsearch CROSS e-book, 1991.

_____. *The Complete Biblical Library Greek-English Dictionary, Delta-Epsilon.* Springfield, MO: Complete Biblical Library, WORDsearch CROSS e-book, 1991.

_____. *The Complete Biblical Library Greek-English Dictionary, Lambda-Omicron.* Springfield, MO: Complete Biblical Library, WORDsearch CROSS e-book, 1991.

_____. *The Complete Biblical Library Greek-English Dictionary, Pi-Rho.* Springfield, MO: Complete Biblical Library, WORDsearch CROSS e-book, 1991.

_____. *The Complete Biblical Library Greek-English Dictionary, Sigma-Omega.* Springfield, MO: Complete Biblical Library, WORDsearch CROSS e-book, 1991.

_____. *The Complete Biblical Library Greek-English Dictionary, Zeta-Kappa.* Springfield, MO: Complete Biblical Library, WORDsearch CROSS e-book, 1991.

_____. *The Complete Biblical Library Hebrew-English Dictionary, Aleph-Beth.* Springfield, IL: World Library Press, Inc., WORDsearch CROSS e-book, 1998.

_____. *The Complete Biblical Library Hebrew-English Dictionary, Gimel-Zayin.* Springfield, IL: World Library Press, Inc., WORDsearch CROSS e-book, 1998.

_____. *The Complete Biblical Library Hebrew-English Dictionary, Heth-Yodh.* Springfield, IL: World Library Press, Inc., WORDsearch CROSS e-book, 1998.

_____. *The Complete Biblical Library Hebrew-English Dictionary, Kaph-Mem.* Springfield, IL: World Library Press, Inc., WORDsearch CROSS e-book, 1998.

_____. *The Complete Biblical Library Hebrew-English Dictionary, Nun-Ayin.* Springfield, IL: World Library Press, Inc., WORDsearch CROSS e-book, 1998.

_____. *The Complete Biblical Library Hebrew-English Dictionary, Pe-Resh.* Springfield, IL: World Library Press, Inc., WORDsearch CROSS e-book, 1998.

_____. *The Complete Biblical Library Hebrew-English Dictionary, Sin-Taw.* Springfield, IL: World Library Press, Inc., WORDsearch CROSS e-book, 1998.

Gill, John. *John Gill's Exposition of the Entire Bible.* In Rick Meyers, e-Sword, Version 10.2.1, 2000-2012. <http://www.e-sword.net>, n.d.

Green, Joel B. and Scot McKnight, eds. *Dictionary of Jesus and the Gospels.* Downers Grove, IL: InterVarsity Press, WORDsearch CROSS e-book, 1992.

Guzik, David. *Guzik Commentary on OT and NT.* In Rick Meyers, e-Sword, Version 10.2.1, 2000-2012. <http://www.e-sword.net>, n.d.

Harris, R. Laird, Gleason L. Archer, Jr. and Bruce K. Waltke, eds. *Theological Wordbook of the Old Testament.* electronic ed. Chicago, IL: Moody Press, 1999.

Hastings, James. *The Christian Doctrine of Prayer.* Edinburgh, UK: T & T Clark, 1915.

Hastings, James, ed. *A Dictionary of Christ and the Gospels.* 2 Vols. New York: Charles Scribner's Sons. In Rick Meyers, e-Sword, Version 10.1.0, 2000-2012. <http://www.e-sword.net>, 1906.

Hawker, Robert. *The Poor Man's Commentary on the Whole Bible.* Birmingham, AL: Solid Ground Christian Books, n.d.

Haydock, George Leo. *Haydock Catholic Bible Commentary.* In Rick Meyers, e-Sword, Version 10.2.1, 2000-2012. <http://www.e-sword.net>, n.d.

Henry, Matthew. *Matthew Henry's Commentary on the Whole Bible: Complete and Unabridged in One Volume.* Peabody, MA: Hendrickson Publishers, 1994.

Hermas, Shepherd of. *Similitudes 5.3.5ff.* In Rick Meyers, e-Sword, Version 10.2.1, 2000-2012. <http://www.e-sword.net>, n.d.

Hirsch, E. G., ed. *The Jewish Encyclopaedia.* 12 Vols. New York: Funk & Wagnalls Company, 1901.

Jamieson, Robert, A. R. Fausset and David Brown. *Commentary Critical and Explanatory on the Whole Bible.* Oak Harbor, WA: Logos Research Systems, Inc, 1997.

_____. *A Commentary: Critical, Experimental, and Practical on the Old and New Testaments.* Toledo, OH: Jerome B. Names & Co., 1884, WORD*search* CROSS e-book.

Josephus, Flavius and William Whiston. *The Works of Josephus: Complete and Unabridged.* Peabody, MA: Hendrickson Publishers, 1987.

Keener, Craig S. *The IVP Bible Background Commentary, New Testament.* Downers Grove, IL: InterVarsity Press, WORDsearch CROSS e-book, 1993.

Keil, Johann C. F. & Franz Delitzsch. *Keil & Delitzsch Commentary on the Old Testament.* Peabody, MA: Hendrickson Publishers, In Rick Meyers, e-Sword, Version 10.1.0, 2000-2012. <http://www.e-sword.net>, 1996.

Kent, Charles Foster. *The Founders and Rulers of United Israel: From the Death of Moses to the Division of the Hebrew Kingdom,* The Historical Bible. New York: Charles Scribner's Sons, 1908.

_____. *The Kings and Prophets of Israel and Judah: From the Division of the Kingdom to the Babylonian Exile,* The Historical Bible. New York: Charles Scribner's Sons, 1909.

_____. *The Life and Teachings of Jesus: According to the Earliest Records,* The Historical Bible. New York: Charles Scribner's Sons, 1913.

King, Philip J. *Amos, Hosea, Micah—An Archaeological Commentary.* Philadelphia, PA: Westminster John Knox Press, 1988.

Kittel, Gerhard, Geoffrey W. Bromiley and Gerhard Friedrich, eds. *Theological Dictionary of the New Testament.* electronic ed. 10 Vols. Grand Rapids, MI: William B. Eerdmans Publishing Company, 1964.

Kittel, Gerhard, Gerhard Friedrich and Geoffrey W. Bromiley, eds. *Theological Dictionary of the New Testament: Abridged in One Volume.* Grand Rapids, MI: William B. Eerdmans Publishing Company, 1985.

Knowles, Andrew. *The Bible Guide.* 1st Augsburg books ed. Minneapolis, MN: Augsburg, 2001.

Lange, John Peter. *Commentary on the Holy Scriptures: Critical, Doctrinal, and Homiletical.* Philip Schaff. ed. 25 Vols. In Rick Meyers, e-Sword, Version 10.2.1, 2000-2012, <http://www.e-sword.net>, n.d.

Lewis, C. S. *The Problem of Pain.* New York: Macmillan, 1962.

Lewis, Theodore J. *Cults of the Dead in Ancient Israel and Ugarit.* Harvard Semitic Monograph, 39. Atlanta, GA: Scholars Press, 1989.

Lloyd-Jones, Martyn. *Studies in the Sermon on the Mount.* Grand Rapids, MI: William B. Eerdmans Publishing Company, 1960.

M'Clintock, John and James Strong, eds. *Cyclopedia of Biblical and Ecclesiastical Literature.* 12 Vols. New York: Harper & Brothers, Publishers. In Rick Meyers, e-Sword, Version 10.1.0, 2000-2012. <http://www.e-sword.net>, 1895.

MacArthur, Jr., John. *The MacArthur New Testament Commentary.* Vol. 1. Chicago, IL: Moody Press, 1985-90.

Mackrell, Paul. *Opening Up Jonah, Opening Up Commentary.* Leominster: Day One Publications, 2007.

Mays, James Luther, ed. *Harper's Bible Commentary.* San Francisco, CA: Harper & Row, 1988.

Merriam-Webster, Inc. *Merriam-Webster's Collegiate Dictionary.* Eleventh ed. Springfield, MA: Merriam-Webster, Inc, 2003.

Murphy, Charles M. *The Spirituality of Fasting, Rediscovering A Christian Practice.* Notre Dame, IN: Ave Maria Press, 2010.

Myers, Allen C. *The Eerdmans Bible Dictionary.* Grand Rapids, MI: William B. Eerdmans Publishing House, 1987.

Neff, LaVonne, et al., eds., *Practical Christianity.* Wheaton, IL: Tyndale House, 1987.

Newberry, Ian. *Available for God: A Biblical and Practical Approach to Fasting.* Translated by Peter Coleman. Carlisle, UK: OM Publishing, 1996.

Nicoll, W. Robertson, Jane T. Stoddart, and James Moffatt, ed. *The Expositor's Dictionary of Texts.* In Rick Meyers, e-Sword, Version 10.2.1, 2000-2012. <http://www.e-sword.net>, n.d.

Nicoll, William Robertson, ed. *The Sermon Bible: Isaiah to Malachi.* Vol. 4. In Rick Meyers, e-Sword, Version 10.2.1, 2000-2012. <http://www.e-sword.net>, n.d.

Orr, James, ed. *International Standard Bible Encyclopedia.* In Rick Meyers, e-Sword, Version 10.2.1, 2000-2012. <http://www.e-sword.net>, n.d.

Packer, J. I. *A Quest for Godliness: The Puritan Vision of the Christian Life.* Wheaton, IL: Crossway Books, 2010.

Paschall, Franklin H. and Herschel H. Hobbs, eds. *The Teacher's Bible Commentary: A Concise, Thorough Interpretation of the Entire Bible Designed Especially for Sunday School Teachers.* Nashville, TN: Broadman and Holman Publishers, 1972.

Philo of Alexandria, Charles Duke Yonge. *The Works of Philo: Complete and Unabridged.* Peabody, MA: Hendrickson Publishers, 1995.

Piper, John. *A Hunger for God: Desiring God Through Fasting and Prayer.* Wheaton, IL: Crossway Books, 1997.

Polzin, Robert. *Samuel and the Deuteronomist.* San Francisco, CA: Harper, 1989.

Porphyrius, of Tyre. *De Abstinentia.* Morden, 1655.

Raymond Brown, Edward, Joseph A. Fitzmyer, and Roland Edmund Murphy. *The Jerome Biblical Commentary.* Vol. 1. Englewood Cliffs, NJ: Prentice-Hall, 1996.

Richards, Larry and Lawrence O. Richards. *The Teacher's Commentary.* Wheaton, IL: Victor Books, 1987.

Richards, Lawrence O. *The Bible Readers Companion.* Wheaton, IL: Victor Books, 1991.

Roberts, Alexander and James Donaldson, eds. *Ante-Nicene Fathers: The Writings of the Fathers Down To A.D. 325.* Vols. 1-5. Edinburgh, UK: T. & T. Clark, WORDsearch CROSS e-book, 1867.

Sanders, Frank K. and Charles Foster Kent, eds. *The Messages of the Apostles.* Vol. XII, The Messages of the Bible. New York: Charles Scribner's Sons, 1900.

Schaff, Philip and David Schley Schaff. *History of the Christian Church.* Vol. 2. New York: Charles Scribner's Sons, 1910.

Schaff, Philip, ed. *The Nicene & Post-Nicene Fathers of the Christian Church: First Series.* Vol. 1. Edinburgh, UK: T. & T. Clark, WORDsearch CROSS e-book, 1886.

_____. *The Nicene & Post-Nicene Fathers of the Christian Church: Second Series.* Edinburgh, UK: T. & T. Clark, WORDsearch CROSS e-book, 1886.

Schultz, Samuel J. and Gary V. Smith. *Exploring the Old Testament.* Wheaton, IL: Crossway Books, 2001.

Simeon, Charles. *In Horae Homileticae or Discourses.* London: Samuel Holdsworth, Amen Corner, Paternoster Row, 1836.

Smith, George A. *The Expositor's Bible Commentary: The Book of Isaiah.* Vol. 2. London: Hodder and Stoughton. In Rick Meyers, e-Sword, Version 10.2.1, 2000-2012. <http://www.e-sword.net>, 1889-90.

Smith, James E. *The Books of History: Old Testament Survey Series.* Joplin, MO: College Press Publishing Company, 1995.

_____. *The Major Prophets. Old Testament Survey Series.* Joplin, MO: College Press Publishing Company, 1992.

_____. *The Minor Prophets. Old Testament Survey Series.* Joplin, MO: College Press Publishing Company, 1994.

Spence, H. D. M. *Pulpit Commentary.* In Rick Meyers, e-Sword, Version 10.2.1, 2000-2012. <http://www.e-sword.net>, n.d.

Stedman, Ray C. *Ray Stedman: Commentary on Selected Books of the Bible.* Copyright © 2010 by Ray Stedman Ministries, <http://www.raystedman.org>, In Rick Meyers, e-Sword, Version 10.2.1, 2000-2012. <http://www.e-sword.net>, 1971.

Sternberg, Meir. *The Poetics of Biblical Narrative: Ideological Literature and the Drama of Reading.* Bloomington, IN: Indiana University Press, 1987.

Stevens, George Barker. *The Messages of the Apostles*, The Messages of the Bible. Frank K. Sanders and Charles F. Kent. eds. Vol. XII. New York: Charles Scribner's Sons, 1900.

Towns, Elmer L. *Fasting for Spiritual Breakthrough.* Ventura, CA: Regal Books, 1996.

Trapp, John. *A Commentary On the Old and New Testaments: Ezra to Psalms.* W. Webster and Hugh Martin. eds. Vol. 2. In Rick Meyers, e-Sword, Version 10.2.1, 2000-2012, <http://www.e-sword.net>, 1601-1669.

_____. *A Commentary on the Old and New Testaments: Matthew to Revelation.* Vol. 5. W. Webster and Hugh Martin. eds. In Rick Meyers, e-Sword, Version 10.2.1, 2000-2012. <http://www.e-sword.net>, 1601-1669.

Tylor, Edward Burnett. *Primitive Culture.* Vol. 2. Boston, MA: Estes and Lauriat, 1871.

Unger, M. F. *Commentary on Zechariah.* Grand Rapids, MI: Zondervan Publishing House, 1962.

Utley, Robert James. *New Testament Survey: Matthew, Revelation.* Marshall, TX: Bible Lessons International, 2000.

_____. *The First Christian Primer: Matthew.* Study Guide Commentary Series. Vol. 9. Marshall, TX: Bible Lessons International, 2000.

_____. *The Gospel According to Luke.* Study Guide Commentary Series. Vol. 3a. Marshall, TX: Bible Lessons International, 2004.

VanGemeren, Willem A. *Interpreting the Prophetic Word: An Introduction to the Prophetic Literature of the Old Testament.* Grand Rapids, MI: Zondervan Publishing House, 1990.

Vine, W. E. and F. F. Bruce. *Vine's Expository Dictionary of Old and New Testament Words.* Vol. 1. Grand Rapids, MI: Fleming H. Revell, 1981.

Wallis, Arthur, *God's Chosen Fast: A Spiritual and Practical Guide to Fasting.* Fort Washington, PA: CLC Publications, 2011.

Walvoord, John F. *Daniel: The Key to Prophetic Revelation.* Chicago, IL: Moody Press, 1989.

Walvoord, John F. and Roy B. Zuck, eds. *The Bible Knowledge Commentary: An Exposition of the Scriptures.* Vol. 1. Wheaton, IL: Victor Books, 1985.

_____. *The Bible Knowledge Commentary: An Exposition of the Scriptures.* Vol. 2. Wheaton, IL: Victor Books, 1985.

Watson, Richard. *A Biblical and Theological Dictionary.* New York: Lane & Scott, 1849.

Wheddon, Daniel D. *Whedon's Commentary on the Old and New Testaments.* Hunt & Eaton, In Rick Meyers, e-Sword, Version 10.2.1, 2000-2012. <http://www.e-sword.net>, 1875.

Whitney, Donald S. *Spiritual Disciplines for the Christian Life.* Colorado Springs, CO: NavPress, 1991.

Wiersbe, Warren W. *Be Comforted*, "Be" Commentary Series. Wheaton, IL: Victor Books, 1996.

_____. *Be Determined*, "Be" Commentary Series. Wheaton, IL: Victor Books, 1996.

_____. *Be Satisfied*, "Be" Commentary Series. Wheaton, IL: Victor Books, 1996.

_____. *The Bible Exposition Commentary.* Vol. 1. Wheaton, IL: Victor Books, 1996.

Williams, Peter. *Opening Up Ezra, Opening Up Commentary.* Leominster: Day One Publications, 2006.

Wolston, Walter T. P. *The "Forty Days" of Scripture, Sixteen Addresses.* Third edition. Edinburgh, UK, In Rick Meyers, e-Sword, Version 10.2.1, 2000-2012. <http://www.e-sword.net>, 1909.

Wood, D. R. W., I. Howard Marshall, et al., eds. *New Bible Dictionary.* 3rd edition. Downers Grove, IL: InterVarsity Press, 1996.

Internet Resources

Brianchaninov, St. Ignatiy, 1807-1867 AD, <http://www.sfaturiortodoxe.ro/orthodox/orthodox_advices_fasting.htm>, Accessed on September 3, 2013.

The Didache or The Teaching of the Twelve Apostles, Tim Sauder, trans., <http://www.scroll publishing.com/ store/Didache-text.html>, Accessed on September 3, 2013.

"*Diversity at Work Series: Fasting in World Religions*", RRAE Unit, OPC September 05. <http:// www.beliefnet.com/Faiths/2001/02/Fasting-Chart.aspx>, Accessed on September 3, 2013.

Eusebius of Caesarea, *Historia Ecclesiastica*, 5.23-25, <http://www.ccel.org/ccel/schaff/npnf201.html>, Accessed on September 3, 2013.

Freedman, H., ed., *Babylonian Talmud: Tractate Shabbath, Folio 64a.* <http://halakhah.com/shabbath/shabbath_64. html>, Accessed on December 4, 2013.

Herodotus of Halicarnassus (484-425 BC), *The Histories*, <http://www.swartzentrover.com/cotor/E-Books/misc/Herodotus/THindex.htm>, 3.89ff. Accessed on November 28, 2013.

Moodley, Silva, *A Practical Guide to Fasting*, <http://www.lpm.org.za/sermon2.html>, Accessed on September 3, 2013.

Plutarch. *Themistocles.* Trans. by John Dryden. <http://classics. mit.edu/Plutarch/themisto.html>, 75 ACE. Accessed on September 3, 2013.

Ryan, Thomas. *Fasting: A Fresh Look.* <http://americamagazine.org/issue/563/article/fasting-fresh-look>, Accessed on June 13, 2013, n.d.

Saint Basil the Great, 329-379 AD; Doctor of the Catholic Church, <http://www.sfaturiortodoxe.ro/orthodox/ orthodox_advices_fasting.htm>, Accessed on September 3, 2013.

Saint Athanasius the Great, ca. 296-373 AD, <http://www.sfaturiortodoxe.ro/orthodox/orthodox_advices_fasting.htm>, Accessed on September 3, 2013.

Stanley, Charles. *The Benefits of Prayer and Fasting.* <http://www.northsidecitychurch.com/pdf/bopf.pdf>, Accessed on June 1, 2013.

Tacitus, Publius Cornelius, *The Histories*, 109 ACE. Alfred John Church and William Jackson Brodribb, trans., <http://classics.mit.edu/Tacitus/histories.html>, Accessed on September 3, 2013.

Towns, Elmer L. *Fasting for Spiritual Breakthrough Study Guide*. <http://digitalcommons.liberty.edu/cgi/viewcontent.cgi?article=1016&context=towns_books>, Accessed on June 13, 2013, n.d.

<http://danielfast.wordpress.com/2007/12/13/types-of-fasting/>.
<http://diet.lovetoknow.com/wiki/9_Types_of_Biblical_Fasting>.
<http://fasting.ms11.net/fasting.html>.
<http://users.stic.net/fortress/pr-fast-8fasts.htm>.
<http://www.allaboutfasting.com/history-of-fasting.html>.
<http://www.allaboutprayer.org/types-of-fasting-faq.htm>.
<http://www.enterthebible.org/resourcelink.aspx?rid=477>.
<http://www.faithcycleministry.org/Fasting/Fasting4.html>.
<http://www.fasting.com/fastingquotes.html>.
<http://www.rcnzonline.com/fnf/a191.html>.

Sheldon Juell is available for speaking engagements and public appearances.
For more information contact:

Sheldon Juell
C/O Advantage Books
P.O. Box 160847
Altamonte Springs, FL 32716

sheldon@fastingforspiritualpower.com

To purchase additional copies of this book or other books published by
Advantage Books call our order number at:

407-788-3110 (Book Orders Only)

or visit our bookstore website at:
www.advbookstore.com

Longwood, Florida, USA
"we bring dreams to life"™
www.advbookstore.com

CPSIA information can be obtained at www.ICGtesting.com
Printed in the USA
LVOW09s2208100516

487644LV00011B/69/P